VIRTUAL GEOGRAPHY

Arts and Politics of the Everyday
Patricia Mellencamp, Meaghan Morris, Andrew Ross,
series editors

VIRTUAL GEOGRAPHY

Living with Global Media Events

McKenzie Wark

INDIANA UNIVERSITY PRESS
Bloomington and Indianapolis

The paper used in this publication meets the minimum requirements of American National Standard for Information Sciences—Permanence of Paper for Printed Library Materials, ANSI Z39.48-1984.

Manufactured in the United States of America

Library of Congress Cataloging-in-Publication Data

Wark, McKenzie, date
Virtual geography : living with global media events / McKenzie Wark.
p. cm. — (Arts and politics of the everyday)
Includes index.
ISBN 0-253-36349-7 (alk. paper). — ISBN 0-253-20894-7 (pbk. : alk. paper)
1. Mass media—Social aspects. I. Title. II. Series.
HM258.W37 1994
302.23—dc20 93-48986

1 2 3 4 5 00 99 98 97 96 95 94

Contents

preface

Hell is truth seen too late.
—G. W. F. Hegel

New Maps of Hell

We live every day in a familiar terrain: the place where we sleep, the place where we work, the place where we hang out when not working or sleeping. From these places we acquire a geography of experience.

We live every day also in another terrain, equally familiar: the terrain created by the television, the telephone, the telecommunications networks crisscrossing the globe. These "vectors" produce in us a new kind of experience, the experience of telesthesia—perception at a distance. This is our "virtual geography," the experience of which doubles, troubles, and generally permeates our experience of the space we experience firsthand.

This virtual geography is no more or less "real." It is a different kind of perception, of things not bounded by rules of proximity, of "being there." If virtual reality is about technologies which increase the "bandwidth" of our sensory experience of mediated and constructed images, then virtual geography is the dialectically opposite pole of the process. It is about the expanded terrain from which experience may be instantly drawn.

In his book *Virtual Reality* (Secker and Warburg, 1991), Howard Rheingold used his descriptions of the latest developments in the perceptual technologies of virtual reality to defamiliarize the reader just enough to create a window in which to speculate on these new perceptual experiences which so rapidly become an unconscious part of everyday life. In attempting to defamiliarize the other end of the spectrum, the virtual geography of places from which ever more information seems potentially to flow, I have had to develop quite a different method. Rather than look at the "normal" state of media flows from around the world, in *Virtual Geography* I look at exceptional moments in the emerging world of globalized media experience.

So this is a book about weird global media events. "Events" in the sense of singular irruptions into the regular flow of media. "Global" in that there is some linkage between the sites at which they appear to happen and the sites where we remote-sense them. Some kind of feedback across national and cultural spaces takes place. They are "weird" in that something about them seems to break out of our conventional mappings of the relationship between political, economic, or cultural events and their representation in the media. When those representations start feeding back across global spaces and between radically different cultures, something odd is going on. Four such events occupy this book: the Persian Gulf war, the fall of the Berlin Wall, the Beijing massacre, and the "Black Monday" stock market crash of '87.

I'm interested in singularity of the exceptional events. So I look at four recent detonations that took place solely within the space of information flows. *Virtual Geography* is about how the media's order of discourse reveals its logics in its failed attempts to exclude its other—noise. Just as reason reveals itself in the disciplinary apparatus via its attempt to exclude its other—madness—so the rationales of global media events revel in their weirdness at the point where noise overwhelms the codes and narrative strategies meant to exclude it.

Virtual Geography is a book oriented toward the future: the future of culture under the impact of globalization; the future of cultural studies as a practice under the impact of emergent cultural forms. I am trying to think about history, in a media culture in which it gets hard to remember what happened yesterday. Do you remember what was happening in the televisual world in the late '80s, early '90s? Will I remember myself, should I pick this book up some years hence—this objectified piece of media memory?

As I write, the television plays in the corner of my eye. Distracted, I notice once again the news footage of children being airlifted out of Bosnia. Unable to find a narrative which might organize and make some sense of this event, the media resort to telling tales about wounded children. The result? Children flown to hospitals in Europe, outside the war zone. Life imitates the theatrical promptings of the media to a degree which would have fascinated—and horrified—Oscar Wilde.

Elsewhere in the news, file footage of a Somali "warlord"—the same file footage we've seen for weeks—rolls by. Pictures of UN troops, montaged up against pictures of Somalis, some demonstrating, some not. One is reminded that had it not been for televised images of the famine, these troops might not be here. The grain might not have arrived. People might have starved. Pakistani troops, under the UN flag, might not have opened fire on Somali civilians. Somalis might not have killed U.S. troops in their UN "good guy" hats with a mine. Pictures of Somalis montaged against pictures of President Clinton. The president, the warlord, the British prime minister appear in successive shots, as appearing to respond to the other, an instantaneous global dialogue in a virtual narrative space, which organizes appearances on the surface of a strange new virtual geography. This is the form of appearance of the space of the vector, the matrix of possible trajectories in which events occur. This is the subject of the essaying inquiries of this book.

Writing Cultural Studies

Each of the four weird global media events I write about here ought normally to fall partly under the jurisdiction of a particular subset of experts. The Gulf war is the province of the Middle East area specialists, the Tiananmen Square events of Sinologists, the stock market crash of those who speak the foreign tongue of finance. Yet something escapes the areas knowledge so neatly defines in the world. Vectors of movement, of information flow, traverse any and every sphere of the world which knowledge may take as a separate object. This is something that does not belong by rights to any discipline at all, least of all to "interdisciplinary studies," which still takes the traditional "field management" system of knowledge for granted and contents itself with wandering along its imaginary borders.

A more radical approach to the problems emerging out of the intricate traceries left in everyday life by the vectors of information flow is the cultural studies pioneered at Birmingham by Stuart Hall and others. Cultural studies started with the event—the event of Thatcherism. It worked back through the vectors which form the contours of its powers, and very pragmatically picked the eyes out of a whole range of specialized knowledges which might help create a practical knowledge organized around the horizon of the event. That approach is still valid today, only the events requiring a critical cultural intervention are increasingly global in scope, and exceed the bounds of any particular national culture and hegemonic class order. If one starts from everyday life, as cultural studies did, from the experience of an ever-shifting combination of dominant, residual and emergent cultural forces, then it is still possible to practice a kind of cultural studies, even when the vectors of power one must trace vastly exceed the bounds of the national popular.

Starting from my experience of four weird global media events, as a media consumer, or more truthfully, a media junkie, I tell stories about them and extrapolate the elements of a theory about them. These stories have an improvised quality. They are not all necessarily compatible with each other. They are an attempt to recover an art of serious writing which takes as its starting point the cultural and political temporalities of everyday life. I read Karl Marx, Antonio Gramsci, and Walter Benjamin as doing exactly that—writing out of the conjuncture. I don't claim to write as well as they did, simply to honor their memory. In particular I value their struggle to write about things that were difficult to theorize, but important, rather than to give importance to things that were easy to theorize, but of scholastic interest only. This is the role of the kind of critical theory they each reinvented for themselves: to enable writing about unfathomable powers, to enable communication about the things that concern us, to create out of such small steps a community of interest in the issues thus brought however dimly to light.

Many of the short sections which make up the eight chapters began life as occasional pieces for *Australian Left Review, Impulse, New Statesman, Tension, New Formations, The Australian, Arena, Meanjin, Island,* and other journals of the left, the arts, or of the mainstream. I take this opportunity to thank the various editors for the opportunity to write about events at a speed which could tag along with the time of their unfolding. I believe it is important, in doing cultural studies, to try to develop and maintain organic links with the media and skills at media practice. It is particularly important to connect research to the time of lived experience and the media's ebb and flow through that time, so that we might teach each other about that world of experiences, beyond the archive and the classroom.

Besides practicing the art of the essay in the face of mediated crises, this book is about speculating on the underlying causes of those events. Here it tries to revive the long-term, historical thinking about culture practiced by Raymond Williams and Georg Lukács. I look for the tendencies which one might attribute to the ongoing and accelerating phenomena of weird global media events. I do not do so in systematic fashion, but as the occasion arises, within the process of telling stories about these events. I do not want to abstract weird global media events too far out of the time of lived experience in everyday life in which we find them. Not least because understanding them means coming to grips with what has come of the experience of time under the impact of the proliferation of media vectors with which we live. Henri Lefebvre saw the importance of these connections a long time ago. Fifty years after his *Critique de la Quotidienne,* one still has to argue, again and again, for the spirit of a critical thinking which can uproot itself from the tradition of viewing culture from the outside and waft into the thermal currents of culture as experienced. We no longer have roots, we have aerials. If this is increasingly true of our lived experience of everyday life, and I think it is, then we need to adapt our critical writing to an emergent cultural form where all experiences are mediated and inflected by global vectors of communication.

Under the sign of a somewhat different temperament, Theodor Adorno well understood the need to find the connections between the fragments of what appear as minute and particulate differences in everyday life and abstract relations. In particular, the abstract relations which create this appearance of separateness as a fetish. Abstract relations which also create the dependence of objects and experiences in everyday life on the process of making and remaking the "bad totality" of modern social life. I think there is a new abstract relation, a new "general equivalent" at work in the world—the abstract relation of the vector. It intersects with, but has a distinct trajectory from, the trajectory that the dynamics of capital trace through culture and the world.

In these pages I relate the isolated images which fall from the satellite sky into our lives from the vector into an understanding of the very real and powerful abstraction of the vector that strategic and corporate interests have let loose on the world. I concentrate on weird global media events because they are at one and the same time the most particular, fragmented, everyday experiences, yet they are also the product of the most abstract, global, interconnected relations. They are the moments which reveal in everyday life something of the abstract form of the emergent virtual geography lacing the world together via the various technologies and cultural forms of the vector.

If cultural studies is to avoid becoming just another type of fetishized scholarship about fetishized differences among things, then it has to trace the connections between the experiences it finds in everyday life, in popular culture, in the rhythm of events as they appear in experience, back to fresh imagining of process, becoming, totality. The discovery, forced into critical consciousness by

Michel Foucault, Jean-François Lyotard, and Gilles Deleuze, that totality is invariably bad totality, that historicism is invariably false historicism, does not give us license to abandon imagining the whole and speculating on its future tendencies. It enjoins us rather to attempt to create a fresh art of writing speculatively about what lies beyond the routine boundaries forced upon us by the academic division of labor, by the self-evident correctness of uncritical moralisms, by the banality of the relentless accumulation in our archives of the reified facticity of difference.

This book is in the main about the virtual geography of the extensive, global net of mainstream media vectors. One of its subtexts is a modest proposal for rethinking the virtual geography of the archive and the disciplinary apparatus of an ever-expanding academic discourse. Media vectors are no respecters of borders, be they cultural or geographic. In order to write along the line of such an agent, one has to think again about the borders within scholarship itself. What I practice and advocate is a writing which follows the contours of the event rather than staying within the boundaries of any academic discipline or specialty. Its first fidelity must be to the time of the event itself, rather than to neatly partitioned space of the archive or the "gentleman's conventions" dividing the academic fields.

Feminism showed the limits of those conventions in the way they parceled out the continuities of women's lives between the experts. I've learned a lot from feminist scholarship, particularly from the early days of feminist screen theory, where the tracing of the organic continuities and breaks in the everyday lives of women was taken to be more important than the formal breaks and continuities imposed upon "the field." This may seem like an odd lesson to draw from Laura Mulvey and Claire Johnston, but I imagined when I first read them and firmly believe today that their work has importance far beyond either feminism or screen studies, as examples of a radical form of critical practice. If the relations of gendered perception traverse the bounds of the disciplines, then critical thought must transgress those bounds and write along the lines of gender. If the relations of globalized perception traverse the bounds of disciplines, then one must follow those transgressions too. If scholarship is to claim itself to be "radical," then it must take a radical approach to scholarship itself as well as to its subject. If radical scholarship formerly went to the root of the problems of both method and material, now it must tune in to the frequencies of everyday life upon which the vector reshapes everyday life and its scholarly accomplices.

Antipodean Cultural Studies

One of the virtues of living and writing in Sydney, Australia, is that the pressure to fetishize knowledge, to force one's forays into the archive into a narrow number of shelves, to divorce one's work and life from organic connection with the living work of making an antipodean, multicultural, postcolonial culture—

these pressures are considerably less than they are in some other contexts. Sydney poststructuralism, as I learned it throughout the '80s from people like Meaghan Morris, Paul Patton, Ross Gibson, Paul Foss, Stephen Muecke, and Liz Grosz, was a range of conceptions of intellectual practice, all of which were determined to make their own connections with political and cultural life and to live and breathe connected to the time and space of collective cultural projects. We all succumb to the pressures of institutional definitions of our practice sooner or later, but the lesson of the period was to try to do it on one's own terms. The version of cultural studies that arises out of the '80s in Sydney knows itself not just to be about culture, but to be culture, and to insist on taking as much of that doubled conception of praxis into the academy as possible.

The challenge that living up to the legacy of this tradition poses is to create a postmodern style of writing about postmodern culture, without thereby producing just another reified knowledge, lacking all organic connection to the emergent cultural forms and norms it was designed as a response to in the first place. Let the dead bury the dead. The problem is the living of this fabulous and eerie new life with all its pleasures and dangers. In other words, there are quite particular challenges and obligations I felt I had to honor in writing about the global from a very particular site and out of a very particular culture within the matrix of an emergent virtual geography. Sydney poststructuralism at its best was a response to a certain experience of globalization, if not a terribly conscious one. My dialogue with the writings of Morris, Gibson, and Muecke is to read them and apply them in this light.

The Historical Imagination

Marx saw clearly and early on that capital is the virus of abstraction. It enters into any and every social relation, corrupts it, and makes it manufacture more relations of abstraction. It is a form of viral relation which has a double aspect. It turns every qualitative and particular relation into a quantitative and universal one. It is the very virus of totality against which the philosophers now uselessly speculate. It is a relationship to which attaches great mysticism. It is in general an unequal relation, yet it is sold as a fair one. It is allegedly the source of productive growth and wealth, yet it is cancerous and destructive. It makes possible the connection of any and every particular relation into an uncontrollable whole, yet it generates the illusion of identity, individuality, agency.

Marx saw too that it cannot go on forever, that it too must strike against a limit or limits. But it can be overcome only by something even more abstract, something which takes further capital's radical abstracting of relations from that which relations relate: people, places, and things. The limit of capital is that it is a quantitative relation. It reduces the attributes of people, places, and things to quantities relative to each other. But how can one value these values, abstracted from particularities of people, places, and things? Only by setting loose an equivalent flow of qualitative abstraction.

It is not the people who have nothing to lose but their chains, but the flow of qualitative information about people, their places, and the things they produce, in short their "culture." Culture which ceases in the process to be culture, and becomes instead a postculture or a transculture. Express it how you will, but the fact remains that cultural studies has arrived, like the owl of Minerva, within the academy at just that point where its object has taken leave of our senses and headed elsewhere. Culture is something that will be overcome—whether we like it or not.

This, finally, is the only sense that the postmodern can have. The postmodern is a notion which ought to inspire joy and terror in intellectuals the way Nietzsche's "death of god" did for believers, long ago. The postmodern is our interregnum. What has ended is a period in which capital dissolved all practical control people could have over nature, the body, and the products of their own labor, yet collectively retained some control over their means of thinking and knowing the world.

Increasingly, culture too abstracts itself from all particularity. But this does not mean that the social relations of culture become identical with those of capital. On this point one sees in Adorno and Horkheimer only the failure of their imagination. One sees instead the construction of a whole new terrain of collusion and conflict between at least two kinds of abstracted relations, both viral, both of which use bodies and minds as the raw material of their endless and quite pointless growth, proliferation, and self-reproduction.

If the importance of the writings the classical Marxists produced in the context of events seems more important to me than it once did, the corpus of "theoretical" Marxism seems to me to have shrunk somewhat. Yet there are a few texts that still seem positively luminous. A few pages of Marx's 1844 manuscript on money and estranged labor and in the *Grundrisse* on the world market; a few pages of Lukács on "second nature"; and the "chiliastic serenity" of Guy Debord's *La Société Du Spectacle*. From meditating on these emerged my understanding of virtual geography—even though it may have little to do with either the virtual, or geography, or academic Marxism as it is usually understood.

I am largely silent in these pages on the work of Fredric Jameson and David Harvey, although they in turn are silently present in them. This is because I wanted to think through a classically Marxist trajectory more sympathetic to cultural studies from some of the same intellectual sources, but thought specifically in terms of my quite spatially particular and temporally contingent experience of events. If one is to do Marxism rather than talk about it, this, I think, is the way to go.

Equally silent here is a dialogue with Jean Baudrillard, whose full-on but one-sided development of the theoretical abstractions of Guy Debord I try to remedy with a return to the horizon of lived time and the failures of simulation which appear for brief moments in weird global media events. Once again, from where I am, the French tradition looks as particular a take on the virtual geography of the global as the American.

Like Bernard Smith, I want to create my particular understanding of the global, as seen from the antipodes. It's a step toward recognizing that while one cannot escape the necessity of conceptualizing the global, it cannot be thought exclusively from the metropolitan centers. It is only by "provincializing" the metropolitan, as Dipesh Chakrabarty says, that an intellectual practice up to the task of thinking the emergent form of virtual geography can emerge.

When I hear the word "postmodern" I reach for the remote control. I want to change channels immediately, before I get instantaneously and totally bored. The scholarly apparatus has hammered the very word itself into unreflected conventionality. But if we are to take so terrifying a word with anything like the respect its uncompromising self-negation deserves, then we must face up to the fact that it challenges all of the procedures, assumptions, and categories of the modern, including all those of scholarship, writing, and publishing. Is there still a place in this brave, bloody new world for a kind of critical writing? If so, what kind and where? How can one practice it? I must confess, I really don't know. All I can say is that I tried to write these pages under a steadily increasing overhang of doubt about precisely this. We no longer have roots, we have aerials. Such a state of affairs is still an incitement to write, but perhaps more than ever to try to write differently.

One has to write differently not only because the form of what one writes about changes, but also because the community one writes for changes. To borrow again from Howard Rheingold, there are emerging "virtual communities" that are unanchored in locality but are made possible by the ever more flexible matrix of media vectors traversing the globe. We no longer have origins, we have terminals. The challenge is to write critically in organic connection with the emergent forms of virtual perception, community, and geography. This is part of a collective project one can only begin to define at present—to identify the forces for social change scattered throughout the vectors. People who have a shared interest in a free and democratic media practice, emerging out of their identity as producers of perception, community, and geography—virtual and otherwise.

acknowledgments

This is my first book, so there are a lot of people to thank. Meaghan Morris, Andrew Ross, Pat Mellencamp, and Larry Grossberg all made it happen, one way or another. Paul Gillen supervised my earliest thrashings about, from which it eventually emerged. Ross Harley and John Potts read bits of it. Sue Best, Gerry Gill, Linda Jaivin, and Greil Marcus responded critically and helpfully to former incarnations of it. For the follies that remain, I alone am culpable.

David Burchill, Erica Carter, Judith Squires, Ashley Crawford, and Eldon Garnet all published bits of it, allowing this work to accumulate some small public life of its own. I am especially grateful to Jenny Lee, in my view the best editor the venerable journal *Meanjin* ever had. Oddly enough, I am even more thankful to Paul Foss, Stephen Muecke, and Malcolm Imrie for their decisions not to publish some earlier sallies. It would never have found its present, happy home with Indiana University Press had they, in a moment of weakness, accepted it as it was.

Helen Trinca was responsible not only for getting me space in the leading national newspaper, *The Australian,* but for calling me up every Sunday before my columns ran and oxy-welding my prose into a more sturdy form over the phone. Luke Slattery has also been generous with space in the paper. I thank them both for their contribution to my lifelong struggle to write English. Thanks to them I can take a certain delicious pleasure in claiming to be a "lapsed Marxist in the pay of Rupert Murdoch."

The cultural studies conference circuit in Australia is a fairly recent phenomenon, although the discussions in the pub afterwards are a more traditional thing. Many thanks to Graeme Turner, Ien Ang, Tom O'Regan, Zoë Sofia, Cindy Patton, Mark Reid, Stuart Cunningham, Tony Bennett, Simon During, John Frow, Marcus Breen, Dipesh Chakrabarty, and many others who have shared their thoughts with me while "on the road" conferencing every November and December for the last five years or so. A special thanks to Kuan-Hsing Chen, David Bennett, Liz Jacka, and John Hartley for inviting me to give papers to particularly keen audiences in the vicinity of particularly convivial watering holes.

I went into "Tron Mode" on the last leg of writing this book, with the answering machine on, barely talking to anyone, so a big thanks to my email correspondents emr, minh, visionary. Discussions hosted by hlr and steeler of virtual community and open sources intelligence on The Well indirectly helped me think through a few things—thanks for all the ascii.

Students in the Communications program at the University of Technology, Sydney, and in Mass Communications, Macquarie University, sat indulgently or intervened animatedly while I made this stuff up, usually on the spot, in the classroom. The people in the Masters Program in International Communications at Macquarie provided a particularly useful dialogue. I would especially like to thank the program's director, Naren Chitty, for the opportunity to teach this material.

I owe a strange debt to the late Henry Mayer, an important figure for almost everybody who studies communications in Australia. He died while teaching at Macquarie. Since he left no course outline or program, I was forced to continue his course in the spirit in which he started it: a free inquiry on the international power paradigms in the media today.

My colleagues at Macquarie, including Philip Bell, Theo van Leeuwen, Caroline Craig, Phil Hayward, David Clark-Duff, David Mitchell, Fiona Mitchell, and Jan Knapman, have patiently put up with me while I taught full-time and wrote full-time—not something I would ever recommend!

Personal thanks to Vienna (my most inscrutable critic), Jo Evenden, Rosie Wait, Stephen Taylor, Gregory Harvey, Shelly Cox, Cathy Lumby, Gary Campbell, Renata Atkin, Robert Thompson, José Borghino, Shelley Kay, Mary Temelovski, and the Elizabeth Bay posse. A special thanks to a special person, Mahalya Middlemist, on whose lovely back verandah I struggled with some difficult moments of it, under the summer sun.

Thanks too to the cafes I wrote a lot of it in: Mama Maria's, Tropicana, the Craven, and Merivales. Much gratitude to all at 11 Randall Street, Surry Hills, for allowing me to spend the last all-nighter writing in their spacious, funky downtown studio, grooving away to Rick Tanaka's Miles Davis CDs. Very therapeutic.

Long overdue thanks to my family: Ross, Melva, Robert, Susan, and co. A big hello in advance to Scotty, Kate, and Tim. Thanks also to my teachers, including John McGee, Deana Doyle, Bob Connell, Tim Rowse, Sheila Shaver, Judith Allen, Ross Poole, Tom Parsonage, Winton Higgins, and Gil Boeringer. Thanks to the comrades who set me on the path to this, unwittingly: Darrell Dawson, Kay Wicks, Jenny Rutherford, Peter Ormonde, Chris Dodds, David Ross, Glen Henessey, Rod Noble, and the late Laurel Quillan.

Virtual Geography is dedicated to the memory of Joyce Crank and Helen MuSung. I can offer only this book now in return for the brief horizon of your unconditional love.

The following are credits for the photographs reproduced in the text. They include the original captions from the newswire photographs that accompanied them around the world on the day they were issued:

Site #1: 5>LONO5:GULF:BAGHDAD, IRAQ,23AUG90—Iraqi President Saddam Hussein is shown on Iraqi Television with his arm around a British youngster identified only as Stawart August 23 Saddam told Stawart and other westerners that they are not hostages. ptb/Itaq TV via CNN REUTER (Reproduced by kind permission of Reuters)

Site #2: BERWO1C:BRANDENBURG GATE:WEST BERLIN,22DEC89—Thousands of East Germans and West Germans gather around the Brandenburg Gate that was opened in Berlin on December 22. pro Michael Probst REUTER (Reproduced by kind permission of Reuters)

Site #3: PEK23:CHINA,PEKING,JUNE3—A Peking citizen stands passively in front of the convoy of tanks on the Avenue of Eternal Peace on Monday. The tanks did not slow down but did turn and avoid him before taking up positions in another area of the city. The man was not injured. COLOR KEY: Tank in green, man's shirt white. REUTER stf 1989 (Reproduced by kind permission of Reuters)

Site #4: TOKO1-21APR93-TOKYO: Money dealers are busy during the morning session of Tokyo's foreign exchange market 21 Apr. The US dollar plunged 110 yen in mid morning trading, setting a new post-war low for the third day running. AFP PHOTO. KAZUHIRO NOGI/KN #0776 .22/04/209? 13.01 (Reproduced by kind permission of Agence France Presse)

Site #1

Victory Arch, Baghdad

terminal sights . . .

terminal sites

Site #1

1. vector

Saddam/Sodom

Dateline: Baghdad, Thursday, 23 August 1990. Iraqi television shows President Saddam Hussein sitting in a television studio surrounded by fifteen British citizens. These people, now hostages, were residents of Iraq and Kuwait when Iraq invaded its Gulf neighbor. Saddam Hussein appears in a suit and tie with a little white handkerchief neatly folded in his left breast pocket. The Iraqis allow the foreigners to talk to their families while the rest of the world looks on. They listen as Saddam explains that the Western media have misrepresented the situation. "In the past few days," he says, "I have come across articles published in the Western papers urging President Bush to strike Iraq and actually use force against Iraq despite your presence here." Responding to a mother's worries about her child's education, Saddam offers to send "experts from the ministry of education." Putting his hand gently on the head of seven-year-old Stuart Lockwood, he remarks, "When he and his friends, and all those present here, have played their role in preventing war, then you will all be heroes of peace."[1]

While the broadcast appeared on Iraqi television, the program seemed entirely aimed at a Western audience. Western media picked it up quickly and broadcast it around the world the next day. It drew instant and predictable official and media responses. British Foreign Secretary Douglas Hurd called it the "most sickening thing I have seen for some time." Rupert Murdoch's English tabloid press dubbed Saddam Hussein the "Butcher of Baghdad." The American State Department called this event "shameful theatricals." A "repulsive charade," said the British Foreign Office.[2]

More than moral outrage at the hostage-taking fueled this response. Two rather more elusive factors emerged in this extraordinary attempt at direct political communication along the media vector between widely differing cultural sites. One was that Saddam Hussein confounded our most cherished beliefs about the genres of television and the kinds of stories they legitimately tell us. Looking like a cross between Bob Hope and Geraldo Rivera, Saddam appeared to Western viewers as a demented talk-show host, in gross breach of the etiquette even of "reality television," where only crooks, pimps, prostitutes, and unscrupulous used-car salesmen may be treated to raw acts of intimate verbal violence on camera.[3] Or perhaps the format of the program looked uncomfortably close to Oprah Winfrey on a bad day, talking about bondage or child abuse.

This offense to contemporary American sensibilities was compounded by another, much older and deeper one. Saddam Hussein unwittingly presented us with a repetition of an ancient and fearful superstition about Arabs, and what Slovenian psychoanalyst Slavoj Žižek calls the threat to our sense of national enjoyment. "We always impute to the 'other' an excessive enjoyment; s/he wants to steal our enjoyment (by ruining our way of life) and/or has access to some secret, perverse enjoyment."[4]

The "fundamentalists," the only adherents of Islam one ever hears about, fall into the first category.[5] The Iranian revolution, that otherwise unintelligible blow to the forward march of "modernization," was the fault of the fundamentalists, who not only stole the pleasures of the modern consumer way of life from the Iranians, but threaten us, too, with hostage-takings and other high-profile media events. That sacred libation of our everyday enjoyment was at stake here: oil.

Until now, Saddam Hussein had in this scheme of things been "our" Arab, a "moderate," not an "extremist." As such he could be accommodated. When Saddam complained to the then American ambassador, April Glaspie, about a report on Voice of America radio critical of human-rights abuses in Iraq, the ambassador informed him that its author had been sacked from the State Department.[6] "Moderate" means, in other words, that the official story will moderate the worst abuses of tyrants who are compliant allies, so long as they remain as such.

When the Western television news and the front pages of the newspapers carried the close-up of Saddam Hussein's hand stroking the Lockwood boy's head, he changed character in the "Orientalist" vision the West has of the Middle East. Orientalism is a legacy of the colonial days, a collection of stories in which, as Edward Said says, it was axiomatic that the "attributes of being Oriental overrode any countervailing instance."[7]

Saddam Hussein touching Lockwood forced Western viewers to place the gesture in a frame of cultural reference. He did not appear to be a Muslim "fundamentalist," a denier of pleasure. In the absence of any other cultural memory of images of the Middle East, the focus on the gesture of touching encouraged the viewer to read it in terms of the other legacy of Orientalist story.

His hand on that boy's head connects not the prohibition on enjoyment enjoined by the cartoon fundamentalists of journalistic cliché, but its opposite. From Wilde's *Salome* and Flaubert's *Salambo,* to Burroughs's interzone of Tangiers and Trocchi's *Carnal Days* in the sultry sun, there is another string of stories of excessive enjoyment, of "harems, princesses, princes, slaves, veils, dancing girls and boys."[8] Not least of which, the mythic story of the Arab pederast, which turned up most recently in the film *Gallipoli.* A scene contrasts "our" Australian soldier-boys buying prostitutes ("normal enjoyment") with the hint of Arabs buggering little boys (excess). This is the flip side of the story about the puritan fundamentalism of Islam: the Arab "whose libidinal energy drives him to paroxysms of overstimulation."[9]

When Saddam Hussein opened a vector of communication to the West, he obviously did not have these Orientalist fantasies and fears in mind. They are only absurd Western fantasies, after all. According to Egyptian journalist Mohamed Heikal, Iraqi television frequently pictured Saddam kissing babies during the war. "This had succeeded in Iraqi terms, and officials thought they could make it work internationally, but they were wrong."[10] Akbar Ahmed, a Moslem scholar at Cambridge, likewise reads the image in terms of how he thinks the dictator's own people would respond. "In his culture an elder, or figure of authority, often displays affection to children by patting the child or tousling the hair. It is socially approved and appreciated."[11] Even a dictator must practice the political arts of affect. He must tap the common font of feeling with actions and images which cultivate popular acquiescence to his rule. Only at home he gets feedback on how his message goes over from the secret police. In the international arena, there is no such closed loop to confirm and confine meanings.

The trouble starts when one opens a vector between cultures which are not usually in communication with each other and taps the affective responses of peoples one knows only through other images, transmitted along other media vectors. The audience has to decide whether to read the image in terms of "our" frame of reference, or in the frame of what we know about the other. What we know about the other of the Middle East is mostly fantasy: images of our unspoken fears and desires, projected onto a few scraps of landscape and decor, costume and legend collected by long-dead travelers of the imagination.

The problem compounds when an Arab dictator speaks to those Western populations brought up on Orientalist understandings of the Middle East of Western manufacture. As Edward Said says, "The entire premise was colonial: that a small Third World dictatorship, nurtured and supported by the West, did not have the right to challenge America, which was white and superior."[12] It is not just that the other place is a refuge for our lost desires and fears. Built into the spatial mapping is an assumption of the marginality of the Middle East, a zone which, in our presumption, is beyond the bounds of the only moral and reasonable law—"ours." This presumption is not as frankly spoken today as it was in the old world's colonial heyday. The vector creates enough contact between places to create a sort of narrative prudence. Underneath, the assumptions are much the same.

One can, and must, critique such vile cultural presumptions, which is what Edward Said does.[13] One must critique the distortions perpetrated by the American media and the damage this does to American democracy, as Douglas Kellner does.[14] One must speak the truth about the imperial designs of the American state and their effects, as Noam Chomsky does.[15] One must use theory as Avital Ronell does, to explore the perverse logic by which America needs to create a theater of operations, in which it attempts to localize and cauterize foreign bodies, unknown pleasures, addictive creeds.[16] I trust those tasks are in numerically few but trustworthy hands. All around what Paul Gilroy once called the "overdeveloped" world there are people working tirelessly and painstakingly, in the wake of the event, to put the vast slew of flotsam thrown up by it into the sort of perspective the more reflective time of critical writing provides.

What is lacking, particularly in the voluminous reflections on the Gulf war coming out in the United States, is a writing about the kind of *global* media trajectories capable of producing such an event.[17] Sure, there are criticisms of the American media coverage of the war. That is not what I mean. The criticisms, even good ones, are part of the same matrix of relations that produced the spectacle of the Gulf war in the first place. Many of the things conveyed in what George Gerbner calls the media's "instant history" of the war were distortions or outright lies.[18] Quite a few people know that now. How do we know? Through other media. Slower and more considered media, like articles in the highbrow monthlies, or earnest, truthful hour-length documentaries, but media all the same. Both the dangers and our ability to do anything about them tie into our everyday experience of the vector. It is that experience that this book is about.

Through the Looking Glass

I'm lying in bed with my lover and the cat, watching TV, when this hostage thing spews out of the TV at me. By a strange accident of geography, the NBC morning news program is shown in Sydney, Australia, around midnight. So here we are, a cozy domestic scene, lapping up the sweet with the bland, suddenly invaded by hostages and threats and urgency and Bryant Gumbel. Neither of us is really watching the set at the time. It just happens to be on, a boring interzone of banal happenings, vectoring into our private space. I think it is the word "hostage" that trips me into actually paying attention. I watch with an unwilling fascination, trying not to let myself submit to this distasteful but canny image. That's when I see something curious: the medium close-up where Saddam Hussein touches that boy. A dictator caresses his hostage in our bedroom. The report gives the impression that the hostage show-and-tell talk show was a long one, but it's those few seconds of the dictator and the boy that made it into the vision mix. The tape is many generations old, blurred and pixelated, but so too is the Orientalist story it revives from the dead. Curiouser and curiouser. At the next commercial break, I pull on an old track suit and head out the bedroom door. "Where are you going?" my lover asks. "To work," I say. "To work."

So here I am, making coffee with the radio on in the middle of the night. Eating a big feed of avocados from the tree in the back yard. Warming up the computer. Setting the video recorder rolling. Opening some new files. I put on some music, something minimalist and basic. The radio and the TV are too distractedly fascinating. A line from a song leaps into the interzone to comment, *"Radio birdman, up above. Beautiful baby, feed my love. . . ."* I need loud music to drown out the silence of the war.

I turn on the heater in the study—it gets cold in Sydney in August. I could smell trouble. I could sense an event coming on. Months later, I could close the door to this study, with its mountains of old newspapers, videotapes, photocopies with coffee-cup rings all over them. By then, this private zone of disorder would look like a pathetic tribute to the carnage in Baghdad. This little room would become a monument made out of trashed information, jerrybuilt concepts, and emergency rations of toxic espresso and vodka, neat. By then I would realize that I had been writing about this fucking gulf since 1987.[19] I have been diving into each and every looking-glass war on television since then.

On that cold August night in 1990, there was already a strange familiarity about it all. With the unfolding of the hostage crisis, the Gulf war as an *event* can be said to begin. It is a difficult thing deciding the start and end of a media event. It is even more difficult still distinguishing the features of events that are purely media effect from those that might come to have more lasting significance in quite other forms of discourse—in history, in diplomacy, in political struggles, in popular memory.

The processes through which popular memory records these events in everyday life may not be the least important level at which they have effects. How do *you* remember the Gulf war, or the fall of the Berlin Wall? So much information about so many occurrences, all streaming into our waking life and our dreams, as if from a world beyond. So much of the memory resources we all rely upon to think and act are encoded elsewhere, in the languages and institutional bunkers of the media's archives. It is no small matter, then, to learn how to *use* these strange memories that exist, inexplicably, outside our heads.

Memories have progressively become thinglike; objectified in electronic archives, invisible traces on magnetic tape, alongside the more familiar storage forms of books and papers. Michel de Certeau suggests that we need to rediscover an art of memory, but where?[20] Memory resides within the electronic archive, within the space of the media vector. The vector lobs instant images like Saddam touching Lockwood into our living rooms, tossing potential memories our way. We have to find ways of using the media record of power strategies like these. We have to use that record as a tool, as a resource for inventing the tactical moves necessary to outwit the cunning of mediated power. The media spectacle, particularly the quixotic events that seem now to happen with increasing frequency, might form the raw material for such an art of memory. After the Gulf war, this much is obvious.

The most characteristic feature of events is that they expose us to our own ignorance of the world. Events, willy-nilly, thrust unexpected sense upon us from a new viewpoint. Faced with an event like the Gulf war, one can say, with Montaigne, "I am free to give myself up to doubt and uncertainty, and to my predominant quality which is ignorance."[21] Of course, after the event disappears, it may seem to all make sense again. The hole ripped through the narrative fabrics and media swaddling will be gently patched up again. That is why it is important to recall exactly how it felt when Saddam Hussein appeared on TV with his "guests." One should be cautious, however, about attempts to construct scientific sense out of either the text that passes along the vector, or the responses of the audiences that the vector composes.

French semiotician Roland Barthes pointed to something in this respect: "From a musical game heard on FM and which seemed 'stupid' to him, he realises this: stupidity is a hard and indivisible kernel, a primitive: no way of decomposing it scientifically (if a scientific analysis of TV were possible, TV would entirely collapse)."[22] Rather than attempt to penetrate to the kernel of the media event, I treat it here as a primitive, an ineluctable core. One could attempt to exhaust the Gulf war as an event with analysis, but the resulting analysis, like most which approach their objects with the suspicion that the truth lies hidden in them somewhere, will be interminable. Perhaps theory needs to find a pace and a style that allows it to accompany the event, but without pretending to master it.

Satellite Feed

Where do events come from? Do they fall from the sky? Yes they do. From the radio birdman, up above, from the comsat angels in orbit overhead, or thrown from a truck onto the ground in front of your local newsstand. Critical journalism scholar Ben Bagdikian points out that these vectors whence we get the information to form an ongoing map of the world and its events become increasingly concentrated in fewer and fewer corporate hands. These corporate owners are increasingly integrating diverse media holdings to more profitably coordinate print and audiovisual flows. Over the last decade, the number of companies controlling the vast bulk of American newsprint shrank from twenty to eleven.[23] Which is bad enough, but in Australia, the major press owners are basically three. An American citizen, Rupert Murdoch, controls 70 percent of Australian newsprint.[24] No matter how many channels we can get, our main news feed comes from few hands indeed.

Rupert Murdoch is one of a handful of pioneers of a new internationalization of the ownership of the media vectors. Critical communications scholar Herbert Schiller argues that the growth of transnational corporations, which seek rich offshore markets and cheap offshore labor forces, necessitates an internationalization of media vectors. The deregulation of economic flows during the Reagan years went hand in hand with a deregulation of information flows and attacks on public control and access to information.[25] The media that feed us are not only more and more concentrated, but increasingly global in both ownership and extent. Since business consumes a vast amount of media information, and business is increasingly global, so too are the information providers. To some extent the globalization of the media flows pouring off the vectors into everyday life is a byproduct of the globalization of business and business communication.

The global media vector does not connect us with just anywhere. It connects us most frequently, rapidly, and economically with those parts of the world which are well integrated into the major hubs of the vector. Hamid Mowlana, a leading authority on development and communication, points out that the Gulf region has a long history of integration into the international media vector. At the turn of the century, Lord Curzon described British interests in the Persian Gulf as "commercial, political, strategical and telegraphic."[26] Some of the world's first international telegraph lines passed through there. British communications with India flowed along this route. With the recognition of the strategic value of oil for propelling the mechanized vectors of war from 1914 on, the region became important in its own right. The vector of communication developed in step with colonial administration and corporate trade until the rise of anticolonial movements and the establishment of independent states.

As Mowlana says, "Development . . . is communication and communication is development."[27] The oil-rich Gulf states were sites of heavy investment in military and security communication vectors, in national hubs connecting into the global finance vector, and to some extent in national communication infrastructure as part of national development and integration policies. This process had mixed results. The Gulf region became the fifth most important international hub in terms of the sophistication of the vectors and the volume of information flows. Given that half of Kuwait's investment portfolio is in America, this is not surprising. On the other hand, "that the Persian Gulf countries have more communication networks with some power centres of the world than among themselves not only prevents them from concentrating their resources for regional economic, social, political and cultural integration but also creates a condition of vassalage."[28]

Mohamed Heikal complains that in the '50s and '60s, Arab media had a "sense of direction" fostered by pan-Arabist aspirations and culture. In the '80s, Arab states increasingly turned toward using the media vector to enforce national communicational regimes and identities. "The audience drifted away, and became easy prey for Western predators, particularly the Voice of America, Radio Monte Carlo and the BBC World Service. Foreign stations were pumping out 412 hours of broadcasts in Arabic every twenty-four hours."[29] Dependence is not just a matter of a lack of economic or cultural sovereignty, it is a matter also of the relative ability of one's indigenous matrix of vectors to hold the attention of one's people and engage on equal terms with the vector fields beyond.

This very brief sketch of the development of the communication vectors in the region can help account for two things: the way Arab and regional interests were outmaneuvered by the United States in the diplomatic endgame toward war, and the incredibly rapid dissemination throughout the world of the image of the hostages held by Saddam Hussein. The pattern of close vectoral integration into the world markets combined with underdeveloped regional vectors and flows stacked the odds against a regional solution to the crisis at the outset. But I'm getting a bit ahead of the story now. The immediate thing is to account for the instant global circulation of that image of Saddam Hussein stroking Stuart Lockwood.

Proximity to a hub in the vector field is the first factor in its circulation. Its news value is the second. Cultural studies essayist John Hartley suggests that "news includes stories on a daily basis which enable everyone to recognise a larger unity or community than their own immediate contacts, and to identify with the news outlet as 'our' storyteller."[30] The protocols of everyday life appear here as the imagined categories of a far more vast and unevenly global terrain of what I call *telesthesia,* or perception at a distance. This world of telesthesia is organized temporally in terms of "visible, distant visions of order," but where these are highlighted negatively by "the fundamental test of newsworthiness," namely, "disorder—deviation from any supposed steady state."[31] Telesthesia is organized spatially by what Hartley calls Theydom. "Individuals in Theydom are treated as being all the same; their identity consists in being 'unlike us,' so they are 'like each other.'"

Definitions of Theydom may have deep historical roots, as we saw in the case of Orientalism, where the Theydom of the Arabs still hinges in Western fantasy on venerable Orientalist archetypes. Things that happen to "people like us" happen to individuals, like Stuart Lockwood. Things that happen to them happen to typical representatives, who may be called upon to give "typical" opinions in the media but are far less likely to be named and individuated in the way little Stuart was. We can think of Theydom in general in the way Slavoj Žižek proposes, as those who threaten our enjoyment, by participating either too much in the pleasures of it—or too little.

So far we have two things combining to bring us Stuart Lockwood. One is the presence of a vector from where he is to wherever you are. The other is a set of everyday conventions operating to make his plight, as one of us, subjected to the horrid interruption of disorder that being held hostage undoubtedly constitutes. There is a connection and a convention, in time and space, making him fall from the sky into our lives.

There is yet a third factor, which has more to do with the swift and terse responses to Saddam Hussein's hostage talk show from Western diplomatic and political authorities. The latter not only want to impress upon their home audiences their energetic response to the situation, they want to communicate this to a world audience, using the international news vectors. This is because Lockwood's captivity is a small-scale event within a larger one. Iraq's invasion of Kuwait and any response to it affects not only the region, but a whole world of trade, investment, migration, and strategic interest. Since the vectors of interest implicated reach out from Kuwait into the globe, powerful actors wishing to influence subsequent events must use the communication vector to publicize their public views and moves worldwide. This is why such a tiny gesture as patting a boy on the head resonates darkly in diverse cultural frameworks, of which I have mentioned only one. It draws responses also aimed along the global vectors of opinion and influence. It was a signal moment in the story of this weird global media event.

How then can such a weird global media event be conceptualized? The event as I will define it in this book is something that unfolds within the *movement* of images along media vectors. These media vectors connect the site at which a crisis appears with the sites of image management and interpretation. Vectors then disseminate the flows of images processed at those managerial sites to the terminal sites of the process, so they fall from the sky into our lives. In this instance the vector connects a bewildering array of places: Baghdad, Riyadh, Washington, London, Paris, New York. Into the vision mix went images hauled off the global satellite feed, showing us Lockwood one second and Douglas Hurd responding to Lockwood's plight the next. The vector created a space where one can appear quite "naturally" to respond to the other, in the blink of an edit. We witnessed the montaging of familiar and surprising sites into the seamless space and staccato time of the media vector. The terminal site of the vector is the terminal in almost every home the Western world over.

Vectors and Antipodes

> When we can go to the antipodes and back in an instant, what will become of us?
>
> —Paul Virilio

A word on this word "vector." I've borrowed it from the writings of French urbanist and speculative writer Paul Virilio. It describes the aspect of the development of technology that interests him most and the style of writing he employs to capture that aspect. It is a term from geometry meaning a line of fixed length and direction but having no fixed position. Virilio employs it to mean any trajectory along which bodies, information, or warheads can potentially pass. The satellite technology used to beam images from Iraq to America and on to London can be thought of as a vector. This technology could link almost any three such sites, and relay video and audio information of a certain quality along those points at a given speed and at a certain cost. It could just as easily link Beijing to Berlin and Sydney, or quite a few other combinations of points. Yet in each case the speed of transmission and its quality would be essentially the same. This is the sense in which any particular media technology can be thought of as a vector. Media vectors have fixed properties, like the length of a line in the geometric concept of vector. Yet that vector has no necessary position: it can link almost any points together.

This is the paradox of the media vector. The technical properties are hard and fast and fixed, but it can connect enormously vast and vaguely defined spaces together and move images, and sounds, words, and furies, between them. The vector is an oxymoronic relay system: a rigorous indeterminacy; a determinate imprecision; a precise ambiguity; an ambiguous determinism. The technical feat of the vector, so celebrated in cases like CNN's Gulf war coverage, was very quickly applied to the global simulcast of *The Simple Truth,* the band-aid rock benefit that inevitably followed in this primitive media logic.

After that it rapidly became a commonplace. It passes imperceptibly into an unacknowledged part of the information landscape we take for granted. Technology is mentioned only to celebrate it. Resistant these days to such celebration, even critical writers treat any mention of the technical determinants of the possible (which is what the vector amounts to) with a blanket suspicion.[32] Critical writing often refuses to discuss technology on the assumption that any mention of it is a legitimation of technology per se.[33]

So it seems apt to bring the critique of technology back into play in cultural criticism. Karl Marx, Lewis Mumford, and Raymond Williams all acknowledged in their writings the importance of a historical grasp of the technical.[34] Yet they were grappling with different stages of the unfolding of the modern and the technological regime of modernization, in which the technological appeared as something unfamiliar. Nowadays, television and its successors in the vectoral stakes seem to require an intentional defamiliarization to appear at all—so much have they become environmental. By taking extreme moments in the instant before the media recuperate them, perhaps there is a space in which to illustrate the workings of the vector, where this particularly scary story can be told. The Russian formalist critic Victor Shklovsky once said that the real reveals itself in culture in much the same way gravity reveals itself to the inhabitants of a structure when its ceiling caves in on them.[35] When reading this book, I hope you feel a faint sprinkling of plaster landing on your head while you are lounging in the living room taking in the news.

It is not only media technologies that have this vectoral aspect. The SCUD missiles Iraq launched against Israel and Saudi Arabia are also a vector. They had certain fixed technical properties: payload, range, and accuracy. Yet they could be launched at any point within a given radius. On the other hand, one could think of the entire U.S. invasion force that mobilized for Operation Desert Storm as a vector too. The fixed properties here have to do with the length of time it takes to deploy a force of a given size. Yet that force could be deployed almost anywhere. Indeed, in an age of proliferating media vectors, perhaps the public spectacle of a threat to the interests of imperial powers will provoke the deployment of this other kind of vector. The alternative, something we also saw on TV during the Gulf crisis, is the vector of diplomacy: diplomats can shuttle between any series of points negotiating an apparently limitless range of demands with seemingly limited results. The time pressures introduced by the military and media vectors pose a serious problem for the tactful tempo of diplomacy.

The beauty of Virilio's concept of vector is that it grasps the dynamic, historical tendency of international media events, but it is not a concept limited to media technologies alone. It also provides a way of thinking about the other aspects of contemporary events. Virilio also homes in on the apparent tendencies that seem to result from the relentless, competitive development of technical vectors. For example, the tendency toward a homogenization of the space of the globe. Its tendency to become an abstract, geometric space across which powerful vectors can play freely. He grasps the novel kinds of crisis this seems to engender: "An imperceptible movement on a computer keyboard, or one made by a 'skyjacker' brandishing a cookie box covered with masking tape, can lead to catastrophic chains of events that until recently were inconceivable. We are too willing to ignore the threat of proliferation resulting from the acquisition of nuclear explosives by irresponsible parties. We are even more willing to ignore the proliferating threat resulting from the vectors that cause those who own or borrow them to become just as irresponsible."[36]

Perhaps it is worth hitting the video pause button at this point in the replay, just as the image of Saddam and Lockwood comes into view. We can ponder what we remember is coming up, somewhere amid the commercial breaks and station identifications. Saddam, who hijacked the Western media with this hostage image, and Bush, who lines up with the people who own these vectors, are not going to be responsible about this. We can forget the Iraqi military threat, which collapsed under fire from the vectoral onslaught. What bears thinking about is whether this media vector is part of what killed people, what led to the starvation and misery of the Kurdish refugees, or Iraqi people dying from cholera and dysentery in shattered hospitals. Not the technical vector alone, but the vector and the networks and structures of social, political, economic, and cultural power it connects across are at the center of this event.

In terms of vectoral power in general, the media are part of the problem of power, not merely a separate space of reportage or critique of emergent forms of power that exist elsewhere. Needless to say, this book too is a part of that problematic, and does not exist outside, in a neutral space. It is in the worst of all possible worlds: within the regime of power created by the media vector, but relatively powerless there, within. . . .

The same goes for the rest of the great slew of critical outpourings on the Gulf war coming off the American presses. It was difficult, as an Australian, not to experience the war as something that happened in America, performed, acted, and sponsored by Americans, for Americans. On television, most voices were American. All the images looked American. Even Saddam seemed to be an American. As American as Lon Chaney or Bela Lugosi. Iraq seemed to be some place in America. A place like Wounded Knee or Kent State or the Big Muddy. This is why the critical reaction to the Gulf war, while admirable in many ways, strikes a strange note. Out on the fringes of the empire, the little media interzone I call an apartment served as the touchdown strip for not one but two waves of American media onslaughts in the Gulf war. The first was the television and wire service barrage. Then comes the critical response, making all the right points, mopping up the propaganda and the madness of it all. What this critical human-wave attack on the Gulf war missed was its own implication in the vectoral nets. In the information war, critical theory makes as much use of American vectoral power as its enemies.

The massive presence in the media flow of American stories, images, faces, voices, is sometimes all that stabilizes the flow of meaning in the global media net. Take away America's imaginary domination and the domination of the imaginary of America, and meaning would drift and eddy, caught in impossible turbulence and glide.[37] Not only the instant media coverage, but also the critical coverage relies on this stabilization of the referents, either positively or negatively.

In this book, I am more interested in the unpredictable movement of information than in pinning down its floating signifiers, and hence this book acknowledges but doesn't pay terribly much attention to the huge critical literature on the Gulf war coming out of the U.S. That literature is in a sense part of the problem this book sets out to analyze. In any case, this is not a book about the Gulf war, but about the evolution of the vector field which made the Gulf war, and the critical response to it, possible.

This is why the critical task has to be approached differently on the edge of the American empire from the way it is at its heart. What is marginal within the empire can have imperial effects on its margins. On the margins, the enormous flow of information in the vector field appears always as something from without. American criticism of the media Gulf war seldom registers this feeling of being struck by a flow from without. Perhaps the combination of a ready access to American media and the spatial displacement of the entire Pacific Ocean can be turned to advantage here. Even the odd effect of watching a breakfast TV news show like "NBC Today," retitled "NBC News Overnight," can have a displacing effect.

What I am talking about here is mobilizing as a means of critical orientation the feeling which every Australian who grew up after the Second World War knows. The feeling of growing up in a simulated America, in a culture with coordinates which are American, but which somehow don't match the territory at all. It is the opposite feeling to that of the immigrant, who is spatially at home in America, but alienated by language and custom. It is, on the contrary, a perverse intimacy with the language and cultural reference points which nevertheless takes place elsewhere, in a client state on the fringes. Places where, in Foucault's words, one can "listen to those things said on the great surface of the empire."[38]

Nightly Chimeras

By starting with this appearance of the media vector in everyday life, we can trace it back to a general problematic of the velocity of power. The "departure lounge" for this is not some abstract concept of everyday life in general, not the life of others, under the microscope, but *this* life, *these* events. A vectoral writing strategy considers the production of events within the media as the primary process that nevertheless gives the appearance of merely *reflecting* "naturally occurring" moments outside all such apparatus.

This may sound a little counterintuitive, since we all tend to take it for granted that regardless of how much the media construct a particular view of an event the media still *report* something outside of the media. While not disputing the fact that violent and momentous conjunctures arise whether the media report them or not, once the media take up such conjunctures they assume a quite different character. A vectoral approach looks at movements of information *transgressing* the boundaries between what were once historically distinct sites. It looks at the effect of this movement on the outcomes of conjunctures. It looks at the event as a peculiar and historically emergent form of communication—or rather of noncommunication, as we shall see.

The hostages Saddam Hussein held in Iraq connected the "Middle" East to almost all points in the Western world—even if the vector-brokers of the "Far" East remained relatively unmoved.[39] When the media vector out of Iraq showed hostages from the West, this was the point at which the event became genuinely if unequally global.[40] It directly engaged the interest of the viewing, listening, reading, information-rich millions. The hostages were "ours," and "they" were holding them. "They" had invaded some little country, and "they" were threatening "us" to prevent "us" from retaliating against "them." As the event unraveled, the principal focus of the media implicated a Western audience directly with the other.

In writing about the Gulf war as an event happening in a network of global vectors, which made it that much more instant, that much more deadly, writing struggles to recall that we are not just spectators. The whole thing about the media vector is that its tendency is toward *implicating* the entire globe. Its historic tendency is toward making any and every point a possible connection—everyone and everything is a potential object and/or subject of a mediated relation, realized instantly. In the Gulf war, to see it was to be implicated in it. There is no safe haven from which to observe, unaffected. Nor is there a synoptic vantage point, above and beyond the whole process, for looking on in a detached and studious manner. We are all, always, already—there.

As the possibility of war increased, television's role changed, ever so imperceptibly. No longer did it exist in a relation to an audience assumed to be a mass of consumers or a public to be educated.[41] The event turns television into part of a feedback loop connecting the spectator to the action via the vagaries of "opinion" and the pressures of the popular on political elites. The television spectator becomes a vague and quixotic, unpredictable yet manipulatory "delay" in the circuit of power.[42] As an Australian citizen, I had my minor part in the drama. A bit part as a diode in the "public opinion" circuit connecting Saddam Hussein and his "guests" and George Bush's press conferences to the range of options open to the Australian state.

This is the curious thing about global media vectors. They can make events that connect the most disparate sites of public action appear simultaneously as a private drama filled with familiar characters and moving stories. The vector blurs the thin line between political crisis and media sensation; it eclipses the geographical barriers separating distinct cultural and political entities; and it transgresses the borders between public and private spheres on both the home front and the front line.

There is no longer a clear distinction between public and private spaces, now that the vector transgresses the boundaries of the private sphere. Generation by generation, television has wormed its way into every recess. First it breached the walls of the parlor. Then it rapidly made itself at home in the living room. Now many people have one in the bedroom, as I do, although this would have been an unthinkable spatial arrangement in my parents' era.

Worse, having grown up on the stuff, there is no distinction for me between the space of television and the space of my imagination. Television passes through and permeates every pore of my body, which may be 90 percent water in its physical composition, but is 90 percent TV drama and pop songs and other trash that wafted in on the vector as far as its learned information component is concerned. As a song that is seemingly burned into the hard wiring of my memory has it, "I stick the aerial into my skin."

As philosopher of science Donna Haraway suggests, "We are all chimeras, theorized and fabricated hybrids of machine and organism."[43] Our chimerical confusion may result from the dissolution of the spaces which kept aspects of the social order separate. Indeed, one of the defining characteristics of the event is that it exposes the disturbing ability of the vector to disrupt all seemingly stable distributions of space and the more or less watertight vessels that used to contain meaning in space and time. As the Gulf war unfolded, the sacred space bled into the profane domain—of television. One keeps the sense of what it means to be in public life as opposed to private life by keeping them spatially separate. Haraway argues that technology destabilizes certain distinctions. Masculine power keeps itself apart in its imaginary from the animal, the mechanical, the feminine. Yet how difficult these separations become! The sense of horror at Saddam's touching a child has a layer to it which draws on the horror of the separate and excluded part reappearing in the everyday sphere of "normality." There is animal baseness in the Western fear of Saddam's image, and a horror of the "feminine" aspect of the gesture.

The reason why these interpretations should spring to mind has to do with another sense of separation, the separation of such things off from the West and their projection into the East. Yet here they are, returned to haunt us, in an uncontrollable way. Here they are in the interzone of everyday life, intersected by the rays of television. To adapt a line from William Burroughs, in an incongruous yet strikingly apt context: "These things were revealed to me in the Interzone, where East meets West coming around the other way."[44]

The interzone is this space where chimerical and monstrous images become a part of everyday life. Haraway is right to point toward the excluded figures, the figures of the feminine, the animal, and the mechanical, and to insist on their importance as borders which frame patriarchal culture. The evolution of such figures needs to be put in the context of the dynamics of the vector, which is the material means via which such figures, literally, transport themselves into everyday life.

So there I was, hooked on CNN, freebasing on its fractured images of the East, taking the portable TV into the office at the university where I work so as not to lose the thread. Like everyone else I was "totally wired" for a while there, until boredom set in again. Normal patterns of life in time were disrupted while the fascination lasted. Fascination with the Gulf war didn't last long, but there was a more durably intriguing formal quality to the everyday experience of the event.

The distinction between public and private space seemed to have been superseded by a distinction between public and private *modalities of time*. There is a form and a flow appropriate to the virtual enactment of free speech and assembly along the vector, and a format for the private pursuit of happiness.[45] Television traditionally divides its time between a public and a private modality—but the event can interrupt this division.

As cultural studies writer Patricia Mellencamp says, the "intrusion of the real is also the taking over of entertainment by the news division, the replacement of women by men."[46] The Gulf war coverage displaced children's TV. This highlights one of the uses of television which matter to many women and the domestic situations they are frequently obliged to manage. The Gulf war took it away from them for supposedly more important male concerns. Public time intruded on the private, but masculine-coded space also intruded on feminine-coded space.

The Gulf war was a chimerical thing, in the sense that it cut an ambiguous figure in the gendering of television reception. Not only did it disturb the macro-separation of East from West, it disturbed the micro-separation of male from female within the allocation of televisual time between men and women. The event disrupted cybernetic simpatico between child and TV, drawing attention to a vastly more monstrous network of chimeras. (Where, strangely enough, one of the first things we noticed had to do with a child and TV.) This is the alarming and fascinating thing about the vector: it transgresses separations at vastly differing spatial scales.

Letters to the newspapers couched the complaint about the "scheduling" of the Gulf war on television in terms of the disturbing effects of the war coverage on children. Given that it was women who spoke *for* children in making this observation, it is better to read it as an objection to television disturbing the relation of women to children. As a machine for "minding" children in the double sense of pacifying their bodies and rebooting their minds, television mediates the relationship of child-minder to child. The intrusion of the unpredictable time of the event into the daily schedule of school and domestic work signals a disruption of television's usefulness as a domestic tool. The use of television as a predictable device for privatized tasks in everyday life conflicts with its increasing engagement with the public, global time and space of unpredictable events.

Moreover, it weaves an "us" and a vast map of Theydoms together as the light and dark strands of a narrative distinction within the event as it threads its way across these other kinds of borders. In breaking down solid old boundaries, the vector creates new distinctions. Flexible distinctions airily flow through the story-time realm of information. They selectively replace the heavy walls and barriers that compartmentalized information in days when vectors were less rapid and less effective. This cruder narrative structure can be applied to more sudden and diverse events to produce the same effect of apparent narrative seamlessness. The application by the media of simple temporal structures, in a flexible fashion, produces more rigid and uniform stories about events.

There have been many analyses of these wartime bedtime stories that expose the interests of capital and empire that lie behind them.[47] Yet the left tells stories of its own. What matters is telling convincing stories, which show others ways to account for the facts. Or persuasive stories, which help as many people as possible to credit this version of the event over other ones. The democratic forces that want to rewrite this event as a chapter in the story of, say, American imperialism or Orientalist racism or global ecocide, must learn the tools and the tricks of the story trade—and prevail.

As the technology of persuasion grows more complex, the art of telling stories in the wake of events grows both more complex and more instantaneous. If this book is less concerned with telling these alternative stories, it is not because such things are not important. It is because it is also important to understand the nature of mediated political events and the power field of the vector. This is the field of becoming within which a certain kind of power is immanent. A field in which democratic forces need to speak, and attempt at least to make good sense for and with the many against the few.

Who Knows What

As Montaigne remarked, there are certain viewpoints that expose us to our own fundamental state of ignorance. Confronting an event on television is such a viewpoint. This is not to celebrate ignorance, merely to recognize that there are no authorities one can evoke when genuine, full-blown, out-of-control events occur. There is, however, always a store of useful information and sets of conceptual tools that might help. Access to these is a form of power that can be very unevenly distributed. The vector is a form of power. Rapid and effective access to useful information is a vector. Not all vectors are extensive ones, seeking to cover the span of the globe. Some are intensive. They seek microscopic paths through the labyrinthine mazes of data stored in the cores of the information-rich archives of the West. Access to these vectors is a form of power, and hence a line along which the struggle in and around events takes place.

Now, some of the really useful information is "classified." It will be released very slowly and to few people. On the other hand, conceptual tools for extracting the most out of the information that is freely available about any actual or potential event are available to a much wider pool of people. This is the process and the practice this book concentrates on: forming and using constellations of conceptual tools that can be deployed rapidly and across disciplines to grasp the nature of the event. I believe this "tactical response" to the media vector to be a worthwhile skill to learn, to teach, to practice, and to communicate.

In a nominally democratic country such as Australia, one acts as part of a public sphere in the sense filmmaker Alexander Kluge gives to the term.[48] A public sphere—a matrix of accessible vectors—acts as a point of exchange between private experience and public life; between intimate, incommunicable experience and collective perception. Public networks are arenas where the struggle to communicate takes place. Two aspects of this concept are relevant here. For Kluge, writing in postwar Germany, the problem revolves around the historic failure in 1933 of the public sphere to prevent the rise of fascism. "Since 1933 we have been waging a war that has not stopped. It is always the same theme—the noncorrelation of intimacy and public life—and the same question: how can I communicate strong emotions to build a common life?"[49] For Kluge, the public sphere is a fundamentally problematic domain, caught between the complexities of the social and the increasing separation of private life.

One has to ask, however, whom Kluge imagines he is speaking for here. Perhaps there are other experiences of the relation between intimate experience and the public sphere, buried out there in popular culture. Perhaps it is only intellectuals who feel so estranged from the flow of information in mass-media vectors. After all, the mode of address adopted by most popular media doesn't address a highly cultured intellectual like Kluge—or even a provincial one like me. We were trained in quite other ways of handling information, and have a repertoire of quite different stories with which to filter present events. How could we claim to know what goes on out there in the other interzones, in quite other spaces where different flows from different vectors meet quite other memories and experiences of everyday life? After all, we intellectuals keep finding more than enough differences among ourselves.

Cultural studies has among its merits the fact that it takes these other interzones seriously. It tries to theorize the frictions between Kluge's intimate experience and the network of vectors, or it actually tries to collect and interpret accounts of such experiences.[50] This book tends to leave open the question of the audience. It is more concerned with the vector and the event. However, it is necessary to at least attempt to maintain a self-critical relation to the codes and practices of the interzone specific to intellectual media experiences. After all, "our" training, "our" prejudices in relation to the vector might be part of the problem. Nothing exempts "our" institutions and interests from the war of the vector, the struggle to control the trajectories of information.

With the spread of the vector into the private realm, a window opens that might be used to create a line along which the communication of intimate experience and collective feeling might take place. Or it might be used exclusively in the interests of privatized consumption. Anyway, the nature and uses of the media vector are not given in advance. They are neither agents of social domination nor avenues of resistant, diverse, and festive play for creative audiences. It is best not to generalize about the vector. It is best to examine its antics case by case, or *experiment* with the communication process itself. This book does the former, rather more modestly than Kluge's heroic attempts at the latter. What is at stake is not the recreation of the public grounds for a universal reason, but finding the tactical resources for a far more differentiated and diverse struggle to achieve communication, that "simple thing so hard to achieve."[51]

The maintenance of democracy requires a practice within the public networks for responding to events that it was never quite designed to handle. Virilio asks whether democracy is still possible in this age of "chronopolitics." Perhaps democracy succumbs to "dromocracy"—the power of the people plowed under by the power to technological speed.[52] Well, perhaps, but the only way to forestall such pessimism is to experiment with ways of knowing and acting in the face of events. One has to experiment with relatively freely available conceptual tools and practices and base a democratic knowledge on these. This may involve moving beyond the techniques and procedures of the academy. In Antonio Gramsci's terms, the academic intellectual risks becoming merely a traditional intellectual, one of many layers of cultural sediment, deposited and passed over by the engine of capital and the trajectory of the vector. One has to make organic connections with the leading media and cultural practices of the day.[53]

Nevertheless, the historic memory and living tissue of the academy stores resources that are useful and vital. In studying an event like the Gulf crisis, a vectoral writing can build on the best of two existing critical approaches. To the schools that concentrate on the structural power of transnational capital flows and military coercion, it adds a close attention to the power of transgressive media vectors and the specific features of the events they generate. To the schools that study the space of the media text in the context of periodic struggles for influence with the national-popular discourse, it adds an international dimension and a closer attention to the changing technical means that produce information flows. The event is a phenomenon a little too quixotic for either of these approaches. Hence the need to examine it in a new light, as the chance encounter of the local conjuncture with the global vector—on the operating table. The chance encounter of Saddam Hussein with CNN, like the meeting of the umbrella with the sewing machine, has a surreal, "surgical" logic specific to it. It is not entirely reducible to the long-term structures of capital or military power and lies in the spaces *between* national-popular discourses. Writing the vector is not really something that can be practiced with the tools of the Herbert Schiller school of political economy or the Stuart Hall school of cultural studies alone, although it owes much to both.[54]

The event is not reducible to the methods of the "area specialists" either. When studying events from the point of view of the site at which they originate, they always remain the province of specialists who deal with that particular turf. Thus the Gulf war is the province of Middle East specialists, the Tiananmen Square massacre of Sinologists, the fall of the Berlin Wall of Germanists, to mention just some of the events studied in this book. Events often generate valuable responses from area specialists, but these usually focus on the economic, political, or cultural factors at work in the area the specialists know firsthand. They do not often analyze the vectoral trajectories via which the rest of the world views the event.[55]

In an age when transnational media flows are running across all those academic specialties, perhaps it is time to construct a discourse that follows the flow of information (and power) across both the geographic and conceptual borders of discourse. Perhaps it is time to start experimenting, as Kluge has done, with modes of disseminating critical information in the vector field. Perhaps it is time to examine intellectual practices of storing, retrieving, and circulating knowledge. Without wishing to return to the practice of the "general intellectual," it may be worth considering whether the development of the vector calls for new ways of playing the role of the engaged intellectual.[56]

The Event

Events have no particular scale, duration, or topos. The media vector renders equivalent a tiny gesture or a major battle, Saddam stroking or the U.S. air force bombing. Television frequently performs this extreme relativity. The Gulf was at times a matter of metonymic close-ups, at times a matter of vast maps and pointers. The time frame of an event can be as flexible as the scale. Some pundits dated the commencement of the event from the invasion of Kuwait, some traced it back to imperialist legacies. Others linked it to the misty dawning of "Islamicism." The troubling prehistory of Vietnam unavoidably had to be negotiated, not least because it saturates television entertainment via Vietnam dramas like "Tour of Duty" and "China Beach."[57]

The curve of the event can be traced back through any number of historical or narrative lines. The event is where seemingly distinct trajectories that would otherwise be studied by separate disciplines seem to become fused in a white heat of light and combustible commotion. The event nevertheless has nothing to do with the more predictable theater of history. As Foucault said, an event "is not a decision, a treaty, a reign, or a battle, but the reversal of a relationship of forces, the usurpation of power, the appropriation of a vocabulary turned against those who had once used it, a feeble domination that poisons itself as it grows lax, the entry of a masked 'other.'"[58] This list seems to cover interesting aspects of all the events studied in this book, from the stock market crash to the fall of the Berlin Wall to the Gulf war. A further specification needs to be added, however. Here only events which happen at a distance, in the network of vectors, concern us.

The site of the event also shifted from time to time. Did the Gulf war take place in Kuwait, Baghdad, or Washington? Was the site the Middle East or the whole globe? This is a particularly vexing point. If Iraqi commanders order a

SCUD missile launch via radio-telephone from Baghdad, orbiting U.S. satellites may intercept the signal. Another satellite detects the launch using infrared sensors. The American military installation at Nurrungar in South Australia downlinks information from both satellites. From there a satellite relays it to the Pentagon, which routes it to the U.S. command headquarters in Saudi Arabia and to Patriot missile bases in Saudi Arabia and Israel.[59] This is not the only vector involved that crosses borders—the traditional stake in geopolitical struggles. A journalist who files a report via a Satellite News Gatherer (SNG) from Baghdad also sends a signal bouncing around the globe. In this case, via satellite back to Cable News Network (CNN) headquarters in Atlanta, and from there back to Europe, America, and Australia via cable, landline, and satellite. Events, then, are a product of competing technologies that cross borders with impunity.

Underlying the various constructions of the event there are "real" actions and forces at work. However, they are not always independent of the processes of representation. In the 1989 Beijing massacre, taken up later, the event took the form of a positive feedback loop. The constructions of the event made by foreign journalists, editors, and other vector-brokers fed back into the event itself via a global loop encompassing radio, telephone, and fax vectors. They impacted back on the further unfolding of the event itself.[60] While it may be desirable to attempt to establish the reality underlying the appearance on the evening news, this is becoming increasingly difficult.

This is especially the case where complex media vectors increase the volume and velocity of salient news information flowing across increasingly vast distances. Information which is available "live" from the other side of the world can flow straight back there, just as fast and just as "live." The volume and velocity of information the vector generates may bear no relation to the significance or scale of the event. Hence extremely volatile interactions between constructions of events where and when they occur and in international news vectors elsewhere are possible, and indeed increasingly common. Almost all the world is an open field for the vector.

The event is a complex of vectors. As the volume, velocity, and flexibility of the media vector proliferate, events appear more suddenly and connect quite disparate sites together in tightly coupled form.[61] The propagation of media vectors has not made events any easier to understand or any clearer. The more quickly the media get to the scene of an event and the more rapidly they transmit information about it to the rest of the world, the more impossible it becomes to disentangle the conjuncture itself from the vectors into which it is inexorably drawn. The spectacular doubling of the crisis in a new, vastly expanded terrain captivates the indigenous roots of the crisis. The event irrupts through the routine occurrence of news, always a little quicker than news professionals and other vector-brokers can stuff it back into acceptable formats. The acceleration of events triggers endless series of little crises in the narrative management of discourse.

As Walter Benjamin once said, "It is hardly possible to write a history of information separately from a history of the corruption of the press."[62] It is undoubtedly true that in most instances, those that play a brokerage role between the site of the event and the flow of the vector take vested interests into account. Yet here this form of corruption is doubled by another, equal and opposite one. Just as the execution of power corrupts the flow of information, so too does the flow of information corrupt the execution of power. The form this reflux takes is the irruption of the event. The fact that the news audience rouses itself from boredom and pays attention to the screen of the event may be symptomatic of a widespread intuition that these are the moments when information bites back. They thus have a special status in the history of information, alongside the story of the corruption of the press by the Beaverbrooks and the Murdochs.

By taking the failures of narrative seamlessness as the point of departure, I hope to defamiliarize the seductive, sticky little stories that pour out of the media and pass through us, pawing at consciousness, seeping into the pores of the unconscious mind. In looking to where narrative rationality breaks down, where the logic of sensing the event bombs out, the aim is to understand the workings of the vector field as a rehearsal for intervening—next time around. It is a preview of the countertrajectories that democratic counterintelligence might mobilize in future events, the scale and significance and fear we can only imagine, but *must* imagine.

Public Image

To return to our point of departure: the Gulf war. The moment Saddam Hussein took hostages, an added moral dimension was inevitable in this event. Holding hostages at strategic sites was a lurid weapon, particularly when coupled with another weapon—television. The message was that he held some of "our" people in "his" domain. The vector inserted this message as close to home in the West as it is possible to go: right into the living rooms of millions. With few weapons with which to take the conflict to the Western powers, Saddam found a way to lob a logic bomb directly into our sumptuous laps. While thousands of third world refugees fought for food in Jordan, the image of a few Western women and children, released with impeccable public-relations timing, captured the attention of the world media. A cynical business all around. There are already many powers, it seems, big and small, hegemonic or despotic, learning the new language of force and terror that is the media vector.

Here television was the trigger for yet another weapon—public opinion. As French essayist Jean Baudrillard aptly remarks, the "masses" formed by industrial capitalism, who replaced the "public" of the liberal era, have in turn been transformed into a kind of "black hole." As he says, "All power silently founders on this silent majority, which is neither an entity nor a sociological reality, but the shadow cast by power, its sinking vortex, its form of absorption."[63] These new masses, hunkered down in front of the TV, do not interpret the media vector according to their own code and speak back, as they might in a public sphere. They silently absorb the light of the media vector into themselves.

The vector must make this silent mass speak, and this is the role of public opinion, of surveys and questionnaires and phone polls and the like. The institutions that produce public opinion create an interlocking grid of representations of the public. These private institutions have thus taken over a function that was formerly the task of the liberal public sphere on the one hand, and of representative government on the other. These institutions also become vectoral.

The public opinion poll has two principal functions: to construct a representation in the place of the collective body of citizens and another in the place of the collective body of consumers. The "private" functions of the old bourgeois private sphere were individual economic activity based on self-interest and rational debate on the issues of the day by citizens with a stake in the general interest. These now appear as an effect of intensive and extensive vectors. The masses, too, feel the effects of the vector in the image it creates of them.

One of the most central vectoral movements is the rating of television audiences. As cultural studies scholar Ien Ang argues, the ratings institutions do not really measure "audience," they create and manage an image of it.[64] This process is a necessary part of the development of the media vector. Without some image of the audience it creates, neither the technical nor the cultural evolution of the media vector has any grasp on its own effects. Vectoral institutions need benchmarks of success they can use to promote themselves to corporate sponsors.

Thus the proprietors of the media vector have an interest in the ratings game, which has striven over the years to produce ever more rapid, more accurate, more diversified collective portraits of its imaginary other half—the viewer. From the diary method to today's Peoplemeter and Homeunit recording devices, TV ratings have accelerated from monthly to weekly to now daily records of alleged audience size and the share. The Peoplemeter method relies on the viewer pushing buttons on a handset like the TV remote control. It retains subjective and active elements, but the choices made by the sample audience can be collected via computer and phone line for instantaneous collation. This microvectoral circuit culminates in the delivery to the station programmers of a result the following morning of the previous night's survey. Hence decisions can be made quickly—such as the decision to curtail the round-the-clock coverage of the Gulf war as ratings started to fall.

Television ratings create an image of the black hole of the masses as consumers, as a quantity of corneas. This mass of captured corneas, which one might call the TV eye in honor of Iggy Pop, is a nominal creation with very real economic effects. The agglomerated TV eye is a commodity that, neatly sorted into "demographics" according to age, gender, and buying power, can be sold to advertisers.[65] The institutions that manage the image of the masses do not merely imagine it as the subject and the object of a commodity relation. It also exists, nominally at least, as the citizen mass.

The sociologist of culture Pierre Bourdieu analyzed this process of the formation of public opinion from the point at which the system breaks down, the point where people answer "don't know" to exactly the questions that citizens are supposed to answer. Bourdieu argues that the opinion poll assumes the universal ability to make rational judgments that Habermas attributes to classical bourgeois conceptions of the public sphere.[66] As the example of the polling on the question of American involvement in the Gulf war shows, the assumption of a universal competence in public matters is far from warranted.[67] Confronted by questions about a part of the world most people know little about, informed by only a few thirty-second bites on the television, it is no wonder that many poll subjects gave apparently contradictory answers or refused to respond.

This refusal constitutes a turning away from the image of the public that polling creates and that answering questions only serves to legitimate. As Bourdieu argues, contemporary liberal society denies most people the means to form an opinion. It refuses this entitlement to all but a tiny fraction of dominant classes. So it can hardly complain if many refuse to have anything to do with the creation of an image of the public over the void of the mass. Polling is a system of intensive vectors that make the information displaced continually around the vector field appear to keep moving. It is an institutionalized partner to a dialogue, repeating to the media vector what the media vector has already said, but voiced as if it came from the place from which the public would speak, if it could.

This institutional matrix of polling can be made to perform quite mundane tasks, like appearing to answer in the place of the public about which TV sitcom the mass prefers. Or it can serve a more sinister function, echoing back to power a loving refrain for its worst excesses. The Gulf war comes under the latter category, but also the former. Simultaneous with the launch of the war was the launch of the media coverage and its shadow—the polling ritual. This ritual sought to establish the seemingly mundane—whether anyone liked the programmed display of air attacks and homely chats with the "boys" in the desert. It also sought something darker—a legitimation of the displacement of information in an increasingly violent circle.

When the Iraqis put the image of the hostages held on Iraqi TV into circulation, they had not counted on the complexity of these filters. The stately ritual of official response, the simulated sagacity of media-brokered cogitation, the carefully manicured impression of populist upsurge, the corporate management of the free commerce of opinion by the polling vector—these are formal strategies which publicly frame the emotional drama of the hostages. Captured by this circuit, this electric cage of information channeling, those poor people the Iraqis held were no longer exactly hostages. They were prisoners of war, for the news bite has eliminated the distance between the front line and the home front as effectively as has the vector of nuclear missiles.

Saddam Hussein fought with missives where he lacked missiles, talking heads where he had no warheads. While the Iraqi SCUDs had sufficient range to reach Tel Aviv, only by playing to the bondage fascinations the Western media has with hostages could he launch an intercontinental attack with image ballistics. The Western media were not exactly in a position to take a moral stand against the hostage-taking. They rushed right in to present the hostage spectacle, and compromise themselves in the semiotic violence. The media willingly gave Saddam Hussein his fifteen-second news bite at the succulent cherry of temporary fame. Like all celebrity, it was a tragic performance, for once alienated from its intent and dispersed into the vector, it was out of its maker's hands, and in the hands of other, more powerful forces. Some of these were human forces, adjusting the "spin" on the image, turning it to advantage. Some were inhuman hands. For the vector itself is a "player" now, only relatively under the control of even the most powerful interests.

Images displaced around the media vector are weapons now, but of a different kind from the old-fashioned warheads of the military vector proper. Like the weapons of the cold war, these can backfire, and in this case clearly did. Fascinated and horrified, implicated and repelled by the nightly visitation by the Saddam-hosted horror show, TV viewers became a captive audience for media-brokers and opinion-pollsters. The pollsters invited their subjects to substitute patriotic revulsion against Saddam's solemn celebrity for televisual complicity with it, and thus recover a kind of distance. Opinion was rallied behind President Bush, the sheriff's badge pinned on, authorizing him to deliver us from television and deliver to Iraq a thousand points of incendiary light. And so the good television drove out the bad. It seems that these days the president's first duty is to mobilize a host of belligerent and patriotic information with which to rally the public-opinion data, that legitimating talisman of the hyperreal polity.[68]

Orienting the Other

Meanwhile back at the missile farm, the Pentagon's professional military "managers" of the Colin Powell stripe handled the military mobilization proper. While the military could harness some army surplus plans for countering a Soviet threat to the Middle East for use in this new event, the narrative problems faced by the media's vector-brokers were a little more intractable. The Western imaginary immediately associated the taking of hostages with an "evil" image of the Middle East. Newspaper reports hauled out long strings of stories that proposed an image of a long-unfolding event, including hostages held by pro-Iranian groups when tension between Iran and the West was at flash point. The fact that Iraq received "our" support at the time, the fact that the U.S. started making overtures to Iran, passed the TV eye by in stately silence. Ignoring inconvenient data was not so much a conspiracy as a necessity, as media tried desperately to identify the bad guys.[69] Moslems and Arabs—indistinguishable in the Western imaginary—make easy television villains, but only so long as the black hats and the white hats are clearly marked and distributed.

As we watch the wheels of television's supple if obtuse imagination turn, we are watching Orientalism at work. As Said says: "One aspect of the electronic, postmodern world is that there has been a reinforcement of the stereotypes by which the Orient is viewed. Television has forced information into a more and more standardized mould."[70] The stereotypes built up during the Western conquest of the Middle Eastern edge of the Orient in both literature and imperial reports are at one and the same time a powerful knowledge through which Western power still asserts itself in the region, and a misleading discourse that gives us demonically simple images of the Middle East. Or as Burroughs put it: "So East screams past West on the scenic railway over the midways of Interzone."[71]

Said does not supply an explanation for why television should exacerbate Orientalist clichés. Part of the answer, it seems to me, is that the *speed* with which television brings the force of events to bear on public consciousness requires simple but subtle, standardized but interchangeable narrative constructions.[72] These narrative tactics prevent the event from rupturing the seamlessness of televisual discourse, which is to say national-popular discourse. Thus the Saddam Hussein who strokes the hair of the child hostage on television is at once the devious pederast that the Orientalist imagination deems this behavior to signal and a national enemy.[73]

It was an unremarkable fact that the Western media roundly denounced this spectacle. From a human-rights construction of the event, it is surely convincing to present things as a moral story, emphasizing the double wrong of the hostage-taking coupled with the television display. Now, one could argue that there is a certain hypocrisy in denouncing Iraqi hostage-taking. After all, the greatest example of hostage-taking in history was the cold war. It worked exactly by taking hostage the populations of almost all the Western and Eastern worlds, and a few million innocent bystanders as well. This Byzantine hostage-taking was called deterrence.

Hostage-taking, viewed as an event with a long and sordid history, might have left Western commentators with a little less secure ground to stand on in condemning Iraq's crude application of the practice. Professional media-brokers always try to build event horizons that exclude the space in which their constructor actually stands. In contrast, a critical approach to the event has to find the blind spot around which the vector-brokers weave their narrative constructions, the hole where the solidity of the ground required for the brokering melts into air. For the media, difficult events have to be brokered in such a way as to preserve the distance between it and us, but a critical approach should try to locate the vector that is always threatening to eliminate that ground. The professional manager of the event needs to stand on "our" side of the event to project it as belonging to the other.

For the folks at home, the event has to engage "us" at some fundamental level of belief. When events blast through the routine of information, they must be quickly captured and interpreted in an acceptable narrative framework. The difficulty is that the very pertinence of an event frequently derives from its uninterpretability, from its resistance to existing narrative frameworks. The critical task is to isolate this intractable level of the event that is the element in the media construct that points back to the real crisis at its source. The crisis the event illuminates is never the one indigenous to its apparent site of origin. We may never know what "really" happened in the Gulf crisis, or the "Black Monday" stock market crash, or any other event. The crisis the event reveals is the crisis of the vector, not the site. It is a symptom of chronic problems that the historic dynamic of the vector introduces into the realm of communication and other systems of movement.

Writing along the line of the vector, one deals less with the object of a media event than with its trajectory. In the place of a content analysis or a semiotic interpretation, I look at relationality itself.[74] The object of analysis has an uncanny habit of outwitting the subject, as Baudrillard has argued in his infamous essays. Vectoral writing contends that the difficulties with the object derive from its mobility. In the Gulf war, the object caught both journalism and critical analysis off guard because it was never where it was supposed to be. Modes of discourse which still want to "grasp" the facts or get "to the bottom" of "things" have a hard time with objects endowed with electric mobility. Hence the need for an analysis which does not "look" at "things," either factually or critically. To substitute a more appropriate metaphor, one learns to listen for the off beats in the regular rhythms of mobile information.

This substitution of relationality and mobility for the object of analysis takes critical theory off in a different direction from the dominant tendency in cultural studies—the return of the subject. Feminism did criticism a huge favor in unpacking the notion of the subject and reconstructing it from the ground up as a differentiated and decentered term. Analysis which wants to address the subject now has to deal with it in its radically differentiated form. Vectoral writing is in no sense meant as a criticism of this tendency, but is rather a counterpoint and complement to it. By looking at what became of the object, rather than the subject, it hopes to tune in to the tendencies toward totality and aggregation inherent in the dynamics of media globalization which the subjective turn in critical analysis has pulled apart from the subjective end.[75]

In the blinding shell-burst of the event, a critical eye can see critical conjunctions of objects and images, oddly grouped together, and frozen in an arc of impetuous light. The media can't ignore the unusual groupings of things which their floodlights will catch in their indiscriminate glare, but their finely tuned sense of narrative discretion will start to filter them out as soon as the tapes are rolling. The collision of things and the crash of time, glaringly clear under the lights on the operating table, can be considered more fully only in the twilight of critical analysis. Analysis, too, must work fast to save this chance encounter from the trauma of forgetting. Critical analysis, too, has its narratives, and does not welcome interruptions from the wings. Still, there is time enough to trace out the movements of these objects and images, to consider in their radical juxtaposition the histories, movements, and relations between instances that might be considered related at all in the narrative times of either the media or scholarship. In the flash-gun glare of the event there is a moment in which to peer through the rent in the fabric of the spectacle, to glimpse unexpected and powerful relations between things that the division of intellectual labors would normally consign to different patches of the crazy-quilt of knowledge.

2. event

Ozymandias

Dateline: Washington, 16 January 1991. Operation Desert Storm began today at 23:30 hours Greenwich Mean Time with the attack on key targets in Baghdad by radar-evading Stealth bombers. "These are times that try men's souls," intoned President Bush, quoting Tom Paine in his televised address to the nation. He reassured the American public that "this will not be another Vietnam" and that "when we are successful, we have a real chance for a new world order."[1]

What follows is a well-known story, or at least some things about it are well known. I won't talk about the "weapons systems," at least not yet. As a telephone poll conducted by Sut Jhally and others found, those watching at home were more likely to know the names of the weapons than the name of, say, Colin Powell. As the researchers conclude, "The more TV people watched, the less they knew."[2]

I want to go back to the day before the massive bombing campaign began, and tell another story. I want to switch sites, from Washington to Baghdad. The day before the bombing, the Iraqi troops paraded under the giant Victory Arches in Baghdad. Schools, shops, and factories closed, and people gathered in the streets for a mass rally which was as much festive as martial.[3] Saddam Hussein watched from the reviewing stand in the middle of the two Victory Arches.

The arches are remarkable structures, composed of crossed swords with gently curving blades. The bronze hands bursting out of the ground that grip the swords were cast from the hands of Saddam Hussein himself. Opened in August 1989 to commemorate what the government declared a "victory" over Iran, the arches were actually commissioned in 1985. The steel swords are cast from melted-down weapons of Iraqi military "martyrs," while huge metal baskets containing 10,000 helmets of Iranian war dead are attached to the rising Husseinian fists. The crossed swords supposedly represent the defeat of the Persian empire by an invading Arab army in 637. The spread of Islam into the region which is now Iran dates from this. Saddam Hussein opened the archways himself, riding on a white horse. By usurping this Shi'ite emblem, he perhaps wanted to signify the unity of Sunni and Shi'ite in the defense of the nation.[4]

Baghdad began acquiring monumental works in the late '70s, constructed in anticipation of the 1982 Summit of the Non-Aligned Movement. The Ba'thist regime no doubt wanted to make a show of assuming the mantle of third world leadership from Cuba. There are other vectors along which information and stories about the world flow, and this is one of them. While the Ba'thist reconstruction of Baghdad did rate a cover story in *National Geographic* in 1985, its self-assertion weighs more heavily along the lines of regional, southern, and third world vectors. Like the mythical Ozymandias in Shelley's poem, the tyrant says with his monuments, "Look at my works, ye Mighty, and despair."

Iraqi television broadcast the big parade, and in a sense it played to at least four separate audiences. It played to the domestic audience, synchronizing with radio and television and regional rallies the more or less compulsory expressions of national unity throughout Iraq. It played to a regional audience through radio stations aimed at specific interests in the region. The Voice of Egypt of Arabism station created a vector for a more secularist, pan-Arab story. "The oil of the Arabs is for the Arabs," it might say. On the other hand, Holy Mecca Radio aimed more at holders of the faith: "Have pity on the holy land of Islam, defiled by the American infidel." There was also a Voice of Peace station aimed mainly at African-American soldiers, in the vain hope of stirring up a bit of mutiny. Its line might be more like "Look at what the gasoline emirs are doing with the American girls."[5] The big parade appeared on CNN and was no doubt meant to be seen by a Western and a Southern audience. The Iraqis no doubt hoped to win kudos in the south and in the region for standing up to American presumption and aggression, and to display strength of numbers and purpose to the enemy.

The difficulties of negotiating between these different stories and vectors ought not to be underestimated. On the one hand, Iraq wants to appear as a leader in the third world, yet on the other it seeks and gets Western assistance in the war against Iran. On the one hand Iraq wants to appear as the champion of secular development in the region, yet on the other it appeals to Islamic brotherhood when politically convenient. On the one hand, Iraq is a one-party state with total control over the internal media vector and over what it projects out into the region and the world. On the other hand, it is in a state of dependence, not only on the military hardware of the superpowers, but also on the global vector field of communications over which it has no control. One might pause to wonder if there is a relationship between the repressiveness of such a state in terms of managing the vector within, and its total dependence on the vector without. Western dominance of the vector might very well act as a negative inducement for any possible attempt to combine a pluralist and open approach to the vector within and an independent relation to the big powers.

This is not uniquely a third world problem. Attacks on the plurality of the American domestic vector field, particularly in the McCarthy period, were usually based on an inflated claim of "infiltration" from without. The closure of the plurality of stories which flowered in the popular front period of the '30s took place in the name of a threatening external vector. Radio, television, and cinema were all subjected to a stringent weeding out of those not following the correct storyline.[6]

Iraq attempts to assert a power over both the historical vector and the geographic one. The Victory Arches attempt to hegemonize the future's relation to the past with their monumental permanence. They can also form an impressive backdrop for staging spectacles to distribute out over the geographic vector, to whoever will look and listen. Perhaps it is significant that the Ba'thist regime chose the day before the last deadline expired and the war began to create one of its greatest "Nuremberg meets Las Vegas"–style spectacles.[7] Whatever the outcome of the war, the regime had this one last chance to disseminate an image of military resistance to America as widely as possible, hoping to seed it in memory throughout the region and throughout the south. As Mohamed Heikal reports, "Millions of Muslims, even in countries which supported the coalition, regarded the Americans rather than the Iraqis as the originators of the conflict."[8] As one Egyptian editorial remarked grimly, "By pitting the rich Gulf states against Iraq, the West was turning Arab wealth against Arab might with the aim of destroying both together."[9]

While many were no doubt skeptical about Iraq, here on these lone and level sands was an image of resistance, and a reminder that "resistance" is not always as morally encouraging a spectacle as those who make a fetish of it like to believe. When the powerless resist power, we feel morally uncompromised, supporting people who lack the means to betray our trust by falling off the white horse of resistance. When minor tyrants with the "sneer of cold command" confront the superpowers, resistance is exposed as being within the game of power all the time. The redemptive story of resistance failed to appeal to opposition movements in the West, and one might have hoped its bankruptcy was exposed in the process. Nevertheless, Iraq's aggressive resistance did appeal to those without the dubious benefit of opposition within the most powerful states, whatever its merits.

In producing such spectacular parades, such monumental structures, Saddam Hussein cannot control how others outside his borders will respond to such images. The power of his police does not extend that far. These images, blown across all borders by the crisp wind of the vector, fall on rich and fallow ground, depending on what narrative bed they land in. They might end up as images of resistance in a story about American empire. They might end up a "colossal wreck, boundless and bare," in a story about the futility of tyranny itself, culled from a Western poem. There are stories everywhere, just waiting for the gusts of the vector to offer up fresh spores.

Brokering the Vector

One hears a lot these days about the decline of American democracy and the evil role played by the media in this.[10] One wonders when exactly the golden age of American democracy supposedly occurred. Perhaps it's just that America's colonial wars come home to roost along the line of the media vector now, whereas before they were obscure telegraph reports in the margins of the newspapers. The various stages of the integration of America into the world of economic and strategic realpolitik have moved along side by side with reorganizations of the vectors of command, control, and communication. The Office of War Information, set up as one of a plethora of narrative management units presiding over the expanding vectors of Roosevelt's interventionist state, is just one example of the administration of the vector necessitated by industrialized war.[11] The mobilization of the population of the nation requires a national coordination of the vector and its narrative forms. As the management of empire becomes an increasingly global affair in an increasingly integrated global economy, the vectors reach out into international media spaces, searching for narrative tactics which can mobilize the still nationally and regionally distinct territories and populations.

A particularly pressing task, particularly in a nominally democratic polity, is managing the gaps that appear in narrative continuity by the disjunctures of political alliance and misalliance. The work of repairing the holes rent in the narrative fabric of public discourse by events rarely takes place in the electronic media, but in media that work at slower rhythms, so it is necessary for criticism to follow the trace of events through these too. It is work carried out by "off-line" editors, as it were, in state and private think tanks.[12] Tracking the response of these second-order discourses about events is a matter of following the discourse in the responsible journals that work out the narrative line of realpolitik and the critical response to those narrative forays in the journals of liberal, radical, or area-specialist opinion.

As Saddam's Western hostages were released, only to be tied again in yellow ribbons, as the U.S. air-freighted its troops to the Gulf and George Bush put together the UN resolutions and the new "Delian League" in a matter of days, the Gulf became a military theater of operations. Yet there was another theater of operations working overtime, attempting to furnish narrations to the media vectors that would fit this twist of events. The invocation of Orientalist images is the popular edge of the narrators' task. These weave in with the more complex designs of the "shifting sands" of interest. This is a particular challenge when events stretch like explosive chain reactions back through recent time—as in the Middle East. Or where vast and powerful narrative sureties are at stake—as in the cold war. The Gulf crisis thus comes piled up on top of any number of crisis events—there appears indeed to be a "storm blowing from paradise."[13] Consider the recent wreckage added to the pile of progress: The Tiananmen Square massacre gave the lie to the myth of Deng Xiaoping the "liberal reformer." The fall of the Berlin Wall flatly contradicted the story about how totalitarian regimes had a total ideological domination over their populations in contrast to merely despotic or dictatorial ones.[14] In short, the narrative structure of the cold war was unraveling event by event.

The invasion of Kuwait was perhaps not such a shock. Geoffrey Kemp, who headed the Middle East section of the National Security Council under the Reagan administration, summed up the prevailing view: "We really weren't that naive. We knew he was an SOB, but he was our SOB."[15] Despite the candid cynicism the foreign-policy elite reserves for its own, it is not above pressuring journalists into tarting up realpolitik with moral homilies. Having dutifully portrayed Saddam as an ally and a "modernizer," the more tractable sections of the media obligingly reversed the story. As Edward Said laments, it was only too "symptomatic of the intellectual will to please power in public."[16] Given the simple narrative grid applied to the Middle East, the change was surprisingly easy to effect, and applies retrospectively to the historical past of media "background reports" as well.

That might be all right in the calculating discourse of realpolitik when nobody outside of an elite circle of friends had ever heard of Iraq—let alone been consulted about it. Once the vector had dragged Iraq all the way around the globe and into the media arena, it demanded the invention of a new language, a new history—and a fresh new alibi. The difficulty the vector causes to power is that it confuses two levels of discursive management that normally remain quite distinct—popular opinion in the narrative world of television entertainment, and the supposedly "realist" language of elite geo-strategy. The event exposes more of the realpolitik calculations of violence to the media than the specialists in the latter are used to exposing. On the other hand, the pressing need for moral stories for mass consumption often finds its way, in a confused fashion, back into the discourse of realpolitik for as long as the storm blowing from the event lasts.

Out of the great plethora of stories and stories about stories about the Gulf war, I want to follow along the line of one which helps us get to the heart of the problem of hegemonizing the story-fabrication process itself. According to the critical arms-industry analyst Michael T. Klare, the argument in elite discourse at the time of "Desert Shield" pitted a geo-economic view of the future of American power against a geo-strategic one. Klare summarizes the issues underlying the divergent narrative lines thus: "At issue are such questions as (1) who will control America's foreign policy establishment in the years ahead; (2) which of the giant federal bureaucracies will prosper and which will fall into decline; (3) which of our states and communities will be the beneficiaries of government spending and which will be deprived; and, likewise, (4) which giant corporations will receive lucrative government contracts and which will not."[17]

When Japanese and German corporations are decimating American machine-tool firms and semiconductor manufacturers, even buying out famous Hollywood studios, a geo-economic focus on investing in research, development, and industrial recovery had powerful advocates.[18] The stock market crash stories picked up later follow the lines of this crisis of Fordism in more detail. At the moment, what matters is that those calling for policies oriented toward that geo-economic crisis were thwarted by events. Or not so much by events as by the superior ability of other interests to articulate the media spectacle to another narrative line. Turning to good profit the Gulf events, those who stood to gain thwarted the acceptance of a post–cold war narrative. "Recent events have surely proven that there is no substitute for American leadership," as Bush told a national and international television audience in September. Or as General Colin Powell, chairman of the Joint Chiefs of Staff, put it sometime earlier in the debate, "We have to put a shingle outside our door saying 'Superpower Lives Here.'"[19]

Thus the projection of American forces in the Gulf becomes a model for the post–cold war style for the "spin control" of events themselves. After a brief period of confusion and bet-hedging, the networks trooped into the fray with a primetime primer on the geo-strategic understanding of the future. A new imaginary war was warmed over to take place of the long, cold one.[20] Having extracted themselves from the debris of cold war, both the discourse of realpolitik and its tall story alibis, both political power and media vectors, now had to concoct new rationales and new stories that would correspond to American intentions.

Curiously, this took on the appearance of a relation between two kinds of *television*. The vector makes the political conjuncture take place before a mass audience as an event. Thus it forces power elites into a rapid translation of elite discourse into narrative form, forcing the elite at times into thinking aloud. According to Bob Woodward, this was General Powell's problem with George Bush. The latter kept leaping out of helicopters, giving press conferences, searching for the narrative threads that could connect him and his office to some course of action that appeared to make sense. As he did so, his commitment to the use of force grew and hardened.[21] The temporal pressure of the event forces elite discourse to think directly in popular terms, rather than at some remove, protected by the obscurity of its forums and a cultivated mass indifference. The exceptional event is thus the point at which the machinery of brokerage and the theaters of operation are most likely to stand exposed.

Just as Gilles Deleuze thinks there is a breakdown in classic cinema in the relation between action and events, a similar problem appears in the news media.[22] It gets harder and harder to portray events as the outcome of the actions of either leaders or the masses. Time, as it appears on television, does not appear to be the product of people acting in time. It appears to move of its own accord, or to be the product of the vector itself. Whereas cinema could make an art form out of this new perception of time unrelated to action, for the "spin doctors" of politics and the media, it is more of an ongoing crisis. There is too much stray information shuttling about in the vector field to neatly pin events to the causal logic of leadership. While President Bush and "Stormin' Norman" managed to look decisive for an instant, the complexity of events, or rather, our perception of them via the vector, overtook this momentary image of action with predictable effects.

Despotic Television

As Samir al-Khalil points out in his dissident critique of Iraq, *Republic of Fear,* television plays an important role in the Iraqi state. Throughout the '80s, the Ba'th had assumed total control of all communication media, combining television, print, radio, and education into an effective and massive propaganda effort. Iraq is interesting as an example of authoritarian media because the Ba'th regime introduced television into a country with a very low rate of literacy, and used it as a tool for creating it, in combination with special classes for adults and a mass education campaign for children. Thus television was an integral part of a strategy for producing a society made up of quite sophisticated consumers of incredibly crude ideological artifacts.[23] Saddam Hussein himself appears as the crudest and most central such artifact. The Ba'th created a literate, modern society with a strategy that combined police repression with mass media saturation. In the place of traditional society with its multiple ties and obligations, the Ba'th established a modern cultural regime with a unified array of images, symbols, and slogans.[24]

Saddam Hussein as a charismatic figure is one of a particularly televisual kind. Attributes such as heroism, oratory, and prophecy do not form the basis of his authority, although they are the classical sources of charismatic power.[25] His is an administered charisma, elaborately rehearsed, staged, and edited.

> Saddam's appearances on television lasting several hours a day in various guises are masterpieces of calculated duplicity. . . . The propaganda is so "bad" that even some Iraqis will pretend to dismiss it; yet they bring their children up to applaud it. Imagine endlessly varied film clips of Saddam Hussein in local Arab attire one day and Kurdish dress the next. Picture him crouching around trenches in camouflage fatigues, standing erect in full parade uniform, embracing foreign dignitaries at the airport in the latest Pierre Cardin suit, handling machinery, reading the Koran, meeting Shi'ite religious notables, opening new buildings, giving lectures on architecture and the environment, looking grim, smiling, berating officials, sucking Cuban cigars, fondling babies, dropping in on "unsuspecting" citizens for breakfast, as a family man, and reviewing the latest captured military hardware.[26]

Thanks to CNN's Gulf war, we have all seen a little of this, although Samir al-Khalil's elaborate program schedule gives something of a feel for the context of our brief glimpses of Iraqi TV. The morning after the first bombing run on Baghdad, Iraqi TV staged a "Saddam at large" program. The leader dressed in casual battle fatigues. He walked around a seemingly deserted city, or launched out of a sedan to shake hands. It was a poignant counterpoint to the excerpt from the day before, showing a mass of Iraqi soldiers marching beneath the huge crossed swords to the theme music from *Star Wars* that Western viewers saw courtesy of CNN.

Television vectors could send images across the battle line with ease, but once through to the discursive domain of the other, the images lost the resonance and associations they would connect with in their "home" discourse. Thus the Iraqi TV pictures of Saddam served perfectly as images of a vain, treacherous, excessive, Oriental enemy in Western news television. The shots of Iraqi crowds shouting and waving guns in the streets could easily be contextualized as a synthetic frenzy whipped up by a totalitarian regime. On the other hand, Iraqi TV could broadcast images of Western demonstrations against the war, but they recontextualized these tokens of the strength of Western pluralism (as Western commentators would insist) to show a lack of resolve to fight. In both cases the image, to a far greater degree than one might expect, was given significance by its context rather than its origin, although its origin still has a curious role to play.

CNN's bombastic owner Ted Turner launched the now famous station by saying to his employees, "See, we're gonna take the news and put it on the satellite, and then we're gonna beam it down into Russia, and we're gonna bring world peace, and we're gonna get rich in the process! Thank you very much! Good luck!"[27] But in the crisis atmosphere of the event, the international news vector is not a form of *communication*. No mutually accepted "messages" passed through this channel from one community to another. There was no commonality between encoding and decoding practices at either end.[28] Rather, the vector allows each side to exploit images that come from the other in a narrative framework which constructs the attributes of the other entirely at "our" media sites. The fact that the image is an authentic product of "their" media merely legitimates a construction of the other that is entirely "our" doing. This magical "us" that appears as the central thing threatened by the other is itself a product of this projection of an other. The image coming from the place to which we project our other version of this other is what legitimates our version.

More precisely, the guarantee of "our" identity comes not from "our" intrinsic qualities, nor from our difference from the other, but *from the vector itself*. The vector makes this other possible, and makes an "us" possible. The vector creates these shifting nodes of "us" and "them" that provide all of us with the trickster syntax of unexpected crossroads. As much as we may want to differentiate, the vector keeps throwing us together, pitting us against others, and legitimating the conflict with the contraband of images it traffics from one place to the other. The vector has the potential to constantly renew this interzone of nonidentity within which others may with any luck reconstruct images of identity that may be somewhat more constructive.

It makes possible a George Bush supported by 90 percent of Americans surveyed, at that triumphal moment when he appeared before Congress to make his victory speech. He referred in that speech to television, and the televised repeats of the occasion montaged the speech together with the TV images he referred to. Bush spoke of a moment that brought tears to his eyes, the moment when GIs hauled Iraqi troops out of hiding and an American soldier said to them, "It's OK now. You're all right." Here the public and private merge totally in the metonymy of the public performance of the president's private tear. Here "we" come together as witness to the image of the vanquished other, and the television vector assumes its place at the center of the construction of the event. Regardless of whether Ted Turner gets rich off it, regardless of whether it is a cold war order or a new world order, this is not communication.

The symbiosis of the vector with power creates a movement of information, but one that legitimates a noncommunication, not one that creates the grounds for a dialogue. Even dialogue is scripted. It occurs within the event as "we said this, they said that, so we were left with no choice but to. . . ." This dialogue is part of a double narrative that the parties engaged enact so that it will "play" simultaneously at home and at the other's home. In each version, the other's speech appears as quoted speech, actively assumed into the monologic voice.[29] The real winner here is the power of the vector, a power that appears to have vanquished the Iraqis and did; which appears under the control of the president but is not; which appears to serve a vast televisual audience which is trapped, as the deadly poll of "public opinion," within its vast and instant reach.

It is difficult to know how symmetrical this process is—if at all. Clearly there are differences between Iraqi and American media. The Ba'th used a combination of the media vector and police enclosure to eliminate civil society. The Ba'th attempted to pulverize traditional allegiances to religion, clan, region, family, and substituted allegiance to the fetish images of Ba'th ideology. In eliminating civil society, the Ba'th eliminated the resistance, not to mention common sense, which civil society can counterpose to a state monopoly of the vectors. The Ba'th achieved speed and unity of action this way—and a license to folly. One wonders if they were the only party to this war to do this. Between the speed of the military and media vectors, one has to wonder if there is still a space and, more important, a *time* for civil society in the West either. Perhaps it has been eliminated, or at least curtailed, by other means.

The American media's ruminations on their role in a military event offer cause for alarm on this score. Some American commentators echoed cold war themes. They beat their breasts about the "vulnerability" of democracies to media manipulation versus the complete media control Saddam and the Ba'th Party have in Iraq—almost as if they might prefer the latter. To some extent this misses the point. States with totalitarian media are "vulnerable" too, if not in quite the same way. While Iraq stated as a matter of policy that it wants the Americans out of the Gulf, on an ideological level it seemed to need them there very badly. The Ba'th regime based its legitimacy, its justification for the terror, the show trials, the suppression of dialogue, the militarization of everyday life, on a paranoid ideology. It stressed the need for strength against the three great evils of imperialism, Zionism, and Arab reaction. As American military ships disgorged their elaborate cargoes on Saudi territory, imperialism and Arab reaction appeared to be very close indeed.

The bizarre accusations made in Iraqi media early in the piece, that some U.S. troops were really Israelis in disguise, was clearly an attempt to make it appear to Iraqi citizens that all the enemies the state has taught them to fear are massing at the borders together. The Western media dismissed these accusations on the grounds that they weren't true, but that misses the point. In the Iraqi media enclosure, implicating the Israelis was a logical part of the story. As necessary to the narrative as the attempt in the West to make Saddam a personification of Islamic evil. That Saddam as a mad mullah was an even less truthful image than disguised Israelis is neither here nor there. Both are logical excrescences of paranoid ideologies responding fearfully to events going out of control. The global media have the unfortunate effect of bringing these monstrous myths face to face on TV, blowing them up to grotesque proportions, spattering them like fallout across the globe. Television is no longer an innocent bystander. The vector forces TV onto the front line, and forces the front line into our living rooms for nightly salvos. The old cold war might be over, but television is still sharpening its teeth.

From CNN TV to WAR TV

About fifteen minutes after the passing of the UN deadline of 15 January, the media—and everybody else—woke up to the fact that the anti-Iraq war was to be a TV war. "The first war ever to begin on live TV," as one reporter gleefully put it. It established the supremacy of CNN's style of coverage, forcing the other U.S. networks to imitate it. President Bush, Defense Secretary Cheney, Egyptian President Mubarak were all reported to be avid CNN watchers. Even Saddam Hussein had a private receiving dish, according to CNN's Peter Arnett.

CNN has certainly had a considerable effect on television news. It has taken advantage of satellite vectors to break the transmission monopoly of the American broadcast networks. Being a twenty-four-hour news service, it does not have the luxury of collecting evidence of an event for hours before the nightly newscast and compressing the available data into conventional journalistic and narrative form. On the contrary, CNN has introduced the queer concept of "live" news coverage—an instant audiovisual presence on the site of an event. Consequently, CNN reports frequently lack focus and narrative direction. In seeking to speed up the audiovisual news vector, the station has dispensed as much as possible with the narrative strategies of American network news practice, if not with its visual conventions. It has also dispensed with expensive, authoritative anchorpersons. In a news strategy based on pure speed, which increases the possibility of error, the Dan Rather style of narrator really has no place. CNN concentrated on attempting to establish a news vector hours or at least minutes before the competition. Employing satellite linkages, CNN can base itself in Atlanta without too much disadvantage compared to the New York–based networks. It enjoys one considerable advantage, being able to set up business paying rates far below the relevant awards with nonunion labor. Information industries, it seems, can also fall victim to the "runaway shop."

On the TV current affairs talkback show *Donahue,* CNN had to defend its coverage in front of a hostile audience, many of whom quite candidly preferred news managed and censored by the military to any attempt at open and critical journalism. CNN's Ed Turner tried to defend the station's approach in terms of the liberal understanding of the freedom of the press and the distinction between propaganda and information. His respondents, like the opinion polls, said they wanted propaganda. This is a curious aspect to the whole event. It seems that TV viewers are even more aware than CNN that the vector does not communicate, and resented the station's feeble attempts to make it do so. They preferred to view the other through the promptings of the president and the "bloodless" stage diagrams of the military briefings. Television has a narrative function and exists in the private theater of the living room. CNN was trying to legitimate it as an information service, invoking a liberal conceit about the role and rights of the public sphere. The vector has already crossed the boundary between public and private sphere, and the event has already taken on a narrative form linked to the projection of the other. CNN was popular with some public figures because it raised the vector to a new velocity. It met some popular resistance for attempting to preserve a liberal understanding of news. This idea of the place of news was from an era before the volume and speed of media vectors broke down the flimsy partitions of the liberal imagination.

CNN's coverage is best on sudden events rather than regular, scheduled photo opportunities and press conferences.[30] The networks still excel at producing news according to conventional notions of the information schedule. Press conferences and the like are still usually timed to coincide with network programming, and this provides the national, daily information cycle with a certain predictable rhythm. CNN, on the other hand, has created a form of abstract news time which corresponds to the new abstract, global space of the vector. The vector now delivers news, complete with a satellite feed of video pictures, almost anywhere, any time. This flexibility in the organization of news flows comes up against the limits of network news schedules, which derive their structure and form from a previous era in communications technology. CNN reveals the limitations of the broadcast style of news, because CNN is premised on the new vectoral possibilities opened up by the satellite.

The success of CNN in "catastrophe" coverage forced the American network news services to imitate it a little, offering their affiliates news information with the same speed and extending the length of their coverage. After the passing of the 15 January deadline, this reached the ridiculous point where CNN, ABC, NBC, and CBS were all offering hours of almost identical coverage, conjuring stories out of thin air as the warplanes were dispatched on their "surgical strikes." Thus the viewer could watch NBC announcing heavily laden F-15 bombers leaving Saudi Arabia, then flip idly to CNN just in time to see White House Press Secretary Marlin Fitzwater declare that "the liberation of Kuwait has begun." CNN then flips thousands of miles across space to Baghdad, where the former CNN gardening correspondent describes the sound of the U.S. attack beginning on the city. Change channels again and an expert on NBC is pointing to a map drawn up in the conventions of a weather report, only the lines on it are not cold fronts but troop fronts. In Britain Channel 4 dispensed with the pointers and chromakeyed elaborate computer graphic images on a simulated map of the principal theater of operations. Little digital images of tanks and troops glided about as if in an arcade game.

Yet not even color graphics could prevent the war from sagging as the sheer lack of pictures or hard information blocked the unfolding of a tellable *story*.

The media filled in the dull patches by reporting about *the media* reporting the war. At this point in the program we are entitled to ask whether the usual liberal soul-searching about war, censorship, and the media really goes far enough. Television entertained us with the Pentagon-controlled pool footage, and explained it all in Pentagon doublespeak terms, even showing the workings of a weapon with the arms manufacturer's video simulation.[31] Perhaps we should entertain the hypothesis that the media have become a dangerous weapon in war rather than its liberal conscience. As the CNN reporter in Baghdad with the unlikely name of Bernard Shaw said: "Wherever you are in the world, ask yourself, why are the governments of Iraq and the U.S. allowing this report from Baghdad to get out of here to you?" He should know. Chinese security police cut him off, "live" on air in Beijing, as Deng's troops closed the media out of the feedback loop before going in to retake the city.

TV was implicated in the process that led to war. In competing with each other, the U.S. networks fought to implicate themselves in the diplomatic endgame toward war. As Alexander Cockburn wryly commented on the early days of the confrontation, "In the absence of military conflict most Americans have settled back to enjoy the war of position and manoeuvre being fought by the television networks on the edge of the fall season and facing a declining share of the market."[32] ABC's Ted Koppel dined with the Jordanian royal family, then secured an exclusive briefing with the Iraqi foreign ministry to pass on the message he had elicited from Jordan. Not to be outdone, Dan Rather went after and got an exclusive interview with Saddam for CBS. The political talking heads followed news-anchor celebrities into the fray. Bush sent Iraqi TV an eight-minute videotape stating the U.S. position. Saddam replied by sending U.S. TV networks a ninety-minute videotaped reply—which adds a new dimension to the military concept of "escalation." On the eve of the U.S. counterinvasion of Kuwait, James Baker, George Bush, and Iraqi Foreign Minister Tariq Aziz all appeared live, while prerecorded Saddam beamed in from Iraqi TV.[33] When a diplomatic letter can take three days from out tray to in tray, why not go live on CNN and blast off a diplomatic retort and a propaganda release for the public at the same time? New media technology is eliminating the time taken between diplomatic moves and countermoves, not to mention the line between diplomatic gambits and publicity stunts.

While the networks fight each other to get a piece of the action, the politicos and the military carefully rehearse their setups for these overeager image-suckers. Stage-managing the Bush campaign was Sig Rogich, a former Las Vegas advertising man with interests in property and casinos.[34] Rogich had a set specially built at Dhahran for Bush's prewar warmup visit, complete with neat rows of F-15 and F-16 warplanes lined up in shot as a backdrop. Rogich choreographed images of Bush walking tall against desert sunsets, Bush the war veteran talking man to man with the troops. The purpose of these image bites was to trigger familiar narrative associations and cement a collective subjective response to it as an event—and it worked. The popularity of this no-expense-spared, never-to-be-repeated Bush–Gulf war double-bill extravaganza surged in the polls.[35]

The Pentagon has also learned a few tricks about how to use TV as a weapon. One wonders if it is any accident that the U.S. airstrikes seemed timed to make the evening news on the East Coast of the United States. Veteran journalists have been reminiscing about how in Vietnam journalists "told the truth" about the war and hastened its end. Which just goes to show what a slim grasp on history much journalistic writing displays. Most Vietnam reporters wrote about the poor quality of the command and the disturbing and obvious fact that the Americans were losing. Only a few independent journalists stood against the tide of imperial opinion.[36]

Even Peter Arnett, who won a Pulitzer Prize for his Vietnam coverage, was hardly a voice of conscience. When asked why he did not raise the outcry against the murder of civilians by the U.S. forces in Vietnam, Arnett replied, "We didn't make judgments because we were witnesses. . . . Surely it was not for us to be judge and jury."[37] If in war killing is exempted from the moral prohibitions against murder, then war journalism seems exempted from the moral duty to call it murder also.

Just to be on the safe side, the Pentagon has greatly restricted media access to its dirty little wars—not to mention the complete lack of coverage of those fought by the CIA.[38] Before the invasion of Grenada, the U.S. military ensured a complete media blackout by sealing off the whole area. The White House released video pictures of the invasion after the event, which the networks broadcast without comment. Nor did the media report the fact that the White House press office misled them about the invasion. Official denials of any possibility of an invasion were still being issued as the war machine moved in on the little island.[39] This little invasion, of which General Norman Schwarzkopf was deputy commander, was a brilliant public-relations success as a media event. The degree to which it was a military fiasco emerged only later. Emblematic of both the state of the military operation and the role of the vector in it is the story of the U.S. soldier in Grenada who was forced to use his credit card to call Fort Bragg long-distance via satellite to request air support for his beleaguered unit.[40]

The communications problems encountered in the invasion of Grenada were tackled afresh in Operation Blue Spoon, as the invasion of Panama was originally known. The *Communications-Electronic Operating Instructions* for the assault was a stack of papers three feet high. Just as important was the assault on the public-relations front. According to Powell, "Once you've got all the forces moving and everything's being taken care of by the commanders, turn your attention to television because you can win the battle or lose the war if you don't handle the story right."[41] This may account for why the name of the attack was changed from Blue Spoon to Operation Just Cause, a moral justification and a slogan all rolled into a catchy title. Given that CNN reported the exchange of gunfire between the Panamanian troops defending Noriega's headquarters and American forces just two minutes after it happened, the concern with the speed and spread of information in the vector field is an understandable one for a commander. The military in effect manage two communication systems, their own and the global news net. Strangely enough, military practices may be quite appropriate for both. Given that military training stresses both a precise, disciplined execution of thoroughly laid plans and the ability to seize initiative and react quickly to crisis situations, the management of the vectoral event can be seen as a military discipline not unlike the management of the military event.

Given the multinational nature of the anti-Iraq force, they set up an office called the Joint Information Bureau (JIB) to coordinate the manipulation of what we saw from the Gulf.[42] In going in to battle with each other for ratings, the media happily surrender to the demands placed on them by the JIB. Even when they firmly believe they are shooting in the cause of liberal good sense and free speech, they violently defeat that objective by turning the moral need to know into sheer fascination. Meanwhile we flip channels from the tennis to the news and back, to keep track of the score. This deference of television to the military stems in part from the ability of the military to block news vectors out of territory it controls and operates. Military secrecy creates gaps and blanks in the illusion of televisual ubiquity. To extend its vectoral potential into military zones, television has to reach a *modus vivendi* with the war machine. Here the competitive imperative toward a global vectoral system for television, a desire for the potential to put a vector between any and every event, anywhere in the world, and the massed living rooms of the target audience, takes precedence over the professional ethics of journalistic propriety.

Not surprisingly, print journalists, saddled with yesterday's vector, with no other advantage left to them besides time to pause and reflect, frequently criticize television coverage. They have every reason to complain when the wire services such as AAP, Reuters, and AFP start reporting what just happened—on CNN! Yet even television cannot compete with the effectiveness of military communications vectors. This is the other reason television finds itself deferring to the military. The military are specialists in the development and implementation of communications vectors. Indeed, most of the technologies now accessible to television, including satellites and SNGs, are the downstream, civilian progeny of technological developments that have their headwaters in research for military applications.[43] Portable video is a spinoff from military needs, as are the new cameras that incorporate gyroscopes to prevent wobble. These arose out of the need for stable images shot from aircraft that generate a lot of vibration. The little charge-coupled devices (CCD) used in contemporary video cameras have an even more spectacular origin. They were designed for real-time satellite reconnaissance of the type performed by Keyhole satellites over Iraq. During the war, television began to make extensive use of night-vision lenses, originally designed for night fighting. This was not a new technology for the military, but it was a novel experience for television. What the military saw in the last war, television will show us in the next.

Television itself is in a state of war, now that a range of technologies have made the TV vector far more flexible and cost-effective. In Europe, the EC wants to counter the influence of CNN with a European news service. In Asia, a CNN proposal to lease transponders on the Indonesian Palapa satellite, which has a footprint extending from Darwin in northern Australia to India and southern China, is up against regional contenders. The Hutchinson Wampoa publishing and communications group has created HutchVision, a company which intends to bring BBC news in Asian languages via the AsiaSat 1 satellite to a vast area, from Darwin to Cairo to Vladivostok. These two developments in turn led to renewed interest in a much older proposal emanating from within Japan's huge NHK broadcasting concern for a pan-Asian news service centered in Tokyo.[44] Whatever the outcome of these particular developments, the main point is that the development of the vector leads to an intensification of the struggle for control of the spaces of movement and flow it makes possible, whether in strategic space or in information space.

Bloodless

While the development of the vector leads to conflict, as new routes and moves through formerly opaque and hermetic space, the experience of conflict becomes ever more remote. The same technologies that make possible the projection of force around the globe make possible a perception of war which removes the bloody and visceral. American bomber pilots flew missions over Iraq with the heavy-metal music of Van Halen pumping through their headsets. Graphic simulation displays helped them guide their bombs to their targets. Back on deck, they could describe strafing retreating Iraqi forces as a "turkey shoot." In short, everything appears as in a video game, as many commentators noted.

Yet it was not a video game. In the slot-machine arcade, all of the possible outcomes are programmed in advance, and the player, in the end, always loses. There is a remorseless teleology to the video game. The future is programmed in advance from a limited repertoire of possible presents. The experience of using virtual-reality simulators to bomb civilian targets is different from this. Nothing predetermines this target, these deaths. If there is a point of similarity between them, it is in the degree of abstraction involved in these two quite different forms of action. Both are actions which present no *tangible* result to the actor. They are actions which present an outcome purely as an index, a sign. They are actions which emanate from the body, but do not present the actor with a bodily rejoinder. They are actions which are not, well, *messy* in any way.

They are examples of *telesthesia*, a handy, ready-made word meaning perception at a distance. From the telescope to the telegraph and telephone, from television to telecommunications, the development of telesthesia means the creation of, literally, *dislocated* perception and action. Dislocating the action from the site via the vector allows the use of power over the other without implicating power in the scene of the other.

Telesthesia can produce a fascination with the image of destruction or suffering which is pornographic. This aspect or form of telesthesia would be those instances when it attempts to reduce the other to its image. The image appears in this relation as a stand-in for the other. No further reference is made to the other, but the image is nevertheless legitimated by an other which is presumed to exist, elsewhere, at a safe distance. In its pornographic form, telesthesia presents an image "surgically" removed from the site via the technology of the vector, but this image is usually accompanied by a grid reference, a scale, a citation, or some other secondary piece of information which authenticates and legitimates it. In the case of the live-to-TV military briefings held during the Gulf war, some useless figure was usually provided, so that the journalists and the TV audience could rest assured that the image of the action did indeed have a referent someplace on the territory it claimed to represent. These statistical indices can perhaps be thought of as *telemetry,* or measurement at a distance. On the other hand, thinking of them as "vital statistics" highlights their pornographic function. The bodies of bombs, like those of porno models, have dimensions. The site of an action, like the centerfold, has a location in space: the attack was in the north, Pamela grew up on a farm near Chicago.

As Avital Ronell remarks, "This recent desire for a 'bloodless war' has shown us that men's horror of blood has got to be dealt with."[45] The vectoral mode of perception seems to lend itself to a symptomatically masculine desire for an abstracted, formalized form of control through action. In the vector field, everything can be rendered discretely, can be "taken out" as an object, free from consequences, free from implications. The vector displaces the palpable complexities of the physical into the information realm, where an attempt can be made at a remote control. This was a pornographic war, where even the strongest emotions, felt at a distance, had no reciprocal impact on the sites from which the images came. It was OK to feel excited as the bombs went off. It was OK to feel remorse when the pictures of the refugees and the children passed as a glimpse across the screen, for none of these feelings involved the viewer in the other.

"Pamela Peters, like most Americans, was glued to her television during the Persian Gulf conflict and said a prayer every night for the valiant fighting forces."[46] Pamela Peters was Penthouse Pet of the Month for October 1991, and she is "an all American farm girl who loves her country." She appears in the centerfold, lying prone on a sand drift, with the American flag draped across her rump and a staple through her middle. Elsewhere she poses in camouflage fatigues and a helmet behind a wall of sandbags, or resting a large gun on her naked hip, or naked with a huge yellow ribbon strapped to her backside. "You have to give those guys credit, " she says of the American troops. "Most Americans don't know what a war looks like up close, but these men and women stared it in the face and won." It might be more appropriate to phrase this the other way around, that most Americans who look at TV know what war looks like at a distance, as a stream of images, just as most men who look at pornography know what a naked woman looks like, at a distance, a similarly abstracted, formalized, and bloodless stream of images.

Missile-Cam

Only the military can produce reconnaissance pictures showing the aerial bombing of strategic sites in Baghdad. Grainy black and white images show the bomb falling earthwards, dropping through the lift well of the building, exploding several stories further down, blowing out the side of the building. Even more extraordinary: pictures from the nose cone of a missile, homing in on the target. Television has for some time been trying to capture images of extremely fast vectors. Race-cam pictures from the cockpits of sports cars and similar images from skiing and surfing prepared us for the ultimate vertigo of missile-cam images. The Star Wars film *The Empire Strikes Back* anticipated this image.[47] In the bombing run on the death star, computer graphics and animation simulate images of the bomb dropping into the airshaft. That these images were so prescient was no accident, given that George Lucas consulted with Pentagon technical experts on what the public could be expected to see and know, twenty minutes into the future of weapons technology. Increasing sophistication in the technical presentation of the mass image is closely coupled to the development of the technical imagination of the military.

With missile-cam the vectors of destruction and information become almost completely synonymous. Only at the point of impact does the terminal sight fail, the screen turning to white noise as the warhead hits its target, the interruption of the arc coinciding with the violence of impact. The random white noise on the screen after impact became an instant metaphor for the disorder and death the vector could not show. Television cannot match such a trajectory, so becomes complicit with it. Television gives the armchair viewer a missile's-eye view of the vector itself, suturing spectator and weapon together until the last moment. This one missile becomes also the million viewers stitched, eyeball to eyeball, with its line of flight into enemy territory. We become complicit with its violation of that territory. The beautiful, historic city of Baghdad, home of so many architectural treasures of the Middle East, becomes home to pure, naked targets—rather like bombing Venice.[48] The vector has so overwhelmed territory and its defenses that recording the rape of territory by the projectile is not only technically feasible but publicly celebrated as an emblem of triumphant American machismo.

All wars are wars of the vector. Military competition has for some time been a matter of states attempting to get missiles with ever longer ranges. Some, including Iraq, were attempting to develop satellite reconnaissance to add a vector of vision and precision to the random trajectories of their missiles.[49] The media war has accustomed us to the image of war as something always ever faster, ever more destructive. From the terror bombing in Iraq by the RAF under the British mandate, to the saturation bombing of Tokyo or Dresden, to the threat of instant nuclear exterminism, war gets bigger and faster—exponentially. The Gulf war showed another side of this. It showed that flexibility and precision are just as much a part of the proliferation of vectors. During the Second World War, the saturation bombing runs were lucky to hit the right city, let alone the right target. In the Gulf war, precision became an almost aesthetic fetish.

Actually, the satellite surveillance may not have been nearly as complete or as useful as techno-fetishist stories in the media might lead us to believe. It seems that some of the information about targets in Kuwait came from the Kuwaiti resistance, armed with the ultimate fifth column vector: a portable satellite telephone and fax. They were able to fax out maps of strategic installations, and boasted of being able to direct-dial President Bush via satellite from safe houses and hideouts in occupied Kuwait. Hence wars of this kind, "brush-fire" wars in the old cold war rhetoric, thrive on flexible vectors, and we can expect demands for military hardware to reflect this newfound virtue. Completion of the global surveillance vector of Keyhole satellites will, no doubt, be a high priority as well: the capacity to see the enemy is equivalent to the capacity to kill. Missile-cam is the *reductio ad absurdum* of this coupling, given that not only is the vision of the target connected in real time to its destruction, but an international audience gets to see the event later the same day on television. We can only await the pilot episode of the event that features live missile-cam attacks with a certain unstable mixture of dread and fascination.

Against this the best the Iraqis could manage was a display of Western prisoners of war on television. This quite rightly raised the ire of the Western press. A Murdoch tabloid headline beamed: **HANG SADDAM LONG AND SLOW.** Yet the missile-eye view of destruction is surely just as much an expression of the horror show which television becomes in war. More frightening than the human tragedy of capture, the pure, disembodied vector turns war into a ceaseless violation of the spatial integrity of other spaces, other bodies. The simple geometry of the blowing up of blockhouses denies any human dimension.[50] As John Pilger pointed out, the U.S. deployed against Iraq many antipersonnel weapons it perfected in Vietnam. No mention was made of this amid the rhetoric of "surgical" precision and the avoidance of "collateral damage," to use an expression coined at the time of Vietnam. The human becomes simply an appendage, hidden from the view of the vector. The vector appears as a power over and against the human, even against the social relations that built and guided it.

The vector makes an appendage of the spectators at either end: the televiewer at home, sucked along in the slipstream; the poor spectator down below, who sees only her or his death as an imminent, inexplicable terror. The irony of missile-cam is that while it appears to aim the vector at the other, in reality it aims it at us. As we watch the blockhouse come closer and closer, the vector captures our home space as much as that blockhouse with its black and white gaze and deadly power. The vector holds us all in thrall and hostage. It is the real victor of this and other imaginary wars. To the vector, the spoils. As the screen turns to pure white noise on impact, this perverse communication ends, but the channel remains open, broadcasting the white noise of events on the threshold of control.

Site #2

The Berlin Wall

from roots to aerials

Site #2

3. wall

> The fall of every figure with totalitarian power reveals the illusory community which approved him unanimously, and which had been nothing more than an agglomeration of solitudes without illusions.
>
> —Guy Debord

Vision Mix

Dateline: East Berlin, 12 November 1989. East German workers tear down a section of the Berlin Wall with heavy cranes, opening a crack in the wall at the center of old Berlin, the Potsdamer Platz. Thousands of East Berliners pour through the gap, across the site of the old Potsdamer Platz, once a busy and historic center of the city. West German authorities in Berlin hand out maps and shopping money to the Easterners. The mayor of East Berlin, Erhard Krack, and his West Berlin counterpart, Walter Momper, push through the crowd on the Potsdamer Platz to shake each other's hand. Krack presents Momper with a model of the traffic light—Berlin's first—that had formerly stood on the site in 1924. Meanwhile many thousands climb the wall and party; champagne and music in the air.

The media quickly capitalized on this event. *The Guardian* newspaper announced: "Europe seems to be a different place this week."[1] On the American television news program "NBC Today," cold war veteran Arthur M. Schlesinger Jr. announced that the cold war was "over." Gorbachev made a statement in Moscow: "Not long ago we were at the crossroads—where was the world going? Towards further confrontation, the aggravation of ideological hostility, the whipping up of military threats; or towards co-operation, mutual understanding and the search for agreement? The choice has more or less taken place."[2]

The curious thing here is the grammatical construction: Schlesinger did not say "we ended the cold war" but "the cold war is over." Gorbachev did not say "we made our choice" but "the choice has taken place." Lines phrased in the passive voice. Events proclaimed without causes at their head.

If the cold war has indeed ended, it had nothing to do with the rational decisions or dialogue between the parties. Events did not appear as the outcome of particular or definable leadership actions. The historical end has simply "taken place." The place history took was a stretch of wall running from

Checkpoint Charlie to the Brandenburg Gate in Berlin, via what used to be Potsdamer Platz. It ran, in other words, from the symbolic arch famous from the history books as the one Napoleon marched through victoriously, to a place made famous from spy movies of the cold war years as the site for those tense exchanges of agents with the enemy. But it was not so much "history" that took this place, but the "angel of history"—the international television camera, and the particular storyline it makes take place—the event. The comsat angel forms an image out of the rubble blasted from the past into the present. It frames an image of the crash of moments.[3]

NBC news interviewed the mayor of West Berlin. It turned out, conveniently enough, that he spoke excellent English. His head and shoulders appeared on the screen with the wall in the background, and the caption underneath said simply: "Berlin." On closer inspection, it turned out that the mayor wasn't actually standing in front of the wall at all, as pictured. NBC chromakeyed his image together with live footage of the wall, and mixed sound recorded at the wall with his answers to the off-camera reporter's questions. The mayor was in a studio somewhere, presumably in West Berlin, while the image behind him showed the wall from the East side. The lighting of the mayor's talking head was designed to match that of the wall, but did not succeed entirely in mimicking that peculiar second-hand daylight of northern Europe.

The caption "Berlin," placed underneath by NBC, was not actually referring to the physical space of Berlin itself. It referred to an electronic space constructed in the studio, which mixed images made on the East and the West sides of the wall into a single vital center. There was no great "distortion" of the facts of the situation here. If anything, this simulated nonfact seemed a more appropriate rendering of the situation than a more straightforwardly representational image would have been. This was simply a matter of contriving the mayor and the wall together to form an appropriate image in the easiest way possible. In the electronic space of "NBC Today," the wall had already come down, and images from both sides could be combined by the vision-mixer. NBC rearranged the furniture of the site to suit itself. The wall itself may still be standing, but it is no barrier to certain vectors and flows of information, if indeed it ever effectively was.

The fall of the wall was as much a problem for the media as it was for the municipal and state authorities on either side of the breach. In their role as global vision-mixer, the various media were in a bit of a state as to which visions to mix. Three narrative lines dominated the commentary on this event as it happened. Each relied on a set of simple narrative conventions, generated out of a relatively stable structure of very basic elements. I am tempted to call these elements "vectemes," only they are more lines of narrative *movement* than elements of interchangeable structures. The first of these three narrative movements of event-containment is "the cold war"—a favorite with the American vector-brokers, and scintillatingly televisual. The good guys were the West and the bad guys were the Communists—and they had just collapsed as an antagonistic pole of power. Archival footage showed the wall going up . . . and coming down. The juxtaposition of some ghostly black and white stock footage of Hitler, Stalin, Roosevelt, and their tank divisions gave this cold war story the grain of media history. If the wall coming down was not the result of a discernible leadership action, at least the wall going up looked like it was.

The cold war narrative frame was perhaps the easiest to pronounce upon but the most difficult to grasp in any meaningful way. While the television coverage did not trouble itself with the details of this shift in the balance of power, it did inevitably pose a difficulty for itself in adopting a triumphalist stance. If the Eastern other has collapsed, how does the West define itself and the necessity of its massive armed response to the threat of the Eastern other? It took another catastrophe—the Gulf war event—to untangle some of the narrative debris of the post–cold war power game. As Zygmunt Bauman argues, the collapse of the Eastern "other" left the space of otherness to the West open.[4] The combined power of military and media vectors showed in the Gulf war that the other can become any state, any force, anywhere in the globe: Panama, Grenada, Libya, Lebanon, Iraq. Stay tuned to CNN for ensuing episodes. . . .

Less triumphalist was a second narrative strategy for the containment of this event. The "people" formed the narrative core of the second, and perhaps most common, framing. In this version, the Communists were still the bad guys, but it was the people of the East who were the active agent who overthrew the tyrant. Whereas the time frame for the cold war narrative was a matter of decades, in this version it could all be compressed into a matter of days. If the satellite feed needed a historical grounding, then a couple of grainy images of the 1953 riots in the Russian sector, shot from the West and showing Potsdamer Platz and the other side of the Brandenburg Gate, would do. The mix could montage these with comparable shots showing those sites today, from the same angle. The same amorphous, humanist swell of "the people" could thus be pictured, milling about today, sans tanks.

Cut to a vision mix of supple, ineluctable crowd shots, defying the bristling porcupine skin of the armed state with their movement. The mass, by virtue of its impenetrable, obtuse obviousness, was something upon which every Western ideological angle could be projected. Any and every demand could be projected onto the crowd: liberal democracy, conservative restoration, social radicalism, free markets, twin overhead cam fuel-injected turbocharged power. Liberals, conservatives, leftists, and marketing managers alike could claim this crowd as their own. Indeed a lively discourse sprang up overnight in the West, trying to pin this wandering mass down as a free-floating story that might drift opportunistically over to support this or that new narrative line. With a little judicious editing, the AWOL images of the Easterners dispensing their own liberty and decamping to the West were corralled into new containments and captures in the narrativizing aftermath of the event.

Cut to a one-shot of a "typical East Berliner," microphone angled to the face. The image of the people could easily be captured—shots of crowded squares and streets filled the screen. Attempts to make the image *talk* were another matter. When interviewed individually, they never seemed to know what was expected.

Their statements were always a little less and a little more than "representative" views. "It's unfathomable," according to a fifty-one-year-old man. "I can't believe I'm here," says an elderly East Berliner. "This is what we have dreamed of for all these years," says another; "I can't describe it," says a young woman with tears in her eyes.[5] Frank, endearing, but not exactly helpful.

Perhaps we can excuse them for this. They were not professional talking heads. It is the professional's role to guess the trajectory of the story and provide the lines that link the immediately witnessed action to the imagined plot. The amateurs, these nonrepresentative representatives of the people, were not telling a story, they were living, and enlivening, an event. It was left to Helmut Kohl: "Let us avoid the temptation to assume that a solution to the German question can be arranged in advance with a script and a calendar. History doesn't follow a schedule." But Chancellor Helmut Kohl certainly does. It says in his script, "There is no script," and the press conference was scheduled for him to say, "There is no schedule." Politics is certainly rather more opportunistic than Kohl's mythical "history," but no less organized, it seems. Even the populist narrative that claims to follow the moods and tempers and nightmares of the people is still a story after all. It is one which keeps one eye on its audience and modifies its tale as it goes along to suit their expressions. One almost imagines Walter Benjamin had someone like Kohl in mind when he said, "History knows nothing of the evil infinity contained in the image of the two wrestlers locked in eternal combat. The true politician reckons in dates."[6]

A History Lesson

For those who find Kohl's guest appearances in their living room distasteful, there was always Willy Brandt, that most unheroic social democratic hero. In retirement from active politics, this former chancellor of West Germany, who had been mayor of Berlin when the wall went up, could afford to put the fall of the wall into his own historical storyline. "This is a beautiful day after a long journey," he said.[7] Especially for those families who are "unexpectedly but tearfully reunited." A veteran politician, he begins with the affect of the wall in everyday life, not its effect in history, that mad tyrant of an abstraction.

The substance of what he has to say concerns that history, and is an attempt to vindicate his and the social democrats' part in it, in the light of this most recent event. He states his credentials to tell such a story as a person who did a lot in and for West Germany "to reduce tensions in Europe and who fought for the greatest amount of practical connections and human contacts obtainable." And so he did. "We had to say: Berlin must live in spite of the wall. . . ." But "we were instructed to keep the path to Germany open." There's that passive voice again, that alibi of history.

Whether contact and connections with the East German state helped the East German people or merely prolonged the reign of that state is the moot point some of his critics might raise at this point, but that assumes that the East

German state *could* have gone on, that it was a self-perpetuating monster, as the hawkish theory of totalitarianism held.

Brandt feels that the alibi of history is on his side, not theirs: "It has always been my conviction that the concrete partition and the division through barbed wire and death strip stood in opposition to the course of history." A brave claim, and one he expects to be vindicated, as he suggests preserving a little piece of the wall "as a reminder of a historical monster." With one eye on future historical time, Brandt can see the value of monuments that persist and remember for us. With the other eye on past historical time, Brandt feels obliged to nominate a beginning for this story. It does not start with the wall going up on 13 August 1961, but with the "terrorist Nazi regime."

The mere mention of this sets the tone for Brandt's meditations on the present. Germany will not seek solutions to the problems raised by the fall of the wall that are not in accord with Germany's responsibilities toward Europe. This statement explicitly addresses not only a German audience but the other NATO powers, the Soviet Union, and Germany's Eastern neighbors. The instant communication of these words to all of the above conditions the context of the speech itself. The space in which Brandt speaks is a doubled one: the steps of the Berlin town hall are one space; the matrix of the vector is the other.

Brandt congratulates the East Germans on taking an active role, demanding in particular the vectoral liberties of free information flow, travel, and assembly. He reiterates his vindication of the social democratic view of history: "This slow movement towards stability and towards dismantling rather than fostering the arms race is now paying off." He speaks, at last, about the future. One where the West will no longer legitimate itself with the self-congratulatory slogans of the cold war. The West will be judged now by what it builds, "in intellectual and material terms," for the future. "I hope that in regard to the intellectual aspect, the cupboards are not empty. I also hope that there will be some cash flow."

Looking back on events since the fall of the wall, on the rise of racist attacks, on the wholesale asset-stripping of the East by Western interests, one can appreciate why Brandt's optimism on the home front was so muted. His wider sense of historical mission, where "the parcelling of our continent must gradually be overcome," looks to be stalled, not least by the instability in European economic integration caused by the debt-financing of the economy of the former East Germany.

Cold comfort for the Easterners: the terms of currency unification favored Western carpetbagging of Eastern assets, and destroyed the export markets even of viable Eastern firms. West German firms move into the Eastern market, while Eastern businesses close up shop. The state was left to foot the bill for the unemployed.[8] East Germany's role in the new, "unified" Germany and in integrating Europe is to be a dependent one, like the former dictatorships of southern Europe.[9]

The one-to-one exchange rate (but only for the first 4,000 marks) provided Kohl with a politically useful bout of instant gratification for the Easterners, and a bonanza for Western suppliers of consumer goods. In so doing, the Westerners defined the terrain of third nature with a steep slope in their favor. Everyone in the East could suddenly spend their cash reserves on Western goods and look forward to a future of being unemployed with a microwave and a color TV. Not everything about the West proved to be at all satisfying for the Easterners, however. The social welfare system wasn't as good. No daycare, no job security, less right to public housing, fewer real jobs for women. And all those Western managers coming over! Then there were the blacklists, the politically motivated sackings. All in all, more like a colonization than a unification.[10] So much for the euphoric slogan, which seized hold when the wall came down, **WE ARE ONE PEOPLE!**

What Willy Brandt referred to as the overcoming of "the parcelling of our continent" also means a massive influx of refugees. West Germany's liberal asylum laws presupposed a parceled Europe. With the vectors of travel opening to the East, a soul-searching debate on immigration law ensued. WE ARE ALL FOREIGNERS read one sticker, plastered everywhere in response to the ugly racist attacks on refugees and guest workers.[11] Particularly alarming were the firebomb attacks on refugee hostels, such as in September 1991 when a vicious mob attacked a hostel in Saxony for several nights.

So in a sense Brandt was right to nominate the Nazi regime as the beginning point of his story about the events leading to the fall of the wall. The site of the Brandenburg Gate had still to be actively purged of their memory in 1993. In place of the wall between the two Germanys is not reunification, but the vector of unequal exchange. Far from furthering unification, it actively prevents it. Helmut Kohl, the true politician, seized the day the wall came down. A practical man, in his plan for integration he explicitly mentions greatly increased telephone links and an expansion of the East German phone system. It is from the matrix of vectors that integration, on whatever terms, has to begin.[12]

One can forgive Willy Brandt for feeling cautiously optimistic when he spoke, in those emotional days, from the steps of the Berlin city hall. One can understand and sympathize with his use of the occasion to vindicate himself and his role in postwar German history. After all, it was the discovery of an East German agent on his personal staff which forced his resignation as chancellor in 1974. Perhaps, at another break in history, his understanding of its trajectory will also be vindicated. The remaining puzzle about the Easterners who packed the trains to get to the West, who forced the lifting of travel restrictions, which began the movement that finally undermined the wall, is: What did they want? Why did they agree to unification on these terms? The answer to that lies along the vector between West and East.

The One-Way Wall

What did the East Germans really want? That tack is really the prerogative of the small army of sociologists and opinion-pollsters who have no doubt descended upon the former East Germans from the West. The answer will no doubt be of intense interest to the political party machines and the marketing managers, but is not to be confused with a critical reflection on the event. A critical approach to the event has to view it through the prism of its own mediations in space. More precisely, upon viewing the videotape replays of the East Germans kicking down the wall, alongside the question "What did they want?" another question arises: Why were the Western media so fascinated by the spectacle of this clear and obvious enactment of the most obscure and ineffable desires?

As the Slovenian philosopher Slavoj Žižek puts it, "Democracy, which in the West shows increasing signs of decay and crisis, lost in bureaucratic routine and publicity-style election campaigns, is being rediscovered in Eastern Europe in all its freshness and novelty. The function of this fascination is thus purely ideological: in Eastern Europe the West looks for its own lost origins. . . . The Real object of fascination for the West is thus the gaze, namely the supposedly naive gaze by means of which Eastern Europe stares back at the West, fascinated by its democracy."[13] Here Žižek offers the beginnings of a possible line of writing into the event. What remains to be decided is whether there is a kind of universal form of relation between the object of desire and the desiring subject as Žižek, in the spirit of Jacques Lacan, would most eloquently like to persuade us. Perhaps a critique of the relation between the East and the West has to be understood as a much more historically constituted form of relation, a relation between flickering images cast by the firepower of the vector in the dark recesses of both Eastern and Western perception.

This brings up the third and more difficult story that sometimes surfaced through the grid of the two just mentioned. The cold war story sees "our" way of life vindicated in the collapse of the East; the democratic uprising story sees it vindicated indirectly, in Eastern admiration for it. The third story had a somewhat more paradoxical ring to it. It stressed the influence of Western commodity culture as a subversive and destabilizing element in the territory of the East, particularly as carried there on the strength of West German television signals. More than one Western reporter mentioned that there were only two parts of East Germany that could not get Western TV, jokingly referred to as the "valley of the unenlightened."

There are some who would not find the joke very funny. Like the late Theodor Adorno, who saw television as part of the dark side of the enlightenment. Adorno once suggested, in an elaborate meditation on the relationship of culture to industry, that it was important not to place too much emphasis on the critique of culture as a sham ideology covering up for a mendacious system of economic domination. Nor was it wise to place too much hope in culture as carrying within it a utopian image of a better life than the existence-minimum that modern capitalism furnishes. Looked at either way, one should not "throw the baby out with the bath water": "in face of the lie of the commodity world, even the lie that denounces it becomes a corrective."[14] The irony is a melancholy one. It is the image of the commodity world, wafting over the borderlines, which is the lie that denounces the "culture" the East German regime tried so desperately to put in its place.

Stefan Heym, an East German novelist, published for the most part in the West, summed up this massed wall-jump thus: "Never before in the history of mankind has a state been plunged into crisis in such a ridiculous fashion. . . . No reformer proclaiming new theses here, no general riding into the capital city at the head of tanks. No, this acute crisis has arisen as a result of the population running away; instead of barricades, a mass exodus; instead of strikes and demonstrations, the occupation of embassies; instead of clashes with the police, trips to Hungary." The mass, in this account, is the prime mover, as in the second narrative line, but what occasions it to move? East Germans may have run westward, provoking a crisis, but they were running in the direction whence images of the good life came. The wall notwithstanding, there is still "the vision on their screens evening after evening of a richer world, a world without boundaries and which is said to belong to the industrious. . . . No wonder that the people of the country run off at the first opportunity."[15]

This is the crux of the third version, which stresses the agency of the comsat angel, the media vector. In this story, the agency that propels the event forward is an inhuman, ethereal one. It is not the people who make history, but the images of their action, taking on an independent life, which in turn sparks actions at some remote time and space. Lenin had been right to call the newspaper of the party in exile *The Spark*. Little could he have imagined that the spark of telesthesia, of perception at a distance, would take on an independent life.

Television attracted East German viewers like flies to shit. It was the strange attractor of desire, the wall notwithstanding. Until in the end the wall withstood no more. Clearly, television cannot be credited all on its own with fomenting a social revolution. Yet its influence may be a clue to the peculiar place of the media vector in what otherwise looks like a classically popular and public uprising. As East German communications scholar Helmut Hanke says, "It is not only sociologists who note that in the German Democratic Republic by about 6PM, even in city centres, the streets and squares have emptied. . . . After work has ended, the media really come into their own."[16] The media, Hanke says, especially television, "put us in touch with the real and fictional worlds which are not, or not yet, within reach. . . . Media culture and particularly music, is constantly opening up new, alternative worlds which are in marked contrast to the world of everyday experience." Writing before 1989, Hanke thought that the Western media vector grew out of a far more internationalized sphere of cultural production than was the case in the East. "In this respect, the media—with their objective dependence on internationalization—can perhaps act as a pacemaker towards our future development."

The East German cultural intelligentsia resist this pull of the West, Hanke notes. What he doesn't say is that they have a vested interest in this. The East German state reached a compromise with the intellectuals, because it needed an effective and well-funded national culture to legitimate a state which was in every other respect an accident of history. The pull of Western television and pop music is in this sense a failure to maintain an autonomous national vector field of cultural circulation. The East German radio station targeted at young people, DT64, played pop music like its Western counterparts, but in doing so it was competing with the Western vector on its own terms, in itself a sign of difficulty. In a society as highly tuned to the vector as East Germany, the fact that people tuned in to Western television "as if it were the most natural thing in the world" is a sign of defeat.

The interesting question is this: What relation can the image of the West furnished in the homes of the East by the vector of the West possibly have to the events of November '89? The West German philosopher Jürgen Habermas sums up the odd juxtaposition of a classical revolutionary mass movement with this historically new modality: "It was, in other words, precisely the sort of spontaneous mass action that once provided so many revolutionary theorists with a model, but which had recently been presumed dead. Of course, this all took place for the first time in the unorthodox space of an international arena of participating and partial observers, created by the *uninterrupted presence* of the electronic media."[17] A primetime global event, in other words, which may be a little beyond the compass of some prevalent theories of communication. Beyond those based on the national framework of hegemony and those based, a little more discreetly, on concepts of an idealized common ground, like the communicative rationality of Habermas.[18] It may also pose some difficulties for Žižek. To indulge for a moment in the hyperbolic style of the media, not since May 1968 in Paris has an event taken on the full form of what Henri Lefebvre called the festival. Like May '68, November '89 will someday have its theorists, just as Hegel answered the enlightened French republicans before him. For now we will have to make do with a more humble task of sifting for the traces of the elusive contours of the event in the rubble of commentary.

Writing along the line of the vector entails placing the narrative frames of the high-speed media vector in the context of the slower rhythms of magazines and journals that explicitly frame the event in the contemplative tempo of more complex historical or analytical narratives. The raw coverage of the event catches ideology off guard, reducing it to its bare reflexes. In the later commentary it can usually be found attempting to reassert challenged hegemonies over the sense of history, drawing on its deepest resources. These two kinds of fallout from the event can illuminate each other. Going one step further, comparing the explicit commentaries produced after the event to implicit ones produced by a rereading of texts preceding it can illuminate the event in new ways. At the limit, the eye-blink of the event can be contextualized by viewing it in juxtaposition to far more slow-moving forms of discursive space—a task that will be put off till the following essay.

Having specified the shifting temporal layers of event critique, it is worthwhile reiterating the questions which specify the point of incision through those layers. The questions which might, in a sense, orient critique are directed to the East and the West, and regard in each case the specific form of its relation to the specular image of the other. To the West side of the divide, one might ask: What was the object of fascination in these images of the East? How does the framing of the other in this or that storyline implicate the West's own self-image? To the East: What was the relationship between the image of the West coming from the media vector and the action that ensued in the territory of the East? Two somewhat different questions, addressed to quite asymmetrical images on either side of the two-way mirror of the wall. Our story begins (that is, *appears* to begin) in the East. . . .

A Small Step for Mankind

The opposition churchman Werner Kratschell recalls driving through the breach in the wall, and his wife wanting him to stop the car in the West. "She wants only to put her foot down on the street just once. Touching the ground. Armstrong after the moon landing. She has never been in the West before."[19] It is appropriate that the pathos of this remark stems from its evocation of the moon, such an austere image of another place, the "other" place, conquered once and for all when Armstrong put his foot on it. Of course, it was not his *foot* that touched down, but an airtight boot. Armstrong traveled many thousands of miles and *still* didn't touch the moon. The other is an airless place, a mirage, an image; even when one travels to it, sets foot in it, one still does not quite touch it. There is something there to touch, to be sure, but it is not quite the other mapped out for you in advance. The moon shot produced the *image* of man passing through the looking glass, but it was an imaginary conquest.

The extraordinary thing is that the West existed in this imaginary form in the East and that it could become tangled up in such a movement. It existed in much the same way as the moon existed as an imaginary other for "mankind" in the mind of President Kennedy, when he ordered a civilian missile program to target the imaginary other of the moon, just as he ordered a thousand Minuteman missiles from the Boeing corporation to target the imaginary other of the East.[20] Had Armstrong really touched the vacuum-sealed real of the moon with his foot, he would not have lived to speak of it and us. Had Kennedy's missiles touched the real underlying territory of the East, neither would we. In a relation with the other, everything seems to hinge on maintaining the proper distance. Now that the vector keeps closing the distance, bringing whole worlds into view with the eye-blink of an edit on the evening news, maintaining the proper distance becomes a considerably more difficult task. The vector is like an asymptote, approaching closer and closer to the baseline it can never touch. Yet this infinitely closer yet still achingly untouchable relation to the other disturbs all those senses of being in the world that orient us, individually and collectively, to others.

Imaginary projections of an other, held at an appropriate remove, are always a necessary step in determining who we "really" are. This is what novelist Peter

Schneider meant when he argued that the wall was the only thing keeping the Germanys together. Each could fix an identity relative to the other because the barrier between them was a fixed point in a floating world, a rare point of stability, and hence something solid to dream of overcoming.[21] The relationship of East to West had a firm boundary, and this could form a fixed, if mostly absent, point of reference for the vector that passed over it. Like the character in Schneider's novel *The Wall Jumper,* who switches between Eastern and Western television stations, as it was possible to do in either Berlin, and remarks: "Network executives on both sides are laughably alike: in their own camp they let only the rulers speak; in the enemy camp, only the oppressed."

We can hold an image of ourselves only when we are standing in the line of such a trajectory. The question for vectoral analysis is not *what* is your identity but *where* is your nonidentity? What points does it lie between? Along which lines does it oscillate? This is not an abstract question, but a very concrete one: what are the channels, what are the frequencies, what are the sources at your disposal to orient you to the world? What the vector does is make identity oscillate between more and more points. Along every line is a story, and so there are many stories now that act as the vehicles of discovery, between where we think we are and where we imagine the other is. Hence there are two effects which the proliferation of media vectors emanating from the West might have had on the East. One would be to give the appearance of a gradual, incremental increase in proximity, a contamination of the spatial and psychic borderlines between self and other. Another effect is the proliferation of other points: an other and an other and an other. So many stories, so close to home. So many lines of nonidentity to act along, so many others to become. Thus, when the wall came down, the rather different and possibly incompatible currents of leftist thought were in a rather confused state. The lines along which they placed themselves imploded. Until they forged a new identity along another line, in opposition to the Gulf war.

Returning to our moonwalkers: Kratschell and his wife might feel like real actors on a real terrain, touching strange earth. The theatricality of the act of stopping the car, stepping out of its capsule, making that small step gives the lie to the degree of imaginary travelogue mixed in with this border-crossing. The act itself takes place on a "real" terrain, but the motivation behind the act is in part imaginary. The Kratschells might feel the whole experience is real, but like method actors, they focus on the interiority of their roles. Viewed from a distance, preferably from the other side of the world, they look more like actors on a set. Just like Kennedy on that platform we have all seen in television documentaries, the one which frames him on a stage in front of the wall for the cameras. Armstrong on a moon we can only imagine. The Kratschells appear in the long view to be acting on a specular map of imaginary identities. In Kratschell's metaphor of touching the moon, the two halves of Europe have become the whole world, as if nothing else existed. Seen at a distance, the whole of Europe looks like another place, a tiny speck somewhere over *there.* A place that holds a mirror up to itself, sees the other in itself, and does not notice the rest of us at all. One thinks of Europe in 1989 as the opening night at the theater where the curtain goes up and the audience comes face to face—with another audience. Each thinks the other is the spectacle, themselves the real audience. One has to be outside the theater altogether to see the whole thing together as one big spectacular show.

Remote Sensing

This is why I could watch it all on Australian television, watch the fall of the wall that went up the year I was born, and laugh with a cynical joy. This is the event of a lifetime—for somebody else. The Germans are making revolution, and I'm waiting for the casserole to warm up. I pick up two remote controls. Two fingers on two buttons, and the TV sound fades down and the stereo fades up. I load the CD player with a melancholy song, just for the occasion. "I am the passenger," it sings to me, "and I ride and I ride." I can smell the casserole bubbling. "I am the passenger. I stay under glass." Later, after dinner, I pick a book up from the random pile that always seems to accumulate on my coffee table. It's by the novelist David Ireland. I know it contains a line which sums up my place in the world, riding the vector from out here in the antipodes: "We are no one, just whites marooned in the east, by history." I am no one, alone with my TV and my food. "He sees the things he knows are his." I am part of the TV eye that now attaches itself to any catastrophe, like the fall of a state or the start of a war. "And all of it was made for you and me." We are all no one, just the terminal points in a growing, global grid of telesthesia, riding the vector, cruising for action. "Let's ride and ride and ride. . . . Tonight we're bearing down on Germany. On with the show, this is it.

Pick up the remote. On line to Potsdamer Platz, city of Berlin. Here are the East Germans, stepping into the West like astronauts. These actors appear to be within a spectacle, but this spectacle is a *double* one. One is the external spectacle on our TV screens of the breach in the wall, the champagne spray, the pickaxe chipping the old wall away. The other spectacle is the one that the East Germans experience as interiority, which they are reacting to from within. Rather than simply crossing a border, they are also starring on *two* separate screens, each a lopsided mirror of the other. In the imaginary of the West, the West itself figures simply as existence, an everyday thing. It seems the most natural thing in the world for the East to want to climb through the looking glass to join it. In the imaginary of the East, the West does not appear as everyday existence. It appears as something other. An image juxtaposed to those the East makes of itself. In the domain of images, the policing of the referent so common in the spectacular world of the East is no match for the inventiveness and proliferation of the spectacle of the West.

That very inventiveness becomes a screen onto which to project a yearning which the spectacle of the East cannot match. Everyday life in the East is marked by "a certain boredom," says Helmut Hanke.[22] Stephen Spender puts it more strongly: "Life under a dictatorship of old style ideologists . . . is extremely boring. Moreover, owing to modern systems of communication people living under dictatorships are made aware of the boredom of the system: the flow of information from the outside is unstoppable."[23] In this sense, the crossing of the border was a revolt against the spectacle, but one that used the presence of a neighboring spectacle as a mirror to work off, with which to critique the unreality of Eastern life. The unreal image of the West exposes the unreality of the image of the East. Not exactly a classical recipe for enlightenment, but something considerably more interesting than the narcissistic self-affirmation that the collapse of the Eastern spectacle afforded the Western imaginary.

In geographical space there was a wall, no doubt about it, a physical constraint on movement. But, as Timothy Garton Ash remarks, in the psychogeography of East Germany, on the specular map of places and spaces, "the Wall was not round the periphery of East Germany, it was at its very centre. And it ran through every heart."[24] The wall not only partitions one set of actors from another, it interpellates those individuals, it structures their sense of who they are, particularly in the East. While the physical wall was ever-present, information blew through it like radiation, slowed but unstoppable. East Germans, the bearers of oppressive social relations, were also the bearers of an unbearable contradiction between the physical space with its rudimentary divide running at its most sensitive spot between the Mitte and Tiergarten districts of Berlin, and the spectacular shopping-arcade landscape beyond the mirror of West German television. Whereas in West Germany television holds up a specular mirror to the social relations of capital and those who bear them, to East Germans it was a mirror to pass *through* into an enchanted land. They *imagined* a real world behind the mirror which their Western counterparts have grown used to assuming is really just an *image*. So they passed through the mirror, and redrew the map. The remaking of the real, of course, has yet to catch up.

Yet the breach in this specular mirror landscape is a not insignificant fact. East Germans ceased to forbear the unbearable, to forgive the unforgivable, to stew in their own juices. They ran off at the first opportunity, a trip to the moon. On his visit to East Germany shortly before these events, Gorbachev had said: "Life itself punishes those who delay." So as the wall melted into airborne transmissions of radio waves, pictures, sounds, East Germans hurried off, stage right. Honecker was left behind in a Russian military hospital while the new masters of East Germany debated the most suitably tragic punishment for him. As the playwright Heiner Müller remarks, this was the first revolution in Germany "from below."[25] Rather than constitutional revolution organized by the Social Democratic Party, or counterrevolution organized by corps of Brown Shirts, this one lacked a social force motivating it, "on the ground" or "at the grass roots," as the usual expressions would have it. Of course, there was resistance, organized within the social and spatial bases of the churches. The churches could function as such because of a certain immunity, a degree of impermeability to influence from without. Yet this feature of the church as a cultural structure was both its strength and its limitation. As events exploded toward the breach, the dissident organizers were forced to follow the lead of the led. The mass that flocked through the wall to join the partying were not responding to the crook of the political pastors any more than to the pastoral social realism of the party's crook ideology, but were freely grazing on the spectacle cultivated in the West. They followed the loaded star of television through the looking-glass screen to its imagined source in the West.

Maps and Territories

Stephen Spender—of all people—wrote most convincingly of the events of 1989 with an élan and aura of revolutionary optimism. An optimism, unfortunately, which may not have been too securely based. "If the present revolution is stopped in any one place, to be superseded by dictatorship, the media will assure that the consciousness of a democratic world, flooding in, will sooner or later break down the prison walls of dictatorship."[26] The optimism about the role of the Western media, as one which has a transparent relation to a set of ethical ideas on the one hand (Democracy with a capital D) and to political practice (democracy decapitalized, if not decapitated), may seem a little misplaced. It may be that what was significant was the clash of opaque and false media with a false society, one falsity exposing the other, but without exposing itself. The difficulty, then, would be to sustain a critique of *both* Eastern social reality *and* Western media in this encounter.

Spender chances upon a fundamental thing. One has to examine an event such as the fall of the Berlin Wall through the medium of a number of stories, one of which is the development of the media vector. "What we see may now show that we have moved beyond the nineteenth- and twentieth-century cycle of revolutions—murder followed by counter-revolutions, also murderous—to a period when great political cultural changes are acts of recognition of changed states of consciousness, among people, made apparent as *faits accomplis* by the mass media." Yet by clinging to the concept of consciousness (like that of "heart" in the remark by Ash), this idea fails to go far enough. One cannot pit the insides of people's heads against the outside of political and cultural reality. In Spender's conception, it is as if the contents of millions of heads suddenly and spontaneously flip-flopped from one world view to another, which then had to be acknowledged by a corresponding change in exterior reality. Things may indeed look like that, but the concept of consciousness is in this context misleading. One would have to assume that consciousness fell from the sky. Rather, one would do better to view subjectivity as formed within *two* sets of exterior relations, both external to individual subjects and their "consciousness," both equally real. Those two relations are the *map* and the *territory* upon which people locate themselves and form their sense of place.[27]

The territory is a set of social relations, a particular physical space of interactions, including relations of production and reproduction, places of habitation and work, public and private spaces, including the Potsdamer Platz and the wall that used to run through it. It is that second nature we construct and reconstruct socially to free us from mere survival scratching in the dirt.

Covering the same space as the territory is the map. Whereas people and their interactions fill the territory, broadcast areas, satellite footprints, telephone networks compose the map, together with the signs and images that accumulate through interactions in this abstract, placeless space of media vector fields. It is a "third nature" which grows out of the migraine of perplexities, disruptions, and alienations second nature gives itself as it grows in complexity and depth. Maps keep track of territories, but territories never quite reveal themselves in any map.

The territory generates conflicts and identities rooted in particular places—Prenzlauer Berg, for example. Prenzlauer Berg was a traditionally working-class district of Berlin which by geographical chance ended up in the Russian zone, and hence in East Berlin. It had been a Communist stronghold before the war, holding out against the Nazis. Even after being terrorized by Nazi storm troopers, a week after the Reichstag fire 44,000 people voted Communist in the local elections. Lately it has been notable for the lack of enthusiasm for voting its residents display. In local elections in 1979, 5,000 people refused to vote at all.[28] Call it resistance if you will, but behind the mapping of this territory produced by these electoral statistics is a form of life which is not of itself knowable to any kind of external knowledge. Except perhaps the secret police. The latter may infiltrate the territory, for it is knowledge of territory that secret police specialize in. Their knowledge of the territory can function precisely because it does not circulate on a separate plane; it accumulates secretly, quietly, discreetly. Yet even the East German secret police, the Stasi, cannot prevent the undergrowth of territorial tactics from flourishing, like aspidistras, in the dark corners of urban space, between the "meagre public statements and the luxuriant rumours," as Christa Wolfe puts it.[29]

Poet, singer, songwriter, and exile from the East Wolfe Bierman describes a journey back through the breach in the wall, back to Prenzlauer Berg, where he watched punks fighting skinheads in the street. He watched the children of the leftist semi-opposition, who have colonized Prenzlauer Berg, scrapping with marauding skinheads. "These half-children, our 'skins,' are drawn from everywhere, but most are the children of functionaries, police and Stasi men, who, out of a job, now brood at home in front of the television, drinking. There's continuity amid the upheaval: the children of the opposition of yesterday beat up the children of the establishment."[30] It is here, in the territory, beneath the flight path of the vectors, that the genealogy of struggle remains.

A point to remember about this concept of territory is that it is a form of experience fundamentally unknowable to outsiders. The secret police, to really know territory, must become part of it. This is what distinguishes them from sociologists and journalists, who retain an identity apart from it, and hence never really belong. One can describe the tactics and ethics that bind people together in a territory, their codes of behavior, speech, gesture, silence, but such descriptions are already a mapping, an attempt to capture territory in a portable form. As Michel de Certeau insists, one has to approach this operation very carefully. Social science likes to treat these territorial tactics as a kind of otherness. It makes itself a trajectory along which it can make sense of it, organize it scientifically, speak the truth about it of which territorial intelligence is supposedly ignorant. This is the problem with Pierre Bourdieu's concept of "habitus." It maps territory but forgets itself in the operation. It forgets that social scientists, like everybody else, live in territories. Some territories are weak and defenseless agglutinations of people. Some are strong and allow people to exist in a space saturated with surveillance, like Prenzlauer Berg. In the fascination with such territories, ethnography reveals a longing for territorial resourcefulness by people much more trapped in vectoral space.

Another problem with ethnographies of territory is that they like to think that they are the only form of mapping that is taking place. They forget that within the territory there is a connection to spaces of mapping already, in the way people use and share the vector of television, in the way they form networks with the telephone. These maps generate quite different forms of interaction, ones not rooted in place, but tuned to an abstract space mapped over the territory. In the territory, people know who they are because they have roots there. On the map, people know who they are by tuning in to it; here we no longer have roots, we have aerials. The experience of the map is the experience of *telesthesia*. It can be a pornographic experience. It can be a rich experience, particularly in places where a dense and deeply rooted territorial intelligence meets a complex intersection of vectors, as in East Germany.

The West in the East

In what follows, I want to try to rewrite the third version of the story of the fall of the Berlin Wall, the version that makes the Western media into the primary agent, in terms that don't turn them into a heroic bearer of the spirit of Democracy. The problem with that version of the story, as presented, for example, by Spender, is that it attaches to Western media an identity that seems rather too good to be true. Just as East Germans learn to be suspicious or even contemptuous of socialist realism as an identity borne by the more vulgar forms of Eastern media, so too most Westerners are suspicious of the "capitalist realism" of Western media—and particularly of their leading genre, advertising. In arguing for a positive role in the East for the capitalist realism of Western media, one ought not to accept the easy assimilation of advertising's market choices to a genuinely transparent democratic realm. One ought not to take the Western media's "self-identifying" at face value, in other words. Rather, it might be more profitable to look *along the line* that the vector opens between East and West. To do this requires a bit of a theoretical detour, through another kind of story, as it were.

The great chiliastic revolutionary writer Guy Debord took an unusual interest in the uprising in East Germany of 1953. It set him off on an unusual line of thought, free from some of the terrible traps the bar of the wall put along the line of leftist thought between East and West. Debord paraphrases and develops Marx thus:

> The worker does not produce himself; he produces an independent power. The success of this production, its abundance, returns to the producer as an abundance of dispossession. All the time and space of his world become foreign to him with the accumulation of his alienated products. The spectacle is the map of this new world, a map which exactly covers its territory. The very powers which escape us show themselves to us in all their force.[31]

The spectacle is a temporal and spatial map of the process of alienated labor which takes the form of an endless image and imagining of that labor's products. This map is a network, and past a certain point of development, the other will now always be an *image* that appears within the network, not beyond and outside it. The other that appears on this map as the product of a socialist, undivided labor is just that—an appearance. Even Marxism and socialist labor must appear as images of themselves on the map of the spectacle. As he remarks of the image of the Eastern other: "The ideology which is materialised in this context has not economically transformed the world, as has capitalism which reached the stage of abundance; it has merely transformed perception by means of the police."[32]

There is a double process of spectacular alienation here. In the West, the image of unalienated socialist labor is nothing more than an image. The images of the East which succored generations of Western Marxists were nothing more than images. That they were necessarily only images is more interesting to Debord than that they were false. The crisis of Marxism has as much to do with the becoming-spectacular of the labor movement, its inclusion within the spectacle as it extends its map over the whole world, as it does with the exposure of the falseness of the image of the East. In the East, what interests Debord is not the exposure of the banalities of stalinoid socialist realist ideology but the process of constructing this image in the first place.

Reconsidering Spender's remarks in this context, one could say that the new form of political action, witnessed on TV, takes place doubly, on territory and map, and doubly *again:* on Eastern and Western territories and maps. Both the map and the territory (East and West) had images of the same line through them: differing images of the same wall. The wall was the figural surface on which the mirror was projected. This double mirroring places the apparently simple movement of "the people" through the Berlin Wall on four separate terrains. However, one must be careful to keep in mind the asymmetry of this situation. The *territory* of the East was maintained as an image of the other within the map of the West; the *map* of the West was the other put into covert circulation in the territory of the East.

The Eastern walkabout thus appears as an elaborate dreampolitik forcing the hand of realpolitik.[33] This dreampolitik takes the form of using the map of the West as a critique of the *gap* between the map of the East and the territory. This was not a flip-flop of consciousness forcing a change of reality, recognized post factum by the media. Rather, the gap between the sense of space and self formed on the map and the sense of place and self forged on the territory caused a playing of the Western map against the Eastern map, in which the Western map was *misrecognized* as the real West.

Two features of this situation, this doubled terrain, appear to be novel. Firstly: where the territory does not correspond to the map, this does not expose the map as "false consciousness."[34] It exposes the territory as a false infrastructure underneath the map. Everything *appears* as if social relations have to be modified to bring them into line with the symbolic order of the map. Secondly: while it is always in relation to an outside, to an other place that one's own sense of place forms, that sense of place now takes place on two planes: map and territory.

The connection between these coterminous planes of map and territory is narrative. Stories dominate the maps of both East and West, stories told and retold tirelessly. In the territory of both East and West, the symbolic marking out of territory with monuments reinforces the rapid diffusion of instant narrative. As Harold Innes maintained, stone was classically the medium for stabilizing the dispersal of a communication through time, whereas paper was the means of ensuring the dissemination of a communication across space.[35] These two methods, vectors, as I would call them, have historically had different relations to each other. In the present situation, broadcast media have greatly increased the spatial reach and tempo of communication, without a corresponding intensification of the temporal anchor of the monumental. The emphasis the East German regime put on the careful monumental marking out of the territory seems to have been in vain, given the ability of the Western map to waft into this same space with apparently ever-new, ever-different images.

While both monumental and broadcast vectors can have quite strong effects, neither state nor capital has ever succeeded in perfecting its control over either the map or the territory through them. In both still reside the tactical reasoning and resources of everyday life that Michel de Certeau calls "a polytheism of scattered practices."[36] These practices exist, in rumor, in jokes, in modes of speech, in memory, and have a presence on both map and territory. Media vectors are never free of this ambiguous residue of heteronomous potential. They too find themselves colonized by a subtle proliferation of ambiguous stories, lessons in tactical betrayal. In both the territory and the map, these other markers of the past still exist, and in some cases, like East Germany, thrive. Existing within the matrix of the vectors and enclosures are a series of quite other trajectories and memories, confined by walls and defined by vectors to be sure, but within such limits, freely chosen.[37]

On both map and territory, power acts strategically to mark out a territory or a temporal image flow with the imprint of the law. Power objectifies places in territory and time in broadcast vectors, with an impersonal stamp. On the other hand, the residual practices of everyday life subjectify the objects and images that power presents as mere things. The statue placed in a square, the television news broadcast narrating a particular event, both present the place or the event as a positing of a thing, objectively fashioned. The tearing down of a statue or the occupation of a television station is a recuperation of the authority of space or the command of the flow of media time for the subject, for the subjective. Power attempts to deactivate space and time, to mark them out in advance, subordinate them to abstract planner's grid and schedule keeper's timetables—if need be Helmut Kohl's opportunistic one. The irruption of the event signals a subjective break, rising out of the tactical resources kept alive in the interspaces of abstract grids. Is it any great surprise that the great upheavals in Berlin over the 10th to the 12th of November took place over a weekend? Or that the church bells rang on a Saturday and that the Potsdamer Platz became the site of a festival on Sunday? Or that by Monday most people were back at work, and the event fell, once again, into the stewardship of professionals? Hidden in the cracks of time are the resources to affirm something new. They can surge into the empty markers of symbolic space, take off on the wings of the vector. In any case, there is always a Monday morning when things will revert to the schedule, to business as usual

Communicative Irrationality

In using the image of capitalist realism as a fixed point beyond, tactical power was able to call up vast reservoirs of subjective power, to reactivate the streets, to paralyze the grid. By misrecognizing the map of the other, by being seduced by its promise, by confusing it with the territory of the West, the gap between the territory and the map of the East emerged as what it was: a meaningless chasm over which sense was enforced by the police. But while the East Germans policed the territory, they had no answer to the map of the West, wafting over the border. In seizing upon that map and forming themselves in relation to its otherness, the East German border-crossers might have seized upon a false image, but its effectiveness is in no way diminished by being a misrecognition. Indeed, this falseness may be an absolutely necessary precondition for transforming inchoate social needs and desires into effective and affective action. In relation to the false image of the other, the map of the West, the East knows itself and can speak, speaks itself and can act, acts itself and becomes—even if it is not clear what it is becoming. When all that is solid melts into airwaves, people are forced to face, with delirious sense, their real relations, and bring them into line with "consciousness," or rather with unconscious desires. False consciousness must be realized, actualized, lived—to be overcome. Irony is the wetnurse of history.[38]

The irony is a manifold one, in that what is at stake here is a misrecognition of a false image, which forms the basis of a genuinely critical movement that leads to the undoing of a regime premised on false images truly recognized as false consciousness. The result is a positive one in a negative sense: the collapse of East Germany. (Or perhaps the transgression of East Germany would be a better expression.) This was not a negation of the distorted and unfree space of the East by transformation into a positive alternative. It was not a rational process. It appears as an event that bears no relation to the narrative model Habermas prescribes as an ideal goal for communicative action.

In the place of the utopian models of free association of direct producers—the very model of communism so perverted in the East—Habermas proposes another, more abstract one: "In the framework of a society with a large scale political integration, let alone within the horizons of an international communications network, mutually supportive coexistence, even conceived in its own terms, is only available in the form of an *abstract* idea: in other words, in the form of a legitimate, intersubjectively shared expectation."[39] Habermas sees this model of a rational communication as the implicit ground which makes the rather less perfect communication in actual situations take place. But was this the case here? Was this communication at all?

Were it conceivable that the real was rational and the rational was real, the normative model would be workable, even if only as a regulative ideal or "shared expectation." In the spectacular space mediated by the vector, what appears is good and what is good appears.[40] The media vector field and the manner in which it interpellates its subjects is far too removed from the rational model for it to be any guide to action. Indeed, were rational communication even remotely possible, events such as these simply would not occur. Crises, to the extent that they could not be averted through rational dialogue, would not take this form. Yet occur they do—on the basis of the power of contradictory and equally irrational uses of the vector.

Habermas is right to view communications historically. Any theory of communications has to begin from its present historical form—the international vector field. In specific, singular events it is possible to grasp the constellations of historical temporalities and forces that shape the dense matrix of the vector fields and the powers that move upon them. It may even be possible to speculate on what unrealized potentials the vector has in store and base criticism on an openness toward the possible developments in the form of communicational power. Yet there is too much optimism in the substitution of an abstract ideal of communicative rationality for a model of a free association of producers. If the former has its roots in a nostalgia for Germanic peasant life on Marx's part, the latter has its roots in a nostalgia for the direct encounter of men of reason in the enlightened salon. Neither grasps the new space in which aerials substitute for roots, in which one vectoral relation crosses many different social territories, in contradictory but all equally opaque ways. Neither approaches the form of time the vector creates. The event does not take place in the abstract, in empty time, but in times marked out by the rhythms and collisions of punch-drunk power and blind desires. No wonder, then, that Habermas seemed to think of these events as a missed opportunity, where the rational debate on constitutional democracy was elbowed aside. It was not an opening of a discursive space, but a vectoral space imploding on itself. It was not an even notionally transparent medium for political dialogue, but an obscure encounter at terminal velocity along a vector grown too strong for the barriers separating one of its terminals from the other.

The transparency Marx sometimes dreamt of realizing in relations of production cannot be transferred onto a desire for transparent relations of communication in their place. The latter, too, become increasingly differentiated and murky. This is especially the case as vectors cross national and cultural thresholds more frequently. Having the other thrust in one's face nightly on TV is not likely to lead to a desire for a common space, but to either a violent urge to punch the other in the nose (as in Yugoslavia) or a desire for the difference the other represents (as here in East Germany).

The East in the West

In the West, we watched professionals like Schlesinger react to the fall of the wall. In the cynical West, it seems, we have professionals to "react" to events like this for us, sparing us the trouble. Our relationship to the map is as cynical as that of our Eastern counterparts, administered by fewer police but more advertising account executives.

Where the West appears to Easterners as a map, the image of the Eastern other that most commonly appears in the West is the image of the East as territory. It looks like a vast set of bureaucratic and ineffectual social relations distributed in a monotone hue across the landscape. A territory nevertheless armed to the teeth. The implosion of the map of the East seemed cause for celebration in the West. Not only is the abstract map of the West thus proven "superior," because more popular, but the collapse of the ideological map-space of the East seems also to remove the threatening aspect of its otherness, the East as a military territory nailed shut with tanks and guns. The next sentence of this paragraph, as I wrote it in 1990, said, "A consequent shift of Western identities and of otherness can't be far away."[41] The Gulf war has since confirmed this in spectacularly troubling ways. The West now takes its enemies wherever it can find them.

The presence of the wall allowed Kennedy to make his "Ich bin ein Berliner" speech to rapturous applause. The platform he made that speech upon is gone now, along with the wall that buttressed it, causing Timothy Garton Ash to comment: "Europe's 'Mousetrap' had ended its 28 year run. Clear the stage for another show."[42] Where now is the site in Europe where an American president can claim center stage? Then again, perhaps this is not the historical analogy one ought to draw. The city filled and cleared the Potsdamer Platz for a performance by Pink Floyd of "The Wall." Its composer, Roger Waters, dreamt of "a symbolic act of cooperation on-stage. If I can get soldiers from East and West playing 'Bring the Boys back Home' I will be smiling."[43] The boys, far from being released from monitoring the borders of the real, were released for other duties necessitated by the shift of the edge of the other elsewhere on the spectacular map of military and media spaces: Kurdistan and Armenia, Kuwait and Lithuania, Bosnia and Somalia, and so on. . . .

Noberto Bobbio stated the narrative problem which appeared ever so briefly in the European conception of the world in 1989 very nicely with this ancient saying: "Today there are no barbarians. . . . What will become of us without barbarians?" The crisis of the Eastern European states, what Bobbio calls the "catastrophe of communism," was also the beginning of the end of a certain narrative trajectory in Western cultural and political thought. This is because the West mapped its concepts and self-image against the backdrop of the Eastern other.[44] The Western liberal tradition sees confirmation for its own beliefs in the fall of the Berlin Wall and the triumph over the "barbarian" other. This may in the long run turn out to be a fatal optimism. Eastern enthusiasts for liberal ideas want to reconstruct the state on the basis of democracy, freedom, and law, and this would appear to be nothing less than a sane and sensible desire. Yet democracy, freedom, and law provide the necessary foundations for a *limited* polity, one that knows its place; a polity that prefers to subtly regulate rather than massively dominate life in the marketplace, the public sphere, and the bedroom.

The paradox of liberalism is that while it maintains the fiction of a separation of public and private spheres, it has at the same time acted as the presiding ideology over the massive penetration of the vector into the private space of the home. Indeed, liberalism maintains the fiction of a separate sphere of the private even as the private increasingly comes to be manufactured socially. The social psychologist Joshua Meyrowitz expresses this in a wonderfully studied language:

> The separation of people into different situations (or different *sets* of situations) fostered different world views, allowed for sharp distinctions between people's "frontstage" and "backstage" behaviours. . . . Such distinctions in situations were supported by the diffusion of literacy and printed materials, which tended to divide people into very different information worlds based on different levels of reading skill and on training and interest in different "literatures." The isolation of different people in different places also supported these distinctions. This led to different social identities based on the specific and limited experiences available in given locations. By bringing many different types of people to the same "place," electronic media have fostered a blurring of many formerly distinct social roles. Electronic media affect us, then, not primarily through their content, but by changing the "situational geography" of social life.[45]

Hence in the West, liberalism tolerated the creation by the vector of a situational geography which, in the end, was antithetical to the divisions of public from private on which it rested. The decidedly illiberal regimes of the East held out rather longer, but have finally caved in under the radioactive pressure of the vector, passing through its walls. The barrier that it depended on was not the division within between public and private, but a line without, walling off East from West. The vector crossed this external partition just as easily as it crossed into the private world within.

The West German filmmaker and writer Alexander Kluge expresses this as the domination of the "public spheres" of experience by the sphere of production.[46] The metaphor of the vector accounts for much the same phenomena, but without the "productivist" assumption at its base. Liberalism consecrates the domestic space with a spiritual aura while it legitimates the colonization of that realm by the vector of socialized cultural production. The vector penetrates so far into the hidden recesses of the allegedly private that it leaves its trace in the most intimate particulars. The storm blowing from television is a prime carrier of viral information, which, in Baudrillard's wan expression, "has wormed its way into everything, like a phobic, maniacal leitmotif, which affects sexual relations as well as kitchen implements."[47]

Nevertheless, this penetration of the vector is hardly a totalitarian takeover of the psyche. It still leaves a latitude of everyday autonomy—often a most remarkable one. The spontaneous surge out of the socialized space of the private, into the public spaces of the East, on into the shopping malls of the West, is a testimony to the quixotic potential of the vector to disseminate, and of the territory to gestate, unpredictable events. They do not simply extend the iron cage into the most private domains. The liberal ideology of the rule of law and the separation of the public and private, far from breaking up into a host of micronarratives, persist. The vector still strives to overtake them. It does not recognize the lines drawn in the social sphere by any metanarratives—Eastern or Western.

Democracy, freedom, and law have nevertheless failed to provide the same things that the Eastern states have failed to provide: a realized social utopia. Hence the only real solace events in the East can offer to Western liberalism is the comfort of knowing that "our" failed political master narratives are so much nicer to live with than "theirs." Whether Eastern liberals will feel more comfortable with a soft and easy failure than with a harsh and tyrannical one is another question. Whether it will really deliver a better material standard of living, not to mention a more equitable one, is also open to doubt. More pressing still, the West dwells in the gap between the promises and freedoms of the map and the mundane existence lived on the territory in a particular way: cynically. To borrow Peter Sloterdijk's delightfully cynical term, we live in a state of *enlightened false consciousness*.[48] This cynicism is nevertheless different from that of the East. Eastern cynicism is famous for its jokes at the expense of the Eastern spectacle, jokes that nevertheless bear witness to a certain tactical resourcefulness, to a promise of an order where dreampolitik and realpolitik might meet. In the West, these things belong to separate domains, and our cynicism takes the form of a Balkanization of consciousness, which keeps dreams and promises compartmentalized strictly within the imaginary domain of the map.

The Triumph of Communism

Conservatives suffer a much greater sense of crisis over the catastrophe of communism, as it is a pillar of conservative thought that barbaric and totalitarian regimes in the East are immune to the political vulnerabilities of regimes that are democratic or merely tyrannical.[49] Conservative anticommunism hinged on this premise, and the hinge appears to have just given way. One has only to cast an eye over the strenuous tirades against the left mounted by cold war conservatives since the fall of the wall to see the crisis of conservative thought at work. The ridiculous charge that the whole of left-wing opinion is condemned by the fall of the East is nothing more than a flip-flopped version of the old Communist bluff that all liberals and social democrats are really social fascists in disguise. Hard conservatism always worked in a paranoid way, by drawing a line through reality that put everybody to the left of Winston Churchill on the *other* side. That other side was a fearful thing, threatening, subversive, manipulative, indefatigable, a horrible thing that must be resisted at all costs. Now that this paranoid fear has revealed itself as a mirage, conservatism of this kind must enter deep crisis. So much the worse for them!

Socialist thought, and in particular Marxism, has of course always had a complicated relationship with the Eastern states. Marxists were always the most lucid critics of the Eastern regimes *and* their most blinkered worshippers, suggesting that the relationship between Western Marxism and its Eastern other was always a complicated one. One interesting aspect was the strategy of reversing the relationship between the barbarian other and civilization: Marxism sometimes made *capitalism* the barbarian half of this mirror image, and upheld the Soviet model as civilization, to use it as a critical tool for examining the West.[50] This critical tactic should have remained exactly that, a tactic for critically reversing the relationship of the West to its other, but it did not. On the basis of this experience, Marxists face the transformation of the tactical playing off of the Western spectacle against the drab East into an imitation of Western political ideologies in the East with a certain fatigue and despair. To misrecognize the other is one thing, a useful thing for figuring out who "we" are. To want to *become* the other, on the other hand, to extend the tactic into a project, is a dangerous game that might implode in the vacuum.

The increasing flow of information out of Eastern Europe undermined pro-Soviet thought. The great narrative collapsed under the weight of countless, relentless little stories of terror and futility, not to mention a few great ones. One need not mention Solzhenitsyn, were it not for the fact that the left had ignored the great narrative cycle of Victor Serge.[51] The undermining of the fable of the socialist motherland was a gradual process, but the collapse of its conservative counterpart may be rather more sudden. Any narrative strategy that banks heavily on a paranoid relation to a great other seems likely to be undermined very quickly by the old mole of the vector, burrowing straight across the line of the wall paranoid thought builds between itself and the other.

Breaking free of this imaginary game was the painful process animating Western Marxism, making it vital and lively, from Rosa Luxemburg to Michel Foucault.[52] The break with the East tore Marxism loose from its moorings in an imaginary political space and dispersed it to the four corners of cultural and political discourse in the West. Josef Skvorecky, still gazing into the mirror of the barbarian and the civilized, the other and its other, complains that "at universities in the West professors still preach the theory which was the backbone of the longer-lasting of the two deadening social experiments in our century."[53] Yet things are not quite so simple as that. In response to the deadening experience of the Western Communist parties, Western Marxism broke the simple, oppressive link of theory and party, and took off. A hundred flowers bloomed, a thousand schools of thought contended: Marxism gained a new diversity and richness, but lost its identity in the process. Given that its identity had hardened on a false and dangerous image of the other, this complete loss of identity was no loss at all, it was a whole new project. A project now possible in the whole territory of Europe.[54] The triumph of communism lies precisely in its extinction, for it takes away the last prop holding up the corroding armor of the old cold warriors.

Fear and Loathing in Minsk

While the East may have ceased to be a bogy to the West, the reverse is not necessarily true. Seen the other way around, the mirror does not present a symmetrical image. The Eastern other appears in the Western imaginary mostly as territory; the Western other appears in the East primarily as a map, populated with the signs of commodified abundance. The collapse of the wall means the extension of that map over the territory of the East, and a remaking of the territory underneath in its image (as the dole lines get longer and longer . . .). The other in this instance has a dual aspect of seduction and repulsion. For example, Russian émigré writer Andrei Sinyavsky reminds us that the rise of nationalism in Russia has its paranoid side. The Leninist and Stalinist idea of "bourgeois encirclement" is alive and well, positing a motherland threatened by the soulless nihilism of the cultural map of the West: drug-addled, pornographic, and violent.[55] The horde at the gates here is a spectacle, a host of sexy information, demon images, yet for all that no less real in its effects. The pornography of telesthesis is on its way east.

There is something touchingly simple-minded about such concerns. As if there were really any hopes of holding back the flow. Yet this Eastern naiveté has its counterpart in the Western mind. Stephen Spender again: "If the present revolution is stopped in any one place, to be superseded by dictatorship, the media will assure that the consciousness of a democratic world, flooding in, will sooner or later break down the prison walls of dictatorship."[56] The reduction to pornography of the flow of spectacular images characteristic of the information landscape of the West is as one-dimensional as the assumption that the free flow of information is somehow synonymous with democracy. The *ambivalence* of the information landscape in the Wonderland world of the West: part democracy, part pornography, part free speech, part bondage and discipline, that is perhaps the curious quality that might more fruitfully be discussed. Perhaps in a simultaneous satellite hookup of "NBC News Today" and the now-televised debates of the Parliament of the Commonwealth of Independent States.[57]

The collapse of the mirror-image other that held together those Siamese twins, East and West, might finally help put on the agenda another kind of mapping. A mapping of the very real flows of information and the subjectivities and collectivities they form, rather than the specular mapping of obsolete territories. One sees precious little sign of this, however. (Has anybody heard mention of the "South" lately? Did somebody say "third world debt crisis"?) In the East, a paranoid reaction to West European nihilism, shading into irrational forms of racism; or pure seduction, a complete misrecognition of the map as if it really described the territory of the West. In the West, the same irrationalism; even more insidious, the smug, self-satisfied smirking of conservatives basking in their own narcissism. For a few brief, electric seconds, old Europe looked in the mirror and liked what it saw; both sides enjoyed a holiday on the moon, relishing each other's otherness. The honeymoon is over.

One could sum this up with a paradoxical parable:

The East and the West were lovers, but they didn't get on terribly well. They occupied opposite ends of the house, rarely communicating. One day both decided, quite independently, to go to the Masked Ball. Off they went in separate cars, unaware of their joint decision. On that enchanted evening, across the crowded room, they recognized each other's masks. They decided to adjourn somewhere quieter, without the others. In the private salon, they took off their masks. The East took off its mask, and the West said, "But you are not the East, you are a stranger to me, masquerading as the East!" Then the West took off its mask, and the East said, "But you are not the West, you are a stranger to me, masquerading as the West!" After this shocking revelation, they got down to a quiet chat, and found they had rather a lot in common, even if the faces they wore under the masks were not what they should have been. Even if the faces under the masks were yet more masks. And they lived, if not happily ever after, at least in adjoining rooms.[58]

4. site

The Archaeology of Knowledge

Dateline: Berlin, 30 January 1993. Thousands of candle-carrying protesters march through Berlin for the Lichterketten. It is a controversial event, although it does have the support of some artists and intellectuals such as Otto Sander and Peter Zadek. The protesters gather in front of the Brandenburg Gate and spell out the words **NEVER AGAIN** *in thousands of candles on the ground. Sixty years ago to this day, Nazi Brown Shirts marched through the Brandenburg Gate, marking Hitler's rise to power. The Lichterketten demonstration is meant to signal opposition not only to the rise of neo-Nazi groups, particularly since the fall of the Berlin Wall, but also to the arson attacks on refugee hostels and other racist violence.*

The Lichterketten was a preemptive occupation, preventing the neo-Nazis from claiming the accumulated memory of the site as their own. It was also an assumption of civic responsibility for history, manifested in a tending of the memorial sites and times of the past. Not everyone was impressed. Micha Brumlik, writing in *Die Tageszeitung,* saw a danger in staging spectacles "which remain in the symbolic space defined by the Nazis."[1] He criticized both the "civic religion" invented by the demonstrators, and also its stagy form of performance art. Brumlik argued for the skeptical illumination of the enlightenment over this affective candle-play with the signs, sites, and times of historical memory.

One cannot deny that the columns of the Brandenburg Gate carry an immense burden, a historical impediment. The whole of Berlin does. As Mayor Walter Momper had said in the heady days of November 1989 when the wall came down, "Berlin is the place where European history is made."[2] Quite so. It is a site to which adhere many powerful associations. Berlin may be "the place that can propel Europe forward," but it can also be the place that drags it backward again. It's time to sift through the layers of rubble underneath this site, as a way of narrating some of the buried country which keeps resurfacing whenever a Berlin story catches the attention of the global media vector.

At the site of the first bulldozed breach of the wall, Potsdamer Platz, a geometric figure was just visible on the ground on the Eastern side. This eight-sided shape is a palimpsest that records not one but many processes of erasure and rewriting of the site in history. In the twilight of the Berlin Wall, only some of these prior inscriptions appear illuminated. In particular, a history of walls and breaches takes shape in the festive air. On the site of the Achtek, the eight-sided figure at the center of what was once Potsdamer Platz, a whole history of the vector can be read between the lines.

The event has no history. Or rather, it has no fixed beginning, no determinate time scale, no general form. This is its most curious feature: it stands for a moment outside the conventional streams of narrative time, hoping to catch hold of another current. To grasp it and communicate it at all, we have to nail it down to the time of a story. Almost any kind of story will do, narrating almost any kind of time: the time of journalism, of chronicle, of fable. This could be an ironic time, a moralizing time, a tragic time. So far I've tried a little of each, but now I want to tell a story about the site of the event in an abstract time. The preceding sections assayed a rather contemporary period but a rather general space—the whole of Germany, East and West, no less. In what follows, the essaying begins from a rather more strictly delimited site, but longer periods of time. In the retelling of the event, both its temporal shape and the space it dances across can be defined at many levels, which all interact within the construct of the event. The scale of the site and temporal rhythm can be fixed at the outset, and the event recounted within these parameters. Or it can wander or jump from one site to another, one tempo to the next. Writing along the line of the vector, true to the nature of the field the vector is creating, is an open, abstract space within which many combinations of information about the event can be figured and refigured.

More and more, the vector is the line along which stories circulate. We no longer have roots, we have aerials. So to try to tell the story of the vector itself is to attempt to speak a metanarrative, a story about the condition of possibility in our times for story itself. It is not a story which guarantees a happy ending. It does not legitimate anything in the present by claiming to speak along the line of the vector's historical tendency. It doesn't ground a claim to truth, merely a place to start speaking. It does not claim to unearth the truth, merely to follow a line of movement, abstracted from the territory in a line of prose, abstracted from everyday life. I make no claim other than to be searching for a way to write about the strange experience of the most abstract, instant, and global vectors turning up increasingly in all aspects of everyday life.

Metanarratives may be unfashionable in theory, but in everyday life they abound. Every day we are bombarded with little stories torn loose from events. Our media are full of them. The more disparate the sources, the more instant the bites, the more abstract the metanarratives which gather the fruit of these global media vectors must be. It is not that people become "incredulous" about metanarratives, as French philosopher Jean-François Lyotard would have it.[3] Whether we believe them or not isn't the point, we need them anyway. Regardless of our lack of faith in them, we need metanarratives to order the ever more abstracted fragments of information into an understanding of their import or their trivia, their warnings, or their offerings. It is not that metanarratives can somehow be superseded as a form of knowledge, it is that we must understand how to use them differently, to understand the abstraction let loose in the world by the ever more rapid, flexible, and instant displacements of bits and bites of story by the vector. The metanarrative that matters is that of the vector itself, the story of stories.

In every blink of an image conveyed by the vector, there are hidden stories, not least about the vector itself. The sites from which every blink of an image is extracted are a reservoir of past events, past accumulations of the developmental story of the vector's effects. Sites like the Brandenburg Gate and Potsdamer Platz are story accumulators, storage sites for stories that can never totally be commodified, packaged, and sold. Storage sites for stories about events which can never quite be captured in the story form or packaged in the commodity form. In what follows, I want to make the gates of old Berlin open up to some of these stories, to some of the events shaped there by the conjuncture of vectors.

To return to the octagon, scorched into the earth at Potsdamer Platz. The Achtek was designed in 1737 as part of the Prussian monarchy's expansion of Berlin.[4] Building on the administrative and military success of the absolute monarchy, Berlin was to grow a new, rationally planned and executed wing. In the place of the peasant-tilled traces of nature a new order would form. A rational, autocratic order traced out in straight streets and geometric parks. Two of these parks, which marked points in the newly expanded perimeter of the city where there were major openings, would later feature as central sites in the media spectacle of the fall of the Berlin Wall. On the new northern edge of the Prussian city, a square park and the Brandenburg Gate. Facing west, the Potsdam Gate and its octagon.

This expansion of the city was the last extension of the fortifications that had enclosed the city since 1237, although not the last time Berlin would wall out the world. There have been three types of enclosure in Berlin's history, and each has been a response to the historical force of the vector. The first kind of wall that surrounded Berlin was a military enclosure, designed to protect the city from the then state of development of the military vector. The history of the relationship between military vectors and fortified cities like Berlin is a relationship between the velocity of military assault and the braking effect of fortification.[5] Up to a certain stage in the development of the military vector, the fortification was an adequate response. It was indeed possible to absorb the impact of the vector. It was once possible to resist the formation of an abstract vector field of power.

This resistance through the braking effect of the barrier was not to last. Lewis Mumford traces the history of this dialogue between military vector and urban fortification.[6] As he points out, there is a threshold beyond which fortified defense no longer has the strength to absorb and retard the velocity and power of the vector. The terrain of battle becomes an increasingly open vector field, unimpeded by barriers and obstacles. The Achtek was built before the military vector had developed to the point where its movements could not be impeded by stationary obstacles, but only by a countermovement. Movement is no longer pitted against static barriers, but against other movements in a space of movement—a *vector field*.

"This morning I saw the Emperor—this world-soul . . . dominating the entire world from horseback."[7] This is Hegel, describing his brush with Napoleon after the French victory over Prussia in 1807. Of particular interest here is the idea of domination on horseback—a mobile power. The great German philosopher of this power was to be not Hegel but Clausewitz, theorist of the reconstruction of Prussian military capacity along the lines indicated by Napoleon's mobile citizen army. Clausewitz might belong in another great canon of German philosophy, one involved less with the canon of Kant, Hegel, Marx, and more with cannon and bayonets, archives and transmitters. As the American philosopher Richard Rorty suggests, "One could try to create a new canon—one in which the mark of a 'great philosopher' was awareness of new social and religious and institutional possibilities, as opposed to developing a new dialectical twist in metaphysics or epistemology."[8] Clausewitz would belong in just such a canon.

For Clausewitz, war was "the shock of two hostile bodies in collision."[9] Like a perversely critical theory, Clausewitz analyzes war first in the pure potentialities of its unleashed vectors, freed of all material impediments. "Thus reasoning in the abstract, the mind cannot stop short of an extreme, because it has to deal with an extreme, with a conflict of forces left to themselves, and obeying none other but their own inner laws."[10] Clausewitz conceives of war as a competition between pure vectors in an abstract vector field. War is a pure reciprocal action, tending to violent extremes. Clausewitz then posits limit factors: the strength of the will to fight, the throw of chance, and the famous concept of "friction." The territory of the battle is not a pure vector field, it imposes constraints, it brakes the colliding forces. Chance and confusion exact their toll. Mud and sand slow the forces down. Communication breaks down amid the fear, the noise, the chaos.

Yet in posing the problem as a critical contrast between an abstract map of the military vector field and its imperfect realization on the ground, Clausewitz points to a powerful conception of space, which the state and capital may have reason to use as much as the war machine. He is also pointing to the possibility of the *logic bomb*. By logic bomb I mean that contradictory moment of crisis and disaster embedded in the gap between a virtual geography and the crash of actual forces on the ground. This is the sense in which one really can see the traces of a potentially critical theory in Clausewitz—the theory of the logic bomb, of the dangerous imperfections of the workings of the vector.

The walls around the city of Berlin gave way to the new Prussian army, a mobile power to counter the mobile power, the effectiveness of which Napoleon had so dramatically shown. Henceforth the wall would have another purpose. The Brandenburg and Potsdam gates served as customs barriers, regulating the increasing mobility of money and trade. The technical development of the vector fed into another power besides the military—it contributed to commercial power. It aided the development of a vector field of exchange. This is *cameralism,* the state regulation of the terms of vectoral flow. Cameralism, the theory of the management of the flows into and out of the princely treasury chamber, was always a theory of the management of the vector. In classical cameralist theory, the amount of revenue extracted depended on the extent of the territory, and the extent of the territory depended on the military vector. Rather than seeing cameralism as a discourse and a practice superseded by political economy, it might be more useful to view it as one that the state adapted to control the space of flows with vectors of information rather than direct military coercion.[11]

The Prussian state regulated this other vectoral power at Potsdamer Platz and other sites like it. They are the points at which the city in this stage of its development regulated its relation to its environment. As such the gates remained an important symbol for the braking or regulation of the vector of commerce—at least until Stalin's blockade of West Berlin in 1948. The overcoming of that siege with a massive airlift composed of 272,264 flights stands for a new relation between the city and the vector, dominated by the vector of the air, and regulated via the airport rather than the gate.[12]

To return to the Achtek—it appears as a striking geometric embellishment on the otherwise unadorned grid of the extensions to Berlin. Both are an absolute, rational order imposed on a medieval symbiosis of culture and nature, and meant to replace the maze of feudal relations with the land, where nature and culture weave unconsciously together, with a new consciousness of reason as something separate, something alienated from the land. Not a symbol but a construct of the dialectic of enlightenment: freedom from domination by nature, but also a new domination of nature.[13] In the geometry of the Achtek, a new order covers over nature. A new order that perceives nature from without. An ideal order replaces the mysteries of the natural one. A new nature paves over and traverses the old. This is an order, historically new yet apparently timeless, in which an absolute monarchy tries to control the unfolding of history through its cameralist mastery of physical space. Hence the Achtek was to be the site of a powerful monument. In the 1790s, it was to be the site of Gilly's monument to Frederick the Great. In 1814 it became a site for Schinkel's monument to the victory over Napoleon. The world spirit, it seems, switched horses in mid–historical stream in between. Neither was built, but Schinkel's gates went up on the Potsdamer Platz, in 1823. The mundane conjunctures of social forces and their conflicts caught up with the grand designs of architecture.

As the vectors of commerce and war sped through the ancient territories of Europe, they brought with them an intense insecurity. One can read Marx's famous lines on the dissolution of the old order in this vein: The "constant revolutionising of production, uninterrupted disturbance of all social conditions, everlasting uncertainty and agitation" that are the hallmark of the modern can be understood as the leveling of the hereditary spatial boundaries and restrictions of feudal order by the constant development of vector fields of movement and the development of the instruments of vectoral power itself.[14]

Nor does it stop there. Walter Benjamin will revise this rhetoric at another conjuncture, where "we begin to recognise the monuments of the bourgeoisie as ruins even before they have crumbled."[15] In the various levels of competition between powers—between state and state, between state and capital, between capital and capital, between capital and the working class, between the working class and the state—the development of the technical forces of the vector and their deployment become a stake and a weapon of conflict. While the ruling powers, be they military, political, or industrial, try to bend the vector to the will to power, the vector is not a tractable instrument. Every vector field is an opening, a clearing of densely defended military, social, or cultural spaces. The vector presupposes a plane of action that is also a plane of freedom. In the West this competition between powers impelled the vector forward, overtaking the power of the collective subjectivity of each and every class. As we shall see when we reach the last site on the itinerary of this book, the monuments of the bourgeoisie also stand in ruins. Meanwhile the vector continues to develop its objective power over collective subjects, be they family, class, or nation.

Just as the fortification and the customs wall were barriers to the vector in space, so monumental architecture was a barrier to the vector in time. Monumental architecture—and there is a sense in which nearly all architecture is monumental—takes a snapshot of the social conjuncture of the day from the point of view of the powers that commission it, and reforms that impression into an ideal form. It then imposes its imagined form of the idealized moment on the site and on circumstances which, perhaps from the moment the monument comes into being, will wear away the significance the monument momentarily held. This is why architecture is always out of step with events, and why, as the vector accelerates, its redundancy occurs ever more rapidly. As the architect Aldo Rossi puts it, architecture *persists*—it preserves a trace of perceptions and desires that the vector obliterates far more rapidly in other discourses. Monuments are "a past that we are still experiencing."[16] Despite the demolition and conversion of architecture, the ruin of the past persists. Its hard white bones jut on the lone and level sands of the vector field. This is what makes architecture a complementary object of study to the vector—even if the extreme movements of modern communications and the extreme persistence of monumental architectures do not seem in the least cognate areas or overlapping disciplines. The dialogue of television and the Berlin Wall suggests in extremis that they indeed are.

Social Dromocracy

Monumental architecture is a barricade in time that attempts to resist the malicious whims, as Isaac Deutcher called them, of history. It preserves an image of what power neurotically strove to preserve just as much as it records the failure to preserve power itself. Potsdamer Platz is the terminus for Leipzigerstrasse, which passes through the octagon and meets the customs wall at the gate on the edge of the city. The revolutionaries barricaded Leipzigerstrasse in the revolutions of 1848, and Potsdamer Platz in 1918–1919. The bodies of Rosa Luxemburg and Karl Leibknecht turned up in the canal just where it passes under Potsdamerstrasse, the road leading toward Potsdam from Potsdamer Platz at the edge of the old Prussian city.

An expression Paul Virilio attributes to Weber sums up the tragedy of Luxemburg and Leibknecht: "They called to the streets, and the streets killed them." Virilio goes on to add, "The masses are not a population, a society, but the multitude of passers-by. The revolutionary contingent attains its ideal form not in the place of production, but in the street, where for a moment it stops being a cog in the technical machine and itself becomes a motor (machine of attack), in other words a *producer of speed*."[17] The mass in this sense is a vector, a particular mode of dispersal in a particular space—the movement of massed bodies in the street, or the street brought to a halt. The revolutionary barricade is also a tactic in the war of the vector, and revolutionary insurrection is above all a struggle to control movement in a given territory. Through the struggle to block and unblock movement, the social forces of revolution and reaction transform social crisis into spatial struggle. As it happens, the revolutionary struggles of 1918–1919 were lost.

Every vector has its limitations. The Spartacist uprising deployed the mass, occupying space directly on the territory, mobilizing and maneuvering on the streets. Curiously, they occupied the offices of the SDP newspaper *Vorwärts* rather than the telephone exchange or the telegraph office. Outflanked in the streets, Friedrich Ebert and the social democratic "government" reached a modus vivendi with the military, in the interests of "order." "Ebert has his beard trimmed, now looks more like a Chairman of the Board, and dresses accordingly," as the dada artist George Grosz recalls.[18] As that veteran of '68 Guy Debord says, the aim of spectacular power is to turn secret police into revolutionaries and revolutionaries into secret police.[19] By these standards, Ebert's career was a spectacular success.

This smells like a sellout, but it makes vectoral sense. Ebert's main contribution, to social democracy in general and the German Social Democratic Party (SDP) in particular, was the introduction of accounting and filing. A party based on illegal work, used to burning everything, took a while to see the power and importance of managing the intensive vector information as well as the extensive one of mass-media propaganda. Ebert was precisely this kind of political technician. That he should find a way to work with the military, that other breed of political technician, and join forces with it to stop the Spartacists from smashing the state both depended on is not surprising. Ebert and his henchman Noske used their telephone and radio contact with the military commanders to outmaneuver the Spartacists. The military sent the Freikorps in to the *Vorwärts* office, where the Spartacists defended their position, in a terribly appropriate manner, using giant rolls of newspaper as barricades.

The significance of the defeat of the Spartacist uprising for Guy Debord lies in the social democrats' joining hands with the forces of reaction against the workers. While this interpretation is intentionally tendentious, it does recover a premonition of disturbing development from the bodies floating in the canal under Potsdamerstrasse. What defeated the workers was an organization that acts in the *name* of the working class yet which does not necessarily act in the *interests* of the working class. The image of the working class is beginning to separate out from its membership. For Debord, the SDP combined revolutionary illusion with reformist practice. Bernstein at least sought to bring the imaginary projections of the class in line with the actual practical projects of its organization. On the other hand, Lenin would attempt to realize the revolutionary imaginary on top of the ruins of the old SDP, broken by the war. Lenin, in Debord's terms, was a "faithful Kautskyist."[20] The SDP was more interested in connecting with the abstract, mediated image of the people via representative government than with the immediately constituted power of the mass on the street.[21] In this they opted for the developed forms of second nature, rather than the primal energies of the mass and the territory.

The gap that opens between the revolutionary imaginary of the working class and its actual existence, organized in space by the associations of union and party, is a curious phenomenon with many causes. Debord calls this state of separation the society of the spectacle. It isolates what for him is "the state of affairs which is at the heart of the domination of the modern spectacle: the representation of the working class radically opposes itself to the working class."[22] This representation will develop after the war and the failure of the Spartacist uprising in two different directions: Eastern, revolutionary communism and Western, reformist social democracy of the kind typified not just by the banal unscrupulousness of Ebert but also by the thoughtful realpolitik of Willy Brandt. Debord's point is that neither representation should be mistaken for the working class itself. The practice of representing the class comes to separate off from organic connection to the class represented. The functionaries that do the work of representation acquire interests and goals of their own, independent of the working class. Perhaps they belong to a class apart.

Rather than play the game of East versus West, real representation against false, Debord draws our attention to a more radical schism between class *composition* and class *representation* that does not permit a simple juxtaposition of the true representatives to the false ones. Nothing represents the working class. Neither the West German nor the East German organizations which pose as the inheritors of the working-class tradition, the SPD and the SED. Not their challengers from within, such as the ultra-left opposition in the West and the dissident socialists in the East. This was evident in the vast gap that opened up between the direction of the mass and the diversions of the various leaders during the events of November 1989. The fall of the Berlin Wall buried the story of social democracy under the video rubble of the collapse of communism. In some respects, however, this event may have more to do with the historical trajectory of social democracy, and in particular the role social democracy plays in mediating between the struggles of the industrial past and the simulated events of the present.

As the map of the media vector grows in density over the social space of the territory, so the representations of the classes and social forces come to join combat on a terrain increasingly removed in organizational terms from the territory, even as it penetrates ever more fully into its recesses. The history of the German Social Democrats illustrates this historic trajectory of the vector. Operating under restrictive conditions, the SDP in Wilhelmine Germany used social clubs for organizing territorially. Singing clubs, theater clubs, cycling clubs—these territorial forms of organization were able to keep social democratic organization alive by burying it within the territory, and provided a minimal means of networking across the underdeveloped vectoral map.[23] Singing provided the intensive vector of popular memory, cycling the extensive one of physically linking the party members across the countryside.

When the political opportunity presented itself, the SDP made full use of the media vector, and produced no fewer than sixty newspapers by 1890. This was a period of technical innovation in the media vector: the telegraph increased the geographic area from which news could be collected; the high-speed printing presses increased the number of people catered to by a single edition; with railway distribution, this allowed the SDP to create an alternative vector field of wide scope and rapidity within which its supporters could be reached. The SDP used this vector field to report scandals and intrigues, creating a space for the play of media events and providing the narrative line for interpreting them simultaneously.

As such, the SDP was able to constitute what Oskar Negt and Alexander Kluge call a *counter-public sphere.*[24] The English rendering of this idea is unfortunate, for it is neither "public" nor "spherical." It does not define a sphere so much as a trajectory across the territory of everyday life. It is a radiation of lines, not a circle. How far and fast a story can travel depends on the technical properties of the vector. What the SDP constitutes is a vector, connecting private experiences of the same abstract machinations of capital across the territory, which creates an articulation of these experiences different from the dominant matrix of vectors. Different in the sense that it articulates privatized, alien experiences as if they were typical, shared experiences. The SDP networked together the private experience of many people, separated by the territory, by social convention, by the division of labor. It created an abstract being at the level of the reach of its vectors, by putting a vector across these boundaries and territories. It used this vector field to narrate, even to create, the events of the day, not least with its famous scandal sheets. Yet it does not in any sense compose an equivalent to a "public sphere." The sense of belonging and becoming articulated in the abstracted space of the vector isn't the same as the sense of belonging in a public meeting, a crowd, an assembly, a communion. Its novelty is radically distorted by reducing it to any such model.

Telesthesia, perception at a distance, perception abstracted from the particulars of place, is a different thing from being present at a site, together with a crowd of any kind. Stories, of necessity, take on a new form in this context. Traditional stories, rooted in place, are designed to persist through time, passed on from old to young, old to young. Vectoral stories, abstracted from place, are designed to transmit across space, from site to site to site. To successfully create an abstract belonging, ever more extensive vectors require ever more abstracted forms of story. As its reach, in expanse, increases, its credibility, in particulars, diminishes. Here is Lyotard's "incredulity" toward metanarratives—only it is not created by the break of postmodernism, it grows slowly with the progressive abstraction of the vector. As the vector spreads its reach, the organizational form legitimating itself as the gatekeeper of stories becomes progressively more abstracted from everyday life, more specialized as a manager of media vectors alone. From the church to the party, from the party to the culture industry, metanarratives persist, but the organizations they legitimate become progressively more banal, using the vector to legitimize their power in turn to offer eternal salvation, social amelioration, temporary pleasure. With the media vectors of the Social Democratic Party, we reach the midpoint in this development, a point to which there is no return.

The high point of the SDP's self-legitimation on the basis of the metanarratives it spread through the press vector was at the outbreak of the war in 1914. The combined circulation of the party's press reached a million and a half.[25] As historian Alex Hall remarks, "In the years immediately after 1890, the founding of new journals was more important to the SDP than the creation of party cells."[26] With the development of a presence on the vectoral map, a tension arose with the territorial space organized in the cells. As the cells became organs supporting the media vector propelled by the party center, the party became a creature of the map rather than of the territory. The question remains: How did this separation come about, and how and what are its material means and relations? The deaths of Luxemburg and Leibknecht mark the beginnings of this schism. With its suppression of the revolutionary option, added to the huge overdraft on its proletarian credibility the party incurred in voting for war credits, the SDP began to lose its proprietary rights to the image of the working class. The franchise was on the market.

Third Nature

The martyrdom of Leibknecht and Luxemburg was commemorated for a while in a monument by Mies van der Rohe. More durable will be another monument to the struggle of vectors built in Potsdamer Platz in 1924—Germany's first traffic light. When East German mayor Krack gave West German mayor Momper a model of this same traffic light in 1989, when they met across the breach in the Berlin Wall, it was as if it were the signal for a backtracking to another story, another modality of history. Perhaps the history Willy Brandt spoke of in 1989 on the steps of Berlin city hall. The historic trajectory of the overcoming of the parceling out of Europe's territories. That traffic light is emblematic of the vectors of movement that cut their way through the city walls in the modern period, and the accelerated cycles of capital that seemed to propel capital across all borders.

In Manfredo Tafuri's remarkable writings on the urban policies of German social democracy between the wars, a picture emerges of a reformist movement attempting to invent and apply techniques for stabilizing the flux and stress experienced in the modern city. The instrument for this was a collectivist housing policy.[27] Tafuri's analysis concentrates on the contradictions inherent in a partial strategy that seeks to redress the dynamic imbalances of capitalist development with a partial socialization of the circuit through which capital reproduces itself and its dependents, namely, a social housing policy. Tafuri dissects the work in Berlin of Martin Wagner and other architects to show how the attempt to consolidate a space for workers that would also contribute to efficient and productive accumulation had to fail. Social democracy partitioned social reality into discrete objects which it met with piecemeal solutions—Ebert's filing cabinet mentality at work! For Tafuri's pessimist Marxism, the inescapable workings of the totality always impose the limits and expose the contradiction in such strategies. Social democratic Berlin could not in the end contain the dynamic powers of capital. Nor could it contain that other dynamic, closely related but not identical with it, of the vector.

While Martin Wagner was working out a social democratic politics for the urban space of Berlin, Walter Benjamin was attempting to intervene in quite another, equally modern, politics. Benjamin's radio programs of the Weimar period addressed the youth of Berlin and attempted to "teach their young audiences to read both the urban landscape and the literary texts generated within it as expressions of social history."[28] Benjamin was acutely aware of the impact of new media technologies on social space, beginning with the introduction of mass-circulation newspapers distributed by rail in the late nineteenth century. With the newspaper, information can be distributed over a large territory in a short period, thus effecting the pattern of information that would prevail simultaneously and affecting the perceptions, judgments, or actions of an increasing number of people in a wider and wider space with greater and greater rapidity. The vector of the newspaper begins to usurp the ancient territorial privileges of labyrinthine rumor and the murmuring crowd. Benjamin comments: "When the electrical telegraph came into use . . . the boulevards lost their monopoly. News of accidents and crime could now be obtained from all over the world."[29]

From this juncture, the vector of information begins to create a new terrain that will impose itself on top of the second nature of labor and its accumulated products. Toni Negri writes, concerning this second nature: "Just as the hammer which forges the iron must be made of iron; and the progressive movement of the method traces the progressive movement of manufacturing, the transformation of nature into an instrument and of the instrument into new nature—second nature, constructed nature."[30] The odd syntax is somehow appropriate, for Negri is describing an open circle, where practice and language transform nature into second nature. At each cycle of the process, that which appears as raw material to be worked and as the means of working it appears at higher and higher levels of transformation, abstraction, differentiation. Second nature grows in extent and depth by rendering raw nature useful, but also by rupturing its wholeness. In rendering it discrete and manageable, both in language and in its materiality, second nature creates a useful space but also creates its own obstacle in the form of fragmentation. In overcoming this fragmentation, the extraction of information from second nature becomes a distinctive process in its own right. Information begins to form a *third nature,* reconnecting the differentiated fragments in the space of second nature, by turning it into a differentiated flow of information across its space.

While the Brandenburg Gate once stood proudly on the ground of the feudal past, announcing a second nature, covering the old terrain, the gate has itself been appropriated. It now forms an image in circulation on the much vaster and more nebulous terrain of third nature. This third nature finds its most historically effective form in television, at least at the time of the fall of the Berlin Wall. In postwar West Germany, the struggle over the production of power had occupied this terrain. One way of understanding the political struggles of the so-called young German film and new German cinema is as a struggle for third nature. The history films, and in particular the broadcast of critical films on television, were a struggle over the extraction of information out of second nature, in particular, out of the bloody past of German history.[31] There is every possibility that development of the vector field of third nature will not stop there. Alexander Kluge, the Clausewitz of critical German media, became a "proprietor of time" as he describes it, on a satellite channel called SAT 1.[32] As the vector proceeds into orbit, the struggle over the transformation of the information landscape goes with it.

In Benjamin's time, radio, film, and illustrated magazines joined the vectoral armory. Benjamin, like Brecht, saw the importance of carrying social struggles onto this new terrain. In a sense, Benjamin's radio work was a barricade in this new dimension, trying to hold back the attempt by the Nazis to swamp the vector field with the mire of myth, the simulated earthiness of blood and soil. That such a struggle was necessary shows an aspect of third nature that will reappear with the fall of the Berlin Wall. The loss of unity resulting from the separation of instrumental reason from the land makes a great leap in productivity possible. It also creates a second nature of the products of abstract, divided labor that confront people as an alien and intractable territory. In overcoming the limits through the imposition of the abstract vector fields of production and circulation, something is lost and something gained. The gain in freedom from material necessity matches the loss of unity of place. The modern experience of fragmentation and anomie has its sources here.[33]

In third nature, an overcoming of anomie appears to be possible. Benjamin tries to think its possibilities and to act upon them. But third nature cannot end the tyranny of separation and fragmentation because it is an overcoming of separation *by means of separation*. Only in a separate vector field will a space open for a unification of the space divided by the one-way street of the vector cutting through the city. The spectacular map of third nature will throw up images and stories of a most spectacular unity, from fascism and socialist realism to the chanting crowds who transformed the radical slogan "we are the people" into the imaginary unity of "we are *one* people," in 1989, as the wall collapsed.

In the Weimar years, the democratic forces and the organizations of the working class struggled for third nature, for control of what Humphrey Jennings perceptively calls the *means of vision*. The means of vision are "matter transformed and reborn by imagination, and turned into an image."[34] While

Wagner and others struggled over the means of social reproduction, Brecht and Benjamin attempted to theorize and participate in the struggle over the means of vision waged on the vector field of the media.[35] The latter would become a contested terrain for at least three levels of conflict that would convulse Berlin between the wars: the struggle to insert a dynamic into everyday life based on a perception of time which matches the rhythm of production and consumption of commodities; the struggle against this complicity of the vector and the commodity in the name of the interests of the nation or the interests of the working class; the struggle to militarize everyday life, forging a complicity between media and military vectors.

Ornament and Crime

Architectural space could not help but be drawn into the struggles of third nature. Besides being a failed site for monuments to monarchic power and barricades thrown up to oppose it, Potsdamer Platz became a site for quite a different monument—the department store. In Weimar Berlin the old Achtek became the form around which clustered a growing complex of stores, hotels, cafés, and the remarkable Kampinski's House of the Fatherland, a fabulously kitsch agglomeration of cafés and entertainments. These were the surfaces of the city that fascinated Benjamin, who lived at the time quite nearby.[36]

Benjamin's fascination with obsolete forms of bourgeois street life is a tribute not only to the power of the logic of capital but also to the trajectory of the vector. The abstraction of capital spreads over the vectors of second nature, coagulating in the physical spaces of consumption and production, coursing through the great arteries carved through the city as a vector field for the movement of labor and commodities. The commodity also comes to assume a second form. The particular use values of Marx, his famous coats and yards of linen, had a second, abstract aspect as exchange values. They had not only a law of equivalence and exchange that made them commensurable but also a physical realization of this potential in the vector space of transport and display. Benjamin's fascination was with use values of precisely this kind, use values left behind by the further development of the vector. With the arrival of the coterminous space of radio and mass-circulation magazines, commodities are beginning to acquire a threefold form. The particular form of the use value coexists not only with an exchange value but with what Baudrillard calls a sign value.[37] The commodity also exists as a disembodied image, establishing a presence throughout the social space, competing for attention with more traditional images. Advertising is the seductive face of third nature.

Of the many faces of the vector, military, commercial, and democratic, it was the commercial which had the upper hand here for a while. In the 1930s a structure was built that tried to avoid association with either: Potsdamer Platz's first genuinely modernist building arrived in the early '30s—Columbushaus, by the great modern architect Erich Mendelsohn. Unlike the gaudy commercial buildings around it, Columbushaus broke with the myths of the past and the illusions of the present. This elegantly proportioned structure with its smooth curtain walls tried to slip smoothly through present difficulties onto a rational plane somewhere in the future. It too would be overtaken by events.

Built as a commercial venture, Columbushaus was a moment in the movement of capital as it transforms second nature in its image. Marx tried to create a discourse which could grasp the workings of this second nature, but the relations and movements he examined do not exhaust the forces at work in its territory. For example, some of the minute but terribly important details of the texture of everyday life are absent from Marx's critique of the nexus between the commodity and everyday life. The experiential aspect of shopping itself, so important to the creation of Columbushaus, is absent. The relation that was coming into being between the commercial space like Columbushaus, the experience of the most powerful vectoral technology of the time, cinema, and everyday experience, is absent from any theory which cannot grasp all of the heterogeneous lines of power that are coming into being at this time. Patrice Petro has recovered an important part of the process by which capital transformed second nature in its image with her examination of women's experience of cinema in Weimar Germany. The creation of a mass female audience for cinema, she argues, is a hidden but disturbing aspect of many discussions of Weimar modernity.[38] A complex set of relationships between public space and private space; between traditionally female and male social places and roles; between the public act of shopping and the private act of domestic work; between private and public zones of pleasure—all of these spatial arrangements are being refigured along the line of the vector, as capital transforms as much of second nature as it can into an abstract zone of commodified flows of information.

Too much of this goes unrecognized in classical Marxist analysis. In the latter, the worker is other to the capitalist, but that is about the limit to the differential play of power. The other of the other, be it the silenced role of women or the invisible presence of the marginalized, is absent. This not only omits important types of powerlessness, it ignores important forms of power: "Political economy . . . does not recognise the unoccupied worker, the working man in so far as he is outside this work relationship. The swindler, the cheat, the beggar, the unemployed, the starving, the destitute, and the criminal working man are figures which exist not for it, but only for other eyes—for the eyes of doctors, judges, grave-diggers and beadles."[39] These too have their place in second nature, and are part of the powerful logics of abstraction that are some of its necessary counterparts. They may even occupy the same space.

Columbushaus featured modern engineering as much as modernist form. Mendelsohn was able to create generous spaces between supporting beams, making the interior space flexible, and the structure incorporated modern service elevators. While this might have made it a functional commercial building, it also rendered it available, with little effort, for quite other purposes. The Nazis used it as a prison and a torture chamber in the '30s. Converting the top floors from commercial to exterminist uses did not disturb the shoppers on the lower levels. This form of power—policing and regulating territory, partitioning and controlling space, maintaining bodies in place in a grid—might seem to have more to do with Foucault's panopticon than with Virilio's vector, and indeed it does. The relation between these two forms of power, which develop in a related fashion but along distinct temporalities, is a complex one.

Foucault's model of the panopticon is a model of the disciplinary society. "Our society" he writes, is one of

> surveillance; under the surface of images, one invests bodies with depth; behind the great abstraction of exchange, there continues the meticulous, concrete training of useful forces; the circuits of communication are the supports of an accumulation and a centralization of knowledge; the play of signs defines the anchorages of power; it is not that the beautiful totality of the individual is amputated, repressed, altered by our social order, it is rather that the individual is carefully fabricated in it, according to a whole technique of forces and bodies.[40]

This extraordinarily resonant passage is, among other things, a careful refutation of the Marxist tradition, or perhaps more properly something to place alongside it. It is also an eloquent statement of the role played by the military technique, the technique of discipline, in cementing in place a spatial order within the city. The space of exchange, reordering the old places of the city according to its abstract principles, requires as its double quite specific techniques demarcating spaces, creating and circulating information. Alongside the logic of capital is a logistics of power.

Yet there is another modality of power besides the abstract law of capital and the meticulous grid of discipline. The vector field is like capital in that it projects itself outwards, it tries to open space to the full potential for mobility of bodies, weapons, information, and commodities. It requires a technology of movement and a control of time that permits an instant response to any and every conjuncture. As such it is an overcoming of the separations imposed upon urban space by discipline and capital. The binary division of labor and the minute classifications of discipline are both traversed and reunited, in their separation, by the motive power of the vector. Capital divides time in a binary opposition of work and leisure, while discipline unfolds its meticulous schedules. The vector is a form of power that does not mark off time in even portions but seizes the moment, rapidly and violently.

The time of the vector is the time of the *conjuncture*. With the development of the doubling of the vectors of transport in the vectors of communication, the time of the vector will become the time of the *event*. With the fall of the Berlin Wall, the power of the vector will triumph over disciplinary power. The crude partitioning of the city, the obstinate retardation of movement in the East, all the disciplinary obsessions of bureaucratic power will cave in in the face of the vector. The media vector will undermine the neat partition of spaces and times between East and West. The vector of the mass, seizing freedom of movement in physical space, will paralyze a regime too used to meting out disciplinary correctives on individual bodies. Yet the mass movement of bodies seizing the vector, hoping to cash it in at the KaDeWe and the other department stores, will rupture the polyrhythmic time of capital in the West as well.

Thus we can add the vector to the list of the logics of the modern city. The logic of the law of capital; the disciplinary techniques of power; the tactics of everyday life; the extensive vector, traversing the space between the city and its other. Not only is the identity of the individual fabricated and maintained in a disciplinary apparatus of statements and visibilities, the identity of places is also fabricated and maintained in an apparatus of vectors. Virilio and Foucault can thus be seen as writing in singularly complementary ways about analogous disciplinary techniques, albeit ones with distinct histories. Deleuze comments that

> Virilio believes he opposes Foucault when he claims that the problem of modern societies, the problem for the "police," is not one of confinement but concerns the "highways," speed or acceleration, the mastery and control of speed, circuits and grids set up in open space. But this is just what Foucault has said, as is proved by the analysis of the fortress carried out by both authors, or by Foucault's analysis of the naval hospital. This misunderstanding is not serious in Virilio's case, because the force and originality of his own work testifies to the fact that encounters between independent thinkers always occur in a blind zone.[41]

Conquest and Shopping

Dateline: West Berlin, 10 November. The East German government lifted restrictions on travel to the West today. Within hours, tens of thousands of East Germans had swarmed across the Berlin Wall, experiencing that tiny piece of the West in the East known as West Berlin. The mass crossing began about two hours after Günther Schabowski, a member of the "politburo," announced at a press conference that permission to emigrate would be granted without preconditions. Following this announcement on radio and television, the tentative trickle of East Germans testing the new rules "quickly turned into a jubilant horde," as the New York Times *put it. "I knew as soon as I heard it on the radio what it meant," says Stani, a nineteen-year-old East Berliner on a day trip in the West. "It's wonderful, but how is it all going to end?" asks the novelist Stefan Heym. Former West German chancellor Willy Brandt, also a former mayor of Berlin, said, "This is a beautiful day after a long voyage, but we are only at a way station. We are not at the end of our way." On the famous shopping street of Kurfürstendamm, the stores have stayed open late, and many offer discounts and trinkets to their Eastern patrons. It is as if they had won the lucky prize on a West German television quiz show, and about as patronizing. In the BMW showroom, young men stand around the seductive metal form of the twelve-cylinder luxury sports model, "whose engines seemed light years beyond their own antiquated little 2-cylinder Trabant."*[42]

Watching it all on television, two architectural images seemed to predominate: the Brandenburg Gate with cheering people atop it, and the extra hole in the wall at Potsdamer Platz with crowds pouring through. Television charged these very old sites with many layers of accumulated memory, with new significance. To the foreign viewer, these former meanings were silent, but still present. Some old historical sites become memory magnets, drawing new events to them. The coupling of these time-accumulating sites with the power of the vector creates powerful resonances. The vector's easy familiarity with the site erases and at the same time affirms the former significance of the Brandenburg Gate and Potsdamer Platz. What does it matter that Napoleon passed through these very same gates, when they can instantly become a global symbol of the collapse of Soviet Eastern Europe? Does it matter in that instant that Napoleon stole the chariot of victory that sits atop the Brandenburg Gate, now that souvenir hunters have carried off bits of it as personal mementos?

While the Prussian state could retrieve the chariot from Paris, returning it from one public domain to another, the present German authorities may have rather more difficulty recovering the little bits of bronze that disappeared into private hands. These fragments, wrested from the catastrophe of the past, are now part of many personal memory stores, recording private moments from the great wall-breaking festival.

There were many souvenir hunters in those few historic days. Some chipped off bits of the wall to take home with them. This became quite a business. When the brightly colored, graffiti-emblazoned Western face of the wall ran out, enterprising mythmakers started spraypainting sections of the deathly white Eastern side of the double sheet of the wall. Enterprising indeed, but perhaps not as good an example of avid free enterprise as the nameless freelancer who sold this story to the media, so that it could grace the pages of the business press. Who is really being had here? The Western tourists buying fake bits of wall? The Eastern con artists discovering the "nature" of "capitalism" and how to turn it to advantage? Or the Western media who were sold this story which, if it weren't true, it would be necessary to invent?

In the struggle for vision on the terrain of third nature, it seems clear who won the battle for hearts and minds. The most political part of West German television, remarks East German playwright Heiner Müller, is the advertising. Advertising, as critical communications scholar Armand Mattelart argues, is not only the avant-garde of capitalist realism, it is the leading edge of the globalization of the media vector. It precedes the products themselves into the territory. It creates resonances between privatized experiences in ever more disparate places. It is the advance guard, not only of the culture of the vector but also of capital's integration of territories into its global traceries, mapping demands and supplies.[43]

As for the crowds from the East, Müller adds: "I think they had a right to plunder the food section of the KaDeWe."[44] I can't help wondering how the many women who poured through the crack in the wall must have felt. If they were as tied to the chores of shopping in the public zones and preparing food in the private spaces as their sisters in the West, did this rupture have a particular significance? Patrice Petro says the appearance of many women in public, at the cinemas, in the cafés in the Weimar period was an important source of male hysteria about Weimar modernity. One wonders whether there is a similar hidden layer to the fall of the Berlin Wall. While the young boys were off drooling over West German cars, what did young East German women feel drawn to in the West when the wall came down? Did the passage of Western television through the domestic interzone have an equal but opposite effect to the passage of women into the public zone of entertainment and spectacle in the Weimar years?

In the West the spectacle is seductive—it elicits the subject's fascination in the transformation of material reality by capital. The media vector transmits the rhythms of capital to the subject in its elaborate and stylized forms. In the East, the spectacle was productive—it manufactured an image of a transformation to substitute for the stasis of bureaucratic rule. Yet the vector underwrites both the relation of the law of capital to its spectacle and the relation of bureaucratic rule to its rather different spectacular form.

The development of commodity abundance and the defense of its privileges depend on the vector. The West depends—more than it knows—on its seductive power, on the suturing of subjective desire to objective mobility. In the East, such a liberation of movement, even if it is only a false and dangerous liberation, is impossible. The form of class power based on the containment and regulation of movement and the restricted, imitative development of the vector must repress it. Yet the East European regimes depended as much as their Western counterpart on being able to procure ever-increasing standards of living. There is doubtless an economic factor in the failure of these regimes—since the '70s the improvements have dried up, and legitimacy with them.

A factor that may have increased the speed of this disenchantment in East Germany was the presence of Western television. Young people compare their situation with that in other countries rather than the past, with what they see on television.[45] Their simultaneous memory, their awareness of what was happening in other places at the same time, grows as a faculty compared to temporal memory, awareness of what went before in the same place. The proliferation of the vector fueled this shift in the faculties, promoting a politics based on the former rather than the latter. Thus the fact that things are better than they used to be cuts little ice with people only too aware that things aren't as good as they appear to be elsewhere.

The scorn that Western media heaped upon the East German motor car, the Trabant, its ridicule in comparison with the sleek Mercedes and twelve-cylinder BMWs, is a condensed image of the contrast between forms of vectoral power. The West thrives on the subordination of subjectivity and political power to the vector. The East survived on the subordination of subjectivity and the vector to political power. A popular postwall film, *Go Trabi Go!* treated the Trabant car, affectionately called the Trabi, as a central and sympathetic character. In the film, an East German family take a holiday in the newly opened terrain of the West, and the film recounts a humorous version of this moonwalk. The satire has a light touch. The West German relatives hide the cake when their Eastern brethren pull into the drive. As the Easterners continue south to Italy, a series of mishaps follow, and the unreliable little car becomes the vector of a storyline about all that is lovably second-rate about the East.

There is already nostalgia in this film, not really for the wall but for a life protected from the vector. A life that does not appear as a race of champions, struggling with speed. *Go Trabi Go!* records an unrepeatable moment, a quiver in historical time, where two experiences of the rhythm of everyday life confront each other. Its interest lies in taking the point of view of slowness. Ironically, an East German studio made the film, and like every other firm in the East it faced ruin, not so much by competition from more "efficient" Western counterparts, but from the one-to-one exchange rate and the onerous conditions on converting debts and assets put in place at reunification. This extension of a strong and buoyant identity expressed via the value of the D-mark extracted a high price in unemployment and compromise with the market—one of the more amusing products of which was *Go Trabi Go!*

Today in the East, no more May Day parades. The image of labor has given way to the image of the commodity. The defeat of the military domination of the vector with the end of the Nazi regime left the media vector field open to a struggle along the two axes of capitalist society. Would the image of class struggle or the image of the commodity form prevail? Class struggle comes to be redoubled in a struggle of images. The image of the working class grows apart from it. It assumes a subordinate place in the diffuse spectacle of the West; it assumed pride of place in the East. Either way it is a displacement from second nature to its double in the spectacular land of the electronic media vector, saturating space with new rhythm and rhyme. The struggle for vision displaced class antagonism. So too a simulated global struggle of electronic feints and counterfeints displaced the military vector from the wars of position and maneuver on the tiny territory of Europe.

While it may be the case that these simulated games of power seem to replace struggles at the level of the territory they cover, this is not so. It would be a mistake to make a fetish of third nature, of simulation, as Baudrillard does. A mistake equal and opposite to the denial of the qualitative changes it has wrought upon the event. The significant thing is always the rhythmic interaction of vector and territory, simulation and power, and in particular the moments at which one punctuates the time of the other. The map of simulation does not exist entirely unto itself. Marx showed how the market has its obverse side in production. So too must viable political territories ground the simulated realm, regardless of how freely and insolently the vector seems to circulate above and beyond the parochialisms of territory. This is not to say that one has to always refer back to an infrastructure. Rather, it means that the temporal dimension of interaction between vector and territory is more important than any static, spatial metaphor.

Very important are the institutional sites that connect the advanced vector fields to the territory. One such institution is the advertising business, which connects the qualitative aspects of capital together on the levels of second and third nature. Another is the old parties of the working class, which still try to counter this with a combination of old-style membership via branches and union affiliates, redoubled at a spectacular level with media vectors of doubtful effectiveness. It is an open question these days whether any of the parties of the working class still have any organic links to the class alliances that formed them. It is an open question too whether they have really succeeded on the new and expanding terrains of the vector.

Both the Social Democratic Party in the West and the Socialist Unity Party in the East are imaginary forms of the working class, which both play a role in formations of spectacle. The historical development of the vector, the creation of the vector fields of pure war, pure surveillance, pure commerce, total spectacle, makes possible the redoubling of the conflicts and parties of second nature in the third nature of communication vectors. In the struggle to wrest freedom from necessity in the form of a material surplus, the vector develops. It paves a second nature over the first. Class antagonism drives alienated second nature to accumulate further and further. The vector's development reaches a point where it threatens the very *existence* of nature and second nature. The vector's development further displaces these antagonisms onto a new terrain, a third nature—a spectacle woven out of the total vector field of communication. On this map, which completely covers its territory, the war of the vector becomes a thoroughly displaced war of images. Müller says that the face of war is now McDonald's, and so it is. The face of war is Ronald McDonald and missile-cam: the vectors of inane commodification and mechanized death.

In the East, the spectacle revolved around a collective subject—the working class. In the West, it revolves around particular objects—the luxury motor car, symbol of the masculine pride of German industry, above all. The Eastern spectacle of the working class was an image that obscures the omnipotence of the bureaucracy. The Western, seductive object is the ruse, not so much of the omnipotence of the capitalist class as of the vector that class has tied its fate to as ceaseless development. The bourgeoisie straps itself and the world with it on its unguided mission. The success of the West depends on the free reign of the development of the vector. Its cameralism is now global in scope, as the Gulf war showed. Capital rides on a technology of territorial control which merely perfects the dreams of the Prussian expansionists. The vector is the hope of the West. Sutured to the seductive image of the vector, thrilled by the speed of its movement and mistaking movement for freedom, the exhilaration of existence in the West is closely tied to the rise—and the fall—of the vector, to its cruising ballistic ballet through the stratosphere in perfect parabolic arcs.

Site #3
Tiananmen Square, Beijing

seeds of fire

Site #3

5. intersection

A Thrall of Political Furies

Dateline: Tiananmen Square, Beijing, 20 May 1989. Things are at present tense. Martial law has been declared, yet the demonstrations in the heart of Beijing continue. This is more than a demonstration by workers and students, it is a carnival. For a few intense, electric seconds, Beijing has become the only city on earth, oscillating in a thrall of political furies. A teeming slo-mo dance, relayed via satellite around the globe. Beijing is "on," and the whole world is watching. I write of these things in the present tense, for now that the spectacle of the Beijing democracy demonstrations is recorded and relayed around the world, it will always take place in the present tense of media memory. Taut images from this wild scenario will now always be present, ready and waiting to be replayed, over and over. . . .

The demonstrations in Tiananmen Square by students and workers, loosely held together by the Western media under the banner of the "democracy movement," were a strange and quixotic series of events. Even naming the movement, if it was a movement, prejudices the story: was it a democracy movement, a student movement, or a protest movement? In their anthology of Chinese rebel writings, Geremie Barmé and Linda Jaivin prefer "protest movement" to "democracy movement." They say that "democracy was not one of the movement's strong points. Rather, its overriding theme was that of protest—against dictatorial one-party rule, a lack of both individual and group autonomy, economic and political mismanagement, and government unresponsiveness to its people's concerns."[1]

The movement did not seek, practice, or advocate democracy as most Western journalists or their audience would have understood the term. Yet perhaps it was those journalists and their audiences who have a too narrow understanding of democracy. One of the stories one could tell about Tiananmen Square, about the Berlin Wall, is a story about how people for whom democracy is an assumption, a formal and realized structure, fail to realize what is involved in achieving it. People in Portugal, Spain, and Greece who remember the "crisis of the dictatorships" may know.[2] In the democratic West, what is more common is surprise that democracy need not be achieved by democratic means. How little we know. How much we forget.

As Raymond Williams points out, democracy was not usually a positively valued term in the West until the nineteenth century, and it referred more to the multitude, to the commons, than to any notion of a procedure.[3] The idea of democracy as a representative procedure is largely an American invention. When thought of as a formal process of representation—democracy as the will of the people expressed formally—democracy as the power of the people expressed directly, in the streets, appears positively undemocratic. The politics of the event, of an unstable management of forces day by day, is in any case always opposed to politics as procedure, governed by formal law or imposed convention. Thus the democracy movement embodies a concept of democracy as antithetical to liberal conception as to authoritarian socialist practice. So in calling this a democracy movement, I do not mean to suggest that its participants aspire to liberal goals. The people who came to Tiananmen Square were not likely to be seeking a system in which an elected government represents them. They were more likely there to express the fact that since the present autocracy doesn't represent them, they will represent themselves.

Since representation turned out to be a key issue between the democracy movement and the government, this idea of self-representation is of no small importance. The intersection of an absence of a vector along which to represent themselves, and the spontaneous creation of self-representation in posters and t-shirts and poses for foreign cameras is one story that one can tell about this event, and an interesting one, given the creativity in extreme situations that the democracy movement displayed for their government, Beijing residents, and international media audiences to see. Too bad many of their compatriots, all over the country, may never hear or see this story for themselves, or even hear rumors about it, on the backwash of Voice of America radio. Those of us who saw them, who remember, in a sense hold the memory of the democracy movement on trust for those who didn't, in the silent hope that one day a vector will open, that self-representation will flow.

What was it we saw? What was the democracy movement? A brief chronology may help provide a preliminary understanding of the contours of those events, if not of their motivations. Almost by definition, a catastrophe cannot be reduced to a story without giving a false gloss of necessity to this aimless crash of disaster piling upon disaster, like the radioactive storm that propels the luckless angel of history, backwards into the future.[4] Can events of this nature be understood at all? Forces of quite different orders, from the trajectories of rifles to the vectors of information, intersected here. How much of necessity and how much by chance?

Subsequent sections of this essay pursue these inquiries, but meanwhile let's reduce the apparent chaos of random news bites to a manageable narrative, distilled from the newspaper reports and retrospective accounts. As I suggested earlier, the event can be traced over any time frame. Beneath the Potsdamer Platz lies an ancient history to the fall of the Berlin Wall, as we discovered at Site #2. At Site #3, the ancient city of Beijing, there are even older trajectories to discover, but for the time being I want to concentrate on the micro-temporal texture of the event, considered day to day. The denser the intensive vector of the archive, the more multiple strands the event can be traced along. The more concentrated the telesthesis, the more attention can be focused on the most minute divisions of time. Later, at Site #4, Wall Street, we will discover an event where the vectoral net is so concentrated that seconds become the decisive unit of time within the event.

At Tiananmen Square, a daily chronopolitics is the most rapid tempo that need concern us. So the first kind of story here will be a chronicle of the micro-events, focusing on this issue of democracy as self-representation. I consider the more mediated aspects of the event within the horizon of the day-to-day experience of announcements, statements, moves, and countermoves. Subsequent sections will look at quite other temporalities, quite different temporal horizons of the event. The story which follows tries to explain what one kind of vector, one kind of media speed, said about the event in terms of another: the pictures and commentaries seen and heard in the daily press and on TV, mediated via the later and more considered accounts provided by books and journal articles.

It might seem, on the surface, that these later accounts are more true than the media broadcasts and wire reports. In the eventless time of the archive, this may be so, but there is also a truth relative to time, active within time, active within the horizon of the event itself. To be right is only half the battle in the politics of the vector. The other half of the battle is to be timely. "Hell is truth seen too late," indeed.

Chronopolitics of Disaster

8 April. The Politburo is in session, considering, among other things, the case of political prisoner Wei Jingsheng. Wei is the author of a famous text calling for a democratic modernization of China.[5] A Beijing court jailed him for fifteen years in 1979, on spurious charges. He passed through one of those "atheist's gates to hell" he exposed in one of his more trenchant essays, where the guards "resort to every conceivable means to squeeze the 'last drop of surplus value' from these hapless souls."[6] Perhaps Wei is on the agenda because of all the petitions sent to the regime, starting with an open appeal by astrophysicist Fang Lizhi that a "nationwide amnesty be called for all political prisoners, including Wei Jingsheng."[7]

But this is not what makes the event so significant. The collapse in the meeting of Politburo member Hu Yaobang is the spark that sets this story alight. Hu lost a power struggle in 1987 and had not been the same since. A heated debate on education angered the temperamental little man.

15 April. Hu dies quietly at 7:53 A.M. on 15 April. The *proximate* cause, the immediate trigger for all to follow, is this one tiny piece of information: the announcement over government radio of the death of senior statesman Hu Yaobang at 3:02 P.M. This makes public a very private death—according to rumor, from a heart attack while sitting on the toilet.[8]

Hu was a pragmatic politician and certainly no saint, but he was relatively popular, particularly with urban liberals and intellectuals. He once informed the world, through the pages of the *People's Daily,* that "Marx and Lenin can't solve our problems," although the paper had dutifully corrected that to "can't solve *all* our problems" shortly thereafter.[9] On the other hand, as the maverick literary critic Liu Xiaobo pointed out in an unsentimental essay on the dead leader, Hu had also published a long article in the *People's Daily* affirming the "policy that the media must be the 'tool' of totalitarian thought control."[10] Nevertheless, many people perceived Hu as an honest politician, untainted by the stench of corruption surrounding the families of many other prominent officials. His downfall stemmed from the relative tolerance he showed to the 1987 pro-democracy movements, and his lack of alarm at the "bourgeois liberalization" spreading in China, fueled by the vectors to the West created by Deng's "open door" economic policy. While history may assign a more ambivalent role to this diminutive man, his death, in the context of the hydra of public unease with the many political, cultural, and economic shortcomings of the regime at the time, cast him in a heroic last light.

16 April. And so wreaths in honor of Hu appear in Tiananmen Square. Chen Xiaoping of the Politics and Law University organizes a massive wreath, two meters wide, which he and several hundred students place at the base of the Monument to the People's Heroes in Tiananmen Square. On the pretext of mourning Hu Yaobang, small groups start gathering. Hu's death also provides a pretext for opening some discreet vectors of communication across public spaces like Tiananmen Square, where traditional forms of dialogue can begin. The wreaths have the names of the *danwei,* or work units who subscribe to them, and this in itself is a crude democratic communication, letting other *danwei* know how they feel.

Anonymous scribes post up poems and posters, patiently hand-lettered, which are then even more patiently copied down by others, or read aloud for the gathering crowds. Some people post essays to Hu's memory, and elegiac couplets on the news of his death, like this one:

> National news, domestic news, all the news under heaven,
> The news clouds the clear blue sky.[11]

On learning of these events through the media while in America, the iconoclastic literary critic Liu Xiaobo writes an incisive essay criticizing Fang Lizhi and others who use the pretext of Hu Yaobang's death to mourn the passing of this patron of the intellectuals. He points out the dull irony of Hu using his privilege to protect democracy. There is something distasteful in this for the protector and the democratic forces living in his shadow. "If our strategy in the struggle for democracy is to act like slaves rebelling against their master, assuming for ourselves a position of inequality, then we might as well give up here and now."[12] Figures like Wei Jingsheng who sacrificed themselves for democracy deserve more respect than Hu. Liu's essay is published in New York and

Hong Kong, but will take considerably longer to appear in print on the mainland, and in a rather odd form, as we shall see later on.

17 April. The first procession to the square. A few thousand students march to the square and lay their wreaths for Hu Yaobang. This is the first "illegal" act: municipal authorities banned such marches after the 1987 demonstrations. The police look on, stepping in only to direct the traffic. The British-made remote-control traffic-monitoring cameras, bought partly with Western development aid, swivel on their tall stands, quietly recording.[13]

Tiananmen Square, it must be said at the get-go, is a classically "panoptic" space. The "Bureau of Public Safety" can see you there without itself being seen to be seeing. As Foucault argues, when it works, a panoptic apparatus provides "the automatic functioning of power."[14] Even if surveillance is not constant, those surveyed must assume that it is, and internalize surveillance within themselves. It thus becomes a machine for perpetuating power independent of the people who exercise it. The extraordinary thing is that this didn't work. Panoptic spaces work best in panoptic time—the regular, measured, ordered time of a prison or a factory or a school. What begins here and now is another time altogether, the time of the event, where people become not the bearer of panoptic space but the bearer of eventful time.

18 April. Around midnight, three thousand Beijing University students and several thousand People's University students set off from campus for the square. Some want to stay all morning to make sure their wreaths and posters are not removed. What to do now? Some start to drift away. Wang Dan, a history student from Beijing University, knows what to do. He has organized "democracy salons" before. He organizes one now.

Sitting in a circle in the middle of the vast plane of the square, they formulate their demands, and express their views with a cheer or a snort. *Rehabilitate Hu Yaobang! End the campaign against bourgeois liberalization! End press censorship! Public accountability for the finances of top officials! And their children! And their mistresses!* (giggles) *End Beijing city council's bans on public demonstrations! More funding for higher education! Objective news coverage of the student demonstrations!*[15]

After daybreak, students tender a petition of seven demands to the Standing Committee of the National People's Congress. Only no one will receive the petition. There is no mediating line of contact with this hermetic government. The students have already decided to stay until senior officials respond. They have made themselves an interruption in what Paul Virilio calls "habitable circulation."[16] This is his answer to Foucault: the city is not just a space of panoptic enclosure and surveillance, it is also a matrix of circulations, a gearbox of speeds. The students' actions cut across any number of orderly rhythms, from daily traffic control to the classroom schedules. This is their answer to the machinations of the regime and to the machinery of the city itself: we may be bearers of panoptic self-surveillance, but we can be the bearers of a time all of our own making.

19 April. The state responds by broadcasting a decree over the loudspeakers in the square, like an air shot over the students' heads. Meanwhile the demonstrations grow bigger and bigger; many thousands join in. The demonstrators put a big portrait of Hu on the Monument to the People's Heroes in the center of the square, facing the official one of Mao over Tiananmen Gate. Word trickles out to other cities. Other students in other cities respond. Word comes back on the grapevine vector.

Li Ximing, an ally of Li Peng's, presents the report of the democracy movement to the Politburo. "This is a most serious political struggle," he says. "Suddenly, it is thought 'unpatriotic' not to take part in the demonstrations."[17] His report does not fail to alarm most of his colleagues, none of whom have had any real contact with the movement itself. A little war of nerves begins to fall into a pattern: the authorities try to reassert the normal daily rhythm, but they do it with threats and orders. The students respond by sustaining their dysrhythmia in defiance of these very orders. There is a vector of communication already here between the movement and the government, but communication need not resolve things, it may dissolve things—a vector of noise.

23 April. The day after the dress rehearsal skirmishes with the authorities at Hu's funeral, student leaders from a number of campuses set up the Provisional Students' Federation and elect a steering committee. Most of its members, like twenty-one-year-old Wang Dan, are undergraduates. The students decide on a strike and set up "propaganda teams" to disperse and spread the word throughout the city. That evening the new organization receives its first donation, from Chen Ziming of the independent think tank the Beijing Social and Economic Sciences Research Institute.[18] There will be a lot of donations—and very little accounting for where any of it goes.

Speaking of accounting: newly formed student unions publish their "revolutionary family trees," "genealogies" of nepotism and racketeering among state officials. These handwritten posters and mimeographed flyers sometimes offer quite detailed critiques of the ways the privileged class uses its political position as a form of command over economic assets. Officials can, for instance, use their position to acquire goods at low, state-fixed prices and sell them on the open market for a considerable profit. Or, they can use influence to get import licenses to bring in cars or consumer goods, or export licenses to earn hard currency. They can get loans at fixed low interest, or foreign currency at the fixed low rate. They can then use this capital on the open market to great advantage.

Deng Xiaoping's son Deng Pufang is explicitly named in some of these muckraking flyers, as are other public figures, often the sons and daughters of elite party officials. One handbill draws the logical conclusion: "Why is China's foreign debt so immense? Why is China's economy such a mess? Why does the daily stipend of a soldier remain at 1.65 yuan after all these years, despite rocketing prices? Nowhere else can you find the answer to these questions except in the word 'official.'"[19] Or as a big-character poster at the People's University declares in an ironic set of definitions, "party membership" is "merely a card having utilitarian character and value as a currency of social exchange . . . a shortcut to material prosperity."[20] This "street Marxism" aspect of the democracy movement would have shocked some of the liberal commentators on it, like *The Economist*'s editorialists, had they paid any attention. Still, there is a strong ambivalence in this exposure of the ruling class and its excesses. Are the officials merely excessive, or thoroughly corrupt?

24 April. Either way, the officials are not amused. The standing committee of the Politburo meets in special session. They hear a report from Beijing party secretary Li Ximing and mayor Chen Xitong. The Politburo decides to take swift action to stop the students from spontaneously self-organizing. "This turmoil is a planned conspiracy," concludes paramount leader Deng Xiaoping. "We must quickly put an end to this turmoil. The more the Poles gave in, the greater their turmoil became. The opposition is very powerful in Poland."[21] Hunkered down in his heavily fortified mansions in Zhongnanhai, the sealed compound next to the Forbidden City where all the top officials work, Deng is perhaps in closer contact with the international media vectors than with the people clustered on Tiananmen Square, a few hundred meters away.

A parable posted at the People's University today highlights this problem of the detachment of the leadership from any vector of information which does not pass through self-interested courtiers or the secret police. The parable is "Bo Le Evaluates Donkeys," based on the old saying about Bo Le's renowned ability as a judge of horses:

> The government is in fact a type of donkey. Originally, we used it to pull the cart, but now it has changed into an animal that loves to eat and sleep, into a lazy, bad tempered worker that lashes out at will. It is impractical to sell it and buy another: there is no other donkey on the market. To kill it for its meat is also unacceptable, and furthermore, its meat is too bitter. The only alternative we have is to train it with a carrot and big stick![22]

25 April. The old donkey was not too lazy to take the appropriate tactical action: cut off the enemy's vector of communication and substitute one's own. The Post and Telegraph Bureau cut the phone lines to the university dormitories in Beijing and intercepted telegrams going out to fellow students across the country. That night the state television station CCTV broadcasts the highlights of Deng's remarks. With a one-day lag, everyone now knows the gist of what yesterday's Politburo meeting decided. There are no doorstop press conferences here. No public press releases straight after the event. There are internal vectors, within the party apparatus, narrow channels that work with speed and efficiency; there are external vectors, linking the whole country, broad nets that work at often considerable delay, waiting for someone to authorize the story.

26 April. The *People's Daily* editorial accuses excitable young students of fabricating rumors and attacking the party, creating illegal organizations, forcibly taking over the public address systems in some of the universities, poisoning people's minds, planning a conspiracy or a riot. The editorial makes it quite clear that the party won't tolerate "turmoil"—the word used to describe the chaos of the cultural revolution.

If the editorial is meant to be an authoritarian manner of calming people down, it has the opposite effect—especially that word "turmoil." "A Review of the People's Daily Editorial," one of many posters put up on the subject at the campuses, opines that the entire editorial has "missed the point" or is "without interest."[23] But for many of the students it is of considerable interest. The Provisional Students' Federation announces a mass student march to protest the editorial. Given the rumors that the elite 38th Army is taking up positions around Beijing, and clear official warnings that the mourning period for Hu Yaobang is over, this is a brave decision.

27 April. Next day the "expressive" crowd of mourners gives way to an "aggressive" type of crowd, as George Rude, historian of the French revolutionary "turmoils," might say.[24] The students react angrily to the editorial condemning them. A huge demonstration, of 150,000 or more, occupies the square again and formulates fresh demands. These are: (1) broadcast of a fair debate between the democracy movement and the state; (2) a public apology from the "Bureau of Public Safety" for violence toward students at demonstrations; (3) favorable coverage from official press of the movement. The demands are narrowing down to those that directly refer to the past time of the movement. Its present and future time depends on what the government says about the status of its immediate past. What will circulate in the loopy vectors between government and students now is not just noise, but noise about the noise.

Unaccustomed as they are to speaking publicly to people without the implicit threat of coercion, the party's editorialists misread their audience to the degree that the story they circulate, of "turmoil" instigated by "minority elements," "black hands" manipulating gullible students, has the opposite of the desired effect on the students, although it is debatable whether the students are the audience for this story. The problem with as indiscriminate a vector as broadcast TV and radio is that they make it very difficult to target specific stories to particular audiences. The "turmoil" story is most likely a warning to the workers and residents of Beijing to keep out of this. The regime might be annoyed by the students, but it fears a Solidarity-style mass opposition. Nevertheless, this message put out to scare off other people only incites the students. To scare off the students, the regime threatens force; but this eventually incites the mass movement.

The public story, of mere children misled by conniving "black hands," has a stern and steady consistency to it. But the democracy movement rejects the story written for it. It demands a right to self-representation. Where the state holds a more or less tight monopoly over the vector of communication and its repertoire of stories, the demand for self-representation is an obvious and a difficult one. As one small-character poster points out, the state maintains itself only on the basis of its monopoly on ideological form and military force. How to challenge one without provoking the other?

The big demonstration on the 27th leads to the founding of an unofficial newspaper, the *News Herald*, which is in effect the beginnings of an answer. One of the stories the new independent paper carries is an interview with journalists, where they speak about the "creative journalism" they claim to practice under the regime of party censorship: "If 'down with Li Peng' doesn't work, we change it to 'oppose the Premier of the State Council.' If that doesn't work, then we change it to 'the main target of the attack is the Premier of the State Council.'"[25]

Someone watching the big parade today is in a thoughtful mood: Li Xin, a conservative researcher for the Academy of Social Sciences, sends a sober appraisal of the democracy movement to the Politburo immediately after the show. He points out that the editorializing against "turmoil" has the opposite effect to that intended. Perhaps he thinks that the Politburo are too isolated to judge the situation, and need his unsolicited vector of informed mediation and meditation on matters. He blames it all on the influence of three black hands: those promoting Western thought like Fang Lizhi; those culpable of cultural "nihilism" like Liu Xiaobo; those pressing for extreme reform, like the producers of the television series "River Elegy," including Su Xiaokang.[26]

28 April. Hundreds of journalists throughout the media vector field are sympathetic to the students, but receive mixed signals from their political bosses on what story to run. On the one hand, the editor of the liberal *World Economic Herald* has been sacked. The paper had sponsored a controversial forum on Hu. On the other, propaganda chief Hu Qili reverses his instructions of the previous week to ignore the students. Now he instructs editors to print reports on the actual state of affairs and leave it to the readers to decide. What they will decide, perhaps, is that the party leadership is divided on what to do next, as in fact it is. Nothing reports confusion better than confused reporting. Noise is a sign of noise, and an efficient vector can distribute noise as the sign of noise far and wide.

29 April. Hewing to the principle of cutting off the enemy's vectors of communication and substituting one's own, CCTV broadcasts a stage-managed pseudo-dialogue. Only the leaders of the official student unions are present, further angering the students. Nevertheless, some students who speak in the broadcast at least manage to raise some pertinent issues. One says the term "riot," used in the official press to describe the demonstrations, is a distortion. Another remarks that the telecast is not the kind of dialogue the students demand, as no senior party figures are present and the "student leaders" aren't elected by the students. The dialogue establishes that there is no dialogue.

While propaganda apparatchiks congratulate themselves on this stunt, the students debate what to do next. At Beijing University the students use the "Voice of Democracy," a public address system lashed together by students and funded by donations, for a discussion of the telecast. Most students criticize the official student leaders and call for them to resign. Some also express support for Qin Benli, the editor of the influential and progressive Shanghai paper the *World Economic Herald,* whom the government has just fired.

In these exchanges the new leaders of the unofficial movement begin to emerge. They acquire larger-than-life personalities, as is befitting for actors in a narrative far greater than mere everyday life. Wang Dan: small and softly spoken, yet an experienced organizer. Wuer Kaixi: confident showman, articulate in English, and a favorite with the Western media. Liu Gang: veteran of the 1986–87 demonstrations. Chai Ling: a child-psychology student, interestingly enough, who will later become the emblem of the final suicidal days in the square.

These personas coagulate into types in the Western media, giving these chaotic events some, literally, fabulous sense of narrative order and authorship. Both the narrative and the authorship will appear a bit differently in the popular memory in Beijing from the way they appear in the Western media. The tactical use of memory in the territory is always a different thing from either the tactical deployment of memory in the media vector or the strategic stockpiling of memory in the official archives and memory crypts of the state. Telesthesis creates quite distinct forms of memory of events when compared to proximate memory.

3 May. Have pity on the poor journalists who have to write about this in the official press! They are caught at the screened gate where official truth and street truth collide on their way into the circuit of the media vector. This gate is like the one outside Zhongnanhai, and outside a lot of Chinese courtyards. There is a screen across the gateway stopping you from walking straight through. You have to zig-zag a little. The screens on courtyards are designed to keep out evil spirits, which, as everybody knows, can't turn corners. The screen in the gateway of the media vector is designed to screen out noise. It puts through the zig of scrutiny and the zag of erasure anything which doesn't lie along the trajectory of expectations. When the screen is monitored by party functionaries with one eye on the historicist vision of triumphant socialism, and the other on tomorrow's faction fight in the Politburo, getting an accurate picture of this interruption of any and every time that is the event of the democracy movement is an impossible thing. The door bitch of socialist narrative pragmatics will just not go for it.

The screen at Zhongnanhai has the words "Serve the people" written on it in Mao's wobbly calligraphy. How are the journalists supposed to serve the people, and whom exactly are the people to serve? Here's the rub: On the one hand, there is what observation reveals to journalists who take themselves to be authorities on the recording of observation and comment. On the other, there are the political "author functions" who have to screen their copy according to stories pre-scripted from above. The journalists are experiencing a little class struggle all of their own here: between themselves, the producers of the flow, and the screeners, empowered by the owners of the vector to stop it. Concerned reporters stop work and gather at the Lu Xun Museum to draft a petition of their own. The setting is darkly auspicious. Who knows what to expect at this conjuncture? The acerbic Lu Xun wrote: "Lies written in ink cannot obscure a truth written in blood."[27]

4 May. With thousands of students occupying the square and with Deng Xiaoping's hard-line approach to the problem yielding little by way of results, Politburo member Zhao Ziyang tries another tack. Perhaps he is using the failure of his political opponents to deal with the students as leverage in his own bid for power within the state apparatus. He gives a speech, broadcast all over the world, at the opening of the Asian Development Bank meeting taking place in the Great Hall of the People. Zhao downplays the notion of turmoil and conspiracy propagated by Deng's *People's Daily* editorial. He openly signals the split within the Politburo to the television nation. Students watching the broadcast on TV in the square erupt in applause.

5 May. The very next day the *People's Daily* publishes its first report of the demonstrations in a manner calculated to appease the students. In the following days, Zhao Ziyang continues with a conciliatory line against a background of rising opposition within the various state apparatuses to this solution to the problem. Zhao's approach is working to the extent that student demonstrations wane, sustained only by small demonstrations on the issue of press freedom.

9 May. This is nevertheless a significant development. At the instigation of *Guangming Daily* journalist Dai Qing and others, more than a thousand journalists demonstrate and hand in a petition to the State Council demanding freedom of the press. The producers of the flow of media information take public umbrage at the screening of their observations and recordings.

10 May. Something new! Writers stage a bicycle demonstration in support of the student movement, leading the "Bureau of Public Safety" on a merry chase through the streets and alleys of the capital. Meanwhile, the students formulate fresh demands and wait for an answer. None comes. Silence begets not silence, but more noise to fill the void. The students try opening a dialogue with the state. They refuse to abide by the more usual procedure of the petition. The petition leaves time on the government's side. Dialogue forces the slow old donkey to communicate in the time of the movement. The state refuses this new approach to the game, and meets the students' 8 May deadline for a response to their demands with silence.

10 May. Word comes that the students will get their reply tomorrow.

11 May. Word comes that the students will get their reply tomorrow.

Either the state is trying to play a waiting game, hoping the students will give up in the face of silence and retreat, or its counsel is divided.

12 May. Word comes that the students will get their reply tomorrow. Either the state is playing a waiting game, hoping the students will give up in the face of silence and retreat, or its counsel is divided, or it simply cannot shift gears from the bureaucratic time of meetings to the improvised time of the movement. Ironic, given that, as Virilio remarks, the Chinese Communist Party came to power over the ruins of the old empire as the historical guide who could ride on the backs of the mobile energies of displaced peasants.[28] Now they are not so much stalling for time as just stalled.

The movement is also stalled, or stalling. Numbers dwindle, as putting one's body on the line seems less and less to be an intervention that can stop the clockwork of the city. The postural crime of placing one's body as a breach across the smooth surface of the square doesn't seem to interrupt its panoptic space that much. As is now becoming apparent, it only appears to break the city's stride. The movement needs something new, something which takes the interruption to much deeper levels of the vast ticking engine of city and state.

That something new is the hunger strike. The loosely organized movement now shifts toward a more radical position. It also firms up the sense of collective belonging of the "loose sand" of people who are the movement. The hunger strikers, by dint of the moral authority they become, coalesce the movement around them. But they also commit not only the movement but also the government to a time which is radically an artifact of their will. The threat of the final interruption, the cessation of the body itself, brings the control of the time of the event back under the apparent direction of the movement as a whole.

But all that is mere interpretation. It was Chai Ling who made the hunger strike an effective movement in time itself.[29] According to Li Lu, the Nanking student who was to become her trusted lieutenant, "Chai Ling . . . was in despair. For her the decision to go on hunger strike came from feeling, not from reasoning." She made a speech, through the Voice of Democracy loudspeakers. "We endure hunger to seek truth," she said. Deng Xiaoping often said to "seek truth from facts," a slogan he borrowed from Mao himself to refute the "whateverist" school who argued that whatever Mao said must be right.[30] Chai Ling staked the truth of the democracy movement on the only unfalsifiable fact—the untranscendable horizon of death. "We have decided to take our leave. We have no choice but to take our leave. History demands this from us." The purity and fatalism of this story would affect and effect the rest of the entire course of the public events of May and June. "If we do not speak, who will? If we do not act, who will?"

According to Li Lu, "More than a thousand cassette tapes of her speech were copied and sent off to different colleges. Many more students joined the hunger strike after hearing the tapes." Looking at the text, translated on a page, it doesn't look like much, but it seems clear that it was the tone that moved people as much as the words. Chai Ling discovered a powerful vector of affect—a much-underrated vehicle of mobilization, as Lawrence Grossberg has noted. "Popular culture," he says, "seems to work at the intersection of the body and emotions."[31] What Chai Ling created is an extraordinary example of what Grossberg calls "affective alliances." Such alliances articulate "what matters" for a certain network of people, in a given space and time. Chai Ling's appeal effected an affective alliance around a new definition of purpose, an alignment of bodies against time.

Interestingly, her involvement may perhaps be the reason for the large number of female students who joined the hunger strike, whereas the previous phases of the democracy movement drew more males than females into action. Which is not to say that as a woman only she could mount an affective alliance. All networks of belonging have an affective dimension. Rather, she created a new affective alliance, of considerably greater intensity than the existing one.

13 May. The hunger strike pushes Zhao Ziyang to make dramatic conciliatory gestures to try to end the demonstrations quickly and hold off a counterattack against his faction's methods of handling the "turmoil" from his competitors within the state. The crucial issue is to end all outward signs of trouble before 15 May, the day Gorbachev arrives. A big Gorbachev portrait has just replaced Hu's as the students' figurehead in the square.

Zhao's ally Yan Mingfu tries on Zhao's behalf to find a way to moderate the students' position. Yan, who acted as Mao's Russian translator during the chairman's discussions with Khrushchev, is no stranger to crash politics. He dispatches a minivan and driver to find Chen Ziming and the other intellectuals from the independent think tank the Beijing Social and Economic Sciences Research Institute (SERI), in the hope that they might mediate between the regime and the students. As was clear by now, the absence of any form of autonomous mediation, and the absence of any vector of autonomous self-representation, were critical issues fueling a worsening of the situation. In the absence of a vector to the public or to government, the democracy movement created its own makeshift matrix, but its leaders had little experience, were not united, knew little of what was going on in government, and had thrown up the charismatic absolutism of Chai Ling.

Yan's minibus tours the sites, collecting Chai Ling, Wuer Kaixi, and Wang Dan, but word of the meeting spreads, and dozens of student leaders and leader wannabes appear. Yan asks who represents the students, and Wuer Kaixi retorts, "We all are. The fact that we've come in three groups doesn't mean we're divided. It only means we have three different positions."[32] Yan's response is not recorded.

Wang Juntao from SERI speaks at length for moderation and calm, but to no avail. Wang Dan and Wuer Kaixi are perhaps persuaded, but not Chai Ling. She has never heard of Wang Juntao. He and Chen Ziming and the other liberal intellectuals might have voluminous files with the secret police and might be celebrities in intellectual circles, but they have never been publicly condemned by the official media. They have little or no name recognition with the student rank and file, who might think well of Fang Lizhi because the government spoke ill of him. The lack of a matrix of vectors across time, connecting past incarnations of the democracy movement to the present one, leaves these experienced if somewhat discreet intellectuals without an organic connection to the youthful democracy movement of today. The students respond to the bodily self-determination offered, by example, by Chai Ling, not to the arguments of the pragmatists on all sides, looking to cut a deal.

Chai Ling is a figure much derided by the rationally minded, particularly in hindsight, outside of the strange attractor of the event. One would not want to be too quick to judge Chai or any of the other actors in this event. This crisis exposed the flawed matrix of vectors running between the various milieux of the students, the government, the media, the residents of Beijing, and the working-class rank and file, not to mention the lines of communication out of the city to the regional centers. It exposed its inability to deal with the interruption of the event.

To some extent one must see these actors as playing roles scripted, if not by the cunning of history, then by what Isaac Deutscher called the irony of history.

Or perhaps by what he occasionally referred to as history's malicious whims.[33] We may not know what this history is that in its totality shapes these actions, but we can sense its effects in its everyday tragedies and casual catastrophes. We can certainly feel the flaws in the relation between this industrializing society of great complexity and the crude matrix of mediating vectors binding its dynamic forces to the congealed vortex at the center of the party itself. The contradictions of second nature have found no terrain on which to become conscious of their interconnections, across the time and space of this last great modernizing empire.

14 May. Responding to the hunger strike, the official news agency, Xinhua, promises "dialogue." Finally! Yan Mingfu summons the student leaders to a second attempt to cut a deal. Clearly, the hunger strike is harming the pragmatic, technocratic faction of Zhao and giving ammunition to party ideologues, he says. His proposal for an early end to the hunger strike results in a noisy eruption. The forty-odd students in the room argue amongst themselves. Chai Ling's supporters play a cassette tape of her "last words." Several burst into tears. Another group bursts into the room, demanding that the proceedings end. The meeting is not broadcast over the speakers outside, as promised. Betrayed, the students withdraw.

The last attempt to create the missing vector of direct contact between the movement and the government ends in a noisy fuck-up. The rest will all be a tangled roar of dark whispers. Wuer Kaixi scores the only compromise: he persuades the hunger strikers to move to the east side, away from the Great Hall of the People, so Gorbachev won't see them from the windows at the official banquet tomorrow. A rare moment of politics in what is otherwise an event—which is something else entirely. Politics subordinates the vector to the clash and clamor of interests; the event enmeshes interests in the vector.

Alarmed by the hunger strike, and having inklings of movements behind the scenes, a group of prominent intellectuals issue a plea in the *Guangming Daily* calling for the government to recognize the "patriotic" nature of the movement and urging moderation on the students. Among the signatories are Dai Qing, an outspoken journalist, author of historical exposés of the party's mistreatment of intellectuals in the past. She is from an old party family and grew up in the bosom of the elite. Also signing his name and his fate is Su Xiaokang, one of the scriptwriters of the famous "River Elegy" TV series, an outspoken indictment of cultural sclerosis in China, which was aired under the patronage of Zhao Ziyang.[34]

The movement is not taking the hint. It sticks to its demands. These settle on a surprisingly media-oriented formula. They want (1) a retraction of the 26 April editorial condemning them, in effect a public gesture from the party legitimating the movement; (2) that the *People's Daily* publish such a statement; and (3) a genuine televised debate between elected student representatives and senior party officials.

These demands, tantamount to creating a media vector, between not only government and movement but movement and nation, cannot be countenanced by a state that has survived in no small part because of its monopoly of just such a vectoral matrix. The students are still in the square the day Gorbachev arrives, as are the three American broadcast television networks, CNN, the BBC, and dozens of international news crews. The government's inability to overcome this interruption now becomes an international loss of face.

A Special Guest Appearance by Mikhail Gorbachev

Who will remember Mikhail Gorbachev? Progress Publishers of Moscow will never issue his collected works in fake red leather bindings, in every language under the sun. Perhaps instead Time-Warner, Inc. will issue his greatest diplomatic hits as a compilation videotape. His appearance in Beijing might have made the selection, had not events overtaken him as well.

15 May. The world's richest media organizations have all come to Beijing to cover the Deng-Gorbachev summit. Summoned by the call to a "historic occasion" of the kind announced by foreign office press releases, they find themselves overwhelmed by a different kind of historical time. The TV image of the summit beaming out of Beijing today is of Deng and Gorbachev dining together. In the shot, sometimes shown in slow motion, Gorbachev shows off his chopstick technique, no doubt the result of intensive coaching. Meanwhile Deng picks up a dim sum pastry with a shaky hand and promptly drops it. This minute gesture, so insignificant it is noticeable only in slo-mo, becomes an instant global metonym for the whole sad affair. Australian journalist John Lombard: "Inside, the leaders of the communist world lunched while in the square ambulances queued to take collapsed hunger strikers to hospital."[35]

The Chinese authorities cancel the highly symbolic ceremony of Gorbachev laying a wreath at the Monument to the People's Heroes in Tiananmen Square. This gesture of respect by the then leader of the Communist Party of the Soviet Union for the Chinese comrades is a historic moment, but a far more eventful one usurps its air time and column inches. Gorbachev dines in the Great Hall of the People, where curtains conceal the stately room's panoramic view of Tiananmen Square. Two states, side by side in peaceful coexistence in the global media vector; two times, side by side in the public site of central Beijing.

In public talks with Gorbachev, perhaps picked up and amplified out of all proportion, Zhao states that Deng is still effectively in control in China, revealing the "state secret" that his "retirement" was purely nominal. Or at least, that is how opponents later interpret his remarks. Gorbachev jokes with Yang Shangkun, shortly to become a victor in the power struggle within the state: "Well, I came to Beijing, and you are having a revolution!"[36] It is almost clear by now to the Western media that the "glasnost strategy" isn't going to happen in China. The liberal tendency within the state will not seek to broaden its base by extending qualified freedoms to some strata of the intellectual class in exchange for their support for the fundamentals of party rule.[37] The failure of the Zhao faction to form any such alliance points to distinct and complex differences between the kind of client-patron links in the Chinese and Russian states and a quite different dynamic. Interestingly, journalists aren't stopped from entering the country after the Gorbachev visit.

Meanwhile, tens of thousands of intellectuals take to the streets. In the front row is Yan Jiaqi. Formerly close to Zhao Ziyang and a contributor to many official reform programs, Yan epitomizes the dead end some reformers feel themselves to be at, working within the state, keeping their noses clean. Many will of course continue to do so, but for a few insiders, the May and June events are something of a personal last straw.

17 May. The students organize a huge rally on 17 May, and an enormous variety of people join in the carnival, perhaps as many as one million. **SATELLITES REACH HEAVEN BUT DEMOCRACY IS STUCK IN HELL** reads the banner of researchers at the Chinese Academy of Sciences. "The time will come when we will cleave through the waves," write some female students at Beijing University. Students from the provinces jump trains to get here for the big event. (In this respect there really is a parallel with the "turmoil" of the cultural revolution.) "Linkages" (another fearful word for the regime) grow organically along the lines of transport and communication. The phone, the fax, and the railways thread together a fresh gossamer of self-organization.

The *People's Daily* reports on the big demonstration with vivid details of everyday life. "The peasants came too. A man from Miyun County by the name of 'Old Uncle' Liu told fellow travellers: 'I am sixty-seven this year. In the past few days I have been watching television and have seen how the students are suffering. It was too pitiful. I had to come out.'"[38] The journalists seek safety in numbers by issuing a collectively authored story, but at least it puts in circulation a version of the day based on observation and journalistic convention, rather than a proscribed line.

Yan Jiaqi and eleven other intellectuals present a strongly worded declaration calling on the "decrepit dictator" to "acknowledge his mistakes."[39] The decrepit dictator meanwhile meets with members of the "old guard" within the party. As Zhao has perhaps inadvertently announced to the world in his comment to Gorbachev, Deng is effectively in control.

Or at least, as far as anyone outside the enclosure of Zhongnanhai can determine. This is a secretive government, used to putting up a physical barrier of isolation between itself and the world. The meeting resolved on the imposition of martial law, but it cannot keep the secret. News of the coming of the troops and the coming of the end starts to leak out, quietly. Bao Tong, who is both secretary to the Politburo and an aide and speechwriter to Zhao Ziyang, will be widely suspected of the leak. Ironically, Deng Xiaoping himself appointed this veteran of the '40s underground movement as Zhao's assistant. Zhao in turn placed him at the head of one of his policy think tanks. It is presumably through these latter connections that Bao Tong has spread the word.[40]

18 May. A photo opportunity: Zhao Ziyang and Li Peng visit stricken hunger strikers at a Beijing hospital. In the streets, it's another big day. One million turn out—Beijing residents, workers, intellectuals, even a few party cadres and security officers. Bus drivers, perhaps veterans of the 1985 bus drivers' strike, drive the property of the Beijing Bus Company into the square and slash the tires, adding just a little more permanence to the interruption of the regular urban timetable.

The students' position hardens. Wang Dan and Wuer Kaixi can't persuasively argue for retreat against the uncompromising moral authority of the hunger strikers and the euphoric atmosphere of the big demonstrations. Meanwhile the Politburo decides to take firm measures. Zhao Ziyang's attempts to moderate have in their views failed. Outvoted, he offers his resignation. It is Li Peng who meets the student leaders for the televised debate, which finally goes ahead in the evening.

Li Peng, a hard-line opponent of Zhao's in the Politburo, opens with the patronizing remark to the student leaders "You are like our own children, our own flesh and blood." Wuer cuts him off: "We don't have time for that kind of talk."[41] Millions all over China witness this moment, this minute interruption, replaying the movement's interruption of the square. At this moment Wuer Kaixi becomes a household name. The powerful vector of television puts some of the democracy movement's leading faces and names into the widest circulation possible.

19 May. Zhao Ziyang appears in public in the course of this event for the last time. He goes down to Tiananmen. He signs autographs. He pleads with students to leave the square. Some will later say he cried as he spoke into the megaphone. The 7 P.M. news juxtaposes a demoralized Zhao Ziyang with a determined Li Peng—one of those television moments when the edit editorializes. A meeting of officials gathered, appropriately enough, in the army's General Logistics Department also broadcasts on radio and television. They relay it over the loudspeakers in Tiananmen Square for the students' benefit. All the top officials are there—except Zhao Ziyang. Both the Zhao faction and its opponents signal that Zhao's position has lost and that the army is already involved. The Zhao faction launch a vain attempt to get Wan Li, the head of the National People's Congress, to recall this body, or at least its standing committee. (Ironically, Wan Li is also the architect of Tiananmen Square in its recently revamped form—video surveillance cameras and all.) Zhao plays out his political endgame while the locus of power moves elsewhere.

That night the Western television crews set up their cameras facing down the broad avenues, rather than into the square. Rumors of the coming of the end percolate even down to them. They wait in vain. That night the army attempts to move into the city, but at the key intersections, hundreds of thousands of Beijing residents blockade the way. After many false alarms, the student leaders feel by 4 A.M. that the blockade will hold—for now. The student loudspeakers broadcast Beethoven's "Ode to Joy" as a victory anthem. Once again the hermetic court in Zhongnanhai misjudge their people. The people of Beijing resist military pressure as they resisted political pressure. A poster in Tiananmen Square reads: "Comrade Deng! Lay down your butcher's knife and you shall become immediately a buddha."[42]

Martial Law

20 May. At 9:30 on the morning of 20 May, Li Peng declares martial law in the Beijing area. An hour later, loudspeakers in the square issue martial law orders. Attempting to shut down the bothersome international news vectors, the authorities ban filming and recording in Beijing. The students dip rags and scarves in buckets of water as a precaution against tear gas, while government helicopters drop leaflets on the square.

The Beijing Workers' Autonomous Federation is born on this day. "Through the democracy movement," reads its manifesto, "we have nothing to lose but our chains, but we stand to gain the whole world."[43] The students are largely indifferent or hostile to the nascent workers' movement, despite the many acts of solidarity performed by the workers' groups over the course of the event. Many of the students risk nothing more than bad job assignments for participation in the movement. Rebel workers may more likely be executed.

21 May. A tactic rather like cutting the phone lines out of the students' dorms, only on an international scale: the Chinese start jamming the shortwave broadcasts of the Voice of America (VOA) shortwave radio service. This is the first time they've tried this since 1978. VOA responds by turning its powerful one-megawatt am-band transmitter in the Philippines over to the Chinese service.[44]

VOA provides the vector loop between Beijing and the rest of the empire that the regime would not, particularly in this event. While the movement's demand that the official Chinese media carry accurate reports on what is happening in Tiananmen Square has a significant political dimension, as a demand for a freeing of the media, the information itself is already getting out on VOA. The regime has to try to interrupt the VOA vector in order to assert their monopoly right to control whatever passes along the information vectors of the territory of the empire.

The future of Hong Kong hangs somewhere between the British empire, whose lease on the territory expires in 1997, and the Chinese empire, which it was leased from and to which it returns. By 2 P.M. the day after martial law is declared, 100,000 demonstrators gather outside the Xinhua news agency in Hong Kong—the unofficial embassy of the mainland. By 9 P.M. a million people are in the streets, some 18 percent of the island's population.[45] Perhaps they saw the demonstrators on television and promptly became what they beheld. The Jockey Club opens its gates, allowing the crowds in to watch themselves on the huge video screens. The Hong Kong stock market may take a lonely dive, but the people's spirits rose, together.

23 May. The movement has so far followed a trajectory dictated by the dictators' own mistakes and the people's seething outrage at those mistakes. It has not actively sought to create organic democratic linkages which might take the place of the antique machinery of autocracy. Such is the judgment of Liu Xiaobo in "Our Suggestions," a document put out today in the name of the

Autonomous Beijing Students' Union. Some of the gathering forces try at least to practice what Liu, ever the provocateur, has demanded.[46]

Chen Ziming, Wang Juntao, and other intellectuals from the independent SERI group throw themselves into organizing "linkages" between the student, worker, resident, and intellectual groups. Meeting under several names and in several places, they try to put the pieces together. The threat of a Solidarity-style mass movement, Deng Xiaoping's worst nightmare, is the fragile reality they struggle to achieve. What they lack is the subtle, supple matrix of vectors running through the centralized workplaces and the church which Solidarity could draw upon. Nor do they have the terrain of national-popular resistance to a foreign power on their side.[47] Nevertheless they try. The Joint Liaison Group of All Circles in the Capital to Protect and Uphold the Constitution meets, ironically enough, in the offices of the Institute for Marxism–Leninism–Mao Zedong Thought. It's not much of a linkage, but under the circumstances, it is a remarkable achievement.

Just as the students can't link up with the so-called liberal faction within the party, neither are their forces outside the party strong enough to link with the forces that can affect the outcome now. The intellectual stratum has too much to lose from a frontal confrontation with the state. The Beijing Association of Intellectuals, cofounded by Yan Jiaqi, comes to these meetings, but few intellectuals will follow Yan and those like him, prepared to step outside the bounds of the state's conception of the intellectual's role. The independent workers' organizations have little power. The party ruthlessly cuts down their members, and in each event they crop up again, fresh for the harvest. The students are thus, in the end, unable to form either a factional alliance within the state, a milieu on its periphery, or a social alliance confronting it. They have nevertheless established experimentally, through their actions, that these are the political options.[48] It is no longer just a question of backing factions within the party.

While the Joint Liaison people still think there is space to maneuver politically, the students in the square split, and a new organization called the Protect Tiananmen Headquarters wins student sympathies away from the Beijing Students' Federation. The very name of the new group, led by Chai Ling, indicates a desire to hold on to the square to the last rather than leave empty-handed. "Our presence here and now in the square is our last and only truth," says Chai in an interview in late May. "For only when the government descends to the depths of depravity and decides to deal with us by slaughtering us, only when rivers of blood flow in the square, will the eyes of our country's people truly be opened, and only then will they unite."[49]

What can we make of this? It would not be seemly, sitting outside the intersection of time and the event, to pass judgment on the tactical wisdom of this, but we can say something about the fundamental conception of the event that is at work here, and which separates Chai Ling from those looking all along for a deal with a faction within the government. She seems to have a very different conception of the time and space of political action. Progress for the movement is not to be made within the horizon of the event, by resolving it, but outside the frame of the event, by its very unresolvability. The space of action is not the matrix of smoky meeting rooms within a cab ride around Tiananmen Square. The space is the space of the vectors which radiate out from Beijing as the symbolic center of the empire. The democracy movement is staging the catastrophe of a bankrupt political regime, not bargaining with the forces for change within a regime which might still be at the crossroads, which might still have a path into the future.

It is not Chai Ling's personal fatalism which is the problem here. She embodies, literally, a structural view of the crisis, as surmountable only through the immolation of the regime itself. It is not the rational and voluntarist views of some of the other student leaders, or of the SERI group, which cause them to seek a deal. It is the matrix of possibilities which speaks through them. They enact the fragile vectors linking the regime to the organic social developments the regime's own policies throw up, like inedible chunks of modern bile.

25 May. Part of the problem is the lack of communication vectors and forms of democratic decision-making that could bind the fractious mass of the democracy movement together. It is, after all, a movement, not a structure. The first issue of the paper *Democracy Forum* provides some redress for the lack of the former, and a line along which to raise the issue of democratic practice, even if it means criticism of the movement: "Why, under the great banner of democracy, are there people so practiced in role playing, being wolves in front of sheep and sheep in front of wolves?"[50] There will not be time for an answer.

26 May. The front page of the *People's Daily* has for a whole week contained contradictory statements, and all other press outlets show signs of an internal struggle within the state. Until today, when military units commandeer the press and broadcasting outlets, forming an almost complete enclosure of the democracy movement within the matrix of the state. The author function of the journalist and the editor function of the editor are once more subordinated to the monitor function of the state, but now in the most direct form.

27 May. A day of separate events which all head for collision with each other: The Joint Liaison Committee with the unwieldy name finally gets an agreement from all parties, including an exhausted Chai Ling, to leave the square. Meanwhile the veteran party man Li Xiannian, who has hung onto power through each successive regime, speaks for the victorious faction in a televised attack on both Zhao Ziyang and the demonstrators. Representatives of the Beijing Students' Federation come to the Central Academy of Fine Arts and commission some of the staff and students to produce a statue for the square. They offer 8,000 yuan ($2,000 U.S.) for expenses.

Wang Dan, Wuer Kaixi, and Chai Ling arrive back at the square from the Joint Liaison meeting and argue for leaving, but this proves unpopular, particularly with the provincial students. Students arrive in droves every day, and this floating population of atomized, uprooted individuals attracted by the pictures and the rumors of the democracy movement is impossible to organize. When they cannot be persuaded to leave, Chai Ling switches positions to follow the mood of the crowd, by now down to about 5,000. She will stay till the end.

28 May. The strange attractor of the square also brings into its unstable orbit people and resources and money from Hong Kong. A consignment of brightly colored tents arrives, and soon stand in neat rows. They bring faxes and photocopiers—those commodified, plug-in personal vector tools so essential for the contemporary insurrection. With a fax and a copier, it is possible to receive facsimiles of Western and Hong Kong news stories and pictures, and circulate them among the crowds. These portable tools make it that much more difficult for the regime to seal off the site, when the whole city is a porous filament of phone connections to the country and the world, and where there is a powerpoint almost anywhere.

The internal dynamics of the event have to contend with the powerful and legitimate feelings and interests of the colony of Hong Kong and the intense interest created there by the news media vector. In between collecting souvenir t-shirts, Jimmy Ngai Siu-Yan, covering the event for the Hong Kong edition of *Esquire* magazine, writes about how moved he is when pop star Hou Dejian leads a chorus of his best-known song, "Heirs of the Dragon," in the square. The song, by the Taiwan-born songwriter who keeps a residence—and a famous red Mercedes—in Beijing, is a song born of the diaspora, although it might also be a song of exile. "I've never seen the beauty of the Yangtze, Though often have I sailed her in my dreams." The dragon, of course, is China itself. "Mighty dragon, open your eyes," runs a last verse Hou amended shortly before the troops turned up.[51] "I'd sung 'Heirs of the Dragon' countless times," says Jimmy Ngai, "but I still wasn't prepared for how deeply moved I would be hearing this song sung here in the capital of the 'land of the dragon' in the 'far-off east itself.'"[52]

As Rey Chow points out, Hong Kong's people's relation to the mainland is a difficult one. "Hong Kong currently has a democracy that is as fragile as its citizens' ethnic ties to China are tenacious."[53] Some semblance of free elections, the rule of law, and some press diversity are aspects of Hong Kong life that are the often grudging concessions of a colonial regime, but are more than the mainland offers. The mainland, whence many Hong Kong people fled to Hong Kong, is nevertheless the ancestral place of origin, and hence acts for some as the imaginary site of desire to belong, especially in moments like this. Cultural artifacts from Hong Kong like music or video cassettes often work as a vector along which desire for the other forms for mainland people, imagining Hong Kong. From April to June 1989, the images coming out of the mainland do the reverse, working as a vector of desire for Hong Kong people, whose desire for a unity at the ethnic level with the mainland is strengthened at exactly the same time as political union with the mainland regime appears more threatening.

30 May. Art students cart the Goddess of Democracy, a thirty-foot statue bearing a flaming torch, to the square. Tsao Hsingyuan provides a valuable account of how this extraordinary work, in a brand new genre of "temporary socialist realist monumental sculpture," came into being. The sculptors rejected the idea of a Chinese-style work, because there is no aesthetic tradition "that powerfully expresses a political concept." What is called for, they feel, is an eclectic approach. So they model the Goddess after a statue of a man holding a pole, an academic exercise, but make the features feminine. The style is that of the socialist realist artist Vera Mukhina, "whose monumental statue of 'A Worker and Collective Farm Woman,' originally placed atop the Soviet Pavilion at the 1937 Paris World's Fair, is still much admired in China."[54]

After assembling the four styrofoam segments in the square, the sculptors pour plaster through the holes in the center of the blocks, cementing them together. The sculptors design it so that once erected it cannot be disassembled, but will have to be destroyed. Thus is the art of temporary socialist-realist monumental sculpture born. Unlike Christo's autodestructive plastic wraps, this work takes a figurative rather than an abstract form, and is in a sense asking for destruction at the hands of human agency rather than nature, but nevertheless the parallel is striking. It draws Beijing people, growing tired of all this, back to the square for a look.[55] While the students in the square and the foreign media take heart from this apparition of gleaming foam, the secret police quietly round up the more prominent of the radical workers.

31 May. A sign of the times: The state buses 4,000 peasants, workers, and schoolchildren to an official rally at a football stadium out of town. The Xinhua news agency describes this classic example of bureaucratic spectacle as a "spontaneous display of anger against bad elements." Ironically, it is the inspiration of Li Ximing, one of the most unpopular members of the Politburo. The regime, once proud of its mastery of crowds, grew fearful of them in the cultural revolution. Now it prefers its crowds domesticated.

2 June. Four men begin a new hunger strike. One of them, Hou Dejian, must fly out of the country very soon to make a recording date in Hong Kong. He may be a little late. Zhou Duo, on the other hand, will not be going anywhere. He is an executive of the Stone Computer Corporation, which has made considerable material and financial contributions to the movement.[56] And then there's Liu Xiaobo, who flew all the way home from the U.S. to join the democracy movement in Tiananmen Square, drawn to the fire like a moth to a flame.[57]

"We search not for death but for true life," states their manifesto, which is mostly an appeal to fellow intellectuals to take an active part in the democratization process. "Through our actions we appeal for the birth of a new political culture; through our actions we repent the mistakes resulting from our long years of weakness."[58] The manifesto seems to be largely in Liu's voice, combining the Olympian detachment of Nietzsche with something quite alien to it—a sense of sacrifice to and immersion in the organic process of creating a new, democratic praxis. This is perhaps a thought that intersects with that other errant Nietzschean, Gilles Deleuze; where nihilism becomes the force that wills history on, where philosophy becomes the thought that produces movements.[59] It's a last thought, an afterthought, a footnote for the future. Everyone can feel that it will all be over soon. The crowd on the monument cannot let go. They can only wait, wait for a demand to be met that will not be met. They wait for the sign from the other that will vindicate the crowd and allow its release, dissolving back into everyday life and time. But there will be no release into "true life." The movement inserts itself as a refusal into the workings of the state. It is a negative movement, waiting for the other to come to it, along the vectors the other controls. None but a few brave souls thought this was a crowd gathered to reverse the order of things, topple the tyrants. Liu Xiaobo's call for a new political culture calls in truth for that reversal, all in good time. It calls for the first step, the opening up of autonomous vectors, free of the state. The movement is presently not strong enough to refuse the state and force it to concede small things. So it waits.[60]

Valhalla

3 June. The army and the people of Beijing face each other in an uneasy standoff. If the regime blockades the vectors of communication, the people blockade the vector of the street. After several abortive attempts at unarmed advances, the soldiers finally move decisively. At 11:35 P.M. they fire at the barricades on the outskirts of town, and breach the blockade. Some of them seem confused. They haven't read the papers, they're not sure what's going on.

Voice of America (VOA) starts transmitting eleven hours of news in Mandarin per day, while the BBC broadcasts three hours daily. Between 60 and 100 million Chinese usually listen to VOA, according to Chinese estimates. During the May and June events, its audience may have grown considerably greater. "The only other medium more pervasive is rumor," according to David Hess, who heads the Chinese section of VOA.[61] Whatever information is available in Beijing goes out via the VOA and newswire correspondents, and back in to the country via the VOA transmitter in the Philippines. The only trouble becomes getting accurate information.

4 June. About 2 A.M. the first columns of troops halt on the edge of the square. This divides the remaining demonstrators. Hou Dejian pleads with students not to attempt to resist the troops and with Zhou Duo goes looking for the commander. Chai Ling tells a story: *Once upon a time there was an ant colony which had to flee through fire. The ants formed a huge ball, and as the ball rolled through the fire to safety, the outer layer of ants burned to death, but through their sacrifice ensured a safe passage through the flames for all the rest.*[62] Hou and Zhou come back, telling everybody that the square is surrounded, but that they can retreat through one corner of it. Not everyone is impressed. Some would rather be the burning ants. "I know those of you who remain are not afraid of death. But such a government is not worth the sacrifice," says Hou.[63] Liu Xiaobo insists on a voice vote on whether to leave or not. Returning officer Li Lu can't tell which way the numbers go, but decides prudently that the "leaves" have it. The few thousand students and others leave by the southeast corner of the square.

At 4:30 A.M. the troops advance. Tanks crush the tents in the square, some of which hold the bodies of sleeping, exhausted students. The troops fire in the air when they reach the Monument to the People's Heroes. This leads many to believe that they are firing on students in the square, but there are few eyewitnesses reporting directly to the international media. Spanish and Hong Kong television crews tape some of it, but most of the media have gone, either to meet deadlines or in fear for their lives. Troops drag Richard Roth of CBS and his crew off the square while they are broadcasting—the camera wobbles and points blankly at the sky. Roth hears shots from his detention inside the Great Hall of the People, but does not actually see any shooting.

The myth of the Tiananmen Square massacre, created live this dim morning, like lightning over the wires, over the air, will be a hard one to put to rest. The students were not the targets of the brutal repression in Beijing that night. The people killed by the soldiers were for the most part citizens and workers of Beijing who bravely held back the martial-law forces with their human blockade. But they were merely featured extras at best in the media story, a chorus line behind the students, the stars. Students died in the fighting. People died in the square. Many people died in the immediate environs of the square. One could justly say there was a massacre, but in Beijing, not in the square—and who will ever know what took place out in the provinces, where the military can act without the restraining power of the vector to inform on their viciousness? But killing all the students in the square was not the regime's objective. Kill its own "children," as Li Peng called them? Not unless absolutely necessary. One thing the Western media hadn't quite grasped was that it was not the students who in the main would be held responsible for all this, but the "black hands," the intellectuals and militant workers the state imagined, or pretended, were behind it all.

The task of clarifying what happened is best left to credible independent sources such as Amnesty International.[64] What concerns me is why, in the absence of evidence in the moments straight after the troops reached the square, so many people *assumed* that a massacre in the square itself must have concluded the story. It's a morbid subject, and this is a morbid kind of story. I don't want to dwell on it. The place the students occupied, the place where the action was set, is a stage set for death. It is a *valhalla,* a word which Elias Canetti glosses as "the dwelling of the fallen warriors."[65] The Monument to the People's Heroes consecrates the space to death. The hunger strike consecrated the students' refusal to go along with the remorseless workings of the time of the empire as a symbolic war to the death. Staged in such a way, how could the story end otherwise? Because it was not a story, it was an event. Stories shape events to suit the ends they serve, but events do not end. They are not stories. Stories end. Events fade away—unless remembered by stories. Preserving the memory of the event means falsifying it, deforming it into story. The persistence of the memory of events comes at this price.

As the smoke clears and the cleaners come in to wash the debris and blood off the streets, the regime begins the leaden mechanics of restoring "order," getting the machinery of the city working again. As one witness says, "The entire state apparatus, with its deep roots in society, has remained intact, as have the party structure and the political system. All these are functioning with great efficiency to save a tottering leadership from the most severe crisis of the last forty years."[66] The democracy movement interrupted the circular movements of this machinery, but did not change it, although traces of that interruption will live on, in memory, for the next time.

The Supreme People's Court declares the movement "counterrevolutionary." Mayor Chen Xitong broadcasts the first of many appeals for people to surrender and undergo "repentance and self-renewal." A callow, shaken face appears live on CCTV's English program, for no more than fifteen seconds: "Please will all of us remember the dark day today, June the fourth, when many people, including a few of my own colleagues, were killed."[67] After that, what more can one say? Poet in exile Yang Lian, watching on television, later pens this line: "In this instant the laughter of angels is the sound of gunfire."[68]

Entertainment!

The horror was a guest in our living rooms, uninvited. On the screen, pictures of bodies and blood, and the light of a different day. Television news repeated one image, over and over: that of Wang Weilin, the nineteen-year-old son of a factory worker, who stopped a whole column of tanks armed only with a shopping bag. This image has since become a metonymic substitute for the unrecorded and indeed unrecordable chaos of the massacre that took place in Beijing on the morning of 4 June 1989. It is an image-trigger, exploding the memory of a narrative arc, stretching from Hu Yaobang's private passage to the other world while sitting on the john, to the public space of Tiananmen Square broadcast live via satellite, and back to the private realms of many million living rooms around the world.

I can't remember much about what happened on television, although I have a stack of videotapes to remind me. I remember vividly how I felt. I remember wandering around the Chinatown district of Sydney, which is right near where I live. People had posted photocopies of news reports and stories, many of them wildly inaccurate, on the street corners. Expatriate mainlanders, conspicuous among the mainly southern Chinese locals, milled about mournfully. They bowed their heads. They looked at their cheap shoes.

I felt very differently about this event than I did about any of the others mentioned in this book, because I have been to Beijing. The telesthesia of the evening news mixed in me with more visceral memories. I must have walked over every inch of central Beijing, down the narrow hutongs and along its broad avenues, of Eternal Peace and otherwise. I know Beijing only as a tourist, as an outsider. I took snapshots, and I came home with a memory stuffed full of metonymic detail.

I met some of these students. Didn't like them much—they were a little too haughty and disdainful to socialize with me much. I spent more time in the bars and cafés with the night people. Spivs, hustlers, black-marketeers maybe. People like the two young men in imported jeans I went on a bar crawl with. One of them ended up in a fight which just erupted out of nowhere in a crowded bar. I helped carry him off to the medical center. It was like I had just become an extra in a Bosch painting or a Borges story, lost in a labyrinth, holding tight to the injured man and my wallet.

Then there was the young woman in the American flag blouse. I will swear blind that when asked about it she said, "I like America and America likes me," as if she were Joseph Beuys, but then I *was* blind at the time, so who knows? Who will ever know.

Then there was the rent boy in the sequin and gabardine suit and winkle-pickers. His stiff black quiff looked more stately than Elvis's. These were the people and the places of Beijing for me. People who traverse the cracks and fissures of any big city without leaving much of a trace.[69]

Watching it all unravel on TV, I am immediately sutured back into the wounded man's bleeding hand, into the flag girl's unintelligible conversation. The vector reconnects me to tiny fetish objects and signs, which in turn are connected to experience and people. Telesthesia can be a form of pornography, as discussed at Site #1, or it may have empowering effects, as discussed at Site #2. Here, it is more like the wages of the sin of voyeurism coming back down the line to haunt me. The only way I could cope with this was to call up other people I had hung out with in Beijing who were also watching it in their "safe European homes." Journalists mostly, they had similar feelings about it. They all knew the site intimately. They all knew people who had most likely become walk-on extras for CNN, unwittingly or not.

This was how I discovered something about the fraternity of journalism. Journalists love a great event. If they are there when it happens, it is a red harvest of desire and frustration. If they are not, envy and awe fill the space of emptiness and the longing. If, like me, they have been to the site where the event lurches online and turns bad, mixed feelings follow. Fascination mingles with a unique suffering, as the tiny facts and tactics that are the stuff of journalistic routine play themselves out with a familiar cast and deadly stakes.

Most people hate journalists. Most people resent their neurotic drive to render visible everything concealed. Even sacred secrets about everyday life end up cold and naked in the machine-finished prose of the media. So if it is any consolation, I have seen journalists suffer over the fate of little people they once had reason to turn into data for the vectoral slipstream. In this situation, the vector works in reverse. It usually takes the ineffable complexity of some particular person's everyday life and glosses it as a sound bite or a quote from a "reliable source." When the troops move in, when you know exactly which streets they will roll down, guns firing, the vector pulls a strange switch on you. The image of the "reliable source," the sound bite of the casual acquaintance, triggers memories of actual people who are now in exactly the same leaky boat.

The temptation is to pick up the phone and call China, or at least try. One vector creates the telesthesia of horror and guilt, so perhaps another can relieve it. The telephone sits by the television, but is this a good idea? Are the lines tapped? Will I endanger my Chinese friends if I call them? Maybe I could call some Western friends instead and get some more information. It's all academic in the end. The lines are dead, of course. If the regime would go to the trouble of shutting down CNN's satellite television, they would surely create a complete vectoral enclosure for all but military and party communication. It is events like these that make you realize with whom the power over the vector ultimately lies.

Back to watching it on television with the same journalist friends. The talk turns to an alternative knowledge, of previous events and statesmen long and thankfully dead. At the mention of the Gang of Four I start thinking that they anticipated days like this. No, not the Gang of Four who ruled China but the Gang of Four from Leeds, England, who took some art history classes from the former situationist T. J. Clark and wrote some fabulous songs about telesthesia and everyday life.[70] (Funny how things come around the back way in the interzone, when memories and events scream into one another, long-distance.) Clark once wrote: "How, in a particular case, a content of an experience becomes a form, an event becomes an image, boredom becomes its representation, despair becomes spleen: these are the problems."[71] Or as the Gang of Four put it, set to music: "Watch new blood on the 18 inch screen. The corpse is a new personality. Ionic charge gives immortality. The corpse is a new personality."[72] They had the British media and the coverage of the struggle in Northern Ireland in mind when they wrote that, sometime in the late '70s. Who would have thought that guerrilla war struggle would happen live via satellite. Not that the newscams got close to the violence in Beijing that night, but they would in Yugoslavia in 1991. The Croatian film school would even send its students off to the front with portapaks rather than guns. Still, the Gang of Four were on the right track: "guerrilla war struggle is the new entertainment!"

The vector replaces the contest of the gladiators with the race of champions, the struggle to control the doubled space of territory and vector. It is no longer up to the emperor to give the thumbs up or down at the end, although press releases from the president of the United States play an uncannily similar imperial role in the coliseum of global media events. Entertainment, as the Gang of Four suggested, may be more than mere divertissement. It is not the artifice of the media one need fear, but its ultimate indifference to the propriety of genre.

And what am I to do about this? Start writing. I set down the first lines straight away. Fight vectors with vectors, no matter how personal in form and feeble in scope.

The Last Reel

But the next word at this juncture of our story, or chronicle of stories, needs to go to someone else. Someone who can mark the intersection between the kind of story the West had about China before the "massacre" and the pieces of one the West found itself with afterwards: "The massacres stunned the world," said Simon Leys, a longstanding critic of the Chinese regime,

> and yet they should not have surprised anyone. The butchers of Beijing are entitled to feel genuine puzzlement in the face of the indignation expressed by international opinion. Why should foreigners suddenly change their attitude towards them? What was so new about the June atrocities—which, after all, were still performed on a fairly modest scale, when compared with similar operations previously carried out by the same regime? In fact, it is not the nature of Chinese communism that took a drastic turn for the worse in June; it is the accuracy of Western perceptions that suddenly improved.[73]

Whatever immense, unyielding problems this leaves in China, it leaves a problem of no small importance in the West as well. How to think our *relation* to such a thing? The relation our media created for us.

Particularly as our cameras and reporters were not there for the last act—the show trials of the alleged "black hands" the regime caught. The Gulf war absorbed our attention while the official injustice system meted out its punishments. It took a while for the official story to reveal itself. After all, deciding who was guilty depended somewhat on who was caught. Wuer Kaixi and Chai Ling escaped. So did Yan Jiaqi, Su Xiaokang, and some of the intellectuals who could see what was coming. Fang Lizhi, his wife, and fellow scholar Li Shuxian hid out in the American embassy. Hou Dejian took cover in the Australian embassy; in the end they were allowed—or obliged—to leave.

Less lucky were Dai Qing, Liu Xiaobo, and Chen Xiaoping, who were promptly arrested and eventually released. Among the unlucky players forced to play the part of scapegoats were Wang Juntao and Chen Ziming of SERI, each sentenced to thirteen years' imprisonment. Wang Dan drew a shorter sentence. Zhao's aide Bao Tong got seven years, and was the ritual sacrifice of the losing faction. They were headed for Q1 prison, Wei Jingsheng's "atheist's gate to hell." Zhao Ziyang himself escaped prison but remained under a cloud. There are many other people who suffered at the end of this story besides those few mentioned here. Chinese television showed pictures of rebellious workers with crude hand-lettered signs around their necks, rudely declaiming their "crimes," their heads shaved and bowed. They were taken away and executed.

Nevertheless, global media attention can have its effects. Hou Xiaotian, Wang Juntao's wife, led a brave campaign to interest the Western media and human rights groups in the appalling conditions her husband was held in—suffering from untreated hepatitis in solitary confinement for months on end.

Editorials in the *New York Times* and the *Wall Street Journal* were not without their effect. In September 1991, Chinese television offered the Beijing correspondents for CNN and the BBC video footage of Chen and Wang in comfortable prison surroundings.[74]

This was part of an extensive campaign to rewrite the story, written in pixels. Chinese embassies circulated their own videotapes of their version of events. Video of Liu Xiaobo, presumably shot while under arrest, showed the veteran of the square telling his interrogator that he had not personally seen anyone shot in the square. It was one last farcical shot in the media endgame, where the Chinese regime responded to the false claim that the West's screen idols, the charismatic student stars, died in the last reel by pointing out correctly if not honestly that it didn't end that way.

From Tragedy to Farce

At this point, a provisional summing up, a recasting of the story in terms of a narrative which encompassed a wider span than a day at a time and which tries to classify the characters in the drama according to type.

This was not the first democracy movement demonstration in Beijing, nor will it be the last. As such it replayed and amplified messages from previous demonstrations, broadcasting them into the future with a loud blast of noisy memory. Marx once remarked that in the chaos of events, actors often grab for the familiar types of reassuring garb from previous historical struggles, yet while the first time an event may appear as tragedy, the repetition is doomed to end in farce.[75] An analogous form of repetition occurred in these events chronicled above. It is perhaps more appropriate to say that the problem for all of the media was that while the props and the costumes in these events looked like predictable repetitions from previous irruptions, the actors didn't play true to type and refused to play to prewritten scripts.

It is narrative form that makes subsequent moments of an event predictable based on previous moments. Uncertainty about the appropriate *type* of narrative form to apply to the experience of the democracy movement renders the events of Tiananmen Square in April, May, and June a catastrophe of telesthesia itself. It is too easy to narrate away yet too difficult to grasp in a useful fashion. Rather than see it as fitting into predictable types of story—about China, about revolt—it might be better to narrate these events in several different registers. If one digs beneath the horizon of this event, one finds singular new rhythms, several explanations, overlapping and intersecting, yet not necessarily aligning in any harmonious way.

While the proximate cause can be named with some degree of confidence, a search for final causes for such an event is far less convincing business. To begin with, there is clearly a complex intersection of class and social forces at work here. The democracy movement in China has the sympathy of many but the active support of few. China is still a country in which rural peasants are the numerical majority. The military is still a potent political force. The working class has many grievances, especially against erratic economic "reforms" that lead to inflation and insecurity, but its demands are not always easily integrated with those of the students and may indeed conflict with them.[76] The technical intelligentsia and the cultural intellectuals are more likely than any other class or class fraction to want democratic change, yet democracy can be only a vague aspiration under a regime that inculcates quite other values, practices, and norms.

Anyway, many urban intellectuals would certainly not countenance the idea of a "democracy" that extended the franchise to millions of peasants. For the most part "democracy" is a relative term. It signals a demand for the inclusion of this or that interest group within the fold of the state, not an opening up of the state to a democratic process open to all. Rather than being an absolute concept stemming from universal and rational principles, "democracy" is a sliding signifier, slipping and shifting from one narrative frame and form to another, caught in the conflicting web of interests.

This dilemma, pitting the interests of class fractions or interest groups—call them what you will—against the state on the one hand and against a universal demand for suffrage on the other, leads to a certain complexity in demands and debates that is as much a problem of political culture as it is of politics per se. This is a polity with plenty of police but without a polis. It lacks a matrix of vectors and a process of screening their flows in which competing narrative forms can struggle to articulate interests and demands. It needs an arena where the hegemonic and counterhegemonic forces can struggle to form a bloc of interests through a genuine and uncoerced leadership of political culture.

The democracy movement struggle is a struggle by fractions of the urban intellectuals and technical intelligentsia to advance their particular interests, and also a struggle to create a space for a polity, at the very least to advance a residual memory of what one might be like. It is a struggle to create a culture and a communication adequate to forming a subsequent polity. Despite what the televisual storylines of CNN and CBS might have suggested, "democracy" under these circumstances cannot mean anything like what it means in the West. Democracy here is an appropriated term designating certain urban, educated interests, staking their claim upon the state, resentful of the license and the wealth extended to the new "entrepreneurial" strata by the economic policies of the Deng era. That democracy appears as a compromised concept is hardly novel, and indeed this may be an essential part of the history of democratic struggles, including the French revolution itself, from which actors in this struggle borrowed some costumery.

The struggle for democracy is a struggle to wrest a matrix of vectors and a culture of brokering their flows away from the state and the party. Yet for the most part this struggle inevitably passes through both state and party, and is easily co-opted there. There may be many genuine reformers within the party itself, yet they constantly come up against the institutionalized weight of sclerotic discourses and vested interests—not least among the middle- and lower-level cadre. In any case the ruling elite has a strong instinct to put personal political survival and the maintenance of the state that sustains them above all else.

Besides analyzing the underlying causes in terms of material interest, one can also trace out the outline of the regime of power that works here, from the largest to the smallest level. Vast and panoptic, the party and state which the democracy movement inevitably confronts is a formidable apparatus amenable to neither a war of position nor a war of confrontation. Quite another politics and culture, for quite another alignment of forces, and most particularly, quite another information environment is called for.

The demonstrations in Tiananmen Square form a significant expression of the experimental search for just such a political culture. In May and April 1989 the students managed to turn the monumental power of Tiananmen Square and the moral force of Communist ideology against itself, and managed to plug the staging of their demonstrations into the global media. This is a politics of "detournment," of turning a space and an ideology against itself. It belongs to what Greil Marcus calls a secret history of modern times, enacted as what official history sublimates or excludes: the possibility of its own negation.[77]

In Tiananmen Square the students created their own "democracy university." Ironically enough it was one in the classic Marxist tradition. One in which one learns about the arsenal of power while attempting to scale the slippery battlements of an unpredictable and chaotic event. One in which the resonance of memory and monumentality, the circumvention of walls and hierarchies, the dissemination of movement and will are the essential curriculum, the streets a hard teacher.

An urban site redolent with symbolic meaning; a panoptic political regime struggling to contain its own power in the face of a modernity it both ardently desires and resolutely opposes; the presence of the Western media with their global information vectors: Tiananmen Square in April, May, and June of 1989 was a metaphorical crossroads for the intersection of diverse forces, following different trajectories at different speeds. In Lenin's terms it formed a conjuncture; in Althusser's, a point of overdetermination. As a way of conceptualizing this intersection of different yet overlapping spatio-temporal registers, the next sections deal respectively with the urban site, the political organization, the media network, and the process of producing and recording this catastrophe as memory.

6. lines

Fire

Dateline: Beijing, 3 June 1989. Just before declaring martial law, the authorities cut the satellite links. This is an ominous sign of what they have in mind, as the troops are trucked in from the provinces. Dan Rather of CBS argues live on air with a bureaucrat armed with pliers. CBS broadcasts the whole incident, with the screen going blank at the end. The networks have contracts to broadcast via satellite several more days, yet here are officials shutting them down—a clear sign of the flimsiness of the rule of law upon which the open door policy and the joint venture agreements rest. The Hong Kong stock market takes a deep dive, and everyone prepares for the moment of repression.

Previous student demonstrations exposed the differences in the demands the students make and the needs and wants of the workers. The students have ideological demands: democracy, accountability, a greater role for the intellectual class in political life, and a bigger share of the state's resources. Anyone who has seen the abysmal state of Beijing University will know the very real basis of these demands.[1] This is not exactly the workers' line. Many workers want less reform, not more. Market-driven inflation erodes their incomes and threatens the job security they had under the "iron rice bowl" system. Inflation, as Elias Canetti observed, is a great inciter of crowds. Inflation not only devalues money, it devalues its owner. These devalued owners of money congregate, and seek to devalue something else—the cause of the inflation. Confronted with the need to mass more and more yuan to realize one's self-worth, people mass more and more of themselves.[2] Inflation of numbers along one vector creates inflation of numbers along another; noise in the relations of private exchange leads to noisy exchanges in public.

When the army arrived, the student-centered crowd, grown on the refusal to study, waiting for demands to be met, changed to a crowd grown on the basis of confronting another kind of crowd.[3] People blockaded the streets with picket lines and encircled the railway stations. The issue shifted from the students' demands for democracy to the struggle in the streets for what Virilio calls "dromocracy": a battle over who controls the movement and the disposition of force in the city. As Virilio argues, the Chinese Communists have a long tradition of dromocratic power.[4] The Long March was the ultimate war of movement, and the party applied the lessons learned then to a disciplinary regime based on the regimentation and control of movement, on pack drills and transmigrations.

During the cultural revolution, the struggle between Mao and his cohorts and the party machine pitted the massive movements of Red Guards around the country in the Exchange of Revolutionary Experiences against the party's rigid controls of movement. Mao set loose the greatest transmigrations the world has known, and in the chaos that followed, the army stepped in, countering movement with force and restoring order, a new political compromise and a new party line.

The old men of the party remember all this only too well. As Deng Xiaoping said shortly after an earlier bout of small-scale student disturbances, "During the 'cultural revolution' we had what was called mass democracy. In those days people thought that rousing the masses to headlong action was democracy and that it would solve all problems. But it turned out that when the masses were roused to headlong action, the result was civil war. We have learned our lesson from history."[5] This line has been remarkably consistent and unshakeable since the end of the cultural revolution, for reasons I'll take up later.

This time around, there were more than "disturbances." The people seized the symbolic heart of the country and blockaded the mobile force of the army out. The workers and the students had no clear unity of demands or slogans. Their collective opposition was one of gesture as much as of ideas, a postural crime. As Virilio says of such movements, "Bodies are guilty of being out of sync, they have to be put back in the party *line*."[6] They placed a brake on the circulation of force through the city. An unknown number of people, a multitude, perhaps a million, kept 150,000 troops at bay.

The troops camped at the railway station, a little to the east of Tiananmen. They moved into position on the subway system and through the network of underground tunnels Mao had built as fallout shelters.[7] It's difficult to know how aware the people of Beijing are of the strategic layout and opportunities afforded by their city. There are no accurate, publicly available maps showing all of the possible routes the troops can move along. It was a case of troops from outside, using maps and logistical skills, vs. the local knowledge of the people: a repetition of a very old historical conflict between military technique and popular defense.[8]

As the troops drew a physical net around the city, the audiovisual enclosure also tightened. The radio and TV no longer referred to the students as "patriotic" and began making ominous noises about "counterrevolutionaries." The "conservative" faction, in favor of the economic open door and reform but opposed to political change, used the demonstrations as a pretext to declare its historic compromise with the political reformers within the party null and void. Deng Xiaoping, Yang Shangkun, and Li Peng were by now firmly in control.

As I have already mentioned, there is still controversy about the "massacre" of 4 July. In short, there are three lines of disinformation one can choose from. The official Chinese disinformation, unequivocal and terse: no massacre occurred. Anti-party elements were punished. Western disinformation (cynical version): reports that thousands of people were killed provoked justifiable outrage and prompted the governments of Japan and the Western powers to take appropriate sanctions. The fact that the thousands of people who were killed were not actually killed in Tiananmen Square is a matter of detail, and in any case, the event has greater symbolic power if one imagines that they were killed in the square, given the enormous monumentality of the square and its significance in CPC ideology. Western disinformation (liberal version): initial reports dispatched in the heat of the moment were inaccurate, as one might expect them to be. In the cold light of hindsight, one must admit that few people were killed in the symbolically loaded site of the square, and yet many people were killed in places and fashions that don't make for quite so compelling "news bites." It is more politically important to get the information right than to get a response to the situation, even if horror, condemnation, and sanctions are the kind of response one might want, in order to communicate to the CPC the unwillingness of democratic capitalist states to do business with regimes that act in such an undemocratic fashion *on primetime television*. Which perhaps is a no less cynical view than the former.

The media loop between China and the West was unprecedented. Some lessons were learned. The CPC used the Western media loop as a surveillance system. Chinese embassies in the West taped the news shows and sent the footage home to be used by the police. Western news blurred the faces of demonstrators unwillingly caught in frame after martial law was imposed, but it was too late by then for many people unwillingly convicted by camera crews with little understanding of what it means to open an international media vector out of a police state.

Chinese authorities intercepted an interview taped by American Broadcasting Corporation journalist James Laurie with a forty-year-old Beijing resident. In it, the man vividly describes the massacre committed by the army. Because direct satellite transmission from Beijing had been cut by the regime, Laurie shipped the unedited tape to Tokyo for uplinking via satellite from there to New York. He read the script to go with it down the telephone line from his hotel. What follows flows logically from the near-certainty that the line was tapped. The CCTV aired sixty-nine seconds from the two-minute interview, with the phone number displayed on the screen for viewers to call if they knew the man. Xiao Bing, an aluminum window maker, was later shown on CCTV in police custody. Two women had spotted him from the television pictures and turned him in to the Bureau of Public Safety.[9] Laurie was naturally quite angry with CCTV about this, but Xiao Bing's relatives would no doubt be even angrier with Laurie. How could anyone seriously think that a regime which flouts its own laws whenever it pleases would think twice about the niceties of journalistic convention?

The CPC managed the positive feedback loop of the Western media, which for a while encouraged and incited successive acts of civil disobedience, into a negative feedback loop, discouraging resistance and prompting complicity with the state. Just as the students seemed to be learning how to use the positive feedback aspect of this loop to their advantage prior to the 4 June massacre and roundup, so the state appeared to be learning how to turn it around and use it to its advantage. The tyranny of distance that once separated events in China from the world has become a *tyranny of difference*—a proliferation of mediated messages from this event that can now be used against those who figure in the great gush of information generated by the demonstrations.

The video cameras installed for traffic monitoring in the center of the city proved particularly useful. The definitive video account of the whole event is in the hands of the Bureau of Public Safety. The operators of these remote-controlled cameras could pan and zoom in on the faces and actions of individuals in the square and environs. Being CCD-type cameras, they even work in very low light. Still frames of the faces of prominent activists in the square also turned up on television, broadcast all over the country to catch movement organizers on the lam.

So on the one hand, the regime hauled footage from global broadcast vectors and used it within the space of Beijing to get their man; and they used footage from within the panoptic confines of central Beijing and broadcast it over the extensive vector of CCTV's national network to catch fleeing demonstrators. The vector can be a very useful resource for a police state, a lesson one can only hope the Western media will one day learn. Both the space and time of the contemporary vector and the space and time of memory can serve as tools for any and every political structure or movement. Nevertheless one has no choice but to record and recall all the lessons learned from this and any other event about these resources and how they can be used, and used against one. The dromocratic politics of the barricade perhaps never change. They are a matter of physical tactics, alertness, stamina. The politics of the media vector keep changing as it develops, and the politics of memory are specific to each site and the traces left in everyday life of lessons learned from the past. This is why the second half of these meditations on 4 June look mostly at memory and the vector.

Unicorporate Power

> Would it not then
> be simpler, for the government
> to dissolve the people and
> elect another?
>
> —Bertolt Brecht

> John Stuart Mill said that tyranny makes people cynical. He didn't realize that there would be republics to make them silent.
>
> —Lu Xun

China's post-Liberation ruling class rule from behind the walls of Zhongnanhai, just across from the square. In a way they are not unlike any other peasant army that rode and fought their way to power over the empire, and built a fortress within their newly won capital to keep their country culture safe from urban influences. What Marx called the "contradiction between town and country" was in some bizarre ways resolved here in favor of the country.[10]

One of Deng's famous remarks during the democracy movement days was that the government had nothing to worry about from a few thousand demonstrators when it had a million troops at its disposal. Troops for the most part recruited from the five-sixths of the population still tied to the land. This is not a government which, at its top levels, has much to do with the city it occupies. The urban traditions of self-organization, representation, and the abstract form of government based on the rule of law are still something foreign to their experience. Having never organized the second nature of industrialization on the basis of the abstractions of money and law, they view with alarm the development of the even more abstracted vectors of third nature knitting their matrix quietly together.

The "May 4th" writer Lu Xun once wrote a parable about power in China, where the law is used in the service of particular and contingent power struggles, rather than providing the abstract grid within which they can more formally develop. There is no shortage of statutes, but

> none of these volumes could actually be used, because in order to interpret them, one had to refer to a set of instructions that had never been made public. These instructions contained many original definitions. Thus, for instance . . . "government official" meant "relative, friend or servant of an influential politician" and so on. The rulers also issued codes of laws that were marvellously modern, complex and complete; however, at the beginning of the first volume, there was one blank page; this blank page could be deciphered only by those who knew the instructions—which did not exist. The first three articles on this invisible page were as follows: Article 1: Some cases must be treated with special leniency. Article 2: Some cases must be treated with special severity. Article 3: This does not apply in all cases.[11]

As evidenced by the sentences handed down by the show trials of the democracy movement's supposed "black hands," these rule books are still in force. The democracy wall movement writer Chen Erjin called this kind of regime of power "unicorporation," by which he means that there is no separation of powers, and the same techniques of power are applied to economic, political, social, cultural, and everyday life. Political power, command over economic resources and communicational vectors are fused into one. One consequence of which is that "mere fluctuations within the political line cause major upheavals throughout social production as a whole."[12] The inflationary crisis which preceded the 1989 democracy movement and fueled it with popular grievance is a classic example. "Market Stalinism" was and remains an incoherent and unstable result of shifting compromises and conflicts between economic liberalizers like Zhao Ziyang and central planners like Li Peng. The dual matrix of communication vectors, one for the party insiders and one for the masses, is a logical outcome of unicorporate power. It is the communicational practice of the old peasant army on a vast scale: timely intelligence networks for the commanders and propaganda lines to mobilize the rank and file.

This unicorporate communication order strives to be transparent at the top of the hierarchy, and opaque at the bottom. Information passes up through the layers of bureaucratic baffling, and orders down. Those at the bottom cannot see or hear or know what those at the top see and hear and know. Yet they know that others know. This asymmetrical relationship, this complex class matrix created as the intersection of the unequal flows of information and authority, cannot fail to engender a paranoid relation between the class that sees, hears, knows, and orders and the class that is seen, heard, known, and ordered.

The *People's Daily* editorial of 26 May appears in this light for what it was: an order. Within the spatial grid of central Beijing, the Politburo heard intelligence reports on what took place on their doorstep. Senior officials interpreted those reports, the Politburo heard them and issued its orders. It then made public statements, broadcast on radio and TV, and directly in the square itself. The space of Beijing is still traversed by many powerful loudspeakers, a one-way vector for the issuing of orders. Unicorporate power leaves its traces not only in the form of command and communication, but within the spaces commanded.

Unicorporate communications were inward-looking, at least until Deng's open door policy inadvertently opened some lines of communication between the space of the empire and the vectors of Western "spiritual pollution" and "bourgeois liberalization." Many used to the many baffling layers of its insulation did not approve. It's something of an index of the enclosure of the culture of the regime that Lu Xun, writing before Liberation, had an international range of literary references to draw upon, and wrote about the lawless law of China's masters with such elegant black irony. Yet Chen Erjin, writing in the aftermath of the cultural revolution, has only Maoist dogma from which to shape the same indictment. China's learning curve on the globalization of the vector went backwards for decades. As with its internal baffling, it tried the same thing internationally: an asymmetrical flow of imbalanced data trade. Out came the newsreels, books, and magazines. In came, well, nothing much at all.

Black Walls and White Lies

Beijing today is a classically modern city, dominated at its center by an orderly arrangement of buildings in functional groupings. As such it physically embodies a peculiarly Stalinoid dream of the modern: the modern as a neat, rational demarcation of units of functional space. The modernization of Beijing meant its *organization*. Techniques of modernity for analyzing, classifying, planning have been applied to it to produce a unicorporate form of transparent order, symbolic unity, and productive functioning.[13] Many of the same principles seem to have been discovered and implemented here as in Western or Soviet cities, but the articulation of various modernizing gambits is distinctive. The first principle of this vision of order seems to be a radical emphasis on the demarcation of space over the circulation and movement of people, information, and things. This spatial principle in turn makes possible the unicorporate regime's techniques.

In Beijing, unicorporate power figures spatially as a ground plan of walls and baffles, and a hierarchy of passes and levels of access which restrict the movement of bodies and information in space no less than that of money and goods. This hierarchical and restrictive communication system is mapped onto the spatial arrangement of factories and neighborhoods by the organization of neighborhood committees and work units. Every unit of space has not only its official monitors of identification, but a network of quiet informers. These two matrices of vector report upwards through the ranks of the party according to two kinds of time. The routine monitoring provides a steady flow through time of information on every movement; the network of informers catches the extraordinary moments, the unpredictable bodily deviations. In both cases the point is to cause an internalization of surveillance within the body of the inhabitant. Should this fail, as it obviously did during the democracy movement, it will serve a second function. After the 4 June crackdown, work units each had to produce a certain quota of denunciations and self-criticisms. In this case it becomes the vector not of discovering guilt but of administering redemption. This was something of an exceptional case.

In everyday life, the system of mutual self-monitoring and informing has the more mundane purpose, in a city without genuine law, of regulating everyday life. In a story called "Black Walls," Liu Xinwu tells a blackly mundane story of a man who decides for no particular reason to paint the walls of his apartment black. The neighborhood committee calls a meeting about this, but can't decide whether to inform the police or the hospital.

> Teacher Sun was thinking of slipping off home, but he was too scared to move. He had to be careful to show the right attitude in this matter, so that if the incident was investigated in the future he wouldn't come out looking like a person of confused loyalties. By the same token, when it was Zhou's turn to be vindicated for his actions, Sun didn't want to appear as a man who had taken an active part against him. Ideally he wanted to avoid any form of criticism for any past, present, future actions.[14]

Such is everyday life in a space traversed by this singular matrix of informative vectors.

The point about this unicorporation of all aspects of urban and social life is not that it results in an obscene and perfect machinery of total control, but rather that it *never* succeeds in perfecting itself. Out of its own complexity and rigidity, out of the system of walls within walls comes friction and inertia. The very opaqueness of order makes the intricate lines of order itself visible—even as it makes the social forces it orders and power which imposes order obscure, the subject of rumor and myth. Political culture in such circumstances comes to focus on the visible surface of order, for want of information about what might lie behind its blank screen.

Ironies of Everyday Life

So many walls, so many protocols of the body for each situation: a situation ripe and rife with material for the play of irony. Whereas in the West the vector seems to break down any and every partition, blurring the bounds along which irony might practice its displacements, the subtle minutiae of unicorporate boundaries can't help but produce an everyday culture of ironic displacement or reversal.

In this it is a world away from what Jean Baudrillard sees in *America,* which "knows nothing of irony," because everything appears to be in a state of pure circulation, pure operation, knowing no bounds.[15] Indeed, if there is anything left for irony to operate on in such a context, it is the apparent boundary of interpretability which arises within the globalized media vector. Things un-American may appear ironically, against an imaginary boundary of the American, but even here the cultural organization works to reduce the image of the foreign to the familiarly American.

Which is why Richard Wald, senior vice-president of ABC News, can say of the democracy movement, without any intended irony: "When these very appealing young people with their ideology seemed to speak directly to our history, remembering us as a revolutionary country, it made us feel good and good towards them."[16] So good toward them in fact that they made nice, clear pictures of them and put them on American television to help the Bureau of Public Safety round them up and subject them to the anguish of prison or the boredom of writing lengthy self-denunciations. The American media vector defuses the potential of irony, that playful confusion across a border, by making everyone either an honorary American or an honorary un-American—the internalized and unironic form of negative being. In order to leave open the possibility of irony—even unintended irony—we have to look for the borders of sensibility within the images the global media vector throws up. That is in a sense the strategy risked by this book: an essaying beyond common sense into the unconscious ironies circulating through our lives along the lines of the ever more ubiquitous vector. But I digress . . .

In Beijing, a frequent cultural strategy for living within this maze of secretive vectors and public walls is to invert the terms of order and celebrate a world where the walls appear back to front. Take, for example, Beijing's first rock 'n' roll star, Cui Jian, who used to appear on stage in old peasant clothing or Red Army uniforms from the Long March era, juxtaposing past and present, city and country. His best-known song is "Nothing to My Name," which was sung many times during the occupation of the square: "It's ages now I've been asking you: when will you come away with me? But all you ever do is laugh at me, 'cause I've got nothing to my name."[17] Its appeal lies in part in its inversion of official ideology, which promises its subjects that all the property expropriated from the capitalists and landlords is now the socialized wealth of the people. "Nothing to my name" asserts the opposite—that the state holds everything for itself, that the would-be citizen is denied the object of her or his desires in the dispossession of the state.

Needless to say, the song's popularity is aided by the fact that it takes the affective form of a love song. The singer's voice records the failure of desire due to the fact of dispossession. The blame for this dispossession, by implication, lies with that opaque order of unicorporate power which the song does not even mention, but which forms the blank black wall upon which all appeals might register. This much was recognized when the Beijing municipal authorities curtailed Cui Jian's performances in 1987.

Nevertheless, Cui Jian's music managed to find its way through the fissures and cracks in the social order which arise out of the friction generated by its application to everyday life. It articulated popular sentiment more effectively than dissident poets or post-Marxist intellectuals with its immediacy. Where order is opaque, and thus readily visible, it provides a fixed obstacle for such furtive articulations. They thread themselves around and draw attention to it. When Cui Jian wears the red flag as a blindfold, it becomes at one and the same time an ironic sign of the opacity of order and of his furtive wit within its tightly wrapped darknesses.

This politics, which might be called a politics of the visibility of concealment, is not unique to Beijing, or even China. Yet no matter how often the power of the media vector comes up against the politics of visible concealment, it never quite seems to grasp the nature of the invisible articles which govern it. In Tiananmen Square, under the Victory Arch in Baghdad during the Gulf war, in Moscow during the attempted coup against Gorbachev, the naive lucidity of the vector came up against the same crafty opaqueness. Perhaps these two forms of power form an extreme pair, not so much dialectical as radically incommensurable. One is a spatial politics where the coverup is as plain as day; the other is a chronopolitics of a lucid banality punctuated by evident silences. The resultant intersection is a baffling irony.

As Henri Lefebvre once said, "The very fact that irony is possible immediately reveals the impossibility of any true identification with 'beings' who are not identical with themselves."[18] In Beijing one can still find the locus of power which creates nonidentity in the partitioning of the self in spaces of panoptic life. In some places in the West, where the vector makes all bounds appear fluid, one loses the tactic of irony, but without for all that gaining self-identity. Identity itself becomes a vector, a matter of subject trajectories and speaking trajectories rather than subject positions and speaking positions.[19]

The Persistence of Memory

Beijing is a space of baffles and flows, like any other Chinese city on the mainland. Yet the center in which its geometric lines converge is Tiananmen, and that makes it unique. Tiananmen: a space built very consciously into the fabric of an ancient history, yet also a space made famous by the saturation of every vector within China of its image, particularly during the cultural revolution. It is a space almost every Westerner is equipped to imagine also, from so many years of watching those curious newsreels of those spectacular rallies held there. One thing you can say about the cultural revolution: it created one of the most globally recognizable sites on earth.

Tiananmen Square is a sacred space. A holy space of mythic proportions, and to understand why it is the focus for so many demonstrations is to delve into the many layers of monumentality that is Beijing, one of the world's most ancient capitals. Despite movements toward reconstruction and deconstruction, despite all of the attempts by the CPC to change their symbolic and quotidian functions, the basic grid of the city and the major sites of historical memory, in Aldo Rossi's term, "persist."[20]

The only way to describe Beijing for someone who has never seen it is to say that it looks like Brasilia, Washington, or Canberra—not as they appear now, but as they will look *in a thousand years' time*. The central axis of Beijing passes through the "Forbidden City," formerly the palace of the emperor. To the north is an artificial hill, the only hill in this otherwise completely flat city. To the south of the walled Forbidden City lies Tiananmen Gate, and farther south again Qianmen Gate, both of which formerly had a symbolic and processional function. Only the emperor entered the Forbidden City through these gates. There were other gates for other visitors: the northern gate, for example, was for military officers, as the north was the direction the barbarians came from. The Forbidden City is now a museum. The exterior of the palaces and temples has been "restored." Yet while the palace is no longer forbidden and has been opened to the public, the space immediately to the west of it, Zhongnanhai, has been closed, and forms a new Forbidden City for the new rulers of the old empire. The CPC did not abandon the site of symbolic power, it moved in next door.

The space in front of Tiananmen Gate had become cluttered with shops and stalls, and these were all cleared away. A vast square was created between Tiananmen and Qianmen gates. On the east side of the square the Great Hall of the People was built, and on the west side, a museum. Thus if one mounts the hill to the north of the Forbidden City and looks to the south, one can see a symmetrical arrangement of the old imperial palace, the gates, with Zhongnanhai and the Great Hall just to the east of the axis, and the Workers' Cultural Palace and the museum to the west.

Simon Leys wrote some devastating criticism of the CPC's architectural appropriation of Beijing:

> In Beijing stands one monument that more than any other is a dramatic symbol of the Maoist rape of the ancient capital: the Monument to the People's Heroes. This obelisk, more than a hundred feet high, the base of which is adorned with margarine bas-reliefs, would by itself be of no particular note if it were not for the privileged place it has, exactly in the centre of the vista from Qianmen Gate to Tiananmen Gate. A good sneeze, however resonant, is not

> remarked upon in the bustle of a busy railway station, but things are somewhat different if the same explosion occurs in a concert hall at just the most exquisite and magical point of a musical phrase. In the same way, this insignificant granitic phallus receives all its enormous significance from the blasphemous stupidity of its location. In erecting this monument in the centre of the sublime axis that reaches from Qianmen to Tiananmen, the designers' idea was, of course, to use to advantage the ancient imperial planning of that space, to take over to the monument's advantage that mystical current, which, carried along rhythmically from city gate to city gate, goes from the outside world to the Forbidden City, the ideal centre of the universe.[21]

To Leys's lucid description I can add only two points: firstly, besides being an emotional energy field, this monumental space is also a transmitter, a transmitter of information, information coded in the massive redundancy of the symmetrical arrangement and repetition of massive forms.[22] It is a transmitter tuned to the frequencies of monumental time, to the long duration. It is built to last. Secondly, while the CPC may have intended this symmetry as a massive affirmation of its power and culture, it has also created a powerful transmitter for quite other kinds of messages. Its original design tuned it to the frequency of monumental time, but as such it has already been turned into an image of all that it stands for, an image which can be broadcast on the quite different frequency of the media spectacle.

It is this double transmitter that the demonstrators learned to appropriate as a channel for their own messages. Messages that will be transmitted down the long duration of monumental time, the time of martyrdom and memory; but messages that will also be transmitted over the extensive, momentary network of saturation presence.[23] They are playing a double game with the signs and signifying practices of the revolutionary tradition and of a regime that has appropriated that tradition, reinterpreting those signs, turning them over upon themselves, sending them out into other space and forward into the future.

Their demonstration against the policies and practices of the regime took place on exactly the same site as the demonstrations the regime used to organize in its own honor, such as the giant cultural revolution–era rallies, drilled and organized for days in advance.[24] But where serried ranks of Red Guards would line up in front of the reviewing stands built on top of Tiananmen Gate, for quasi-religious ceremonies presided over by Mao Zedong and Lin Biao, the demonstrators of today sit or stand with their backs to the old reviewing stand, facing in the exact opposite direction. Rather than facing the reviewing stand outside of their mass, the demonstrators focus inwards, facing the Monument to the People's Heroes in the center of the square. The leadership of the movement and the hunger strikers clustered around the two-tiered podium of the monument, self-consciously presenting themselves as martyrs in the making. Perhaps unconsciously, the whole composed itself as a televisual image, and given the degree of support, sympathy, and advice some members of the Chinese media gave to some of the students, this may not be entirely accidental. In any case, given the penchant the regime has for organized spectacles, it should not be surprising if a taste and a facility for them has seeped into everyday life. The regime's own spectacular expertise was there on display, for quite other purposes.

Remember 1919

What is one to make of a democracy movement banner which says **HELLO MR DEMOCRACY** in English, but which has, in its top left-hand corner, the logo for Marlboro cigarettes? Marlboro is a popular brand in China, so perhaps the sign is simply a generalizable sign for desire itself. Or perhaps the logo stands for Marlboro country, a talisman for a free space of the imagination.

In such a radically different context, a cigarette ad performs some very odd semiotic functions. It is stripped of its original context and inscribed in another context, yet the traces of its former context can never be entirely removed. They leave a residue. That residue, an awkward agglomeration of connotations, of freedom, the frontier, elemental struggle, now becomes the whole of the sign. This is not a case of a free-floating sign which the demonstrators have simply reversed. Even in the ethereal world of simulation, signs are lined on the inside with weathered layers of association. It is this weary history of seemingly trivial signs that can be the most disturbing aspect of the third nature of vectoral information trajectories. No matter how much the vector accelerates the velocity of the sign flow, it cannot entirely bleach out old meanings.

These canny demonstrators have combined this high-velocity sign with the slightly slower one, Mr Democracy. Mr Democracy and Mr Science walked these streets on 4 May 1919: the day which gives its name to the May 4th Movement. Yet the students of today know that not all of the passions of 4 May can be contained and appropriated by the party. May 4th was, as Arif Dirlik says, a "communications explosion"[25] during which cosmopolitan intellectuals in Beijing and Shanghai started to receive national attention through their journals and papers. Along the vectors of information established by May 4th intellectuals, capitalizing on the news of the violent clash at the square, would travel the thoughts of a provincial anarchist called Mao Zedong.

The urban intellectuals of the May 4th Movement in China became part of international vectors for the communication of ideas, such as they were in the early decades of this century. Liberationist and cosmopolitan, May 4th culture established the vectors along which socialist ideas would travel into China and come to have significant effects—not least of which was the founding of the Chinese Communist Party (CPC) itself. Many May 4th intellectuals saw China in an international perspective, and adopted universalist interpretive categories borrowed from foreign sources, including Marx. This had its problems: "When [Beijing University] radicals made their first foray into Beijing suburbs in the early '20s, armed with a dictionary of popular usage compiled by the anarchist Wu Zhihui, they found it inadequate for communicating with the people."[26] While Beijing and Shanghai had a growing and often militant working class in

1919, in Shanghai's case comparable in size and energy to that which Marx encountered in Paris in 1848, it was not the May 4th Movement toward the cosmopolitan culture and links with the working class that is recalled by the CPC today.

Built on a peasant base and the goal of national liberation, the cultural ambience of May 4th is missing from the CPC regime's articulation of its memory. Indeed, Mao had to forcefully overcome some of the leading ideas of the May 4th era, which sought to break the Confucian dependency of intellectuals upon the state. The idea of intellectuals as independent producers of culture was crushed by Mao in his famous Yanan talks.[27] Intellectuals were returned to a neotraditionalist role in the fold of state paternalism. The revival in 1989 of the 1919 slogan "Hello Mr Democracy" can be seen in this light. The idea of universal suffrage and a Western-style parliament was far from universally held by the 1989 demonstrators. As Anita Chan points out, not many urban intellectuals want to see sovereignty handed over to the 70 percent of the population who are peasants.[28]

Remember 1976

The particular micro-technics of unicorporate power produce quite particular forms of oppositional power. In 1976, the funeral of Zhou Enlai unleashed a demonstration of popular sentiment against the faction then in power, known since their dethronement and trial as the Gang of Four. Presumably for the benefit of American readers, cultural historian Anne Thurston compares the effect of the news of Zhou's death with that of President Kennedy, in the sense that all those old enough to remember can recall what they were doing and how they felt on that day. During the Qing Ming festival the following March, the traditional time for paying homage to the dead, wreaths and eulogies to the dead premier began appearing on the Monument to the People's Heroes in Tiananmen Square.[29]

For urban intellectuals who had suffered and survived during the cruel years of the cultural revolution, Zhou was a symbol of the last line of resistance within the party to the Gang of Four. Whether he deserved their praise and respect is not really the issue. He became the vessel for the demonstration of popular resistance to the Gang of Four as much on the strength of their vain attempt to pass over the death of their old rival in silence. The wreaths that began to appear in Tiananmen Square did so in defiance of the official policy of silence.

After a terse announcement of his passing, radio and television programs continued as scheduled, as if nothing of note had happened. Orders not to mourn the premier were passed down to the work units by telephone. As far as the Gang of Four were concerned, that should have been the end of that. Telephones were for official use, connecting work units to their superiors. Communication was linked vertically, not horizontally. Movement was even more restricted. Visitors to a work unit would have their names, units, and purpose checked and recorded, discouraging casual contacts across work-unit boundaries. Thus the vectors of movement and information were controlled by subordinating horizontal links as much as possible to a vertical system of surveillance and control.

There were, however, exceptions. No matter how much a regime attempts to partition space and regulate the movement of vectors, there will always exist some potential for the accidental contact and circulation of people. Michel de Certeau speaks of the walker in the city of New York, actualizing the spatial possibilities embedded in the granite-hard grid of the city. In this way, the walker "makes them exist as well as emerge. But he also moves them about and invents others, since the crossing, drifting away, or improvisation of walking privilege, transform or abandon spatial elements."[30] The line traced by the walker's steps is always a singular one, always a unique possibility of encounter.

This is fine if you live in a Western city where "walking privilege" is a practice which for some has been won and can be utilized, but in a city where even walking may attract undue scrutiny, a checking of papers and so on, it is not an alternative. Yet while the tactics de Certeau wishes cultural studies to follow in the footsteps of, as it were, are not universal, there are still practices which can be found in each particular organization of space of power. There were always the buses. In a city where industrial development had for the most part taken priority,[31] transport was chronically overcrowded. In the random and anonymous press of bodies on buses, conversations muttered and murmured, exchanging information against the baffling grain of boundaries and constraints. And there was Tiananmen Square: a vast, open symbolic space in the heart of a city of walls. Laying wreaths to Zhou at the monument at its center was a signal that the regime did not control all of the vectors. That signal was heeded, and people began to come from disparate parts of the city.

On 2 April, telephone directives came down to the work units expressly forbidding this, but in this bureaucratic system there is always some degree of interpretive latitude in how a directive is implemented. Some work-unit leaders announced to their subordinates that if they wished to go to the square they had best go there before 8 A.M. on 3 April, as the directive would not be officially read out until then. And so, in the mornings and in the evenings, before and after work, people would gather in the square and lay their wreaths—hundreds of thousands of wreaths! Each would have the name of the unit on it, and this too was a signal, so other units in the square would know who was with them. Poems were composed and declaimed. Relay teams would form to shout the lines on to the edge of the crowd. Their texts were hung from trees for passersby to read. Groups of strangers gathered and sang "The Internationale."

People placed little bottles and vials on the monument. The name of Deng Xiaoping is a homophone for "little bottle." The communication of this pun to the audience in the square signaled the quiet presence of Deng's allies and supporters in this demonstration, ostensibly of grief for the late Premier Zhou Enlai, obviously in opposition to the Gang of Four, and for some at least in support of Deng Xiaoping. Not that it did him much good: the demonstrations were violently crushed on 5 April. Deng was held publicly responsible and was stripped of his posts. No wonder, then, that when the students demonstrating in Tiananmen in 1989 started smashing little bottles, Deng Xiaoping took it personally. The fate of "democracy" movement demonstrations depends very much on the power within the apparatus of the personality who acts as its sponsor—or at least it has until now.

Unicorporate regimes seem to lend themselves perfectly to the ironic mode of writing—and for that matter, demonstrating. Perhaps this is because, for all the cynicism embodied in the "secret pages" as Lu Xun describes them, unicorporate power still rests publicly on an appeal to law. Not law in the sense of statute balanced by case law, but as statute buttressed by the "laws of motion of history," which is to say, law as grand narrative, writ large. Law as embodied, for example, in Tiananmen Square itself. Much of the wit and humor of successive democracy movements lies in exploiting the ironic gap between the cynical imposition of power in the everyday flux of events and the attempts to justify these intersections as the necessary workings of the law of history itself.

Hence, in 1976 the movement hoisted the image of Zhou into the air, an image legitimate in terms of the narrative law, yet one which implied a critique of Zhou's Gang of Four opponents in the world of realpolitik. The Gang of Four responded by crushing the movement on 5 April, and then hoisted Deng on his own petard as a neat way of simultaneously resolving the narrative by turning out the villain and turning events temporarily their way by dispatching a rival. Thus both the pragmatic threat from within and the democratic movement threat from without became "counterrevolutionary." The former suffered demotions, the latter a holiday in jail.

Temporarily, for Deng had regained enough power by 1978 to reverse the line and declare the demonstrations leading up to 5 April "revolutionary." This by implication meant that the Gang of Four were *not* revolutionary, and had to be deposed. Yet while the reversal of the narrative line about the 5 April incident helped Deng combat his rivals within the state, it also provided the sanctity of law for a fresh outbreak of democracy movement demonstrations. This is the trouble with simple narrative structures—they place demands for the symmetry of justice which mere power cannot meet.

Remember 1978

Not surprisingly, the 1978 demonstrations took place in the name of the April 5th Movement. On 26 November, the first issue of *April 5th Forum* was published—neither the first nor the last of the independent "people's papers," painstakingly stenciled and mimeographed, that were distributed at "democracy wall" near a bus shelter in the Tiananmen district.[32] The first issue of another journal, *Enlightenment,* carried a poem which had been pasted on democracy wall that October. It described what Chen Erjin called unicorporation as a "war of spiritual enslavement": "The war goes on in everyone's facial expression. The war is waged by numerous high pitched loudspeakers. The war is waged in every pair of fearful, shifting eyes."[33] Its author was Huang Xiang, a worker from a knitting mill in provincial Guiyang. He was arrested the following March.

While the April 5th Movement of 1978 was able to exploit the problematic application of the workings of narrative law for a brief period, Deng succeeded in routing his opponents and could comfortably dispose of the democracy movement. Yet in the brief interlude where conflict within the unicorporate state led to ambiguity and vacillation in the application of its narrative law, the democracy movement burst forth with a flood of posters, meetings, and publications. Wedging itself into the cracks in the edifice, it spread like weeds and wild grass, along vectors the regime neither authorized nor explicitly denied.

Some at least of the 1978 demonstrators, like their predecessors in 1976, were aware that this gap in the narrative line was temporary. Some took a chance, throwing their lot in with one faction against another, and were rewarded for their contributions to democracy by marginal sinecures on the fringes of the apparatus, or survived in the growing private sector. Others were not so lucky, and opted to oppose not one faction within but the whole apparatus of unicorporate power. For the most part, they ended up in jail. The former opted for a place in official history—so long as their factional masters keep winning. The latter opted for a place in the secret history of negation—hoping that there would be further gaps in the storyline further down the track to revive their memory.

These demonstrations were like relays, public signals of a continuous, hidden process of resistance. The demonstrators seize upon every opportunity to recognize every moment of historical hope and wrest it away from conformism, and they know that if they do not continue to do so, then in Benjamin's words, *not even the dead will be safe.*[34] It is true that the demonstrators mostly take sides within the regime rather than frontally opposing it, and in this sense they are not student radicals in the tradition of the new left, nor are they dissidents of the Eastern European type. There is a long tradition of advice and dissent from within in Chinese intellectual history, not least under the post-Liberation regime, which has always been both dependent on intellectuals as a source of legitimation and contemptuous of them as a class.[35]

The democracy movement may respond with ironic distancing to the narrative law of the state, yet it is far from clear about what to put in its place. A simple and dangerous game with the Western "other" sometimes appears. The irony here lies at a transcultural, international level. While the Western opposition in the '60s admired the revolutionary purity of Mao's Eastern state, the Eastern opposition of the '80s admires the liberal trappings of Western culture. Other strands of the democracy movement seek a reconstruction of the Marxist narrative along more convivial lines. Chen Erjin's work falls under this heading. This kind of work was popular with Western leftist intellectuals for a while, who didn't want to make a radical reassessment of their own involvement with narrative law. Beyond the synchronic move of appealing to the "other place" of the West, and the diachronic move of rewriting the temporal order, more radical strands of the democracy movement wrestle with the complex and dangerous nature of these events, and the new avenues they open up. Lu Xun would perhaps have admired this latter camp: "Rather than discussing how to reach the future, it seems to me that we ought to think first about the present. Even if the present is desperately dark, I do not wish to leave it. Will the future be free from darkness? We'll talk about that tomorrow. Meanwhile, let us busy ourselves with transforming today."

Forget 1968

"It is an embarrassment," says Greil Marcus, "listening to these stories and these cries, these utopian cheers and laments, because the utopian is measured always by its failure, and failure, in our historiography, is shame."[36] Marcus is writing about the dustbin of history and those scholars and writers, including me, who dive into it. History, he says, "creates its own refugees." The newspaper reports and newsreels push certain realms of barely describable experience to the margins. The experience of the utopian moment, in particular, is left in the trim bins of documentary history. When these other stories, these other cries, break into the seamless montage of history as we know it after the event, they declare their otherness in advance, and their failures past.

Marcus goes on, "There is no special gathering place, not even in historical hell, for the denizens of history's true dustbin; it is a wasteland in which all are distant from each other, because this is a territory, unlike history, without any borders at all—without any means to narrative, a language with which to tell a story." What is missing from this picture? Marcus writes as if the experience of the otherness of an insurrectionary event were always a privatized experience, as if it were not shared by many, passing through the communicating vessels of everyday life. This motif of a solitary, speechless remembrance gives Marcus's essay a melancholy tone of alienated tragedy. Keeping that tone in mind, one can see why Marcus responds the way he does to some lines of mine about Tiananmen that he quotes. Here are those lines, which I wrote on 4 June 1989—a little less selectively edited.

"Taut images from this wild scenario will now always be present, ready and waiting to be replayed, over and over. I try to capture some of the densely pixelated images that are present here and now, reeling between the lines.

". . . This remarkable series of events will be recorded in a much longer, subterranean history. Zhao Ziyang may soon be airbrushed out of official history, but he has become a people's hero, alongside Zhou Enlai and Hu Yaobang. So too have the hunger strikers. They have joined Wei Jingsheng and many, many others in jail—or worse. Yet this event will relay into the future the whole hidden culture of revolt and resistance that are the uncontrollable connotations of the revolutionary heritage the CPC claims as its legitimating moral force.

"It probably all makes sense now. It didn't then, that's for sure. Beware of the smooth surface of history, looking backwards, making everything make sense. It made no sense at the time, like a random series of jump cuts. Indeed, like all insurrections, this one stood outside of time for a moment, hoping to catch hold of a different current, hoping to rise above the flux, hoping whoever or whatever edits history plumps for the right cut. You can still feel this other temporality, this futile hope in the video footage. At least video can now preserve history with all its jagged edges—if we choose to edit it that way for ourselves."[37]

Asks Marcus, "But what is this subterranean history? It is today, little more than a jumble of rumors about the past." Well, perhaps, but Beijing has a reservoir not only of memory, but also of feeling. I thought of Greil when I read an essay by Nicholas Jose about Beijing after the crackdown. Near Zhongnanhai there's a nightclub, and a few months after 4 June, a band called "1989, I Love You" plays '60s classics. It's obligatory to conclude the gig with a patriotic song, so "they turned 'Without the Communist Party There'd Be No New China' into a weird, cacophonous twenty-minute improvisation that could be interpreted as a musical reenactment of events still imprinted on everyone's mind. It was electrifying. Nothing was said, and nothing needed to be said."[38] A little exercise in applied Hendrix, wiring together an affective alliance for the future out of supercharged metal. Memory lies in waiting, waiting for the current to pass through it once again.

In the context of a fresh event, the jumble of rumor quickly polarizes along the lines of magnetic force coursing through the event, like iron filings on a magnet the moment the power switch flips. This jumble of rumors is not just the property of those who were there, either. It is a collective memory, stored away in the stories told and retold in everyday life. Were it not so, then Tiananmen could never have happened in the first place. It did not fall from the sky, it arose in part out of popular memory of events past. Not just events in China itself, either. A popular memory jumbled up with all kinds of images, an aphasic lexicon of longings. In it were the state of liberty, "The Internationale," the May 4th Movement: memories waiting to be charged with a reason for existence.

Marcus finds my essay on Tiananmen "interspersed with the notion, which the writer seems unable to suppress in spite of himself, that this was just a movie. It scans like one, like an entertainment. But the discontinuities of the dustbin are lived, not watched." By who, Greil? Who lives them? Who watches them? The people who were there, they live them. You and I, Greil, we watched them—on TV, in the newspapers, on the radio. This is the eerie experience of telesthesia, of perception at a distance. It is not entirely an anaesthesia. We are not entirely drugged to indifference by watching the tanks roll in, listening to Chai Ling's thin reed of a voice rustling, "I am still alive." No, we are charged with a duty of sorts, to remember. To keep these stray iron filings, these seeds of magnetic fire, stored in memory for the future.

This is a contemporary development, a post-'68 development. The vector now spreads the image of weird insurrectionary events around the globe in a way unthinkable even twenty years ago. There's a nice image in James Miller's book on Foucault of the May '68 events in Paris, which happened while Foucault was out of town. Daniel Defert, Foucault's lover, "called Foucault in Tunis, told him what was happening—and then placed the telephone next to a radio. Like much of the French nation, Foucault thus followed the pitched battle over the airwaves."[39] On the one hand there is something quaint about this, the improvised vector, the lousy reception. On the other it points toward the present, our present. These days, he would be watching on CNN.

There is a history to the subterranean memory of those unspeakable moments, outside of historical time. They are a form of experiencing a connection with history which itself has a history. As Georg Lukács remarks, at about the time Napoleon marched through the Brandenburg Gate, war made history a mass experience. "The extraordinary quantitative expansion of war plays a qualitatively new role, bringing with it an extraordinary broadening of horizons."[40] War in turn begat the development of the vectors of movement and communication.[41] The former development creates a mass involvement and direct experience of the event as history, and of the event as something partly recuperated by the writing of history and partly excluded from it. The second development, the development of the vectors of communication, is something else. The whole possibility of a satellite television transmission, of lightweight CCD cameras, of transmitting video down a phone line belongs to a regime of developments which are also military in origin, but which here serve a civil purpose. It makes possible a memory of the event beyond its experience. A memory which comes in the form of entertainment. I was not trying to suppress, but to express the antinomies of the transmission of the inexpressible via the vector.

Whereas René Char may have thought he "found himself" in the experience of the Resistance, now we mask the memory of the utopian experience as mere stories, but stories which, like Brecht's "teaching plays," are an entertainment which presupposes the possibility of the sound of a different ending. It falls to us to remember and retell these stories, and indeed Marcus has provided an exemplary recording and recounting of these secret histories in his book *Lipstick Traces*.[42]

There is a gathering place for Marcus's refugees from history, in the practices of everyday life, where, as Michel de Certeau shows, people store tactics away in the form of stories. Traced across the spaces surveyed by disciplinary regimes is the spider's web of popular memory. As de Certeau says of memory and its economical condensation of the refuse of history, "Far from being a reliquary or trash can of the past, it sustains itself by believing in the existence of possibilities and by vigilantly awaiting them, constantly on the watch for their appearance."[43] Only memory, this "sense of the other," now has quite other materials to work on than direct experience of the event. It has the experience of the vector. The spider's web of popular tactics of memory and story may connect up to a wider web of vectors, traversing the partitioned space and measured time of disciplinary society.

Rather than a melancholy invocation of the tragedy of the voiceless, it may be better in the age of CNN to find ways to turn the simulacrum of the event into memories of utopian quiverings, outside of history and thus not trapped in the past. Outside of time, and thus a reservoir for the future.

Remember 2000

> Listen, I call you all. Show your cards all players. Pay it all pay it all pay it all back. Play it all play it all play it all back. For all to see. In Times Square. In Piccadilly.
>
> —William Burroughs

As I write this, there are some nervous officials in Beijing, China, and my home town of Sydney, Australia, waiting for what to them is a very important decision to be made. The International Olympic Committee has before it bids to hold the Olympic Games in the year 2000 from Istanbul, Manchester, Berlin, Beijing, and Sydney. Sydney, I can tell you, is in it for the money. It's part of the local poker-machine mentality about economic development: gambling 29 million Australian dollars on winning the Olympics is the developmental equivalent of putting your wages into one of the one-armed bandit poker machines in any licensed club in Sydney, hoping to hit the jackpot. Beijing, on the other hand, might be in this just as much for the political capital it might generate. The last time world media attention connected its vectors to the Chinese capital, it left a bad taste in our mouths. With the usual market Stalinist mix of bureaucratic planning and corporate deal-making, they hope to attract our attention again and this time get it right.

There is, of course, the danger in this that it will turn out like the Olympic Games in Seoul, but that's a risk the regime seems willing to run. At the very least, human-rights lobby pressure on China is increasing, although the release of democracy movement prisoners seems a long way off. If the regime is so confident about repressing the possibility of a democracy movement resurgence in Beijing in 2000, that's gloomy news, but we can at least speculate on what lessons from the past movements might contribute to a more enlightened future, particularly in terms of the effective use of the media vector.

Beijing student demonstrations sometimes take on the appearance of a global positive feedback loop: a few thousand students demonstrate at Tiananmen; foreign journalists report it; Voice of America radio relays that report and amplifies it, saying that hundreds of thousands of students demonstrated; students pick up the broadcast, and while many of them are suspicious of the American versions of the event, it rings truer than the Chinese press reports, so it becomes a self-fulfilling prophecy. The American disinformation is at least less boring than the official Chinese disinformation.

That, in a simplified, stylized form, is pretty much what happened in 1987, when the anniversary of the death of Zhou Enlai became the pretext for students to lay wreaths at the Monument to the People's Heroes in Tiananmen Square, and demonstrations snowballed vainly and bravely until the police stepped in. "Even if these disturbances had been more widespread," Deng Xiaoping told Japanese political boss Takeshita Noboru shortly afterwards, "they would have no effect on the foundations of our state or on the policies we have established."[44] That may be so. Nevertheless, the long-term effects of the integration of the spatial and political orders which structure Beijing life with contemporary global information technologies are still unclear. The 1989 democracy movement demonstrators sometimes composed themselves as specifically televisual images.

Even Chai Ling, often imagined to be the very epitome of authenticity. Hong Kong journalist Jimmy Ngai recounts a story of an exhausted Chai Ling turning up at a hotel for an interview. "In front of the lens, Chai's fighting spirits returned. She gesticulated boldly as she spoke, trying to communicate with the rest of the world."[45] In another interview, for foreign consumption only, Chai gives her "only when the square is washed in blood will the people wake up" speech. Then she pauses. "How can I say such things? The students are so young. I feel responsible for them."[46] I am not saying that Chai Ling was duplicitous or conniving, merely that the connection to the "other space" via the vector creates a sense of projection within you when you are confronted with it and with the other context, somewhere else, it reaches. The proliferation of the vector creates an ever-deepening sense of a playing to an elsewhere. This is a cultural facility that has to be learned, and it is far more advanced in some media environments than others. When American cops appear on TV, they have the "Dirty Harry" walk down pat. When Chinese students appear on international TV, they don't yet have as full an awareness of it and what it can do, but in 1989 this familiarity with this other terrain seemed to increase markedly.

To the extent that the students sometimes turned the movement into a spectacle, making it flow outwards along the lines of the Western media, they could overcome, just a little, the barriers and obstacles placed in the way of the dissemination of information, and hence eventually of memory, by the unicorporate monopoly of the vector. One of the things they had on their side is that the square itself is already a site in the international lexicon of vectoral sites for events of one kind or another.

While the party may have intended the symmetry of Tiananmen Square as a massive affirmation of its power and culture, it has also created a powerful transmitter for quite other kinds of messages. Its original design tuned it to the frequency of monumental time, but as such it has already been turned into an image of all that it stands for, an image which can be broadcast on the quite different frequency of the media spectacle. It is this double transmitter that the democracy movement has now learned how to appropriate as a channel for its own messages. Messages transmitted down the long duration of monumental time, the time of martyrdom and memory; but messages also transmitted now over the extensive, momentary network of saturation presence. They play a double game with the storylines of the revolutionary tradition and of a regime that has appropriated that tradition, reinterpreting those storylines, turning them over upon themselves, sending them out into other space and forward into the future.

In the monumental arrangement of the Tiananmen site and the spatial configuration of bureaucratic power, one finds the monstrous traces of the insomnia of a certain modern form of reason. This is the ratio of the boundary, the partition, the hierarchy, the classification, the grid, the order. Yet alongside the process of modernization, routinization, bureaucratization, jargonization, quite other, less orderly developments have always taken place. Beijing may look like the spatial realization of the iron cage, yet it too feels the effect of the silicon trajectory. Nothing guarantees that information technologies will coincide with a logic of rhizomatic openness, but a certain curious alignment of events opened a vector of opportunity in Beijing where it might be so.[47]

The presence of the Western media in Beijing for the Deng-Gorbachev summit provided a window of opportunity for the democracy movement too good to miss. The world press had turned its attention to Beijing. Two American broadcasters, CBS and CNN, had even set up their own satellite uplinks for live broadcasts of the summit, under contractual arrangements with the government.[48] Here was an opportunity to experiment with the media feedback loop connecting Tiananmen Square to the living rooms of millions around the globe, including policymakers who considered Deng a liberal, and the kind of "opinion leaders" who made him "Time Man of the Year" in 1985.

So with the city full of senior correspondents and camera crews, the students unwittingly stole a pre-prepared set from the government. They appropriated potential for Tiananmen Square to become a giant information transmitter on a massive scale, and the networks were there to broadcast it live to the world. The government intended Gorbachev to lay a wreath at the Monument to the People's Heroes in Tiananmen Square. The students just stole the show.[49] The regime assumed the square was theirs, but in vectoral terms it is not. It belongs to anyone who can claim it. It belongs also to the vector itself, and to us who are its children. It is a site imprinted by the vector in our minds.

The regime invited the media in to exploit their power to make news and the power of the square. They intended putting a new message about the state of superpower relations out over the global media vector. But while it is true that there is a screening process involved in getting something past the gatekeepers who broker the vector, there are many kinds of power one can use there as a calling card. There is the power *in* the image, and there is the power *of* the image. Power in the image: Deng and Gorbachev sitting down to lunch. Power of the image: students—kids just like yours, starving themselves. Does that make you feel concern? Or a mite hungry? Either way it's a powerful image, although not an image of power. This is a picture of an ordinary kid. These are the doctors rushing him to hospital. Powerful images work by using the vector to convey not the abstraction of power, but the power of physical sensation or emotional affect.

The vector of information from Tiananmen Square to the world carried as its storyline not Gorbachev and his wreath, but hunger strikers and slogans. They stole the spectacle and made it their own. The CPC opened this information circuit for their own purposes. The students just discovered how to appropriate it; how to piggyback their line out with the other signals. In the initial weeks of the demonstration, the CPC discovered that by inviting in the foreign media to set up international satellite datalinks, it had set up a logic bomb for itself: the instant relay of video signals became the vector along which the politics of dissent could travel, in the place of the politics of statist diplomacy.

This vector of information from Tiananmen Square to the world was relayed straight back again via informal fax networks over the long-distance phone lines and on shortwave radio services, contributing to other demonstrations elsewhere in the country. Meanwhile, in Beijing, foreign journalists became heroes, constantly asked for news updates from their wire service machines in the foreigners' compound on the outskirts of the city. Suddenly Beijing was as plugged in to the international information network as it was possible to be. No longer could repression be carried out behind a screen of silence.

The democracy movement discovered the difference between the spatial metaphysic inscribed in unicorporate organization and that implied by the vectors of televisual information, and began an experiment in exploiting that difference to their own ends. When considered from the point of view of unicorporate power, Beijing is a city which favors *enclosure;* Beijing presents itself as something static, monumental. One thinks of the most familiar forms of representation of the city: the map, the plan, the elevation. One thinks of an aerial outline of architectural elements, arranged in space. When considered from the point of view of the trajectories of information, Beijing appears as a system of *openings*. One thinks not of discrete entities in space, but of relational pathways, circuits, frequencies, *interruptions.*[50] The architectural space of the unicorporate state has been invaded by the technological time of contemporary Western media.

As one might expect, the democracy movement as the Western media presented it and the democracy movement as it worked itself out on the streets of Beijing were two quite separate stories. Far from being a revival of the universal values which the Western enlightenment once aspired to, much of the propaganda lines of the demonstrators reveal ironic and cynical impulses. Some occasionally seemed to address their democratic rhetoric—written and sung in English—to an American television audience. Some of the students have watched enough TV to have an everyday grasp of media skills.

Others prefer to double the line of the regime's rhetoric back at itself, by taking the stories of martyrdom, socialism, sacrifice and enacting them, dwelling in the abyss between sign and referent. Others prefer to make the storylines of socialism resonate, to make their inner cavities sing, their hollowness manifest. Either way, this is the payback, in Tiananmen Square, in Piccadilly, for repressing the autonomous growth of self-representation, for repressing the organic development of the abstract vectors needed for an increasingly complex field of social production. The unicorporate culture hollows out, becomes ever more ironic, the tiny displacements of value in everyday life reaching higher and higher up the baffled layers of command and communication. By the year 2000, who knows?

A New Space of Memory

The development of the ever more densely knotted mass of noodles that is the vector field not only provides an elsewhere to project an image toward; it also generates images of and from elsewheres that can become part of one's reservoir of tactics. The spaces we operate on and recall operations on is increasingly a doubled one: the space of everyday life, at the site where we live; the space of telesthesia, the elsewhere at a distance. The lines of the latter increasingly weave their way into the contours of the former, like soft wet noodles stirred into everyday broth. And on exceptional occasions the reverse may apply, and our site where we live our workaday lives may end up hurtling over the vector, into the mind's eye of others we shall never know: our unknown neighbors under a television sky.

For example, take the way Gorbachev appeared in Beijing. Not the "real" Gorbachev, not the man himself, but that other Gorbachev, the one that walks the ether of telesthesia. This Gorbachev was a bit of a hero to some of the students. They were aware, one way or another, of the Gorbachev who wrote: "Reason and conscience are beginning to win back ground from the passiveness and indifference that were eroding hearts. Naturally, it is not enough to know and to tell the truth. Acting on the knowledge of the truth and of understanding it is the main thing."[51] This Gorbachev spoke of the kind of process some students want for their own country, a process in which the intellectuals can ally themselves with the reformist elements of the party. So this Gorbachev was there for them. A Gorbachev in memory, in the mind's eye. A Gorbachev from the silver-lined clouds of a television sky. A Gorbachev of fine words widely distributed, rather than a Gorbachev of murky backroom party deals, unseen in far-off Moscow. That's another site, another problem. None of that figures in third nature, in our TV eye, our virtual geography.

The students may not have been aware of some of the other Gorbachevs: the weak, vacillating Gorbachev; the tough, uncompromising apparatchik Gorbachev, or the Gorbachev that Enzenberger described as the "hero of retreat."[52] Given that they were more likely to know Gorbachev via Western media sources than local ones, this fascination was quite understandable. The Western media at that time couldn't get enough of Gorbachev. They were at the height of their fascination. He was both the image of power and a powerful image: he walked in Stalin's shoes, yet he presented enough everyday detail to appear in the Western media as a Gorbachev, not just as the general secretary.

The quite remarkable media politics Gorbachev's office practiced at the time had much wider effects than either his handlers or the Western media brokers intended, most notably in the Tiananmen Square demonstrations and in the fall of the Berlin Wall. The spectacle of the Russian leader, from Stalin to Gorbachev, had always been an image of supreme and sublime significance in a globalizing media vector field overdetermined by the narrative structure of the cold war. As that narrative fabric unraveled, mostly as an initiative of a carefully stage-managed Gorbachev spectacle, very diverse interests and groups in many locations seized upon the image and used it as a weapon. In the end, then, many Gorbachevs being wielded by diverse groups in the eastern bloc, in the United States, in Europe, in China, were barely compatible with each other, fostering many narrative crises in the media. The quite local and reactive politics of Gorbachev's attempted management of perestroika all too often conflicted with the narrative necessities his image was obliged to play to abroad.

There are other foreign sources the students appropriated: a visual style along the lines of the old new left, with its flowers and peace signs. Commodity fetishism: revolutionaries in shades and Nikes. The revolutionary tradition of American democracy: Shanghai students built a three-meter-high model of the Statue of Liberty and paraded it before the party offices. The headbands with slogans appear to have been an idea borrowed from Korean student demonstrations. CCTV broadcast images of the Korean student movement's Molotov street parties during the Olympics, presumably as an indication that all was not well in the much-vaunted Confucian capitalist paradise.

In short, native traditions and symbols of dissent were retriggered and mixed with foreign signs and practices that the students found useful. The resources of dissent in a global information network are themselves global. Which is probably why the Burmese military junta blacked out foreign news altogether during the democracy movement. They have enough trouble with students and popular rebellion without the vector feeding in fresh ideas. They are not about to go opening any doors. Honecker tried the same thing, maintaining a media enclosure on the issue, with considerably less success. Watching the Beijing events on West German television, a Leipzig clergyman observed that "although people were afraid, they were also filled with hope."[53]

The Open Doors of Disinformation

The "open door" policy Deng initiated ten years ago brought in foreign investment, technology, and tourism but brought with it new vectors of foreign culture and information. The campaigns against "spiritual pollution" and "bourgeois liberalization" in the late '80s were a stale line, a feeble attempt to keep the cultural and political vectors closed and the economic and technical vectors open. But as an old saying has it, a door is either open or closed. Deng's door tried, like Duchamp's, to be simultaneously open *and* closed, but with less success.

In any case, China has long been a permeable membrane for foreign ideas coming from shortwave radio broadcasts. BBC World Service, Voice of America, and Radio Australia are all popular sources of news and information about the outside world and about China itself. While the party circulates its *Digest of Foreign News*—one of the biggest-circulation newspapers in the world—only within the party, it cannot control the information available on foreign radio.

During the crisis, more or less accurate reports of demonstrations by sympathetic journalists had to be allowed in Chinese papers and broadcasts, not least because to not report such events would seriously compromise the credibility of the press, when foreign sources are readily available. The openness to the flow of foreign information weakens the central control over the flow of domestic information.

In saying this, one does not have to subscribe to the myth that the Western press is open and free and reports the facts, while the Chinese press is monolithically totalitarian and false. The difference is palpable but may not be quite so simple. It is perhaps more accurate to say that they are quite different systems of disinformation. Disinformation is the process by which more or less random events are articulated together and given form within the overarching narrative structures which organize media flows. Disinformation gives form to the event, and thereby does a disservice to its more nebulous, elusive qualities, but is in a certain sense and at a certain level essential. If you will pardon a somewhat Socratic digression, I want to amplify this rhetorically, so that we can consider this problem of disinformation from another angle to the usual one where it is assumed that disinformation is somehow an unnecessary and immoral impurity that has to be eliminated from the telling of the truth, the whole truth, and nothing but the truth.[54]

All representations are necessarily false. Say you are in a room watching television with Gorbachev, and Gorbachev comes on the TV. You turn to Gorbachev, sitting on the couch next to you, and say, "Hey, it's you there on the TV!" You wouldn't get the Gorbachev on TV and the Gorbachev on the couch mixed up. A TV picture of Gorbachev might be the same color and shape and move the same way, but it's flat and grainy. At some level the image is false. At some level it ceases to be like Gorbachev. Let's say you and your pal Gorbachev go and check out the wonders of the new virtual reality media at the museum, and there in virtual reality is an image of Gorbachev. You shout out to Gorbachev, "Hey, there's a 3-D image of you in here! Check it out!" You still don't confuse it with Gorbachev, because it might be in 3-D and it might move, but it's bumpy and jerky—not like Gorbachev.

But then say you walk into a room and there are two Gorbachevs. Somebody cloned him! An exact replica—but which one is which? You can't tell. This is no longer a Gorbachev and an image of Gorbachev. Now there are *two* Gorbachevs. In the absence of the falsifying flaw, the simulacrum ceases to be a simulacrum and becomes something else. It lacks the trace of disinformation which authenticates it as an image, a representation. Now, this disinformation is usually highly formalized if it is meant for transmission and consumption as flow, along the vector. It is neither random nor artistically singular. It is formal and repetitive. But there are different kinds of formal lexicon by which disinformation can be made to carry information, and there are different gatekeeping procedures for screening raw perception and fitting it to the formal properties of disinformation that are assigned to carry it into the flow.

Disinformation is the narrative artifice which is the necessary medium of perception, the abstraction into another world which makes communication along a vector possible. Disinformation is what opens the door to the communication of perception—it is perception's condition of possibility on the terrain of the vector. But there are different ways of brokering the relation between what is perceived of our everyday environment—second nature—and the medium it will pass into—third nature. In the West, vector-brokers put a premium on speed. Unusual incidents, scheduled spectacles, and events are all stuffed into narrative frameworks as quickly as possible. Hence the narratives tend to be temporary affairs, if no less infused with hegemonic stories for all that.

On the other hand, where the state has a monopoly on news, there may be no such premium on speed. In China, it is quite common for the presentation of news to lag behind its occurrence. Chinese television delayed the reporting of the events in Tiananmen Square for several days. While this may help the vector-brokers craft elaborate narrative strategies, it does tend to undermine the credibility of new ones, particularly when alternative news sources such as foreign radio are available.[55]

Now, raw perception is always grafted into the medium of disinformation in such a way that any radical alterity and immediacy is necessarily left behind. The world has to appear *for us* in third nature. But there are a number of different types of narrative disinformation it could be shaped to fit: the singular, the typical, and the ideal.[56] A singular narrative exists only to convey *this* experience, although it is drawn from a repertoire of narrative forms. A typical narrative fits the experience into one of a number of types which are predetermined narrative forms. These can, however, change if enough cases turn up which don't fit the type. The ideal narrative always shapes the experience to fit predetermined narratives which are always "correct," and determined independently of experience. While these are hardly unknown in Western culture, the typical mode is the pragmatic but limiting form of disinformation of most journalism. The ideal form is more typical of unicorporate inflexibility. The singular is a rare form of communication, where the lines of narrative form are rethought for each and every perception.

The three forms correspond loosely to three kinds of vector-brokering: those where a political apparatchik monitors the flow according to ideal conventions (quite compatible with power pragmatics); those where an editor answerable for the economic viability of the vector applies typical standards, negotiating between the reliability of the media "product" and the production of novelty; those where the producer is autonomous and creates the vector to suit the experience—or where media practice becomes a marginal and radical art. This book aspires to the singular, to a reconstruction of form in relation to particular experiences—although I wouldn't claim to have achieved any such thing.

The CPC operates a dual media system, composed of a mass broadcast and publishing system for the "masses" and a restricted vector field of media outlets, supposedly available only to the political elite. The ideal form of narrative disinformation is more typical of the public media system; the internal system ideally operates more with the formal codes of the typical. Part of the problem with the dual system is that everyone *knows* there is a dual system. Even people who don't have access to the restricted outlets know such information exists, and this knowledge is enough to undermine the credibility of the mass-media presentations. People know that the "model worker" propaganda and other harmless stuff in the mass media has a double, somewhere. When people are armed with this knowledge that other knowledge exists, resistant or negotiated readings of mass media are not uncommon. The audience goes looking for the grains of experience captured in the lugubrious sludge of ideal form.

Another aspect of the politics of the media in the People's Republic is the relative absence of images of the leadership. In stark contrast to the massive presence of Saddam Hussein in Iraqi media, the Chinese leadership exert power through their absence. As might be expected, this can increase their aura in the popular imagination. It does not, however, prevent popular suspicions and paranoias. Shortly after the 4 June crackdown, rumors circulated wildly in Beijing that Deng Xiaoping was dead. Ideally, of course, he should have been. That was from everyone else's point of view what the story demanded, considered as an ideal form. The facts, however, didn't fit that particular popular version of the ideal storytelling form.

On the rare occasions when you see China's elite officials on television, it makes you thankful that they don't appear too often. They have no style. There is not a terribly sophisticated knowledge of how to present the image of political leadership in the mass media. Indeed, the whole feedback loop between audiences and the media vector is somewhat underdeveloped. Since it does not operate on the formal code of the typical, there is not that constant process of examining the categories of the typical into which experience is classified. Ideal forms of narrative disinformation make experience as a whole conform to the categories, not vice versa. CCTV relies on letters from viewers and focus-group research for feedback on programming, and the latter is still a reasonably recent innovation.

There are not the resources within second nature to fully support the formal categories of the typical. In a country where the private telephone system is relatively undeveloped, it is impossible to poll sample radio or television audiences directly and quickly. Hence knowledge of what works and doesn't work in the media is hardly the sophisticated discourse it is in some Western countries.[57] In China, the third nature of vectoral flows and institutions to manage such flows is in an underdeveloped state, and so too is the effective political use of such a mapping of the social.

The problem this creates is a lack of feedback—perception reshapes the ideal categories only after a total collapse of their functioning, like the fall of the Gang of Four and the end of Maoist dogma. The change in ideal categories takes the violent form of the exposure of the leader vector-brokers themselves, their denunciation and even imprisonment. One cannot simply change the categories to a shift in the evidence, since the categories have priority over the evidence. The regime has to accuse the brokers of the old categories of some heinous ideological crime—as defined by the new categories.

This presents serious problems for democracy movement activists, who vacillate between two strategies. One is attempting to force a change in the ideal categories through barracking for the leading faction within the state with the power to remove the old vector-brokers and install the new ideal forms. The other is in changing the organization of the vector altogether: abandoning the ideal form and defusing the assessment of perception by making it merely a process of applying more flexible and contestable types of narrative category.

The open door policy has meant that the underdeveloped, unicorporate monopoly form of the vector in China, where officials massage perceptions into the ideal form of disinformation, has had to confront media vectors of a more developed kind. Foreign information might have some appeal simply in its difference from the opaque wallpaper of Chinese media, but that in itself does not guarantee much of an audience for the international vectors. The American, British, and Australian radio sources, for example, seem to be popular as much as a way of learning English as an alternative news source.

Taiwanese propaganda, which for many years provided an equal but opposite wall of opaque propaganda narrated in the ideal form, subsequently changed tack in a bid to increase its audience. Since the June 9th incident, the Taipei-based Broadcasting Corporation of China, a Nationalist station, has tried a different route into the hearts and minds of mainlanders. The station has regular game shows offering prizes to mainland listeners including motorbikes, microwaves, television sets, and refrigerators. The winners are announced by family name and city only, which is supposed to prevent the CPC authorities from confiscating the prizes. The prizes are collectable through Hong Kong. The station also offers breezy programming, including reports on the gyrations of the Taipei stock exchange and on its ever-congested traffic.

The capitalist "good life" is here insinuated into the programming through everyday, quotidian details of excess. Traffic jams and stock market slumps are supposedly problems mainlanders wish they had. While it is difficult to judge the impact of such a program, it is worth noting that Radio Beijing has responded with game shows of its own.[58] Radio makes possible a transgression of territorial barriers, but ideological barriers within propagandistic radio are still a barrier to articulating any kind of popular sentiment. Were both competing stations to dismantle their ideological ramparts and compete as vectors for subjective allegiance, the battle between the CPC and the Nationalists would become quite a different kind of conflict, basing its appeals on individual rather than collective or national desires, a politics of everyday life organizing its mass appeal through the typification of desires and stories.

Different regimes of disinformation misapply quite different narrative forms in quite different ways. In the People's Republic, the ideal form is complex, but is neatly summed up in a set of four affirmative principles and a set of four negative ones. The affirmative principles are called the four modernizations: the modernization of the army, education, technology, and industry. The mass media present events in each of these fields only after being disinformed by the narrative of modernization, as understood for each of these four domains.

The negative ideal principles disinform by excluding from the public sphere statements which do not conform to certain narrative guidelines. The first two cardinal principles require that media discourse acknowledge the leading role of the party and the principles of Marxism-Leninism. The second pair of ideal principles are that media discourse must also adopt a narrative form which does not conflict with the road to socialism and the dictatorship of the proletariat. The first two of these negative constraints protect the synchronic aspect of the regime of disinformation. The party and Marxism are the sources of authority which ground the narrative in the present moment. The latter two are broadly diachronic. The socialist road and the present stage on that road, the dictatorship of the proletariat, are points along the temporal axis of the narrative structure.

The point about this regime of disinformation is that while it applies narrative tools broadly familiar from our own experience of the media, it is strikingly different in operation. In Western experience, the complexity and differentiation of second nature proceed apace (this is what we call modernity) and the volume and velocity of information in circulation increase along with it, yet in an exponential fashion (this we experience as postmodernity). The net effect, as Lyotard describes it, is an inability of what he calls "grand narratives," or what I would call ideal regimes of disinformation, to cope.[59] A certain complexity and skepticism about ideal regimes of disinformation which inform media discourse is the precipitate of this process. Events appear less predictable, more confusing as a result.

In China, the process is quite different. The complexity and differentiation of second nature certainly proceed. This is the aim and purpose of the four modernizations. Yet the proliferation of information is kept in check by the more or less rigid imposition of an ideal regime of disinformation. Events are compelled to appear in the guise of modernization, or are excluded by the negative constraints of the four cardinal principles. Hence there is the noisy anxiety and confusion produced by an unenforced regime of disinformation, and there is the myopia and repetition of an enforced one. Either way, events are compelled to yield to stories which they never knew they had within them.

Since the open door opened, and particularly since 1989, the remarkable thing has been the exposure of these two different systems of disinformation to each other. It is not the veracity or accuracy of the Western press that matters, but its presence and its difference. Even if one were to assert that the Western reporting on China was entirely false and misleading, it is nevertheless true that an alternative channel of false information, disinformed in a novel way, can be just as powerful a weapon.

In the Chinese regime of disinformation, modernization has shaken the certainty of the ideal diachronic storyline. Even Deng Xiaoping appears not to know what socialism is anymore: "Our basic goal, to build socialism is correct, but we are still trying to figure out what socialism is and how to build it."[60] A certain complexity in trying to fit events onto the diachronic axis of the regime of disinformation has led to a compensatory strengthening of emphasis on the synchronic axis. Hence the violence of the response to the democracy movement, and not just a physical violence.

The power of the media in an event such as the 1989 democracy movement lies in the connective lines it opens between points in an information loop, not in the ultimate foundation of that loop in a referent event and space outside of the circuit. The *occupation of time on the information network* becomes the first principle of this aspect of struggle, and the *occupation of space in the symbolic landscape* is merely a means to that end. One occupies the latter space with bodies and the former with disembodied signs. The referents of those signs can matter as little as the motivations of those bodies.

In politics, it is the *effect* which counts, not the intentional objective or the referential object—and in the emergent space of the global media vector, some strange effects result from the most futile of gestures. I want next to return to a very particular gesture, and work back from there to the outline of a more abstract kind of story.

In the Bag

A man stands in front of a column of tanks. The lead tank stops, then starts, then stops again. The tank and the man do the two-step, jiving backwards and forwards, neither willing to enact their roles with any strong degree of finality. The man does not really want to sacrifice his life to stop a tank. The tank commander does not really want to run him over in pursuit of his duty. For a moment, then, this *danse macabre,* performed in all innocence for the cameras.

Where does it all end? For the tank commander, disciplinary action. For his dancing partner, jail. Meanwhile the image of their strange encounter now stands as a metonym for the whole affair. I cannot watch this videotape routine anymore without focusing, even more metonymically, on the shopping bag the man holds in his hand. What was in that shopping bag? If the whole image of this insane dance now has to carry the whole weight and freight of meaning produced by the Tiananmen Square events, it must be a very strong bag. In looking at the image, we ask, What does it all mean? What sense is carried by this image? I look at the shopping bag, and I ask, What is in the bag? What does it carry? The fact that this second question seems ridiculous makes me hit the pause button. It is ridiculous to ask what this man dancing with power, with death, is carrying in his shopping bag. It is just as ridiculous to ask what the larger envelope of the image itself is carrying as the freight of meaning.

Rather than ask what is in the bag, better to ask what the bag itself does. A shopping bag carries things from one place to another. The man with the shopping bag carries we know not what from one place to another. An image carries things from one place to another. An image is a displacement, literally a changing of place, of we know not what from one place to another. I don't know what sense the image of the man and the tank ultimately conveys. I do know that it is an image worth perpetuating, worth keeping in circulation.

Rather than look at the image and try to unpack it, it may sometimes be just as useful to look at the image and figure out how to utilize it. Not looking and theorizing images, but experiencing and using them. Images, like shopping bags, are ready-made tools. Here they are, in the interzone, the man with the bag and the dancing tank. In a very special sense, images are the only tools we have in this world that are both ready-made and also ready to hand. The world of objects is vast and complicated and beyond my control; the world of images is vast and complicated, but at least I can make what I want out of them. We do not experience the world anymore in the guise of things that are ready to hand, as Heidegger might say.

Nor is the world present itself as a profusion of commodities, as Marx famously put it. Rather, "life presents itself as an immense accumulation of spectacles. Everything that was directly lived has moved away into a representation."[61] As Guy Debord suggests, our experience of everyday life shifts from being to having to seeing. Or as Baudrillard rephrases it, from use to exchange to sign value.[62] Here, in the interzone of everyday experience, buzzes a restless spectacle of stories and images, borne of the proliferating vectors and teeming archives of larval data.

The more these images proliferate, the more useless it seems to theorize them. What semantic analysis of story, what deconstruction of a text, what "reading" of any kind can claim anymore to have chosen the really strategic image, the really critical narrative as its object? For every object chosen to explicate a theory, there is an ever-increasing plethora of images unchosen. Better under such circumstances to theorize the vector along which the bloody stream of images courses than to pick the odd corpuscle from the flow and subject it to the microscope. Better to make of the image a ready-to-hand tool than a message to decode. Theory isn't the customs department, unpacking every bag to inspect its contents for immoral smugglings. Theory is the baggage department, loading images onto and off their vectoral flights.

Pick up a bag, decide where to send it. Do you get it? Like the passport of a refugee, passed from depot to depot, the image collects stamps and imprints, inspections and corrections. But it has, as Chuck Berry said, no particular place to go. Like the luggage of the smuggler, the image always outsmarts the moralizing customs officers. There is always a hidden compartment stuffed with diamonds and drugs, for someone else to deliver, or steal, or find by chance. The one thing the image will not smuggle in by the back door is a closet humanism, disguised as an all-knowing "critique." Critical theory does not master the image, it merely rummages through its underwear.

The image, like a bag, is a tool for carrying things, but it is a far more sophisticated tool. I understand how a bag "works"—it seems silly even to ask. I don't know how a television works, or a chainsaw. Yet I have used them both. I can pick up a tool and use it without knowing how it works. Likewise, images are tools that are ready to hand and useful, even if I don't know how they work. They are always there, in a mundane, worldly sense. Learning how they work requires using them, not vice versa. Thus there can be no semiotics without writing; no cultural studies not founded on cultural practice.

If you think of any vector as a tool for moving images and stories, and theory as a particular type of tool for deciding the destination of certain flows of semiotic baggage, then this implies a certain responsibility. This was very clear in the media coverage of the June 9th movement. Journalists did not ask themselves where their reportage was headed. To the extent that it was headed around the world and straight back again, back into China, this had two consequences. It would feed back into the struggle itself via radio and fax. It would feed back into the party and the state via the embassies and intelligence service. The neat analytics of liberal journalism still imagine the media in a compartmentalized public sphere, but this is clearly not the case. The media are not a place to unpack the baggage of an event and value its contents when those contents will also be revealed to the participants in the event itself. The media are a place where one has increasingly to ask about the destination of the vector. If there are now such things as satellite feeds, then who is eating it all up?

If a camera is a tool that a journalist uses, then what's the use? Likewise, if television is a tool which I use to make cultural studies, then who am I making it for? Foucault had this partly right when he suggested that theory was a toolbox. It would be better to say that the everyday life of the intellectual throws up many types of tools. Books, TV shows, magazines, conferences, the radio, newspapers—all are governed by institutions to be sure. Yet just as shopping bags seem to keep circulating long after their original journey from the store, so too images flow through everyday life in ways never envisaged by the governmentality which regulates each and every discourse. Images and stories leak out into the ungoverned, unrecorded flux of the residues of everyday life. It is in the everyday that a life can be made which uses these tools with other ends in view than the institutionally delimited ones. To pick up a book, turn on a TV, and use it with an end in view means to take a step toward communicative action. A TV or a library is an apparatus through which flows along particular vectors can be channeled, fashioned, edited, styled, and passed along. Nothing ever guarantees this process in advance. There is only the will to make a difference that makes a difference, as Bateson put it, and set it into the flow.

Out of the Bag

In any case, what is the point of analyzing the content of what we know to be banal brain junk? Baudrillard's point is a valid one: the masses are *indifferent* to it anyway. The mass audiences constructed by the vector field have their own uses for the flow. It is a giant set of socket wrenches for turning on amusement, distraction, ambience, electronic wallpaper. The quite artificial distinction between liberal-democratic media segments which imagine they speak to citizens and the mass-entertainment segments which imagine they speak to consumers is breaking down. Far from being a perversion or a decline of the media, this drift is in fact the slow emergence of a more abstract, fluid culture of the vector field in all its purity.

In its wildest imagination, the vector field imagines itself connecting every point to every other point. The vector field is, potentially, a rhizome. Powerful interests prevent it from realizing this potential, naturally. By encouraging leakage, spillage, noise, cultural practice can reveal the vector field *in potentia.* This may involve a departure from liberal notions of the proper place and time for things.

Heidegger speaks of our fallenness in the world, our absorption in being-with-one-another. For Heidegger this inauthentic aspect of being is one of fascination with idle talk, random images, immersion in the other. This "fallenness" does not amount to alienation in the negative, Hegelian sense. One exists mundanely, in the interzone of vector flows, in the worldly circumstances of everyday life. This immersion in mundane existence is the condition for imagining a movement toward something else, for not just being subjected to flows, but subjecting flows of images oneself. Immersion in the banality of the vector field and its products is the condition for thinking its opposite, for imagining communicative actions. This in a sense is the message cultural studies tries to take back to the institution of the humanities from the "outside world": there is no hope for resisting popular culture. The academy is just an institution in the vectoral matrix like any other. Hope emerges from immersion in the vector flow. One must think dialectically about the vector. Which is to say, one must make use of it. One must make use of things like CNN, and one must make use of things like Heidegger. CNN is a tool for figuring out what to do with Heidegger, and perhaps vice versa.

The information flow from the vector field has nothing to do with everyday life. It is quite the opposite of everyday life, yet the vector is a condition of everyday life's very existence in the postmodern world. As James Lull shows in *China Turned On,* his study of television audiences in contemporary China, the vector field provides a steady stream of stories and images into the interzone, in this case the cramped quarters of modern Chinese apartments. There the quite particular forms of family viewing Lull describes make of TV a tool for various purposes.

We are born, we grow up, we think and act in a world where the global vector field is always already there. Every local, specific, different, minor culture is saturated with the constant stream of the vector flow. Yet this does not always put an end to the specificity of distinct and local cultures. On the contrary, if it does not kill them, it makes them stronger. The vector flow from the vector field is the condition of existence and self-knowledge of the local, the traditional, the specific, and the resistant. It is in contact with the other of the other, the vector field itself, that a culture sees other cultures and comes to perceive itself as distinct not only from what has always been near, from neighboring groups, but also from what is distant. This contact with the flow from the other of the other not only may make a culture perceive itself in relation to an other, but may add hitherto unknown dimensions to its sense of boundedness —bounded not only from what is near but from other, distant others as well.

In contact with the vector flow, cultures come to perceive themselves not only as distinct from images of the other, but as distinct from what is most distant of all, from the vector field itself. A culture can come to perceive its difference from, but intimate connection to, third nature itself. Cultural autonomy does not consist of blocking the vector flow, but in seizing upon it as useful, as a tool of self-definition. Thus the same applies to the culture in the vector field as to the individual in the interzone.

Thus the democracy movement had the right idea, not the party. The party is still trying to open the "bottom half" of the door to Western capital and technology, but not the "top half" of the vector field and the flows of images and stories into everyday life. The party fears the shopping bag of the vector, bringing in "bourgeois liberalization" and "spiritual pollution"—and rightly so. It rightly guesses that in the contact with the vector flow, the symbolic resources of Tiananmen Square will be revived, and a movement to autonomous self-creation will be unleashed.

It is thus no accident that foreign signs abounded alongside the repeated calls for a genuine Chinese patriotism in the democracy movement, for the interaction of one with the other, of third nature with second nature, is the uncanny moment out of which arises a changed sense of cultural difference, but also cultural purpose.

Do You Get the Picture?

> A world picture, when understood essentially, does not mean a picture of the world, but the world conceived and grasped as picture.
>
> The fundamental event of the modern age is the conquest of the world as picture.
>
> —Martin Heidegger

Says Heidegger, "The fact that the world becomes picture at all is what distinguishes the essence of the new age."[63] The world appears as re-presentation "for man." In the classical age, to the contrary, "man is the one who is looked upon by that which is." Put simply: the gods used to look upon us and we had a perception that they watched us; now we look at the world and we understand the world as that which we can see. Perhaps the postmodern tends back toward that original, pagan perception. The spectacle of the world no longer appears as it did in the modern era as organized for us. Images of the world no longer appear as the raw material and the outcome of heroic human acts. What Deleuze perceives to be the breakdown of the action image in the cinema seems very similar to this.[64] The modern ends when the world is no longer presented to viewers as a picture, to be subject to conscious rational calculations and predetermined actions with foreseeable ends.

What Heidegger thinks of as the pagan relation to the world may be back with us. Once again we must gather and conserve third nature, the bitter landscape of exposure and unfathomable catastrophe. We still see much more of the world than people ever did before: the relentless development of the vector field which typified the modern continues. Yet it continues way past the point where it seems to empower us by exposing the world to us, by bringing it near. The slogan of SBS TV in Australia, surely one of the world's most cosmopolitan and multicultural broadcasters, is "Bringing the World Back Home." Yet this does not feel quite right anymore. We are exposed to the world; the world no longer exposes itself for us. Fragments, images of it are exposed, placed in proximity *to* us, but not *for* us. We apprehend what comes our way, but it does not re-present itself to us, still less do we represent the world to ourselves. What is apprehended must be gathered and conserved, fashioned and delivered again, elsewhere, elsewhen.

When representations cease to exist for man, then humanism is at last finally making its exit. Heidegger thought the end of humanism as an idea; Foucault traced it in the discourses of modern social science—but it is only in the proliferation of the vector field that the end of humanism becomes a global condition. Under the influence of the vector field, subjectivity appears as a network of nodes subordinated to the vector flow. Not entirely subordinated, however. The outbreak of Tiananmen Square is a fabulous example of the recovery of sovereignty and autonomy out of the residues of sensibility which the friction of the vector field and the disciplinary apparatuses leave behind in everyday life. The condition of subjection to the vector flow is the condition for a struggle toward autonomy in relation to it.

Humanism arises out of modernity, out of the presentation of objects in the form of images before the subject, as the dialectical counterpart of the subjection of people to the monstrous object-world of second nature. Yet humanism is a form of fetishism. In place of the dual relation of people to objects and to images, relations which come increasingly to mediate both territorial social relations and the map of vectoral, communicative relations, humanism makes a fetish of the human-to-human relation, ignoring all forms of mediation. Humanism thus ignores the historical accumulation of the object-world of dead labor that characterizes second nature today, and the simultaneity of events which is the politics of the present in a mediated world.

The development of the vector field once held out the promise of overcoming the tyranny of objects, of dead labor, of second nature. This was the modern desire, to create through representation a theater of operations through which the object-world could be subordinated to human control. The astonishment proper to the postmodern is when the reverse reveals itself, when the vector field appears as an absolute barrier to human control of second nature or to unmediated communication of all that is human. We may "get the picture," we may understand what we see as the vector flow—but it is more appropriate to say that the vector *gets us*.

We must be its image fodder, we must swallow its fictions whole (but with a pinch of everyday salt). We must actively seek to become the nodes of the rhizome to have any idea what is to come. For Heidegger, "That the world becomes picture is one and the same event as man's becoming subject in the midst of that which is."[65]

In the modern approach to third nature, the organizing power of the spectacle struggles to create a vector field through which that power itself organizes and plans the whole of second nature via third nature. "Because this position secures, organises and articulates itself as a world view, the modern relationship to that which is, is one that becomes, in its decisive unfolding, a confrontation of world views; and indeed not of random world views, but only of those that have already taken up the fundamental position of man that is most extreme, and have done so with the utmost resoluteness. For the sake of this struggle of world view and in keeping with its meaning, man brings into play his unlimited power for calculating, planning and moulding of all things."[66] Or so the Chinese Communist Party still imagines—but it is actually rather more like Kafka's great wall of China, and it does not confront another world view but rather the lack of it. It now confronts a world flow.

The symptom of this passage from modernity to third nature is the event. The great monuments of Tiananmen Square might persist in form through time, but they cast a long shadow. In the light of CNN and the global vector, the great monuments to the organization of the world through the world view, through picturing and planning, are rendered invisible in their lengthening shadows. "The shadow, however, points to something else, which it is denied to us to know."[67]

Site #4

Wall Street, New York City

planet of noise

Site #4

7. noise

> The practice of calmness and immobility, of certainty and security, suddenly breaks down. . . . All these pretty, polite techniques, made for a well panelled boardroom and a nicely regulated market are liable to collapse. At all times the vague panic fears and equally vague and unreasoned hopes are not really lulled and lie but a little way below the surface.
>
> —John Maynard Keynes

Immaterial Wealth

Dateline: New York, 19 October 1987. The stock market crashes, as panic selling sweeps the Dow Jones industrials down 22.6 percent. This record decline far exceeds the drop on 28 October 1927. By late afternoon, the transaction tape at the New York Stock Exchange, capable of handling 900 trades a minute, runs 2 hours 15 minutes late. Institutional and individual investors jam brokers' lines, trying in vain to protect their investments. The computer-generated arbitrage and "portfolio insurance" programs prompt surges of sell orders, which culminate in the Dow falling 100 points in the last hour of trading.[1]

THE END OF THE WORLD IS NOT NIGH flashed the banner headline, as if casually announcing that the apocalypse was over and we could all go back to business as usual. There have been times before when a stock market crash on Wall Street has triggered similar falls elsewhere in the world, but never before with such instamatic speed. The market seemed to be the unconscious nerve center of capital itself, and as such betrayed its chronically manic-depressive personality. After responding only to good news through its historic bull market climb, it appeared to turn bearish on a whim: an Iranian missile hit a U.S. ship in the Gulf; Nancy Reagan entered the hospital for cancer surgery; Secretary of the Treasury James Baker let slip some loose talk about German monetary policy. No matter how rational individual market-makers may feel their decisions were at the time, the market as a whole, as a complex net of information, changed its mind in a matter of minutes from buoyant optimism to a nihilism of despair. This change of mood reverberated through the money temples around the globe.

The October stock market crash gave us lay people a new appreciation of what has been going on in the money business. For a moment the opaque tedium of finance, droning incessantly on in the sections of newspapers and segments of news bulletins that most people instantly switch off, came alive. People who had convinced themselves that it was all too difficult for them to understand suddenly realized it was too much for anybody to understand. Those of us with no fortunes to lose could silently muse on the intangible workings of this digital watch that forms the surface effects of the economy. In the thirty-seven revolutions of the global chronometer between 16 October and 21 November, the markets pulled each other down and down and down. The percentage losses were: Sydney, 40 percent; Tokyo, 9 percent; Hong Kong, 42 percent; Frankfurt, 23 percent; London, 25 percent; New York, 16 percent. "There was no escaping the 24 hour clock," as one postmortem put it.[2] Nor has there been for some time now. The difference was that suddenly it was both more unintelligible than ever before and in its mystery far less boring.

History is littered with stock market crashes. Indeed, the October 1987 crash was perhaps the ninth or tenth on Wall Street since 1929.[3] Not that many traders or bankers or arbitrageurs would remember. The globalization of this immaterial style of business seems to encourage the spread of "simultaneous memory" and "historical amnesia." Market-makers are intensely familiar with what happened this morning or last night on other markets, back over the global horizon, but tend not to think too far back into the past of their own marketplace. "Money never sleeps, pal," as Gordon Gekko puts it in the movie *Wall Street,* although it does seem to dream. It is cognizant of all that happens, everywhere at once, and forgets it all in a moment. Or as the Machiavellian banker Maxwell Emery observes in the movie *Rollover:* "Someone sneezes in Zürich and we say Gesundheit in New York." Yet it is in such a state of perennial, restless flux that it is quite unaware of its own historicity. "Every age in the stock market reinvents the wheel," says one "analyst," "convinced it has created something new and quite wonderful while completely ignoring what happened to the old wheel."[4] The old wheels are still in there somewhere, and still spinning.

Perhaps the image of a spinning wheel is no longer appropriate. The oscillating electrons beating time in a quartz circuit may be a more appropriate emblem. Every new circuit, pulsing with information about opportunities and signifiers of wealth, adds a new trajectory along which information may surge uncontrollably, or in which noise may overwhelm information. These vectors are of an immaterial nature, an artifice grown over the old. The philosopher Jean-François Lyotard posed the problem of this immaterial nature in an exhibition at the Pompidou center some years ago. He proposed the idea that the shift to immaterial technologies undermined the concept of the enlightenment project as the mastery of nature by "man." Lyotard has lost faith in a mankind which labors, plans, and remembers, which shapes the material of nature by force, brute or otherwise.[5] Finance capital responded enthusiastically to immaterial technology, making one suspect a close affinity between the abstract social force that is money and the principles of the new technologies.

As Lyotard suggests, movement is the key to the immaterial, the movement of information. There are no stable poles of identification in the immaterial world. It vaporizes the problem of the relationship between objects and subjects, transubstantiating it into a new problematic. In this immaterial paradigm relations come not only to designate but to dominate their terms. The market is not a vector that enables "man" to remember, decide, and plan. It is where man is remembered, decided, and planned.

The historic proliferation of the vector, in other words, is more than just a problem of an increase in "speed." It is a qualitative change in the structure of society itself. Nowhere is this change more thorough and more perplexing than in the world of high finance. Adorno once said that the "almost insoluble task is to neither let the power of others, nor our own powerlessness, stupify us."[6] Nowhere is this more true than when it comes to confronting the financial world. Confront it we must, however. For in that realm the intimate connection between capital and the vector is a self-evident and everyday reality. The concrete, immaterial reality of the vector becomes a technology only too appropriate for the abstract principle of money. The stock market crash displayed the essence of this connection, but before looking to the crash itself, it is necessary to set the stage a little, to see what and who were implicated in the event itself.

Boredom and Apocalypse

The '29 debacle was called a "crash," memorialized in Galbraith's great work, *The Great Crash 1929.*[7] On the other hand, the professional stockbrokers who were called upon to moonlight as amateur vector-brokers called the October '87 spectacle a "correction" or a "meltdown," or a "freefall." Their choice of terms seemed to depend on the underlying fundamental value of the optimism and market faith they had at the time, and their degree of moral exposure. The difference in metaphor reflected a difference in the disintegrating courses followed in '29 and '87. The latter was more of a horizontal skid than a bump. As *Business Week* reminisced, six months after the event, the '87 slide worried other stock markets around the world, but didn't instantly spread down into the domestic U.S. economy.[8] The destruction of $500 million U.S. in immaterial wealth "hardly put a dent in consumer spending." Between the immaterial economy and the totality of economic movements there appeared to be a "shock absorber." For one thing, the material economy is itself becoming a veritable space of flows, and has been busy remaking itself according to its own timetable of regional and sectoral changes.[9]

There seemed to be no shock absorber between the stock market and the media, however, especially television, which narrated the event in its uniquely cool but apocalyptic style. The apocalypse, after all, is the weekly stock in trade of television, and is no longer the cause of any great excitement within television itself. Presenting other people's excitement and panic rather than panicking per se is the mode of advanced television. It seeks out sources of excitement to alleviate its boredom, and allows the viewer vicariously to share this relief. Excitement is still a daily part of the professional world of both finance and news. Since both television and finance operate on daily schedules, the televisual voyeur within the world of finance appears as a natural if necessarily stupid participant in the bull pits of capital.

The daily routine of apocalypse, of war, famine, disease, and disaster in the natural world, is thus occasionally leavened by disasters from worlds of a more synthetic kind. Third nature too has its disasters, its causes for fear and trembling. With financial disasters, tremors and tumors develop every other news week, so something had to be added to the presentation of this one to set it apart. Without breaking out of its habitual coolness, television did tweak up the brightness in the voice, the superlatives in the news copy. It also added a historical perspective. Old newsreel footage of the '29 crash reeled past our screens, providing the anchor for a narrative pinned to the superlative notion that this was the biggest and the best financial crash since '29. The newsreel pictures have become part of television. The events depicted have become a database of possible narrative points through which the vector-brokers can navigate in search of a trajectory for today's apocalypse.

Like every weird global media event, the story began in the middle, leaving the news-brokers and massagers looking under every rock for someone who might have a plausible beginning to tack on the front of the story, after the fact. The business of brokering the event, above and beyond the negotiating with powerful institutions and their vested interests, is a navigation in two vectoral spaces. One is the contemporary space of synchronic memory. In this space, vast amounts of simultaneous little "eventlets" have to be massaged into the highly formal stories of the day. The other is a rather special sort of historical memory. The past too becomes a vector field when a catalogue of images and stories about it exists and can be accessed by the broker in search of a sightly grander narrative line than usual.

In "The Storyteller," Walter Benjamin drew a distinction between the stories that grew out of the everyday life of rural communities, rooted in the territory, and the information propagated by the vector of the press. He did not deign to dignify the latter with the term "story," as news pieces are most usually termed. According to Benjamin, "The value of information does not survive the moment in which it is new. It lives only at the moment; it has to surrender to it completely and explain itself without losing any time. A story is different. It does not expend itself. It preserves and concentrates its strength and can release it even after a long time."[10] For Benjamin, storytelling was a disappearing art, but for us it too appears as something taken up within the network of the vector. When necessary, mere information can be dignified by making it a link in a story. The raw material of this kind of story is no longer everyday life, but an intensive vector field composed of compressed data, images, and monologues, accessible as an abstract map of an infinite range of authoritative pasts. The speed of events in the extensive vector field of the perpetual present has led to the creation and increasing recourse to this intensive vector field, where ever more abstracted presents meet ever more abstracted pasts.

This most abstracted news event called for the recollection of an abstract past. Thirties newsreels, old popular front–style social realist images of the Great Depression came out of their hiding places in the archives to anchor in time the middle of an event which was not anchored in a strong sense of place. When the stock market crashed, vector-brokers scrambled to make sense of the debris. Financial disasters have a peculiar quality to them. As one seasoned analyst put it, "Reporters are always looking for a reason and there isn't always a reason."[11] The media were largely incapable of grasping the significance of a market that could rise in a month more than it used to rise in a year. They were rendered quite insensate by one that could fall in a second more than it used to fall in a week. Unable to play the voice of the one supposed to know, the news resorted to superlative and apocalypse: The biggest disaster in its class since 1929. Does it mean the end of civilization as we know it? Stay tuned. . . .

The Economic Sublime

It was more than 500 million immaterial dollars that vaporized that October. The romance with the culture of fast money vanished with it. The crash devalued the "Roaring '80s" image of fast, hard, young, tough, single-minded professionals, simultaneously serving self-interest and the greater glory of capital. The magic conjunction of obscene amounts of individual wealth and the efficient allocation of social resources now seemed like a less than marketable idea. After the meltdown, many aspiring young yuppies found themselves looking for other employment, as brokering firms shed staff to contain costs in the lean post-crash months. In the week preceding Black Monday itself, Wall Street firms had already shed over 1,000 jobs. In more fragile economies like that of Australia, the fallout from the crash in finance capital was even more severe, but didn't make the world news reports.

Looking back on the mid-'80s, it all seems slightly ridiculous now, a replay of the Roaring '20s more on a cultural level than on an economic one. Perhaps there is a historical amnesia affecting culture too, a casualty of the vast chunks of memory space taken up with synchronic data on the current style map. Money was at the center of the story in the Roaring '80s, but it was an absent center. This was a time of much talk of market forces, deregulation, level playing fields, productivity, restructuring, competition, and the fast track. It was difficult to sort out how much of this was fascination with the free movement of capital and how much with the *means* of that movement. The technical means were now there to turn capital into a bitstream of supple data and send it to the moon and back, instantly changing the identities of those it graces with its power as it comes—and goes. Viewed retrospectively, the crash seemed like a suitable ending, fit for a moral fable, where the speculators finally got their just deserts. In the end the vector-brokers could play it like a Frank Capra movie, conservative but populist. But as we shall see, there were many more layers of narrative caked onto this event.

Before the crash the market had almost acquired the status of a utopian concept. As Fredric Jameson says, "In the postmodern, indeed, it is the very idea of the market that is consumed with the most prodigious gratification; as it were, a bonus or surplus of the commodity process."[12] But it was not just any image of the market that marketed so well. Not the old image of the market, the old bourgeois fictions, but bright, dazzling new ones. This was a sublime market, facilitated by the comsat and the credit card. Instant liquidity was the image that had all others dancing. Suddenly it appeared as if the market had broken loose from the sites that once preserved its image and customs. The market was no longer on Wall Street, nor even on the high street. The market was everywhere, adding its aura to the hemlines of little black dresses, the ice cubes of baroque cocktails, the polished curves of the third Mercedes. "It is the fraternization of impossibilities. It makes contradictions embrace," as Marx put it a long time ago.[13] Now it is *everywhere.* The market sublime crackled like a static charge, bristling on the edges of any occasion from the sex act to singing in the rain. The market, like rust and money, never sleeps.

The sublime can inspire terror as much as lust, awe, and madness. Burning constellations of narrative lines collided in an event that jolted the editorialists and leader writers out of their accustomed narrative postures, at least for a little while. "Share prices can indeed go down as well as up," as the *Financial Times* laconically editorialized. On a more serious note, "there must be lessons here about the instability of the global institutional marketplace, which feeds on fear transmitted from one time-zone to another."[14] This was a lesson that, as we shall see, finance capital largely resisted. The resistance can be felt at work in the twisted syntax of the following judgment: "It is hard not to sympathise with the view that nothing has happened in the real world over the past few weeks to justify such a spectacular collapse. Clearly, the very fact of the slide has considerably enhanced the risks of an economic slump."[15] Which translates as: "The crash was not a response to an impending recession, because no such recession was likely. Now the crash has occurred, one might be."

In the illogic of this relation can be glimpsed a separation of some peculiar kind between the bit of the economy that crashed and the vast part that didn't. That the crash was an event, that it defied economic rationality, at least momentarily, was a conclusion papered over by the columnists and scholars who studied it. Most of them, after all, make their living off the idea that the market is rational, and hence that there is some value in buying a financial newspaper or spending money on expensive academic research.

The crash was a moral crisis and a counterfactual for the story of the market sublime. Or rather, it revealed the underside of that sublime, the abyss of the economic real looking back at us. It was an event which even the best media surgeons, market specialists, and business news operators could not readily suture back into the popular understanding of the story. For a moment the curtain blew aside and a tiny glimpse of something strange and unknown appeared. Something beyond conventional perception. It was just as quickly covered over by the judicious application of freely improvised story. The frenzied compulsion to tell on the part of the media, the strange fascination with watching and listening to the stories on our part, both colluded to produce a network of lines, threading through the break in the skin of perception, weaving the vectors back into a symbolic whole.

This led some news-brokers to make some rather odd statements. "The market's going down because it's going down," says analyst Newton Zinder to *Time,* as if speaking about the weather or the wheel of fortune. Meanwhile in Zürich "a speechless crowd stands, gaping at the Reuters monitor as if they were at the scene of an accident."[16] Besides the interest they understandably took in their own fortunes and futures, they were watching the spectacle of immaterial technology devouring "confidence," wrecking "efficient market theory," putting a value on panic, and other intangible ideological properties. The end of ideology, rolled over and deferred since postwar optimism, since the Vietnam confrontation, fell due again in October '87, and tumbled over again. And who knows what bargain was struck to keep it rolling—Faustian or otherwise. While the good people of Zürich watched the crash on the Reuters screens, everyone else watched them watching—on the evening news. "As Vietnam was the first war fought on TV, so the crash of '87 was the first stock market panic to unfold on camera, the first to be truly communicated around the globe"—so says *Fortune* magazine.[17]

While this may be as hyperbolic a statement as the panicky sell drive to which it refers, Black Monday nevertheless had the feeling of a fresh chaos in the realm of media experience. It appeared as a novel addition to the repertoire of accidents that syncopate the television's everyday narrative rhythms. Watching TV news alone at night, I'm reminded of a line from a song by Nirvana, "In the dark, it's less dangerous. Here we are now, entertain us." Here we are now, a global audience, well fed and bored. Sated on the everyday trope of catastrophe. Here we are now, tuning in on the off chance that the boredom of catastrophe will be enlivened every once in a while by an event. As situations which formerly would have had the shock value of an event become mere catastrophes, the news vector scours the globe for bigger and better trumpet blasts, greater and louder tumbling stones of Jericho.

We *want* to witness catastrophe. The fascination evoked by Benjamin's rural storyteller finds satisfaction today in tales of deep, dark, dangerous third nature. When those sallow newsreel images of depression-stricken people walked in black and white across our screens, it was as if the unburied dead of the economic sublime had come back to haunt us, to remind us that the consequences of economic catastrophe are forever with us. There are no just rites for these people. No one accounts for them. So they come back to remind us that in this story, as in all ghost stories, justice is not served. Far from disappearing in the modern news story, folklore is alive and well. The woods may have been cut down and sawmilled into wood pulp for the newspapers, but the old stories live on.

The walls that came down, ever so briefly, on Black Monday were the walls of the capital of capital. For a moment while the wall was down, all could see that capital is not rational, it is barely even conceivable. Just for a moment the ruler of the citadel of capital did not appear personified as the all-powerful capitalist, but as something barely even human anymore. Just for one moment, the sublime dream of the market came tumbling down again. The failure of the present, which is all an event is, restored the moment of memory once again.

Guy Debord wrote that "the immense growth in the means of modern domination has so marked the style of its pronouncements that if the understanding of the progress of the sombre reasoning of power was for a long time a privilege of people of real intelligence, it has now become familiar to even the most dull-witted."[18] The great provocateur strikes an overly paranoid note here. It is true enough that what Marx called the "sheet lightning" of the press crackles with duties it has been charged with by the powers that be. The media and capital are closely related, but not just as a conscious minding of vested interests. Their vectoral networks are also closely interrelated. So closely that when reason fails in one, the failure appears like a sudden blackout in the other. On Black Monday, everybody could see that finance capital had lost its head. Or rather, that capital is no longer a conscious, rational relation through which a class organizes its interests. The clear outline standing out in the blackout was of a far more monstrous power. Everyone with eyes to see, a paper to read, a news bulletin to catch, could detect, not the somber reasonings of power but that "finally—and this goes for the capitalists too—an inhuman power rules over everything."[19]

Gekkos on Wall Street

Not only the markets but narrative economy seemed to find a new level with the crash. While corporate power remained more or less untouched, the more flamboyantly personalized kind of wealth that typified the '80s seemed to get its comeuppance, as narrative economy would naturally demand. One can imagine a character like Gordon Gekko from the mid-'80s Oliver Stone film *Wall Street,* shouting his wonderfully visceral insults down the phone as the crash unraveled on the morning of Monday, 19 October. As the market lost confidence, share prices started to fall. As more and more sellers entered the market it went into "freefall," crashing down past the level of the "real value" of those shares at some unknown point on the way. Gekko tries like everyone else to offload his shares too—possibly ones he paid a premium price for in some takeover war. Then the portfolio insurance programs kick in, and computers start offloading shares at a lightning pace and trying to buy up other assets in their place such as futures. With the value of the underlying shares gone off a cliff in New York, the futures market built on top of it in Chicago went berserk as well.

For all the aggressive gung-ho individualism of the Gekko ethos, markets function only on an unstated consensual spirit, something akin to Machiavelli's *virtu.*[20] For all the rhetoric about the New York stock market being the closest thing to a working example of a free market, it is the "specialist firms" that maintain the impression of stability. They supposedly ensure that trading in each stock is orderly by buying and selling each stock in a countervailing manner to even out the gyrations of the market. The media and the official inquiries criticized these firms after the crash for failing to hold the floodgates shut against the torrent.[21] In a sense, these firms were on the front line of the ambiguity between collective virtue and solipsistic self-interest, and were unable to uphold the former without taking huge and possibly pointless losses, contrary to the latter.

With virtue deserting the marketplace, every individual holder is out there alone in midair without a parachute. Gordon Gekko would find himself at the end of the day with a bunch of paper worth maybe three-quarters or half of what it was the day before. That might be no great disaster, but Gekko is a speculator. He has borrowed money at usurious rates in expectation of making a killing on some deal, and sometime soon after the crash his creditors will want to extract their pound of flesh—or at least repossess the condo. Worse, he might have committed all his cash to making the *deposit* on a big block of very expensive shares on some provincial exchange where the rules are sometimes a little more flexible. He might be expecting to sell these before he has actually paid for them, a practice known as "selling short." By selling at a higher price before he actually buys them, he can pocket the difference.

This move is doubly perverse: not only would they be sold before they are bought, but the rise in the share price might result from the *act of buying itself*. By going into the market buying up big, this act would drag the price up by its bootstraps. Thus credit fuels perverse speculation that has nothing to do with the actual *power* of the players or the possession of superior information.[22] Gekko could leverage himself into the market with borrowed money, so that he could, as he put it in the movie, "piss in the tall grass with the big dogs"—but only as long as his credit and the bull market hold up. Once the enchanted world stops floating blithely on air and takes a peek down into the abyss, seeing only bottomless void, all is set to come back to earth with a thump. Gekko and co. are going to burn up on reentry, casualties of one of Gekko's magical transferences "from one perception to another."

Perception is indeed the heart of the problem. Adorno asked: "Is not the simplest perception shaped by fear of the thing perceived, or desire for it?"[23] The *Wall Street* movie is certainly framed between the fear and the desire for the becoming abstract of finance capital. In being unable to critically reflect on its desire for the elusive lure of the immaterial, Oliver Stone's film falls short of a clear perception of that desire for the immaterial itself. It may be advisable to shift more toward fear, and look at this sublime, immaterial world from a perspective colored by that fear.

Spectacular Capital

When Marx said that "capital is man completely lost to himself," he might have been describing Gordon Gekko.[24] Or conversely, Gekko personifies capital lost to itself, lost in the vector. The crash is, literally, an index of a more pervasive loss of self-possession. The "market overhang" collapsed in on itself, shooting down past the invisible point at which market value equals "real" value, but of course this real value remains real precisely because it remains unknown. One can benefit enormously from guessing where real value *might* be. Successful investors are people who have somehow glimpsed the real in the market and acted accordingly. This is why the reverence accorded these business sages is not without foundation.

Of course, if we really knew that point we would all be Marxists *and* millionaires. The point is that we don't, and in a fundamental sense, there is no such point. The "economic real" is in some quite fundamental ways elusive, ineffable, unknowable. To assume that there is a "true" price or set of prices at which buyers and sellers will match up perfectly and the market will clear, assumes away everything dynamic and changing in the market. It assumes away time itself. To assume that there is a knowable correspondence between prices and the value of the goods and services they represent assumes that one has access to a knowledge of the movements of the economy which is independent of the institutions and discourses that make it manifest by representing it. Neither assumption is really warranted, and economics, both orthodox and radical, has an alarming tendency to abstract away all the problems caused by the institutional matrix that represents and makes manifest the mysterious workings of the economy, and within which institutions are obliged to calculate, set goals, and risk resources.[25]

One lesson of the stock market crash is that these institutions and agencies, the collective cultures that they spawn, and the network of communication that threads them together do not simply reflect what happens in the economy. The economy is an ensemble of movements and flows, mostly tied more or less rigidly to the physical space of fixed assets that persist in time. The financial vector is a dynamic development that seeks to escape from commitment to such permanence. The movements of labor, capital, commodities make up second nature, which exists when and where the commodity has become "the universal category of society as a whole," as Georg Lukács put it. "Only then does the commodity become crucial for the subjugation of men's consciousness to the forms in which this reification finds expression and for their attempts to comprehend the process or to rebel against its disastrous effects and liberate themselves from servitude to the 'second nature' so created."[26]

As Guy Debord has argued, the dynamic, open-ended process of the self-reproduction of capital goes beyond the transformation of ancient territories into the space of the social factory, where all of social space and the vectors that traverse it are dedicated to the ceaseless making and unmaking of commodities. Even before this process is complete, a "third nature" begins to remake it over again. Where the growth of second nature over the landscape takes the form of private property, in Marx's terms it transforms *being* into *having*. Where the vector develops to the point that it can break with the surface and the tempo of second nature, in Debord's terms it further transforms having into *appearing*.[27]

Now, the vector and capital are complicit in this, but the vector and capital are not identical. Capital drives the vector further and harder, forcing its technologies to innovate, but at the same time it tries to commodify the fruits of this development. The vector may have other properties, values that escape the restriction of its abstract potential to the commodity form. That this potential may exist, latent within the vector, seems indicated by the trouble the vector causes capital—the '87 crash, for example. The benefit capital derives from the vector is not without its side effects. Velocity has its price. Nowhere is this more evident than in the momentary crises that the rhythms of second nature suffer when they fall out of step with the movements of the third.

Debord saw third nature, what he called "the spectacle," as a pure, functional outgrowth of capital. It was to him the logical extension of alienated and reified social relations into the whole sphere of everyday life. To some extent this conclusion seems warranted: third nature does have a rhythm that fits very nicely with everyday life. From nine to five: work. From six till ten: television. Yet there are also divisions between the time of second nature and third. The vector is not always subject to a rational and functional control. Nor is third nature limited to the production of a spectacular realm of consumption. Debord says that the consumer "becomes a consumer of illusions. The commodity is this factually real illusion, and the spectacle is its general manifestation."[28] This deals with only one side of the question of third nature. Debord thinks of a spectacular relation between the commodity, the worker (appearing here in the guise of the consumer), and money (appearing here in the form of wages). There is another such relation, the other side of third nature, which connects the commodity, the ruling class via their agents in the financial sector, with money as capital in its most electrically liquid form. The first side of this relation between second and third nature can be portrayed as a functionalist nightmare, where "capital" extends its domination over the whole of social life. Or as Fredric Jameson says in an extraordinary phrase, where "the prodigious new expansion of multinational capital ends up penetrating and colonizing those very precapitalist enclaves (Nature and the Unconscious) which offered extraterritorial and Archimedean footholds for critical effectivity."[29] The other side shows quite a different picture of capital. One where it struggles with the forces of the vector it has unleashed, but which become a power with the potential to break free from capitalist rationality. Replaying the stock market crash in slow motion, as it were, offers a glimpse of the other side of the relation of capital to the vector.

Two Mondays

The economy is an ensemble of movements and flows of labor, capital, and commodities and is a vector field as extensive as the earth. The finance vector appears as an extension of this that tends to break away from it. It is neither a subset of the totality of economic movements, nor a representation of them. As the finance sector acquires a technology that allows it to act in space and time according to an entirely more rapid rhythm and with far more mobility in space, finance will begin to separate itself from second nature. From now on, the third nature of finance and the second nature of the productive economy will discover their difference from each other when one crashes into or contaminates the other, where noise overpowers their relation. Wild gyrations on the global stock markets, international banking scandals—these are only symptoms. While the barriers come down between national territories in the name of deregulation, the gap between the second nature of production, existence, and survival and the third nature of even more abstract movement and power grows wider. The symptoms are there in the territories that deregulation has flung together: the debt crisis in Poland and Brazil and the capital trapped in ceaseless, paranoid liquidity in Tokyo or New York are signs of the same process of divergence between second and third nature. The costs of which in the territories it infects are, naturally, unequally borne by the people of the third world.[30]

The distinction between second and third nature can be expressed by thinking about two different Mondays. Both are the same day, 19 October 1987. For some, this is simply another Monday. Whatever the big incidents of the day were for them, we don't know of them. They are episodes belonging to the territory, not to the international news vector. Maybe this was a Monday on which they went to work. Maybe they don't have any work to go to. Maybe personal survival was more important to them than the survival of vast immaterial fortunes. Maybe nothing much happened at all, besides the fact that the headline on the newspaper was two centimeters taller than usual. Imagine a regular day in the West: get up in the morning, go to work, come home again, watch TV, go to sleep. Another boring day in paradise.[31]

Perhaps it wasn't a day like that at all. Perhaps it was a day like the following, an electronic day that does not follow the movements of the sun but the electronic dawnings of the world's stock markets. Think of the globe itself as a twenty-four-hour clock. Imagine that it's 9 A.M. in Sydney and the markets are gearing up for the day. Sydney is close to the international dateline, and trading on any given day more or less "begins" here, hence the international interest in Sydney, despite its small size. When it's 9 A.M. in Sydney it's only 8 A.M. in Tokyo and about 7 A.M. in Hong Kong. Everyone will be looking for indications in the Sydney market of what will happen in the other Pacific markets, particularly Tokyo, the biggest of them all. Tokyo and Hong Kong might check Sydney before their trading day begins, looking for trends. When it's 9 A.M. in Sydney it's still between midnight and 1 A.M. in Zürich, Paris, and London, and there is about six hours between the opening of Hong Kong and the opening of Zürich. When it's 9 A.M. in Sydney it's about 6 P.M. in New York, so traders there can check Sydney just before they pack it in for the day. When it's 9 A.M. in Sydney it's 5 P.M. in Chicago, where the big futures and options markets are going through the closing-time rush. When it's 9 A.M. in Sydney it's 3 P.M. in Los Angeles, back over the horizon on the other side of the Pacific. With this somewhat simplified chronography, it's possible to see that during trading hours in any financial capital, big or small, there will be markets positioned around the globe, "before" and "after," trading at the same time, and to which capital can move. So, for example, when the Hong Kong stock market shut down for four days during the October meltdown, investors rushed to get liquid by selling on the Sydney exchange, thus contributing to its near-vertical plummet. Another day, another world.

The Enchanted World

John Maynard Keynes had a talent for speculation, both in philosophy and on the stock market. Perhaps this experience contributed to his sanguine view on the psychology of markets. Keynes viewed the market as a probabilistic space, where the future could appear only as a domain of great uncertainty. In the face of this, the players would be prone to bouts of bullish bravado, rising to the point where they plunge back into the abyss of bearish caution. Keynes sums this up with a striking metaphor: "The Stock Exchange revalues many investments every day and the revaluations give frequent opportunity to the individual (though not to the community as a whole) to revise his commitments. It is as though a farmer, having tapped his barometer after breakfast, could decide to remove his capital from the farming business between 10 and 11 in the morning and reconsider whether he should return to it later in the week."[32]

Keynes has here aptly characterized one of the differences between the map of the vector and the territory it represents. What on one is an abstract field of mutable information is on the other a space of often lifetime commitments. In a wonderful little book on Keynes, G. L. S. Shackle stresses "that thread of thought which runs persistently through the *General Theory* though often concealed, the theme that economic action flows from expectation and is accordingly the creature of uncertainty, mutability and precarious faith."[33] In other words, Keynes was interested in the *experiential* time of the event as it was lived by economic actors, not the logical time of economic or historical abstraction.

In other words, he was interested in what cultural studies calls everyday life. The crucial facet for Keynes is the everyday life of capitalists rather than of the subaltern classes. Cultural studies has tended to deny the experiential aspect of bourgeois existence because it has wanted to see in everyday life some reservoir of resistance or portent for the future. Henri Lefebvre argued that the "true critique of everyday life will have as its prime objective the separation between the human (real and possible) and bourgeois decadence, and will imply a *rehabilitation of everyday life*."[34] On the other hand, Lefebvre did also speak of the "rehabilitation of wealth." As a Marxist, Lefebvre was scornful of moralizing disdain for wealth. Social change would proceed "not by sharing out weakness, poverty and mediocrity—but by seeking power and wealth." The aim was not equality of mediocrity; "the aim is still wealth: wealth that becomes progressively universalised, socialised wealth."[35] One suspects that, for quite different reasons, the liberal Keynes might not have been entirely out of sentiment with such a view.

Cultural studies, on the other hand, shies away from wealth, as much as it may love consumption. It has been at pains to point out the miraculous achievements that subaltern groups have managed on very slight material resources. Now, there is nothing so terribly wrong with a cultural studies which takes the powerless as its subject, its object of study, and—sometimes quite literally—its muse. What is curious, however, is the lack of attention to the everyday life of the extremely rich and powerful. Besides the political sympathies cultural studies has with the subaltern, the most obvious reason for the lack of a discourse on the everyday life of the very rich is the difficulty of actually getting access to them. Practitioners of cultural studies have for the most part succeeded in gaining access to the everyday lives of the subaltern, for the simple reason that such groups usually lack the resources and the presumptions to refuse. Cultural studies has in effect succeeded in studying anybody with less power than cultural studies.

The very fact that the very rich are for the most part invisible in their everyday life is itself a major social achievement. The almost-but-not-really extremely rich often make a virtue of publicity and presence in the media. The really extremely rich do not. They are perhaps the one group which can be visibly identifiable, yet which has the power to create social spaces—whole social worlds—which exclude the vector. No traditional society left on earth seems able to keep the prying eyes of anthropologists out forever. No infamous slum seems able to keep the sociologists at bay for long. No subculture is too obscure and fleeting not to attract the attention of cultural studies before disappearing. Yet the very rich remain an enigma to the precise extent that they deem this necessary to the exercise of power. Indeed, the layer of celebrity beneath them in the social order seems designed precisely as a spectacle of wealth which detracts attention from what really goes on in those well-paneled boardrooms and well-appointed homes.

In the absence of evidence for the everyday life of the ruling class, it remains extremely difficult to know what kinds of rationality its members bring to bear on decisions about the disposition of their immediate wealth and the long-term investment of surplus in fresh cycles of wealth creation. Is it entirely fanciful to suppose that the kinds of uncertainty, insecurity, panic, and doubt that afflict the kind of people cultural studies does know about also afflict those it doesn't? Perhaps the animal spirits of capital flag sometimes. Perhaps magic thinking is not entirely banished among them. Who can tell? Most disturbing of all, perhaps they are no longer in control. Perhaps the process via which control of the immediate labor process is taken out of the hands of the worker also, ultimately, takes control of the totality of the labor process out of the hands of the ruling class. Perhaps the "information revolution" was a last-ditch attempt to impose management on the unmanageable technologies of production and distribution that are the intricate, delicate, and complex engine of everyday life. Perhaps the weird global media event is the symptom of precisely this loss of control.

Power does not seem too perturbed by the world it has made on an average Tuesday morning, like this one right now, as I write. The morning news on the radio indicates nothing other than the silent, efficient workings of a power too intricate to see. Yet in the periodic burst of the event, there may be a symptom of a more complex world yet. A world in which the flow of information wriggles loose, and bites the powerful hand that fed it. The event breaks the spell of the enchanted world of capital, as it appears experientially, from the inside. It is not the dangerous classes that threaten power sometimes, as much as dangerous information.

The Money Power

If the enchanted world is not a rational space, then there is no reason to blindly and blithely support the globalization of the financial vector. One of the most persuasive critics of deregulation is Susan Strange. She points out that in the aftermath of the 1929 great crash, much attention was paid to bank regulation. This regulative effort has been undermined steadily by technological developments in the vectoral movement of finance, and by deregulatory policies. Under the Glass-Steagall and McFadden acts, American banking law had sought to limit the potential for crisis by partitioning different kinds of banking off from each other. These acts erected geographic barriers to the free movement of finance across state borders and across the national border. Capital interests increasingly see these barriers as a fetter to the ever more abstract organization of the economy across space. She quotes the comptroller of the currency under the Reagan administration as saying, "We must begin to work towards a world where government supervision is less important and market discipline more important in guaranteeing a sound banking system."[36] Beneath the fashionable ideological gloss of "market discipline" lies a very real process of abstraction.

It is curious how the market seems to be the central metaphorical term for equal but opposite narratives of legitimation. On the one hand, the market means freedom; on the other, it means discipline. And it seems automatically to know what to let loose and what to stop through the magic of the price mechanism and its effect on the allocation of resources. The wisdom of the market was the cover story for a coming together of the free-flowing energy of capital and the technical means of the vector. The result was a wave of capital mobility around the globe of unprecedented scale and volatility. Deregulation opened the doors between capital as a form of relation and the international communication vector as a force of communication. There was more than just a fashion in public policy at issue here. There was a transformation of the forces and relations of communication.

To the extent that the vector can become a channel for immaterial information which distributes the effects of unreason ever more rapidly and more widely, it acts in a manner quite contrary to any economic rationality. The theory of economic rationality presupposes an adequate distribution of *true* information. The vector, pursuing pure velocity within a market framework of decapitated flows, can guarantee neither accuracy nor an adequate distribution of information. In cannibalizing its own information system and propelling it down the vector, the financial market has destabilized itself. It has committed itself to a permanent state of destabilization, in which flux assumes new and perturbing forms, only to be partially stabilized by new rules or artificial technical constraints. The struggle is now to minimize the negative effects of some flows by hedging on flows which move in a contrary direction. Only the biggest centers of capital can afford to pay for the most accurate and detailed information and the most rapid technical means of shifting capital on the restless seas of the international global vector.

It seems odd that while in the '80s enlightenment assumptions about rationality were under attack in the humanities and the social sciences, they were having a field day in pop economics. That the market is a rational mechanism which is nevertheless beyond the conscious agency of individual consciousness was a bold and seductive idea, but nevertheless wrong. It was up to Keynes to introduce some rationality into the fantasy image of the market mechanism, by dwelling on the psychological reality of market behavior. Ironically, Keynes viewed the market as prone to collectivist thinking. When a given set of conventions appeared to work, appeared to explain away the real, assuage doubts and fears, prove instrumentally useful for investing and reaping rewards, then those conventions would be followed, and might prove self-fulfilling. They might feed back into the totality of economic movements which constitute the real and come *retrospectively* to be a correct representation of it. So as long as the Gordon Gekkos of this world succeeded in their scams, that success would legitimate the world view which went with it. The world view would be shown to be instrumentally correct, regardless of its logical status, regardless of what features it left out of the real economy.

Having separated themselves from second nature, the "players" on the vector field of third nature have not achieved a separation from third nature itself, and are indeed deeply bound to it. Hence a new mythical culture, populated by animistic spirits, grows within the interspace of the vector field. Third nature abounds with cults and soothsayers, mostly speaking in tongues which sound a lot like economics, which is a sort of Church Latin of the finance information vector field. These soothsayers have recycled scraps of wisdom from the cultural data bank, transplanted from the mythic field of nature to the vector field of third nature, equally mythic.

For example, Wall Street historian Robert Sobel tells an amusing story about Joe Glanville, a market soothsayer who was proven right one time by the turn of market events. Joe became an overnight financial celebrity. He took off on a national lecture tour, on which he predicted an earthquake in California and claimed to be teaching a monkey to drive his car.[37] No set of conventional assumptions can explain everything, especially in a market growing ever more complex. After a few inaccurate predictions, Glanville lost the confidence of his audience, just as easily as the more scientific market analysts with their traceries of charts and their newfangled numerology of theorems. Should the interaction between the conventional, enchanted world of economic representation and the ineffable real economy start to build up perverse and damaging effects, the whole might come crashing down. A simultaneous crisis for the real economy and the representation of it might result, forcing a narrative crisis of no small importance.

Administering the Referents

Just such a narrative crisis took place in October 1987. In the week before the crash there was a hint from other representational spaces about other moves taking place on the swings and roundabouts of the world economy that the speculative carnival was over. On 4 September, Alan Greenspan at the U.S. Federal Reserve discreetly signaled an impending rise in interest rates. The signal was lost in the noise of other news on the financial pages, fretting about trade deficit figures, trouble in the Gulf, new legislation mooted for takeovers, electioneering, and concern for the first lady's health. Looking back on it, trying to fabricate a beginning for this story which like all weird global media events appears to begin in the middle, the change in mood on Wall Street dates perhaps from Wednesday, 14 October. This was when the Commerce Department announced the latest trade deficit figures. These showed a small decline in America's trade deficit vis-à-vis the rest of the world, but Wall Street chose to interpret it in a pessimistic spirit—the fall had not been big enough. Friday, 16 October, was a bad day. The New York stock market had its first 100-point fall in a single day. The situation clearly indicated that Monday would see another fall.

Gekko's traders probably went home like the rest and did their homework on the weekend, which would have shown that, technically speaking, the market was past its peak and it was time to sell.[38] The copies of the *Wall Street Journal* they may have read on that Friday would have contained the following stories: "An Iranian missile struck an American owned tanker near Kuwait." Elsewhere on the front page, "In Washington, Reagan left open the possibility of retaliation." In financial news, "Stocks and bonds slid further as treasury secretary Baker tried to calm markets." Baker tried to sound an upbeat note for the last working news day of the week by stating, "I believe Chairman Greenspan and his board when they say inflationary fears are unjustified." In London, the *Financial Times* continued the gloomy mood on the following Monday. "The larger the party, the bigger the mess," it warned. It also saw Baker's outbursts on negotiations with the German Bundesbank as "an extraordinarily abrupt reversal of U.S. economic diplomacy." On the international scene, "The US appeared to be still undecided at the weekend whether to retaliate militarily against Iran following the Iranian missile attack on Friday on a US flagged tanker in Kuwaiti waters." It mentioned that "George Shultz, the US secretary of state, gave an ambiguous response to questions about how the US might react." Such is the bedtime reading that gives financiers sleepless nights. The insomnia of reason breeds monsters.

The market's signals indicated a downward move, and market-watchers had the weekend to toil away at their leisure, analyzing the market information with their computers. The market does not respond just to past price and volume signals, but to all of the information available to it. Indeed, the market is held to be "efficient" in the strong sense by rational market theorists because it responds to *all* potentially relevant information, not just past market movements.[39] All available information which might affect expectations is fed into the market vector field from the international news vector. This includes both political developments and news about international "economic diplomacy." As much as they may resent it, markets and market players still operate in an environment where state institutions make many of the rules and can powerfully affect the totality of economic movements through legislation. The decisions of the more or less autonomous central banks can speed or slow the economy through their influence on interest rates and money supply. Much, then, is in the hands of the state, even if key parts here are not under democratic control.[40] Information about the intentions of state economic organizations is thus highly relevant to the market, which has an informational relation to the state (in the form of a flow) as well as an institutional one (in the form of a constraint).

Market-makers keep one eye on the market and the other eye on the state. Which means that they must reserve their "third eye" for watching television. One extra scintilla which burst into this negative information environment was not foreseen and could not have been more badly timed. Speaking about economic negotiations with West Germany, Treasury Secretary Baker said in a television interview, "If the Germans feel it necessary to toughen up their financial policy at the risk of putting a brake on their economy, they can't expect us to stand by with our arms folded."[41] This indicated that the German Bundesbank was going to increase interest rates. This would slow down the German economy, perhaps cutting the sale of American goods to Germany and worsening the trade deficit; perhaps contributing to a more general slowdown in the world economy, affecting the American economy also. Perhaps this would slow the rate at which the profits from Germany's export-driven economy could be recycled back to deficit-ridden America in the form of bond buyups and stock-buying splurges. Baker's remarks were widely held to indicate that the U.S. might retaliate with a devaluation of the dollar. This could make American exports more attractive, but would adversely affect anyone outside the U.S. who held their wealth in U.S. dollars, or Americans intending to buy outside the U.S. in currencies other than the dollar, such as, say, German D-marks. With so many ramifications, no wonder the markets were wired in one way or another to Baker's TV message. In retrospect, one might add, no wonder such a tiny event could seem to spark the forest fire of 19 October across the world's stock markets. This is one plausible beginning one might write for the story—after the event.

Without going into the details or the ramifications of this peculiar international economic politics, perhaps it is enough to note that the state is engaged here in a politics of third nature. Baker and the Bundesbank played a game of power, fought over the definition of the relative values and movements of many kinds of liquid assets. The relative worth of the dollar to the D-mark and the quantity and price of both affect all of these assets. The market doesn't bypass the state in the deregulated financial environment. On the contrary it is all the more central to it. State institutions, even the constitutionally autonomous German Bundesbank, have a powerful ability to *administer the referents* in the space of third nature.

It is difficult to know what the effect of these events in the *political* economy of third nature was on the overall event of the crash. It is difficult to tell the forest from the trees. Stories told after the fact mostly homed in on the same putative causes, but were reluctant to assign importance to them. "No single event, but a swarm of converging causes—among them the treasury secretary James Baker threatening to beat down the dollar if the Germans raised interest rates—provoked the panic," in the judgment of *Fortune*. The *Financial Times* thought that the markets were responding to "the potentially deadly combination of a falling dollar, rising world interest rates, and a US recession."[42] The problem is that there is no easy way to quantify the impact of news information on markets. News information either increases uncertainty or reduces it. In the Black Monday crash, every scintilla of news seemed to trigger further uncertainty, making it more difficult to assess risk and act. The vector feeds information into the market, but the "efficiency" of the market's response depends on being able to *interpret* that information in an appropriate way.

Moreover, a rational response for an individual to the overall information picture might not be a rational response if everyone else acts the same way. Rationality exists in the flow of time and in relation to other acts and judgments, rational or not. Imagine what would have been going through the minds of Gordon Gekko and his brokers, and their counterparts throughout Wall Street and indeed the rest of the world, on Friday afternoon, 16 October. Their main concern would be that if interest rates rose in Bonn they would rise in New York. A rise in interest rates causes people to leave the stock market, where dividends are likely to fall anyway, and head for the bond or money markets, where the rate of return is now higher.

While it may make more sense for each individual to act in this manner, the sum of such actions may result in pandemonium. If a fire breaks out in a crowded theater, it makes sense to each individual to leave, quickly. As the crowd stampedes the doorways, some may be crushed or killed in the panic, unnecessarily. In this crisis, as in the overheated market, the problem lies with the narrow aperture between the safe and the dangerous zones. Quite a few Gordon Gekkos, and even more diminutive little people end up crushed in the rush. In the market, as in the burning theater, you can count on the big boys to muscle their way out first.

It would be a busy week for another cultural icon of the Roaring '80s, Sherman McCoy, the "Master of the Universe" depicted in Tom Wolfe's novel *The Bonfire of the Vanities*.[43] McCoy was a bond dealer, trading in the increasingly global and liquid world of "securitized debt," meaning debt transformed into an exchangeable financial instrument and set loose on the third nature of the globalized markets. If interest rates are low, the money is to be made from putting your money in stocks and hoping the low interest rates stimulate growth and productivity and fat dividends. If the interest rates are high, the money is to be made short-term in the money markets and long-term on bonds. So the crash would result in a busy time for the McCoys. Stock markets always live in the shadow of the big central banks like the U.S. Federal Reserve and the German Bundesbank and their influence on interest rates. The central banks can (metaphorically speaking) pump money into the economy, cheapening the stuff and causing rates to fall, or they can soak it up, making it scarce and precious and causing interest rates to rise. For the stock markets, a rise in interest rates is a message ("look out!") and punch on the nose (smack!!) all at once: information and action combined.

Baker's TV interview on Saturday preempted the Bundesbank by more or less spelling out on broadcast television what the German economic negotiators had said they were intending to do. Interest rates would have gone up anyway, and the stock market would have come down—there were enough indicators pointing to the end of the bull market to cause a slump on Friday. What might not have been necessary or prudent was adding that little scintilla of information into the enchanted world at precisely that moment. It caused the selloff precipitated by the peak of the bull market to coincide with the selloff in anticipation of interest-rate rises. But then, no one would know until Tuesday morning that the network of information and money tying all this together was a fragile global gossamer web which could transmit not only the information and capital of more or less efficient and orderly markets but the noise and static of chaotic markets poleaxed by the real as well.

Rationality Meltdown

"I call it the nearest thing to a meltdown I'm ever likely to see," said John Phelan, chairman of the New York Stock Exchange.[44] This somewhat intemperate remark to journalists, made in the white heat of the event, can be contrasted with a later one, where he states that the system "has shown its ability to handle an increased amount of volatility."[45] Which still doesn't quite get away from the fact that there was volatility aplenty. While some market narrators had tipped a peaking of the bull market for quite some time, nobody had really predicted the eventful form it actually took. The *Wall Street Journal* quoted Phelan putting the blame on five factors:

1. The lack of a correction for the past five years.
2. Fears of inflation.
3. Rising interest rates.
4. The conflict with Iran in the Gulf.
5. Added volatility caused by derivative instruments such as futures, index futures, and portfolio insurance.

The point about all of these factors is that they were well-known pieces of information for at least a week before the crash, and had indeed led to a downward trend for some days. They may explain the downward trend, but do they explain the crash?

As chairman of the exchange, Phelan was hardly likely to dispense anything but calming bromides, particularly in the tense atmosphere following the crash, where statements from him might really give what the jargon calls a "jittery" market the shits. Information feeds back instantly into the markets, and can rapidly be mistaken for noise. More telling is a comment Phelan made in *Fortune* magazine a few years later on the subject of upgrading the technological systems of the exchange. "That trading floor is the same space where we did 14 million share days in 1968 and it had to be shut down one day a week to handle the paperwork. One day in October 1987 we traded 608 million shares. The productivity of the people working on the floor has gone up exponentially."[46] It's curious that the mad scramble to push 608 million shares through a badly overloaded computer system in a day is somehow an index of productivity. What exactly was being *produced* here? Stock market employees produce share transactions. Their efficiency is a purely relative measure: they do more of them per head than they used to, not least because of changes in technology. Such is the perception of value in third nature, relative entirely to itself. In the rhetoric of market rationality, it must always be assumed that the outcome of a market move is a rational one, so long as the market itself is more or less competitive. Rationality is attributed to the market itself rather than to the actors within it. Not all of the latter need act rationally for the market itself to be a rational instrument. It is simply assumed that more rational players win and less rational ones lose, but the market itself is a rational instrument. Hence if it decides to chuck a wobbly, all that remains is to process its desires as rapidly as possible.

This is why pro-market analysts such as Lawrence Harris can say, after the event, that "future problems can be at least partially eliminated if capacity limits to the flow of information are raised. In particular, orders, confirmation, and transaction reports on the ticker-tape should all arrive at their destination instantly."[47] Presumably this would eliminate things like the fact that when the crash hit London, the screen pages of the London Stock Exchange's Automated Quotation system showed many important stocks as down 99 points because the counter on the screen didn't have a third digit.[48] Not only the transmission of information but the transmission of trades themselves, in Harris's view, must not impede the movements of the market. On Black Monday and the following Tuesday there were 608 million shares passing through the New York Stock Exchange, in a system designed to handle 400 million shares per day. [49] Harris's solution is to increase the capacity of the vector to maintain "orderly" movement, no matter what the velocity.

To Harris, imperfections in the rationality of the market result from the technical imperfections of the system. Perfect the vector and the market will continue to allocate capital rationally, shifting it faster and further. This does seem to contradict another popular remark about the crash, which is made to defend the role of the computer vector in the market. "Computers," as *The Economist* put it, "do little more than help investors respond quickly to information. The real problem, on the way down as on the way up, is that knowing information is not necessarily the same as understanding it."[50] This latter view returns to the question of the rationality of the *actors* in the market themselves, rather than the rationality of the market as a supra-individual entity. If information moves more and more swiftly, down more and more complex vectors, then can market players actually keep up? Or will the *reactions* to movements be increasingly automated too, so that those who can afford it can react in a preprogrammed way to predicted changes, instantly and massively?

There may not be any option, given that the business information firm Reuters is reportedly "spending megabucks" on a system that would provide "quotations for every instrument traded on every significant stock, commodity, option or futures exchange in the world." Already, satellites used in Europe deliver quotes at a speed of 64,000 binary digits a second. As such technology spreads and interlocks, the movement of liquidity becomes more and more tied to the vector and to third nature, less and less to the cumbersome, slow-moving business of making things and selling them, which both debt and equity finance were originally designed to facilitate. The beneficiaries in manufacturing, it seems, are a handful of suppliers offering complex and powerful technical vectors. "It seems likely that within a few years only a small number of large quotation vendors with resources to survive in, and supply, global markets will remain."[51] Presumably their stock prices are pretty solid.

In a special section of the *Financial Times* on the globalization of financial trading, the situation is aptly summed up thus: "Computer technology and improved telecommunications have changed the nature of world stock markets, bringing instant price and news information from around the world to the desks of every professional trader and investor. The responses to the data—buy and sell orders—may be more rapid, synchronised and international than they once were, and in this sense technology might appear to accelerate market movements."[52] This may increase "volatility," but that is a relative term. The volatility of yesteryear looks like small change compared to 1987. Perhaps more significant, what is volatility to a very small player in the market may leave the bigger players unperturbed—or looking for momentary bargains. If one assumes that the market responds to all available information, then volatility results from doubts about assets or from the process of transaction. There is, however, a third kind of volatility, noise-induced volatility. This results not from uncertainty, nor from the trading system itself, but from misinformation.

Efficient market theory, as it is called, proposes that while there are information inequalities on stock markets, a trader who is not "in the know" can infer what others *do* know from the behavior of prices themselves. But if there are some large players in the market who are big enough to affect price levels significantly by their own actions, then competition is imperfect. When this is the case, "the amount of information conveyed by prices is to some degree a matter of their strategic choice."[53] This is exactly what Gordon Gekko was doing in the movie *Wall Street:* using information strategically, rather than translating useful knowledge directly into the action of buying and selling. A gap appears here between the rationality of self-interest and the rationality of the market. Thus Gekko might proceed quietly to acquire stock based on inside information, through dummy accounts and so on, rather than broadcast to all his intentions and his knowledge. On the other hand, he was not averse to creating false information either, "talking up" stocks by generating noise which other buyers mistake for information. This is not to suggest that everyone who plays the stock market is a crook. Yet if there are only a few crooks making "false" moves, this dissimulation may affect the whole market if their movements are taken to be useful information.

Efficient market theory assumes that players who act on noise information will lose their money. The market supposedly irons out irrational imperfections. Yet what if a majority, or even a significant minority, of movements in the market were caused by noise rather than valid information? This situation may not be quite so uncommon. In any case, the distinction between noise and information is an analytic one. How is even the best-informed player to decide if deprived of the time to decide? Michel Serres sees noise as a "third man" present in an exchange of information. "To hold a dialogue is to suppose a third man and to seek to exclude him; a successful communication is the exclusion of the third man."[54] Serres sees this problem of noise, the third party, as more significant than the problem of the other, who appears in communication as the second party. The other allows a subject to form in relation to it, it allows an identity which can say "I" or "we": "As an American, I . . ." or "We Germans are. . . ." The problem of noise exists as a third party in this relation, interfering in the understanding which parties to a dialogue can have of each other.

Hence the need to struggle to exclude the possibility of a third party, so that two parties may form a reciprocal image of each other. The exclusion of the third is clearly very important in communications upon which actions and events may turn, but in a situation where there are many potential parties to dialogue present, all with competing and contradictory interests, a little noise may be a necessary thing. Noise is clearly present in the relationship between Baker and the Bundesbank, or to return to earlier examples, between Saddam Hussein and the American State Department, or between Helmut Kohl and the German people. When others are listening, it may be necessary not to exclude the third party, to send a confused or noisy message. This is the art of politics in the age of the vector.

On the other hand, economics is premised on a kind of quantitative fetish of "noiselessness." "Mathematics presents itself as a successful dialogue or communication which rigorously dominates its repertoire and is maximally purged of noise." The fetish for *quantified* information in the third nature of the finance vector stems from this belief, but as Serres adds, "Of course, it is not that simple." In a mathematical language, "the irrational and the unspeakable lie in the details; listening always requires collating; there is always a leftover or residue, indefinitely. But then, the scheme remains open, and history possible."[55] Or in the age of the instant vector, coupled with the mathematical language of economics, *the event* remains possible. Noise and information may become indistinguishable. Market players may choose to listen to the "demon" third rather than the other. When hot noise hits the cold vector, rationality vaporizes.

In a situation where noise is prevalent but where the dialogue partners are not as finely tuned to it, as in the diplomacy of news media, it may be possible to profit from the admixture of noise and information rather than seek to profit solely from the exposure of noise in favor of valid information. "Investors, with no access to information, act on noise as if it were information that would give them the edge."[56] Rather than being driven out by arbitrageurs who spot the difference between what noise buyers and sellers will trade on and what a more rational view of the market might suggest, it is quite possible that noise may at times prevail. Rationalists might not want to risk proving the misinformed wrong if it may take a long time to profit from that rationality. If a market is being driven in a given direction, say up and up in a bull market run, it may not be prudent to insist otherwise even if the rise is not justified on the evidence. Third nature can thus resist the pull of second nature.

If one suspends the assumption that the markets *represent* the economy as a whole, and treat them as a globalizing vector field rapidly developing their own time and space, then they can become an arena of speculative potential *using* information *about* the economy of second nature. The relationship might be something like the soccer pools, which for many people have nothing to do with soccer. The matches simply provide a more or less random result against which the bets placed in the pool are judged. Likewise, the markets may use information from the economy as the stakes. Information about the statistical image of the economy might constitute a player's resources and skills. The art is in playing the properties of space and time peculiar to third nature rather than concentrating on the market's representational role as an image of second nature.

The markets, in other words, might be becoming a *modern art,* in which the materiality of the tools and spaces of information are themselves the game. Noise becomes a tool among others in what Donald Trump christened "the art of the deal." Profiting from noise becomes equivalent to profiting from information, and in the short term, possibly more profitable. The volume of movement caused by noise in the short term may be more profitable than the tendency of movement in the long run. Which is bad news for the fortunes of the firms that make and sell things on the terrain of second nature. One can indeed make "cash from chaos," as the self-styled pop svengali Malcolm McLaren proposed. The third nature of global finance, like the third nature of global style, admits the *false move* as a profitable option.

If there are noise traders in the market, it is risky to trade against them for another reason. If the basis of their present actions is irrational, then their next action may be irrational too. There is no reason to expect them to respond rationally in future if they do not do so now. Hence "noise traders create their own space."[57] They can actually expect to benefit from the noise created by their actions. A positive feedback loop can arise, where noise traders can drive a market in a given direction, say down into a bearish mood. As the information of their willingness to sell passes through the market, the rational arbitrageurs who wish to buy at their expense may be outvoted by noise traders taking the sell move as a cue and selling more, driving prices down even further. Were such a move to happen very suddenly, would there be terribly much time to gather enough information to decide whether a given movement is rational or not?

Efficient market theory assumes that rational players, who are in the majority, study the available relevant information and profit from the badly informed by knowing more, and more quickly, than they do. There may be a more profitable method, however. De Long et al. remark that "many professional arbitrageurs spend their resources examining and predicting the pseudo-signals noise traders follow in order to bet against them more successfully. These pseudo-signals include value and price patterns, sentimental indices and the forecasts of Wall Street gurus."[58] Rather than continually using statistical or analytic techniques, fathoming the lie of second nature beneath the glistening surface of the market, there may be another strategy, and another metaphor for describing it. In this other strategy, the player studies the surfaces of third nature rather than attempting to find the stable bottom beneath the turbulent surface. In the instant sand-dune shifts of these surfaces, the third nature of the market provides opportunities in and of itself. What matters is the speed and size of the dunes, not what lies beneath them. Or to paraphrase Gordon Gekko, the market is not a second nature where values are created and exchanged, it is a third nature where values are transferred from one perception to another. It is private property in a purer form, detached from tangible, sensible, material substance—property without properties. It is private property all the easier to privatize because it lacks substantial natural or machine-made form.

Markets may not, it seems, be as rational as all that. Or rather, the concept of rationality has to be expanded considerably when thinking about economic behavior, just as it has in the humanities and the social sciences. Economics, it seems, is still innocent of complex motives and unsystemic impulses in its heart of hearts. Perhaps market players are so lost in the bitstream of information that they no longer quite grasp the connection between the signals passing through the ether of third nature and the totality of relations which it imperfectly maps and represents.[59] The turn toward "chaos theory" in market hypotheses might indicate a recognition, to some degree, of irrationality as the other of any form of orderly behavior. The chaos theorists are "sceptical about the concept of rational, basically stable markets, believing the markets to be subject, at times, to unpredictability, volatility, overshooting and what gives the impression of being short-term rationality."[60] The amount of hedging and qualification in this passage indicates that chaos theory is meant to come to the rescue of the basic assumption of rationality by discovering more complex forms in which it can manifest itself and new methods for finding it.

Economic theory likes to imagine *proportional* changes between factors, whereas chaos theory posits the possibility of minute *qualitative* changes which trigger massive quantitative shifts. The stock market crash seems to fit such an assumption nicely. Rather than a rational and orderly transference from "one perception to another," as Gekko might put it, some tiny scraps of information appeared to trigger massive shifts, as we shall see. The wider difficulty with this is that if the combination of news information vectors with financial transaction vectors simply increases the scale and scope of the events crashing through it, then the globalization of financial markets appears far less attractive. Hence the insistence by many that the crash was a "correction," not a freefall or a meltdown. Correction implies an error in an otherwise rational communication of messages. The bull market is thus seen as a correct tendency which just overshot the mark a bit, and had to be corrected back in the other direction. The crash precipitated a rather too drastic movement in the other direction, which was subsequently corrected again with a surge of buy orders on Tuesday. Correction implies that while noise might cause exaggerations at the margin, the general trajectory and form of the market is rational. "What is rational is real and what is real is rational" seems to be the philosophy here, still. The efficient market theorists may want to believe that, but for everyone else who watched the crash on TV, "what is good appears and what appears is good" seemed to more aptly sum up the consensual hallucination of the '80s.

"Meltdown" is a dangerous metaphor, but in a sense an apt one. A meltdown in a nuclear power plant takes place if a controlled nuclear reaction gets out of control and melts through the restraints which regulate the reaction. In place of the controlled release of energy, a positive feedback loop starts: each release of electrons triggers the crash-up of more and more atoms, a tendential process which bursts out of the constraints meant to manage it. The metaphor is apt in that it captures the sense of a positive feedback loop taking the place of the negative feedback loop which is supposed to characterize the market.[61] Markets are supposed to be homeostatic and self-regulating—like nuclear power stations. They grow, but in a manner which automatically seeks equilibrium. Yet as Marx clearly saw, the tendencies of capitalism are dynamic. Capital pushes the development of the vector so hard and fast that it bursts through its own limits, as it did in October 1987. Like a meltdown, the crash was an accident programmed in advance to happen as the system pushed against its own limits.

Kathy Acker writes, "I am giving an accurate picture of God: A despot who needs a constant increase in His power in order to survive. God equals capitalism."[62] This is the god the devotees of the market secretly believe in, even if nobody else does. In attempting to increase its power over itself and the world via the vector, capital encounters obstacles within itself. The event is the symptom of this encounter with the obstacle. Third nature is both the means by which capital extends itself, and the symptom of its inability to do so. The event is thus an *iconoclastic* moment. The event is the autodestruction of the iconology of contemporary faiths. The event is a privileged moment in which to see third nature for what it really is, stripped of its myths and kitchen gods.

From Fordism to the Crash

Although the event provides the negative conditions for a demystification of the stories told about the economic real, it does not in itself enable us to see what by its very nature cannot be seen. The economic real is something terrible and sublime, vast and godless. The enchanted world of economic calculation and storytelling exists precisely because that which it calculates and narrates is too infinite in extent and complexity to be grasped in itself by mere human perception. The logistics of perception exists to present this sublime and ineffable other as if it came with a built-in point of view which matches our sense of scale and proportion. The stories, the statistics, the analyses, the models—all exist to render human what has become posthuman.

In this last story that I want to improvise out of the time of the event, I want to deal in the most abstract way with the relation between the signs of the economy which float through our everyday life and the economic real, basking below some opaque and muddy depth. Readers uninterested in an abstract, speculative mode of writing about the event may want to skip.

While we cannot grasp this economic sublime in itself, other than through the mediation of the enchanted world of appearances, we can still speculate on what, beyond our perception, those appearances may constitute. In other words, one of the stories one can write, one of the ways of brokering the event, is in terms of a kind of organic Marxism. A Marxism which appears to grow out of the event itself, or rather out of what the event reveals. Given that it was the telegraphed news of a looming crisis which incited in Marx the tremendous outpourings of the *Grundrisse* notebooks, perhaps all Marxism has or ought to have this organic quality. Perhaps it can be recovered from the slow and steady time of the academy and reconnected to the abrupt and turbulent time of the surprise guest appearances of the economic real within the host of appearances which make up the enchanted world.

The story one might tell along these lines today is that the very experience of a regular economic temporality and the occasional irruption both owe their nature to a certain developing relation between the economic real and the increasingly abstracted space of third nature in which it appears in both its mundane and terrible forms. It would be a Marxist story precisely because it involves the relationship between price and value; between the perceptible signs of the economic in everyday life and the invisible but nevertheless totally real forces beyond where values are created as a social process and consumed. For our present purposes, we need a story about this relation which does not reduce price to value or value to price. Regardless of the merits of such positions as bits of economic theory—by and for economists—they do not shed much light on the problem of a relation between price as an evident measure and value as a concept for an inexplicable process.[63]

What does shed some light on it is the so-called "regulation school" of economists, some of whom, like Alain Lipietz and Michel Aglietta, take the non-identity of price and value to be a central and useful idea in Marx's thinking.

As Jameson points out, Adorno thought of the exchange relationship in capitalism as fundamentally a relation of identity.[64] And so it is, but nonidentity creeps into it, not merely at the margin, but fundamentally between its appearance in everyday life as price and its social being for no one in particular as value.

The regulationist writers such as Alain Lipietz try to think about the economic real systematically, as the interrelation of three processes. The first is the labor process. They look for distinctive phases in the social and technical development of the labor process, each of which has its characteristic techniques. The second is the regime of accumulation. This is the corresponding historical development of the various branches of production and the forms of consumption which correspond to them. The third is the mode of regulation. This is the matrix of institutional forms which connect the everyday life of workers and capitalists, bureaucrats and caregivers as they experience it to the regime of accumulation. It is the whole set of social and cultural norms and constraints which produce a population of productive bodies on the one hand, and render the process intelligible and manageable to the bodies so produced.[65]

Aglietta identified two modes of regulation of the process of production, accumulation, and distribution of the social product. He called them respectively the competitive and monopolist modes of regulation. What is distinctive about the latter is that it is a phase in which the representational space of economic agents grows enough to allow a fairly systematic process of calculation and forecasting. Aglietta attributes this to the dense network of institutions which emerge to supplement and supplant simple market mechanisms. One could also point to the role played here in the development of forms of communication which make possible a constant mapping and remapping of economic space and its movements. Monopolist regulation depends on the development of third nature to a certain point, where more complex and rapid communications about the economic real are feasible. This permits a matrix of decision-making discourses about the productive and allocative activities of second nature to flow across its vectors. The vector becomes the general equivalent of any and every productive relation of second nature. Just as money as a general thing is the equivalent of commodities as particular things, the vector as a general relation becomes the equivalent of any and every particular productive relation.

This space of calculation is what Alain Lipietz, following Marx, calls the "enchanted world." It is a world of "prices proposed, profits anticipated and wages demanded."[66] One might add that it is a world in which these formerly local acts of calculating and narrating the economic real become increasingly abstracted from particular places and become integrated into a map of such behaviors, the map of third nature. This enchanted world interacts with quite another world, the world of the economic real. Now, one of the striking things about contemporary thinking about the economic is the assumption that because the economic discourse which takes place on the surface of third nature has become ever more universal, this automatically means that the workings of the economy itself are becoming more transparent and ubiquitous. This is not necessarily so, because the apparently universal map of the economy on the surface of third nature is not equivalent to the economic real itself. It is something more than a mere representation of it; it is something less than the economic real itself. The two are, dare I say, dialectically implied in each other, but they are not identical.

The enchanted world is thoroughly interconnected with, but not identical to, what Lipietz calls "the disenchanted world of blind struggle for ownership of the social labour product." A blindness not of the immediate, particular form that the economic takes, but a blindness to its great posthuman whole, the second nature of the struggle to wrest a domain of freedom from necessity, which imposes its own necessities, not least of which is that the struggle with the terrain of nature and its products appears in the form of a struggle between human agents.

For Lipietz, the relation between the enchanted world and its "disenchanted" other is a problematic one. Nothing guarantees that the nominal prices set by the enchanted world will be the "right" ones in terms of a future outcome, although they will continue to regulate the workings of the economic real, or at least appear to, until their inadequacy reveals itself in a momentary break, an acute crisis large or small when the economic real appears as an irruption. Lipietz frequently returns to the image of a cartoon character who has gone over the edge of a cliff and continues walking on thin air, not noticing anything amiss. My favorite version of this is the coyote in the Roadrunner cartoons, who always looks back at the viewer in a Stoic moment, before plummeting to a ground so far below that we cannot see it. All we see is the faint puff of dust as he hits the deck. This is an apt image for the moment when the economic real reveals itself—in its absence.

Lipietz uses this image to illustrate the crisis of Fordism as a regime of accumulation and the way it revealed itself in the '70s. This regime keeps running on credit even though the ground underpinning postwar growth has fallen away. The steady, invisible, incremental increases in industrial productivity have long since ceased to deliver the growth in output that could cover the expectations built into the monopolist mode of regulation that wages and living standards will rise, that the welfare state will be maintained, that employment will remain more or less full depending on the mood swings of the business cycle. Actually, the fall in the rate of increase in productivity is something measurable and known. Indexing this is part of the task of administering the referents performed by economic agencies of the state. What is not known, what is lost in conjecture and in the intricate and dispersed differential details of the economic real, are its specific causes. An index after the fact is not the same thing as a knowledge of the totality of the process as it unfolds in time. That difference is part of the distinction between the enchanted world and the disenchantments of the economic real. In any case, the slowdown in the rate of increase of productivity is in the regulationist view at the heart of a series of crises and evasions, and forms one of the beginnings to a story one might tell after the fact about the sublime middle point where the stock market crashes.

The failure to deliver increased productivity leads to the "stagflation" crisis of the '70s. Workers in the industrialized, overdeveloped West push for the customary round of wage increases, but without the underpinning of increased productivity, the outcome can be only a profit squeeze or price rises. To the extent that there is a profit squeeze, investment slows and the rate of increase in productivity is further hampered. To the extent that there are price rises, this can only encourage a further round of wage demands, more price rises, and so on. An inflationary spiral where the nominal values of wages and prices chase each other's tails but make only temporary changes to the distribution of social product within the economic real.

This brings to an end the growth phase of Fordist regulation, where steady gains in productivity through social and technical engineering of the workplace provided the basis for steady advances in real income for workers, both in take-home pay and in the social wage. This created the basis for a culture of consumption which cleared the markets of the vast stocks produced and steered investment into consumer products. The state came to the party by providing the infrastructure needed to expand consumption: the roads, schools, power stations, and so on. Such was Fordism, as much a culture of everyday life as a regime of accumulation, but where both were held together by an elaborate institutional matrix of monitoring, bargaining, and calculating.

When Fordism started to slow down, when stagnation and inflation descended upon it at the same time, the enchanted world became the focus for a series of attempts to restart the engine of development. The central banks tried fiddling with the money supply. They tried to expand it, in order to ease credit and stimulate demand. Then they tried to contract it, the "monetarist" phase of contraction and shakeouts. They tried a middle way between the two. This third scenario corresponds to the Reagan years, when the credit eased a little but the budget deficit kept growing, pushing along demand. This was financed with U.S. treasury loans from Germany and Japan. The result was that the value of the dollar and interest rates rose. The trade deficit worsened, leading to the "twin deficit" problem highlighted in the media. The government spent more than it raised in taxes, covering the difference by selling treasury bonds. To make these attractive, they had to offer competitive interest rates, thus pushing up all interest rates and pushing up the value of the dollar. Which in turn did nothing to help the trade balance. An overvalued dollar hampered American exports and made foreign goods look comparatively cheap. Which did nothing for the confidence of capital in investing in American manufacturing, at a time when high interest rates made borrowing unattractive anyway. Higher productivity would thus not flow from technical improvement. It had to come from reducing the cost of labor.

Reducing the cost of labor meant not only the attack on living standards across the United States, but the phenomenon of the "runaway shop."[67] In search of lower overheads, firms move to low wage or low tax states, or close their plants in the U.S. altogether and move production offshore. All of these methods may for the individual firm lower costs relative to output for a given production technique, thus improving productivity, but they have an adverse effect on aggregate demand. Pushing down wages means less purchasing power. Lowering taxes to induce businesses to stay or move to your state reduces state outlays and hence demand from the state sector. The shortfall in demand may in some measure be made up by federal deficit spending, mostly on the arms industry, but the dubious benefits of this policy are not evenly spread throughout the economy. In short, the monopolist mode of regulation and Fordist patterns of accumulation broke down.

Autonomous Third Nature

Two movements arising out of this crisis are significant for another story, the rapid development of the vectors of telesthesia in the '80s and the connection between the enchanted world of economic appearances and third nature. One is the already mentioned tendency to move production offshore. The other is the move to "deregulate" areas of business previously kept off limits by state constraints. These two movements extend the modern form of second nature, under the sway of the abstract form of capital, out into the world with a new intensity and into the last holdouts within the overdeveloped world itself. Both movements require an intensive and an extensive development of the vector. Both movements are a seizing hold of the space of second nature, in its crisis, by the intensive and extensive powers of third nature. This is the dual movement of globalization and deregulation, a great, uneven development of the forces and relations of communication at the expense of certain institutional barriers and constraints at a time when the forces of production were not developing qualitatively at a speed sufficient to meet the demands of wage earners, creditors, and the needs of capital replacement.

This at least is one way of telling the story, a beginning for the crash of '87. For the extensive and intensive development of third nature not only facilitated the reorganization of the global space of productive second nature as a space of flows rather than a space of places. It also facilitated a new autonomy for third nature. Second nature can know itself only locally. It cannot know itself in its complexity and as a whole. Third nature, with its endless series of economic indices and electronic transactions, is the consciousness of second nature as a whole. The monopolist form of regulation involved more than just state institutions and a certain culture for economic everyday life, although Lipietz and Aglietta are quite right in stressing the importance of both. It also involved the technical development of the means of communication.

Third nature develops as a form of consciousness of second nature. Yet it is also a consciousness of itself. As its various financial instruments become more abstract, they become properties in their own right, convertible into each other and traded in their own right. Their holders become a class apart. "Rentiers," as Joan Robinson called them—their interests as holders of the immaterial values of third nature detach from the holders of property in second nature. As Robinson comments, "The relationship between the yield and the capital value of placements is very loosely connected with the relation between output and productive capacity for the economy."[68] The enchanted world within which the rentier buys placements and clips the coupons from them operates according to its own consciousness of the relative value of these instruments relative to each other, not just relative to the various standing reserves of values they represent in the productive processes of second nature. Financial instruments may lack substance, but they do not lack qualities. The valuation of those qualities assumes a life of its own. "The typical rentier," says Robinson, "has been brought up in conceptions which echo the morality of the peasant." In other words, they live off what they regard as their entitlements to the terrain—in this case, of third nature.

The rentier class are not a new phenomenon, but they develop in number and influence with the development of third nature and its autonomy from second nature. As Lipietz remarks, "It is only contemporary capitalism which has actually asserted the autonomy of the [enchanted world], particularly in the current crisis."[69] Crashes form something of a paradox for conventional economics, which functions for the most part with a highly nominal theory of value. It recognizes only those values "discovered" in the market. Crashes reveal a fault in the process, a break in the continuous process of discovering value itself. They reveal behind the market something other. Marxists appear to know what that other is, but we might choose to be a bit more sanguine about their claims to have discovered an essence behind the appearance of prices. We can admit at one and the same time that the crash reveals something other, the economic real, the economic sublime, but it is not itself knowable.

In the wake of the crash, a montage of shots stood in for this unknowable. The news showed pictures of checkout lines, close-ups of the cash going into the till. Little fragments of everyday life standing in for the whole. Yet the whole itself is not knowable. All these images do is signal its absence from the scene and thereby attest to its lingering presence in any and every economic scene. The totality of its movements and their connectedness to everyday, sensuous life is a thing of folklore, a popular knowledge. Yet it can appear only through the partial mediation of the enchanted world of third nature which monitors and regulates its movements and presents the sum of those movements in forms which we can perceive. We cannot perceive the economic real itself, as itself, because it is something quite beyond the realm of human perception. It might be of human construction, but it has become a thing apart, a second nature.

The capitalist form of the development of second nature necessitates the development of third nature in a way that the bureaucratic-socialist form does not. Where second nature is organized on the basis of private property, the commodity, and the wage relation, its central problem becomes that of the coordination on an ever-expanding scale of the realization of the product of particular, private, and concrete labors in a social, abstract, exchangeable form. To the extent that decisions about the allocation of the social product of these particular labors lie in private hands, each successful realization of value, accumulation of capital, and expansion of the commodity form across the space of the landscape requires with it the expansion of the enchanted world within which private interests are organized, validated, and effected.

Ironically, it also requires their automation. As the enchanted world grows in speed and complexity, abstract private entities such as companies more and more replace individual agents, while the rational decision-making on behalf of those agents becomes increasingly dependent on the nonhuman intelligence of third nature itself. The maintenance of private interest require its ever more thorough dehumanization.

The space of second nature comes increasingly to depend on the space of third nature, for it is within the vectors of the latter that territories, populations, and resources are monitored and assessed. The more extensive and intensive this process is, the more certainty private holders of capital, i.e., of command over the social product, can have in allocating their resources. The more the space of third nature expands, the more widespread and thorough the process of socializing private and concrete labors can become. The problem being, of course, that the more extensively and intensively the terrain of third nature grows, the more it comes to be a terrain in which the private holders of capital have a stake in third nature itself. It must not only act as a terrain for the discovery and validation of the product of second nature, of tangible commodities, assets, and labors. It must also act as the terrain upon which private investments in third nature *itself* are evaluated.

On the terrain of third nature, agents collect information on the space of second nature, where everything there is framed in Heidegger's term as a "standing reserve."[70] Everything is a quantifiable risk or resource. Even people and nature appear as standing reserves, from the point of view of their instrumental uses. Nature appears as so many acres of pasture yielding a certain quantity of beef or rice, with a certain susceptibility to flood and drought. Or as a mining lease with a certain yield of gold or uranium ore, with a certain cost and difficulty of extraction and transport. Labor appears as a given quantity with a certain level of skill available at a certain price, with a particular historical risk of militancy and ability to self-organize.

People appear here as a resource and risk not only of production, but also of consumption. We appear as standing reserves of demand, categorizable in demographics and taste cultures. The terrain of second nature can be divided by zip codes, each of which can be mapped as containing a certain mix of demographic groups, enabling marketers to closely target potential consumers of this or that product, according to age, gender, ethnicity, sexual habits, and occupation. In fact, all of the things championed by cultural studies as "differences" are also a catalogue of our value of consumers, as mapped on the terrain of third nature. In short, third nature organizes the spaces of the world as an increasingly integrated and increasingly abstracted space of risks and resources. Satellite imaging reveals where previously unvalued mineral resources hide. Ever more complex analyses of the patterns of consumption yield new propositions about our consuming potential. The slow accumulation of aggregate statistical evidence on more and more parts of the global economy enables the integration of more and more parts of the space of second nature into a matrix of calculation and investment. On the basis of this mapping, private holders of capital place their bets. This is the way in which the space of third nature integrates into the space of second nature, at the beginning as well as the end of the cycle of production and consumption. This is where the odds are assessed, where the dice are loaded and thrown, and the winnings picked up from the table.

Yet two things take place within third nature which make it an autonomous terrain, not entirely subservient to the productive relations of second nature. Firstly, forms of credit also appear as standing reserves to be valued and exchanged. As debt becomes abstracted into convertible forms of security, it too is traded, to some extent independently of its connections to particular projects and assets within second nature. A side game develops which starts to affect the main event.

Secondly, any form of credit is an anticipation of a future. A loan extended presupposes its repayment. A bond bought; a coupon clipped and returned. A share of stock bought; a dividend realized. In short, these abstracted forms of third nature anticipate an ongoing process, a certain quantitatively variable relation between moments in time. A process via which private, particular interests and concrete labors, in all their differences, articulated in apparently unsystematic juxtaposition to each other across the terrain of second nature, must nevertheless come together somehow in a totality, unfolding in time. A totality which, no matter how unfashionable it may be as a concept, is nevertheless quite real. It is a real abstraction, existing in the world. An abstraction mapped and monitored by third nature. A map which has only a mediated and unconscious relation to that totality, built out of the flow of data, dependent for its effectiveness on the assumption of continuity in time.

Of all the products of third nature, an exchangeable security is in a sense the most abstracted, most dematerialized, of all commodities. Its degree of abstraction, and hence its utility, lies in the degree of its exchangeability on the one hand and its security on the other. This is its strange tension: it must be as firmly anchored in tangible assets within second nature as possible, yet as freely exchangeable within third nature as possible. The more liquid, the more readily exchangeable a security is, the more it can be said to have the particularly abstract use value of exchangeability. One might say that this is the postmodern commodity par excellence. Its usefulness consists only in its exchangeability for something else. A commodity with the ultimate value of being another value.

This exchangeability, this postmodern value, depends on the continuity of the reproduction of the capital accumulation process. So long as the products of private labor are valorized socially, so long as concrete labors realize their particular values via exchange in the abstract form of money, credit can be extended and exchanged according to established conventions within the enchanted world. These might once have been Fordist conventions, when it could be assumed that the labor process would continue to develop and deliver rises in productivity, when it could be assumed that this rise would produce rising real wages, when it could be calculated that these wages would be turned into so many cars, so many washing machines, so many Elvis records. Now they are what one might call post-Fordist conventions. Productivity is sustained by using the resources of third nature to distribute production around the globe, seeking out standing reserves of cheap but skilled labor. The composition of production has changed in accord with this. Gone are the great mass markets of the West. In their place, products must be targeted at particular demographics. Now that there is a greater disparity between rich and poor, and a growing army of unemployed and semi-employed, a class division arises within commodities themselves, where previously there was a continuum from economy to deluxe. These changes in the regulation of the economic real lead to different investment decisions, based on a different pattern of standing reserves. Credit is no longer extended for the production of the goods of a Fordist mode of consumption, but for something quite different.

To a great extent, investing in productive activity of any kind looks less attractive. Moving production offshore increases productivity by reducing wage rates, but it also reduces consumer demand, precisely by reducing wage rates. Moreover, it shifts that demand from American wage earners to, say, Korean wage earners. What for an individual firm makes perfect sense—reducing costs—has a disastrous effect on the economic real. Aggregate demand falls within the United States, while the offset in rising demand in Korea is not necessarily met by selling American goods into that market. Things look bad for manufacturers, dependent for so long on the Fordist mode of regulation, which kept a predictable cycle of consumption, production, and investment going within the United States for decades. Their share prices drop, in line with the expectation of lower dividends. They find it harder to borrow money: the value of their assets is falling and interest rates are rising. Interest rates are up because the government is selling bonds to attract Japanese and German money, and this money is being used to buy arms. This props up demand within the American economy a little, but it really helps only those parts of the country tied to the military-industrial economy, like California. Keeping the dollar's value high and interest rates high helps create the cliff-edge illusion of a continuity in time of the economic assumptions of third nature, but all the while the contours of the economic real have dipped downwards.

Investment in long-term, productive enterprise on the terrain of second nature looks unattractive. The future is uncertain, demand is low, dividends on industrial stocks are low, interest rates are high. Investors put their money into real estate, fueling the extraordinary land speculation of the '80s. Investors also put their money into high-yield bonds. When interest rates are high, money moves from stocks to bonds, expecting to make a bigger return on the bond coupons than the stock dividend. The '80s were a lively time in the bond market, where an excess flow of liquidity met a lax regulatory regime and the new computerized vectors of calculation and exchange. One of the strangest phenomena of this cliff-edge capitalism was that the value of the stock of manufacturing companies fell below the value of their assets. Thus the takeover boom was born. Money could be made buying up stock, either to force the company to buy it back or find a "white knight" partner, or leading to the takeover of the whole company. The company could then be carved up and sold off. The money for a takeover could be raised by selling bonds to be paid off out of the assets of the target company. This was one of the most characteristic signs in the '80s that third nature not only had diverged from second nature, but was actively cannibalizing it. The combination of this divergence, the technical development of the vector, and the growth of a detailed matrix of information existing at the level of third nature on the standing reserves of capital itself led to an extraordinary period in the history of American capitalism, in which Japan and Germany were heavily implicated as sources of liquidity, and in which the newly industrializing countries were implicated as beneficiaries of the deindustrialization of the landscape of American second nature.[71]

We Built This City on High-Yield Bonds

These were the times when Michael Milken rose to fame as the king of the junk bonds.[72] Milken discovered while in graduate school at Wharton that junk bonds yielded a higher rate of return than one might expect, and that this more than offset the higher risk. As Jeff Madrick, financial editor for WNBC-TV's "Strictly Business" program, says, "In the 1970s, such notions were fairly heretical in academic circles. The financial markets were for the most part thought to be 'efficient.' It meant that profitable opportunities were exploited so quickly that the prices of stocks and bonds reflected almost immediately any news about the underlying companies or the marketplace."[73] Milken discovered that third nature is not a true mirror of second nature—and that one can exploit the flaws in the glass.

Milken raised money with high-yield, low-security bonds for a number of famous takeover attempts. The firm he worked for, Drexel Burnham, had a flash video to show clients, complete with a jingle set to the tune of Jefferson Starship's "We Built This City on Rock and Roll." It showed a *2001*-style space station, replete with flashing lights, orbiting in empty space. The jingle, sung by a woman sounding uncannily like Grace Slick, goes, "We built this city on high-yield bonds." And so the corporate raiders did, building castles in the airless space of third nature. Immaterial fortunes built on intangible values. Conservative columnists would later berate the "instant gratification" sought in finance as in everything else by the "baby-boomers," but there is something else at work here. A familiarity with the abstraction of the vector, born of rock 'n' roll and TV reruns of *2001*.

Milken is emblematic of a certain tendency toward separation on the part of third nature, developing autonomous, specialized movements of its own, no longer necessarily in sync with the rhythms of the production cycle. Credit is built on an assumption of a continuity of time into the future, but it also creates a connection between past and future time, by commanding labors to come into being which can realize their value only at a future time, and thus retrospectively validate the credit extended. But should there be a rupture in the process, should anything force a revaluation of the flow of electronic values circulating in third nature relative to what takes place in second nature, then the side game of trading abstractly the values of third nature against each other will suddenly come crashing to the ground.

This transference of *all* perceptions from one state to another can come from any of the particular flows which cross the screen of third nature. A break in the value of the standing reserve of nature, labor, or credit itself can force open the enchanted world and reveal the inscrutable face of the economic real—its Medusa face reflected on computer screens, wire-service monitors, and eventually the evening news. The enchanted world quite readily adapts to fluctuations in nominal values of anything and everything. That is, after all, the point of it. But a break in the value of a standing reserve is another matter. Not a change in the nominal value, but a *questioning* of nominal value itself. There is a philosophical aspect to crises—they are when the meaning of value itself comes into question.

A revaluation of labor brought about by a sudden burst of militancy, a revaluation of oil brought about by the political manipulation of its price—these are two of the recent historic questionings of value that have forced crises of one kind or another. The militancy of labor in 1968–69, the "oil shocks" of the '70s—each of these questionings of the value of a flow across the space of second nature brought with it crises of global proportions, ramifying throughout all terrains capital has integrated into its dynamic totality. The crash of '87 adds a new chapter to this recent history, one in which a flow of abstract value across the space of third nature triggered the crisis, rather than a tangible standing reserve.

When the future asserts its *difference* from the past, that is the crisis. When an event causes political time, with its storms and stresses, its deals and struggles, to intersect with economic time, with its investments and realizations, its values posited and realized, that is the crisis. It is when the future refuses its continuity with the present and the past as mapped in the economic cartography of third nature. The divergence of third nature from the economic real may indicate a malaise, but it is when an event from another temporality cuts across the screen of the enchanted world that the crisis is triggered.

When this happens, the autonomous side game of abstract values loses its imaginary referent, and a devaluing of all the flows of symbolic value follows. The irony at this point is that the enthusiasm for the technical perfection of the vector in the finance industries which makes possible the ever more frictionless connection of the economic past and present also makes possible the instantaneous transmission of the aphasia of crisis. The enchanted world's disenchantment communicates itself at the maximum velocity engineered into the vector field. To the point where, on Black Monday, a new world record of sorts was posted for the extent to which the ineffable real could be simultaneously and instantly grasped in all capitals of the overdeveloped world.

The rupture between the space of production/consumption and the enchanted world, between second and third nature, has a temporal dimension. It is the forcing open of the gap between two temporalities. The valuations made within third nature of the various standing reserves is an anticipation based on a present assessment of the valuation of the past. These future valuations will, more or less, come to pass if the future indeed turns out, more or less, as a continuum from the past. But if a significant standing reserve turns out not to yield the value expected, then the intertemporal chain breaks. Like any other chain of significations, a final calling into account of the value of the symbolic order of third nature is indefinitely deferred. And just as well. No valuation has any tangible connection on its own to a tangible referent in second nature. It is only the totality of values which succeed each other in the chain of significations which refer as a totality to the referent space of second nature.

Call into question one value, and a price may change, a bankruptcy may rupture across the screen of third nature. Call into question a flow of values, be they values of labor, nature, or credit, and the whole relation between signifier, signified, and referent is called into question. The economic real then reveals itself in the hole which appears in the symbolic order of the enchanted world. Serres's excluded third turns out to be the divergence between second and third nature itself, which reappears as noise when triggered by the appropriate event, like a difference of opinion between James Baker and the Bundesbank.

At this point, the vast proliferation and intensification of the vector, meant to deepen the symbolic order of the economy and hasten the process of every subtle change in second nature, becomes also the means of revealing ever more rapidly and thoroughly the terrible face of the economic real. We are invested in the vector, then, in a double sense. A gold-based monetary system refers value to the past and to nature. It grounds the symbolic function of money in an accumulated reserve, extracted from the earth, of a commodity which does not do much more than offer itself as exchangeable for all the others. A credit-based system refers value to the future and to third nature. As Lipietz says, "Instead of the law being: Gold is exchangeable, it becomes: these values-in-process must be considered as realised!"[74] In the mechanism of credit, as ever more perfected by third nature, we bank on the future's continuity with the past. Credit is extended before the values it is grounded in have been realized, on the assumption that, in aggregate, they will. This puts money into circulation at ever greater velocity, but velocity has its price. Should an event cut across this subtle interlinkage, like feedback noise in a Hendrix solo, the divergences between the temporalities of second and third nature will reveal themselves in a cakewalk into the abyss.

8. crash!

The State of Third Nature

One fairly clear lesson seems to be that it is the *immediacy* of information itself which can create crises. The game of dialogue, where the participants collude to exclude the noise of the "third," has to be thought of as a game that occurs in time. This is not the abstract, logical time of analysis, but the rather more quixotic time of experience. Speeding up the dialogue and increasing the number of messages leads to the situation where information and noise are indistinguishable. Moments appear where the details suddenly leap out and assume a significance of monstrous proportions.

In the October '87 crash, the proximate cause of the stock market slide (as opposed to longstanding political-economic tendencies) can be found in a three-layered sandwich of digital information systems that form a net over the globe. This trinity of information systems is: the defense information network; the business information network; the public news network. (And that is perhaps also the hierarchy of their speeds.) An Iranian missile, an off-the-cuff remark by the U.S. treasurer—each of these bits of information flies by each of the nets, affecting each in turn, each in turn affecting the trinity, each net then producing its meta-comment—a vector field looped around and around itself.

The paradox here is that rather than suffer uncertainty caused by not knowing what is going on, the markets appeared to suffer from knowing too much. They overloaded their systems with stimuli and data, the combination of which could trigger a meltdown when the underlying conditions were ripe for it. This was a clear case of the state of an information system steadily diverging from its referent space, but dragging its referent space along behind it. This system was ripe for the right combination of noise. Noise sent it right back down again, overshooting in the other direction, then leveling off so that the information in circuit on the market comes to more or less coincide in its tempo with the rhythm of second nature once again.

The trouble with all this, of course, is that in the philosophy of economics, one cannot point to "the real" in any simple and unmediated way. The economy appears to us only through the effects of a number of agencies like the ones examined at the first site in this book concerning television and media politics. The television vector needs to create an image to stand in for the audience it cannot see. The politics of third nature uses opinion polls to stand in for the public sphere it no longer connects with. Similarly, the functioning of the economy comes increasingly to take the form of exchanges between abstract entities. The major difference between the institutional abstractions required by the economy of third nature and those of its politics and civil society is that the former requires an information environment provided by a more or less neutral party in the economic war of all against all—the state.

These necessary agencies fall into two categories, the quantitative and the qualitative. Quantitative agencies tell us what is happening in the economy through a simple device known as an index. Anything from the number of new motor registrations in a month to the interest rates at the bank can be an index. These indexes are either retrospective or prospective. Either they indicate what happened in a prior period, as with the motor registrations, or they indicate what others expect to happen in the future, as with interest rates or other prices. Some kinds of information are reactive. They might cause economic actors to behave in certain ways, but depending on how they react to it, how they interpret it. Others, like interest rates, are proactive. They affect the whole system whether you like it or not.

Statistics are for the most part the province of the government agencies. Their task is the impartial creation of a *nominal image* of the whole economy and each of its parts, and for defining it into a number of distinct parts. Statistics may be used as indices for decisions, but are not necessarily directly causative. On the other hand, the state also has a role in defining what constitutes certain kinds of action. For example, taxation law not only distinguishes consumption expenditure from investment expenditure, it *causes* there to be a distinction between them at a certain point by taxing one and not the other. The definition of the objects also affects their existence. If the definition of investment expenditure includes the costs of interest payments on loans taken out to raid other companies or fine art bought to hang on Gordon Gekko's office walls, and makes these things tax-deductible, then they will become an investment and they will happen. This is the peculiar materialism of the complex contemporary economy, which ebbs and flows through a world of nominal referents.

The agencies which name, define, index, and narrate the categories and rules of the economy make the economy exist by providing the flow of information that nominates it. The state becomes heavily involved here in the administration of the referent. In the history of second nature, the state provides physical and social infrastructure which capital is incapable of providing for itself, ranging from roads and dams to schools and police. In the history of third nature, the state develops the basis of an *information infrastructure*. By this I don't mean the channels through which information passes, many of which are as likely to be privatized as state-provided these days. The state is having some of the pioneering tasks it performed in the development of second nature—from building roads and railways to creating communications systems—taken away from it. Yet the state is still necessary to private interests as the provider of the information infrastructure of third nature.

On this terrain, the state has a duty to fix the *meaning* of a range of important infrastructural elements on the information landscape, or to provide the structures where such meanings can be fixed. Legislation, the courts, and the

Internal Revenue Service fix the definition of "investment," for example. It is not fixed for all time, but fixed for the foreseeable future. It is not fixed in isolation, but in interaction with the accounting profession and its clients. Interestingly, as the economy becomes more global, there is a greater and greater need for international information to create the *image* of an international economy, so that the real underlying global economy can be known and acted upon. There is also an increasingly intense struggle between states for hegemony in setting the nominal categories, narrative assumptions, and the raw nominal data that define the international economy per se.[1]

The state gives key *retrospective* indexes to the referent space of the economy. It administers the referent. The state creates the raw data on second nature that third nature can grasp and act upon—second nature as a set of statistical aggregates and abstracts—a nominal, quantitative map that exactly covers the territory. Perhaps one could say that the state is in the mining business—it mines second nature for information, which is the raw material processed by the business of third nature. The state provides very important prospective and proactive indexes. At any moment in time the state is putting out at least two signals. It tells you how much tax you will pay. (Nothing is certain besides death and taxes.) The state will also tell you about something a little less certain: the amount of money it wants circulating in the system and the price one ought to pay for it, as measured by the rate of interest.[2]

The state also provides some key qualitative indicators. When Secretary of the Treasury James Baker said that the Germans were going to raise interest rates, the market signaled its response by taking a nosedive. Likewise, when Iraq invaded Kuwait and the price of oil shot up in August 1990, the market went down, signaling a mix of rational expectation of a recession and irrational panic at the thought of a major Gulf war. Interestingly enough, a new system developed since the 1987 crash that temporarily suspends trading when the volume of transactions moves too quickly stopped the New York stock market from falling too far too quickly. This supposedly prevents irrational, positive feedback loops where the market just keeps going and going, be it up or down. It is also meant to prevent the market from trying to move faster than the technology can handle. There is an absolute limit to the speed at which a market can work, determined by how quickly the computers can process the transactions without lagging behind the trading—or worse, crashing altogether.

International channels for qualitative news information and channels for quantitative business information form a complex interactive network, and it is certainly no accident that the Reuters firm, for example, is involved in both. The quantitative and qualitative networks of information feed into and off each other. Ideally, the quantitative mechanisms of the market form a negative feedback loop. What that means is that when things shoot too far in one direction, the market corrects itself and heads back the other way. If the price of something falls too far too fast, eventually it will reach a point where it becomes a bargain, encouraging players to buy up. As the volume of buying rises, so too will the price. If the price rises too high, the buyers fall away and the price will have to come back down again. Supposedly, the market is a place where buying and selling moves to allocate resources according to what the players in the market really want in a way that can only be described as utopian, which is perhaps why this market cannot and does not exist. Positive feedback loops can and do occur with the potential to repeat and amplify a signal till the circuit breaks, which is exactly what happened when the stock market crashed. Both the stock market crash and the Tiananmen Square events took this form.

At this point, the state steps in as the information bank of last resort. When uncertainty has spread around the circuit like a virus, the state has to rescue third nature from the noise it creates within itself. It has to reassure it that the territory it moves across is still there. This occurs in two forms. Firstly, the easing of interest rates to avert a credit crunch for those caught up in the crash. Secondly, calming statements meant to balm the wounds of the market from the president, reminding the markets that all is well in the rest of the world.

Markets and Metaphors

When we say the word "market," we forget that it is only a metaphor. Like "community," "society," "culture," "politics," "market" is a metaphor derived from a simpler if less eventful time. Lewis Mumford evokes the conditions under which markets rose and flourished during the Middle Ages.[3] This market was a specific place, where all the buyers and sellers could see each other's wares and hear the open outcry of their prices. The buyers could compare prices and quality. The sellers could watch as the buyers flocked from one seller to another, chasing bargains or better-quality stuff. All took place within the protective walls of the abbey. Certain conditions here, such as the unity of place, perfect information, protective guarantee, simply don't exist in most of the real world, and neither do markets. "Market" is a metaphor for far more complex and fragmented processes. In taking the term "market" at face value, we are taking the representational space of the economy for the real thing. Social scientists mostly know this when they talk about other metaphors like "politics," for example. There is no "polis." There is no unity of place and action in the metaphorical drama of "politics." Perhaps it doesn't hurt to remind economists of this, though. By talking about markets as if they existed and persuading others to do likewise, they are moving in a sublimely postmodern information space. A space as devoid of irony as the advertisements Merrill Lynch ran in the business press only days after the crash. Under the headline **IT'S NO TIME TO GO IT ALONE,** the copy reads, "At times like these, it's more important than ever to have continuing access to the kind of information and insight that can help you exploit the opportunities that uncertainty creates."[4]

The concept of the invisible hand, with us since Adam Smith, is a crude metaphor for a negative feedback loop. In theory, it works in a purely quantitative way, as if it were a domain of pure, denotative signs responding with perfect sensitivity to each other. Most elementary textbooks in economics will give a little list of the conditions under which a free market will operate. One condition is that there have to be enough players in the market that no individual player can affect the prices too much all on his or her own. This is more or less the case on Wall Street, but certainly not so on the Tokyo stock market. Four big players dominate the Tokyo market, which works on quite different, oligopolistic principles. Another condition is that resources can be transferred from one perception to another without too much difficulty or time lag. This is perhaps the case only with something like a stock market, where apart from the legal niceties there is nothing to trade but bits of paper that are about as exchangeable as one could get.

Most important, a free market requires the free movement of information, so that all market players have equal access to information that might affect the returns everyone can expect on her or his investments, and can thus base their investment decisions on calculated risk. This condition is very improperly met on some stock markets. In the absence of strong state administration of the economic referents, the Hong Kong stock market allows firms to list without really disclosing terribly much useful information about themselves. The market can enforce behavior only on the basis of individual self-interest and cannot enforce its own conditions of collective propriety. Consequently, many firms in Hong Kong reveal very little about themselves, including the famous Hong Kong and Shanghai Banking Corporation with its wonderful high-modern Foster & Foster–designed office building. This wonderful building looks as if it has abolished history and established itself in a pure present. This is apt for an institution that grew rich off the drug trade with Imperial China of opium and tea and which for the time being issues bank notes for the world's raciest casino economy.

The state also has to enforce rules about fair access to privileged information, something else the market cannot do for itself. The fuss about insider trading is basically about infringements of this rule by people taking advantage of privileged information. Usually what inside traders exploit is not some absolute piece of superior knowledge, but knowledge *relative to time*. The inside trader knows before everyone else some factor that will affect the return on an investment, and moves her or his money toward or away from some asset based on prior knowledge. Speed is essential here. As Marvin, a junior trader in the *Wall Street* movie, shouts down the phone: "I need the information now. In ten minutes I'm history. At 4 o'clock I'm a dinosaur!" The inside trader, like Gordon Gekko, is of course a necessary product of a market economy that pursues self-interest in the absence of collective constraints which ensure a certain standard of virtuous behavior. The market economy without state or other constraints encourages deception and cheating in the pursuit of self-interest. It thus encourages a deviation of the representational space of the economy from the underlying economy, as each deception adds to the unreliability of the information available about the state of the underlying economy. In short, the market presupposes nonmarket forms of communication to function with any level of efficiency.

The utopian metaphor of the market space also assumes that ideally all points plug into the networks of qualitative and quantitative information equally, and that everybody can play. Despite the rhetoric about the global market, this is not so, although many assume it is heading that way. National factors still play a very strong role on equities markets, and not surprisingly so. Stock markets are dependent on the state to set up the nominal landscape upon which the business of third nature can be conducted. Until a supranational agreement establishes some conventions for *translating* between national spaces within third nature, globalization will remain a linkage of distinct national or regional markets rather than a genuine integration. Nevertheless, "a substantial amount of multilateral interaction exists among national stock markets. As can be expected, the US stock market turns out to be by far the most influential in the world."[5]

This is hardly accidental. The whole purpose of a market is to get the best price at any given time. The reason that an actual, face-to-face "open auction" market like the New York Stock Exchange still has a role in the world of the electronic vector is that it can still claim to be a site where there is sufficient concentration of capital distributed among enough buyers and sellers to get a better approximation to a fair price than any other market-maker can offer. While this still may not necessarily be the case, it is the reason why the seemingly incongruous conjunction of a bull pit full of shouting brokers and an international vector field of interested parties has occurred. The global vector does not necessarily have a decentralizing influence. It may concentrate power in sites of information that are in heavy demand. Regulators have to tread a fine line between preserving the integrity of something like the New York exchange as a viable information center from which prices can be distributed to the world, and encouraging business into the market itself through relaxed regulation.

Thus the paradox: the more global capitalism becomes, and the more it desires the global market, the more it also requires the state to administer the referents the market connects and coordinates, and to police the veracity of information companies issue about themselves. Free-market utopians thought they could escape from the state along the vectors of the globalized market, and indeed they have escaped antiquated state regulation. Marxist pessimists correctly saw the dangers in all this for democratic governments and national social forces like trade unions, but missed one paradoxical aspect of this movement. As capital moves in an ever more global space, trying to free itself from the regulatory net of individual states, it flies by one set of nets into a space where it needs another net beneath it. It needs a new administration of the referents without which globalization is always incomplete.

Capital and Vector

The neo-liberal promise of globalization entailed an embrace of technology as a vector out of the clutches of the state. The market-as-utopia connects anyone, as an individual with wants and needs and assets, to everyone else. The paradox is that the more the market appears to reach toward a global state of connectivity, the less it seems to have to do with human agency at all. Of course, the market players are mostly corporate, not individual subjects. A corporation is a legal form of collective subject to which individual wills and desires are subordinated. Yet the market seems sometimes beyond even the corporate subjects who occupy its surface.

Most pundits agreed that computerized trading was a subsidiary cause of the October crash. Around 20 percent of the trading on Black Monday was program trading.[6] The scenario Virilio fears with nuclear war—that the speed of the vectors of war technology will become so fast that decisions pass out of the hands of leaders and into the cold embrace of computers—is the scenario which has already arrived within the immaterial economy. Computerization means that the flows of capital directly interface with flows of information, via a program that supposedly picks optimum "bets" based on the data available to it. For example, "portfolio insurance," a technique for linking the purchase of stocks to related stock futures in an attempt to offset potential losses. In other words, the current prices of stocks are offset against future prices. It operates on a "strike price," which is the price at which the program unloads the stocks it has bought back on the market. In a rising market like the bull market of the '80s, the strike price rises as the general price level rises. This ratchet effect supposedly locks in gains, ensuring that stocks sell on the way down at prices that are still higher than the ones the buyer paid for them on the way up. In the crash, this ratchet effect seems simply to have increased the volume of shares that the programs tried to unload as prices fell. The programs tried instantly to unwind positions in this or that stock that might have taken months to build up.

In other words, an "automation of capital" may be occurring, not completely unlike the automation of labor. On the day after "Black Monday," Wall Street banned computerized program trading, on the grounds of restoring "some human common sense."[7] That sensible, i.e., human, control needed to be restored, or at least that regulators thought it needed restoring, seems to indicate a fear that the technology may become a thing apart from its agents. As the allocation of liquid capital becomes a minute-by-minute decision, or even second-by-second, computerized systems execute more and more decisions according to preprogrammed instructions. So, for example, if a minute gap momentarily appears between the price at which a stock trades on two different exchanges, a computerized system can profit from this instant imperfection. Rather than tending to push the market toward equilibrium, such moves may at times cause volatile movements of their own. As the crash showed, such programs cannot consider the effects of complex interactions—particularly the interactions of a program with the actions of other programs. As all powerful market players have access to the same information, it becomes increasingly likely that they will attempt to move in the same direction at the same time, causing sudden lurches. Thus the paradox of markets that can use the vector to profit from ever more minute and momentary ripples on the surface of capital, smoothing them out in the process, but can also precipitate the tidal wave.

Such movements have been in evidence for quite some time, but were not widely commented on until the crash. While program trading fell out of favor after the crash, it is highly likely that more complex and sophisticated systems will take its place rather than a return to "human common sense." Just as the physical products of labor grow, becoming a power over and against labor, so too one can say that the *movement* of capital becomes a thing apart from the class that nominally possesses it. Labor senses its alienation from its products in the form of the massive physical presence of the commodity realm, the vast bulk of plant and equipment, the inescapable concreteness of second nature. By contrast, the spectacle of third nature appears as something of an escape from this. Within the narrative economy of the spectacle, the utopian desire for a happy ending, transplanted back to reality, can never be eradicated, as Ernst Bloch knew. On the other hand, capital comes to experience its separation from itself in the form of movement, in the lightning-fast mobility of its liquid self. Perhaps this is why capital seeks so often to offset this search for security in mobility with another kind of security, one built of concrete and glass and steel.

Computerized trading doesn't mean much except greater velocity in the system. When it combines with new financial instruments, greater volatility emerges as well. The media noted Phelan's "meltdown" warning in 1986, but didn't pay much attention to it. In 1987, his meltdown metaphor became common property, appropriated overnight by the global media. Events poke through the thin fabric of narrative seamlessness, and have to be stitched back into the line. As this example shows, established narrative strategies have a half-life. Journalists can capture events in the net of previous narrative strategies that they discarded at the time of their formulation. The world is teeming with narratives, a veritable planet of ragged noise. The global media vector picks up the thread of whatever narrative line seems necessary to stitch the event into the seam of things. The proliferation of strands of stories in a narrative economy, like the proliferation of trade-able securities in the financial economy, is a means to security, a safeguard against the "end of ideology" or the "decline of the master narratives." Paul Virilio remarks that "speed is the hope of the west," to which we might add, "hope is the speed of the west." The ability to take any event and stitch it back into the program flow, as just another episode along the way, is the remarkable thing about the news vector.

As Virilio notes, "Manipulation of the need for security takes different forms."[8] These may include superannuation, pension plans, hoards of cash under the bed, gilt-edged government bonds, strong currencies, gold bars, a portfolio hedged by diversifying stocks, or hedged on the same stocks at different times (futures). Forms of capital with a use value close to nil, like securities, pursue the opposite strategy to more tangible assets such as property. Property has value derived from its usefulness and permanence—literally, a stake in second nature. Securities, on the other hand, have value precisely for the opposite quality, their permanent mutability. This is what makes them an instrument of third nature—they exist only on an information landscape, relative to other pieces of information and their owners. The desire to expand the space in which they might circulate is the desire to get greater security for wealth through greater mobility, greater interchangeability between nominal values. The dynamic of capital, which creates uncertainty as one of its very conditions of existence, drives the desire for this third nature of even more mobile and exchangeable values. This is the paradox of capital's use of the vector. It requires ever greater movement in pursuit of stability and security for individual assets and values, but thereby risks the crash of the whole system at ever greater levels of immaterial value.

"It was internationalization, not computerization which caused simultaneous collapses," says the *Far Eastern Economic Review* with hindsight (i.e., a few weeks later). Nevertheless, it is the technology of the vector that makes globalized movement possible. This ought not to be taken for a technological "determinism," however.[9] The technological dynamic has often disappeared so far from the horizon of critical theories that the mere mention of it is assumed to be an invocation of determinism. Technological change is not an independent variable. A complex and contingent logic of power drives it. The tendency of capital is an ever greater perfection of the abstract space of third nature as the result of the deepening and broadening of the extensive vectors of communication coupled with the intensive vectors of data storage and retrieval. The vector is merely the means, the goal is the domination of the space of the globe, appropriated as third nature. The tendency of the vector is toward ever greater speed and flexibility.

Perhaps one could speak here of the possibility of a *geo-economic* homogenization of the globe,[10] paralleling the *geostrategic* homogenization Virilio fears in his book *Speed and Politics*.[11] As discussed earlier at the Baghdad site, the ruling circles in the United States have argued the relative merits of geo-economic versus geo-strategic hegemony. The point here is that *both* require the extension of vectoral technology beyond its present capacity. There are still limits to this process. For example, geo-strategic information vectors are far from providing the Pentagon with satellite coverage of the whole of the globe.[12] The creation of a homogenized geo-economic space of the market within a global network of information vectors requires not only new technology and adaptive forms of state regulation, but the creation of a rich and deep information map over the whole territory. There are many obstacles to this. For example, many countries maintain secrecy laws that restrict the disclosure of financial information.[13] At the other end of the scale are those parts of the world like Burma, where a military regime of an old type simply refuses to participate in the vectoral coverage of the globe at all. Countries like Switzerland find themselves in a difficult position, given that they were able to attract capital from elsewhere by offering secrecy. Switzerland put a partition between the legal space where Zürich is and the rest of the world. There may now be more to gain from being an abstract space of the free flow of information than from a partitioned space that conceals it.

Another factor inhibiting the perfection of the vector field is the uneven quality of "research." "The availability of information has improved with the development of worldwide communications, but the quality of data still leaves much to be desired in many countries."[14] How are equities in different markets to be valued relative to each other, when the information field which gives them their separate values is the province of distinct spaces, mapped out by states harboring very different financial cultures? There are no doubt technical solutions to such a problem, but how then is one to assess the "political risk" in this market as opposed to that market? The event may raise its ugly head at any moment. The Gulf war, the fall of the Berlin Wall, the Tiananmen Square massacre all had their effects on various markets, transmitted as news instantaneously and simultaneously with the unfolding of the events themselves.

The limit to the speed of the stock market plummet was the only absolute measure of time: the speed at which the globe turns. It followed the light of dawn around the horizon. The rhythm involved here seems like that of a two-stroke motor. During daylight hours capital "works," pumping the pistons of profit and loss. During the night, it "cogitates"; it draws in the data on the activities of other cylinders which at that moment are in action. This applies to both the human and technical resources of the market. The automated settlement systems with cute acronyms like CHIPS, CHAPS, and SWIFT, based in the U.S., Britain, and Western Europe respectively, will automatically match up the movements of the day with the new patterns of ownership of this peculiar form of notional property.[15] While the hardware hums into life, the "wetware" will be heading home for some downtime, perhaps reading the *Wall Street Journal* on the way. Who knows what dreams they may have, or how they might find their way back into the unconscious of the vector field the next day?

Perhaps they dream, like Sherman McCoy in Tom Wolfe's novel *The Bonfire of the Vanities,* of being "Masters of the Universe," being the human center of vast movements of capital across the globe, through the vector. Or perhaps they have technofear nightmares of being dominated by the vector, which stands as a dynamic world apart from the human effort that created it and set it in motion, now steadily developing an illogic of its own.[16] The persistence of the market ideology, with its insistence on the primacy of a vast array of rational calculator-brained subjects, whom the vector serves as a neutral instrument of their choices, is perhaps symptomatic of a repressed nightmare feeling that it really isn't so at all.

The everyday life of the financial agents of third nature is a mysterious thing. Their belief in the power and reason and reality of the market is a form of commodity fetishism in reverse. They do not fetishize the commodity, as if the world really is piled high and deep with goodies that one can own and trade. It does not fetishize the object but the *subject* of exchange. It does not detach the object of labor from the space that created it, treating the world as a space of consumption. It detaches the subject of capital from the trajectory of capital, treating that subject as if it were the sovereign master of capital's self-movement. By making a fetish of the subject of capital, it can assume that the autonomy of this subject, the space and time and memory with which it can make rational decisions, is simply something given. It need not concern itself with the problem of the elimination of that space and time and memory by the vector.

The vector appears to serve a subject which simply exists, pregiven—God's eternal entrepreneur. The subject of capital is as much a creation of the technical vector as the objects of labor are of the worker's skill and effort. Both of these aspects of the relation disappear from view in the fetishism of the market as much as in the fetishism of the commodity.

The faith in the rational powers of *homo economicus* and its chosen habitat, the market, seems to become more strident, more fundamentalist, the more clearly the power of the vector seems to overdetermine the space and autonomy of the subject of capital. The vector seems to automate capital no less than the labor process automates labor. Yet the former remains even more of a mystery than the latter, given the tenacious need to believe that the dynamic that provides more than a living wage but power as well cannot be fundamentally flawed or tending to veer out of control. The wetware interspersed in tiny nodes throughout the vast technical apparatus of hardware and software still dreams of mastery, lest it wake in fright and discover someday third nature's increasing autonomy from state and market. The crash was just such a rude awakening, but once the broken narrative threads of the market story were patched back in circuit by an equally powerful media vector, the dreampolitik resumed.

From Telegraph to Terminal

While globalization is still a relatively new phenomenon for stock markets, many other forms of business have been feeling the impact of the globalized vector for some time. Where the movement of stocks or bonds requires some degree of uniformity across the nominal spaces of the old state boundaries, foreign exchange (forex) trading has always thrived on the *differences* between state-regulated spaces. It is not surprising, then, that the use of the vector developed first in global forex markets.[17] While stock markets have been slow to catch up with the use of the vector begun in forex trading, its extension to equities has quite a new significance. Forex trading takes place on the basis of the difference between the notional spaces regulated by the states. On the other hand, the growth of global equities trading implies a creation of a transborder space of third nature, where national difference can be translated and negotiated by capital flows.

What distinguishes stock markets is that traditionally they have centralized locations where brokers meet face to face. Their functioning as a market depends on the unity of place and time and the availability of information to all, simultaneously. Stock markets really are a market in the strict sense, and quite literally have used the "open outcry," the method of markets since ancient times. This unity of place and time has undergone some changes, however, as the stock market and similar institutions like commodity futures markets have interacted with the vector.

In a brilliant essay on the telegraph, James Carey notes that before the telegraph, the term "communication" referred to both the passage of goods, then by road, rail, or steam, and the passage of information, which traveled the same routes by the same means. With the invention of the telegraph, transport and communications became *separate* things, one belonging to the territory, the other to the map. With this separation emerges the distinctive paradigm of information, the problem of the economy and accuracy in transmitting signals. The problem, in other words, of third nature and the distinctive form of telesthesia, of perception freed from some of the constraints and frictions of physical movement. The telegraph begins the integration of telesthesia into economic, political, legal, and cultural life through a spate of institutional innovations.

The telegraph made the modern form of the market possible. As Carey says, "The effect of the telegraph on the market is a simple one: it evens out markets in space."[18] The telegraph tended to eliminate the traditional role of merchant capital, namely the speculation or arbitrage on price differentials in space. Via the telegraph, the supply and demand for goods in all places linked by it will come to bear on the formation of a market price. This makes the market itself a far more complex mechanism, and one now *abstracted* from any particular place. The third nature of economic discourse detaches the term "market" from its historical origins. It becomes a metaphor for an abstract space in the form of a network, not necessarily located anywhere. Of course the communicational apparatus itself will be centered somewhere, and that territorial somewhere will become a locus of power, but the market itself has no place.

Carey notes that once the telegraph unifies the space of trade, speculation moves from space to time, from arbitrage to futures. The telegraph makes prices more certain across space, but adds uncertainty to the movement of prices in time, as movements of demand and supply react upon each other in a wider, abstract territory, much more quickly and in complex patterns. Telesthesia, it seems, can be a giddy feeling. The Chicago Commodity Exchange, still the archetypal futures market, opened in the same year the telegraph reached that city. Fittingly, it was a year of unpredictable and fabulous events, the year Marx worked on the *Neue Rheinische Zeitung:* 1848. As Carey puts it: "Once space was, in the phrase of the day, annihilated, once everyone was in the same place, for purposes of trade, time as a new region of experience, uncertainty, speculation, and exploration was opened up to the forces of commerce."[19] The still rather localized political and economic turbulence experienced by the young revolutionary Marx could take place in a more abstract space. Even the first worker's international was not averse to communicating along the new vector. "An immediate reply, if possible by telegraph, is requested," as the famous circular letter to Bebel says.[20]

The development of futures, the buying and selling of contracts for the sale of staple and standard commodities at future dates hence, is linked to the separation of transport from communications; the separation of territory and map; second nature and third nature. Information about the availability of commodities, such as reports on the cotton harvest, is available long before the goods themselves. "Commodities were sundered from their representations," negotiable paper representing quantities of commodities could circulate freely, easily, and much faster than the commodities themselves. For the market to become abstract, a communicational map exactly covering the territory of capital, commodities themselves had to become abstract, in the sense that they had to become uniform, equivalent, and interchangeable. The more abstract a product can become, the more readily it can be traded. Significantly, futures markets first developed for agricultural commodities, and most recently for financial instruments and securities. The first is the product of nature made into a flow of abstract, quantified commodities, the latter is the product of capital made into a flow of abstract, quantified information. The former occurs when the map of market information comes to cover the territory, the latter when it supplants the territory and subordinates it to the map.

The stock market and the futures market take the form of a classic open outcry market. Vectoral technologies connect these old-fashioned bull pits to vast, abstracted markets. These markets function according to the perceptual logic of telesthesia, thanks to the vector's ability to separate the movement of information and of commodities. There seems something odd in this survival of the most ancient form of the market, still functioning at the center of the network of vectors. Speaking of the future of the stock market in the era of the global vector, one analyst notes that "computerization will add value by transforming stock exchange prices from assets to marketing tools, and clients will pay for them. The central function of stock exchanges—allowing prices to be established—will become its paying business."[21] The point here is that while not all equity-trading business passes through the stock exchange anymore, the exchange still has a role to play in setting prices for those who trade "off the floor," on their screens. The exchange itself thus passes from a market to an *image* of a market, on which buyers, sellers, and traders can discover a reliable indicator of the best price. This image of the market as a whole becomes itself a marketable product. By transforming the ongoing activities of the market into a stream of instant information—and charging for this image-in-process—the stock market becomes a point at which the invisible third nature of movement finds an image of second nature.

It is not a foregone conclusion that the business of third nature need be conducted in such a fashion. There are also fully simulated markets that are not located anywhere in particular. The National Association of Securities Dealers operates the NASDAQ securities system, which exists only as a bunch of telephone lines and screens and has no "floor" at all. It is the third-largest stock exchange in the world, after New York and Tokyo, and is bigger than the cities of London, Zürich, Bonn, Toronto, and Paris put together. Its 460 dealers in 550 separate locations use 125,000 terminals to display data. A centralized system of 30 mainframe computers processes the buy and sell orders. NASDAQ has grown at the expense of floor-based exchanges throughout the '80s, and its more relaxed regulatory environment allowed it to attract business away from the New York exchange. As might be expected, it suffered in the crash even more than the floor-based exchange, as it was even more heavily dependent on the vector.[22] Nevertheless, NASDAQ points to the defeat of national economic territory by the vectors of business information, in much the same way that architectural space and strategic defense fall victim to their respective vectors.

Which leaves us with a lot of technologically obsolete architecture. After fifty-six years the Pacific Coast Stock Exchange building in Los Angeles closed down, and was subsequently turned into a disco called, appropriately enough, the Stock Exchange. Its new owners called the opening-night party "Small Change." Guests danced and drank on a floor littered with fake money—real fake money this time! The trading floor became a dance floor, and the former trading stations served drinks rather than scrip. This stately old building has moved from one side of the immaterial economy (pure money) to the other (pure style) with hardly a missed beat between. Which is perhaps the architectural equivalent of poetic justice![23]

The disappearance of territory as an obstacle to the movement of information and capital can only have profound consequences— including many accidental ones. There is coming into existence "a new order, a global marketplace for ideas, money, goods and services that knows no national boundaries," says Walter Wriston, formerly CEO at Citicorp. "The information standard has replaced the gold standard as the basis of world finance."[24] Yet more and quicker information has not led to more rational and orderly markets, as Wriston prophesied; if anything, the reverse. It has exposed within the being of every market, not the benign machinations of the invisible hand but a heart of darkness, desperate and afraid, yet continually rolling the dice, spinning the wheel, willing only that the dice return, that the wheel spin only to be spun some more. A heart which wills all the more strongly when its darkest secret escapes, as it did on Black Monday: that at its core the market still harbors what J. K. Galbraith called its "suicidal tendencies."

Pure Capital

"Securities finance is cheaper, more flexible and more fashionable than traditional bank loans."[25] The old regime of face-to-face financing by investment bankers in the metropolitan core of the major cities now has to compete with the abstract space, faceless transactions, and exchangeable financial products of third nature. There are a series of changes taking place here, a shift from long-term banking to short-term trading; from raising capital for a fee to taking risks for short-term gains; from establishment banking to finance supermarkets; from cultivating contacts to staring at video quotations; from entrepreneurship to risk-avoidance; from raising venture capital to junk-bonding hostile takeovers, or what merger lawyer Martin Lipton calls "dealing in war."[26] Businesses don't build brands and plants and markets anymore, they simply buy them, and then strip the assets to pay for the most-valued acquisitions. Business, like deterrence, is heading for a steady state of pure war, led by the immaterial economy of banking and trading, aided by information technologies, in which constant increases in velocity are the principal weapon. "My industry leapt at the chance and helped create a Frankenstein," says investment banker–statesman Felix Rohatyn. "The western economic system is now the hostage of the market, instead of vice versa."[27] Or more specifically, the financial mechanism of third nature.

What might all this mean, back in that time and space of that "other Monday"? The one where nothing much happens besides eating, sleeping, maybe watching some reruns of "Dallas"—if you're lucky. Time to tell another Marxist-style story. The immaterial flows of data don't merely circulate in third nature alone. They have the potential to undermine the physical space of the city. The *overaccumulation* of "electromoney" is intimately connected to the *underinvestment* in productive enterprise. The uncertainties generated by rapid mobility of liquidity around the globe are certainly a factor in the reluctance of big corporations to reinvest their surpluses in production. This particularly applies to Japanese corporations, caught in the '80s between the rising yen and the setting dollar. Using "zaitech" methods of exploiting finance programming technologies to switch cash flow from reinvestment to speculation, they have managed to keep in the black at home while acquiring large chunks of architectural real estate and government war debt in America, not to mention a few Hollywood studios.[28]

(Or at least they did until the Tokyo bubble burst in the early '90s—which looked for all the world like a slo-mo aftereffect of the '87 crash in New York. The divergence between the economic real and the enchanted world of Tokyo finance was a rather different affair from New York. In the '80s, demand for Japanese manufactures was strong. Market shares grew. The big corporations put the profits back into expanded capacity. Productivity grew faster than wage levels and domestic consumption, meaning that the surplus had to go into expanded production for the export market, local speculation, and buying up trophies on the international market like movie studios and prime real estate. But the international economy could absorb only so many Japanese exports, and this round of expansion of productive capacity confronted static or shrinking markets. The link between the past and the future severed, the economic real asserted itself in a slump on the stock market and in real-estate values in Tokyo. Since prime Tokyo real estate is one of the principal assets big Japanese firms borrow against, the writing down of its value is a major blow.)

Meanwhile, back in second nature: Alongside the electronic economy, a sweatshop economy flourishes, even in the most affluent of the old world cities. The urban sociologist Manuel Castells calls this "polarized growth." Mobility and flexibility are the key features of both: the mobility of overaccumulated, speculative liquidity chasing the movements of credit and currency prices; labor migrations chasing footloose capital and trade flows. Two sorts of speed operate here, the mechanical, analog speed of the productive economy, ticking loudly away like a trusty old alarm clock, and the "digitime" speed of the speculative economy, with its silent, inertia-less, ineffable workings, like that of a digital watch.

Here is a new geography and *chronography* of flows, where factor inputs become transitive elements in an almost global combinatory "whose meaning is largely determined by their position in a network of exchanges."[29] Business now calculates the comparative advantage of this urban site over the other, in much the same way as the military picks missile targets. "We are living increasingly in a space of variable geometry where the meaning of each locale escapes its history, culture or institutions, to be constantly redefined by an abstract network of information strategies and decisions," according to Castells,[30] and we are "no longer a society of sedentarization but one of passage" for Virilio. He concludes from this: "If in the 19th century the lure of the city emptied agrarian space of its substance (cultural, social), at the end of the 20th century it is urban space which loses its geographic reality"—and disappears. This is the end of the "political and economic illusion of the permanence of sites"[31] and the arrival of "the last postindustrial resource: acceleration exceeds accumulation."[32] Acceleration proceeds along the line of the historical development of the vector, from the telegraph to telecommunications. We no longer have roots, we have aerials. We no longer have origins, we have terminals.

In James Carey's analysis of the telegraph and the futures market, he notes that all the elements of the market transformed by the telegraph are also the elements of Marx's analysis of commodity fetishism. The commodity becomes abstract and quantitative; its useful, sensuous qualities become separated from its quantitative value; it begins to move in a space of pure movement, that which tends to become the world market. The separation of the sign from the thing, and their parallel movement in different but connected spaces—this is the modern world. Perhaps Carey is overly hasty in explaining Marx's concepts in terms of the effects of the telegraph. Rather, Marx's exegesis analyzes in theory the same abstract process that the telegraph expedites and which Carey describes. Marx's interest in the abstract social relations of capital is intimately connected to his experience of the new abstract geography that the *perpetuum mobile* of capital describes across the landscape.[33] "The circulation of money began at an infinite number of points and returned to an infinite number of points. The point of return was in no way posited as the point of departure."[34] This infinite process of money reticulating between abstract points ties in to the process of the circulation of capital. In its movement between points, money turns itself from one thing to another, from wages earned to commodities bought, from commodities bought to commodities sold, from commodities sold to investments realized, from investments realized to credit returned and further wages advanced, and so on, infinitely, indefinitely—until the process crashes. "The circulation of capital is at the same time its becoming, its growth, its vital process."[35] Marx was already clear, in the *Grundrisse,* that the parameters of the *perpetuum mobile* were, firstly, the volume of capital, the velocity with which it circulated, and its geographic mobility.

On the dynamic tendencies inherent in capital, Marx wrote, "The tendency to create the world market is directly given in the concept of capital itself. Every limit appears as a barrier to be overcome."[36] Once capital had imposed its dynamic regime on the whole society in the part of the world whence it sprang, it would seek to extend this. Its movement is a crucial part of this dynamic. He discussed the movement of capital as second nature over the space of the globe, and the central role of money, originally in the form of gold, in that process. Gold was the means for "drawing the dimensions of exchange over the whole world; for creating the true generality of exchange value in substance and in extension." The movement of capital in the form of gold was an abstract flow, devoid of qualitative cultural codes, which could rearrange all such codes around its dynamic. "In fact, it is because of this abstraction, that it becomes such an enormous instrument in the real development of the forces of social production."[37]

The move from gold to paper money reinforced the boundaries of the national. Paper money thus appears as a transitional moment. Paper money was more abstract in its form, more tied to the territorial space of the nation-state. The era in which the nation-state acted as a crucial vehicle for the creation of an abstract if delimited space traversed by the vectors of second nature is overtaken by the creation of an interspace across those territories, but nevertheless still dependent on them. Third nature breaks out of the bounded space of the state, pushing for a space of flows, regulated but free.[38]

That it is the vector which makes this circulation possible was recognized by Marx, but not emphasized: "The more production comes to rest on exchange value, hence on exchange, the more important do the physical conditions of exchange—the means of communication and transport—become for the costs of circulation. Capital by its nature drives beyond every spatial barrier. Thus the creation of the physical conditions of exchange—of the means of communication and transport—the annihilation of space by time—becomes an extraordinary necessity for it."[39] What Marx does not explore fully here is the *separation* of communication from transport, or the development of two distinct *velocities* of movement. The first includes that of labor, materials, and commodities, or of capital in material form; the other includes that of money and information, or the pure and infinite movement of capital in its *potential* form. In the 1844 manuscripts, Marx began his analysis of alienated labor with the premise that the workers produce objects which become a power over them because they are compelled to do so, but "the worker can create nothing without nature, without the sensuous external world." The worker becomes a "slave of nature."[40] Yet already in Marx's time, a map is emerging which will fully cover this territory.

Indeed, the value of Marx's *historical* analysis of the dynamic of alienation, from nature to second nature, has less to do with its theoretical rigor and everything to do with the fact that the analysis can be read as a narrative of his own rich experience. Marx witnessed the final transformation of traditional social space by the vector into second nature. This experience of a revolutionary leap in the vectoral abstraction in everyday life is one that most of us who are grappling with the meaning and tendencies of third nature have lost. The usefulness of Marx is twofold. Firstly, the historical changes of the present have their historic roots in the transformation of nature by capital which took place in his day. Secondly, the *difference* between his experience of that transformation and our experience of the present transformation of second nature by third nature is highly instructive. Both the fulfilment and the supersession of the analysis of the abstract relations of capital can be traced in present events. *Grundrisse* still functions as a narrative which anchors critical thought in the historical conditions of its existence. Of the vast repertoire of narratives, both grand and *petit,* which the intensive and extensive vector make available to critical thought, it still has some value.

Coextensive with the sensuous external world is an information landscape, on which money and information move at a faster rate than labor and commodities, always preceding them. Where the class of alienated workers, the first class, applied themselves to wresting use value from nature, the class of nonworkers, the second class, the bourgeoisie, applied themselves to dominating the first. Yet out of the *perpetuum mobile* of this double domination of nature and of labor arose a third field of activity, and a third class. The object of this third class is not labor, nor laborers, not working, nor even nonwork in the bourgeois sense of appropriating work, but *networking.* The third class knits together the infinite points of action, the endless series of events. Call them the new middle class or the new petit bourgeoisie, call them the impossible class, but even the act of naming them belongs now to this same, third class.[41]

The dynamic of capital propels the technical development of the vector, and the space opened up by the vector, be it road, rail, telegraph, telephone, television, or whatever, becomes a space for capital to colonize. The vector and capital are not the same thing, however, and the vector is not always a functional tool for capital. In spreading itself though the vector, in growing and broadening its grasp, capital's movements are far from an effortless overcoming of traditional space and time. "From the fact that capital posits every such limit as a barrier and hence gets ideally beyond it, it does not by any means follow that it has really overcome it, and, since every such barrier contradicts its character, its production moves in contradictions which are constantly overcome and constantly posited."[42] As the vector extends the reach and range and speed of capital's overcoming, it also establishes new barriers and impediments. "The universality towards which it irresistibly strives encounters barriers to its own nature."[43] At the point where movement encounters the barrier within itself, events proliferate.

A Process without a Subject—but with Goals

In this book, many kinds of time intersect. Indeed, one of the effects of the proliferation of the vector is that formerly discrete times and places intersect and perturb each other in curious ways. Global television comes to Beijing politics; central bank diplomacy blows an instant ill wind through the global markets. Some of these kinds of time are erratic, irregular, sometimes even chaotic. At least one appears directional, nontransitive: the temporality of the historical unfolding of the vector itself.

As I have mentioned before, the tendency of the vector is toward ever greater velocity and flexibility, ever greater interconnection and abstraction. We see this clearly as we enter the postbroadcast age. Indeed, CNN may represent the twilight of the broadcast age, rather than the brave new world many took it for at the time of the Gulf war. The interconnection of the spaces of broadcast television vectors is far from complete, and there will be many more ruptures as it breaks down old cultural and political boundaries.

The postbroadcast age introduces something new, however. The economies of scale of the broadcast era may well give way to economies of scope. Flexibility and interactivity may for audiences who can afford it and have the cultural skills to do something with it replace the cultural forms of broadcast television. With the breakdown of the Fordist regime of economic regulation, with its more or less full employment and relatively continuous gradations of income, comes the breakdown of the economic conditions which favored the broadcast vector. No longer does the mode of consumption in the overdeveloped world call for the creation of mass audiences who can become mass consumers. More flexible and interactive vectors are needed to create and maintain standing reserves of niche consumption. The telephone companies, computer companies, publishers, film and TV studios, news corporations, video game producers, and big research institutions are jockeying for position to create a new phase in the development of the forces of communication as I write.[44] Cultural studies, if it is to have a future, has to speculate on what tendencies these developments represent, or at least that is what I have argued.[45]

One of the most interesting developments in cultural studies in recent years has been the attention paid to institutions of cultural power by the "Griffith school" of Ian Hunter, Tony Bennett, and Stuart Cunningham.[46] Eschewing the focus on "resistance" in cultural studies and the moral valorization of the powerless, the Griffith approach entails a Foucauldian return to the subtle and pervasive mechanisms of "governmentality" within the institutions of culture itself. The Griffith school also renounced the Marxist tendency toward abstraction, preferring to concentrate on specific and contingent forms of cultural institutionalization. Hunter is particularly scathing about "those following Hegel and Marx" who locate the humanist normative foundation of critical discourse in "a special process of historical development, in which the reconciliation of fragmented human interests and capacities is governed by the ethical goal of complete development."[47]

In response to this, one can make three points. Firstly, the Griffith writers point to a need for cultural studies to study all the phenomena of culture, including those where power is deployed, not just those where power is resisted. On this point I would defend what they do from a certain moralizing tendency among their critics. Secondly, the Griffith writers seem to have taken the Althusserian caricatures of Hegelian-Marxist thinking at face value. The dialectic of redemption Hunter criticizes is certainly there, in the literature, but so too are many other versions of Hegelian-Marxist historicism. Although it takes us too far from the subject at hand here, I would contend that there are a number of distinct and indeed incompatible historicist trajectories in Marx's own work. Many of these historicist projections turned out to be wrong. But that was precisely the point of them. In the difference between the trajectory plotted by a historicist theory and the wayward movements of history itself lies a method which allows for a constant writing and rewriting of the pleasures and dangers of the future. A future which critical theory has all but abandoned to professional "futurists" of a corporatist stamp, as Andrew Ross has recently reminded us.[48]

Raymond Williams spoke of residual, dominant, and emergent cultural forms.[49] This historicizing of the issue of cultural form is a welcome change from the endless repetitions of margin and center which have been so much at the center of cultural studies, yet it points to a problem with the Griffith approach. Hunter's work is mostly about the institutions of education. Bennett writes about those of literature and the museum. Cunningham's interests are in cinema and the national regulation of television. Nowhere do they break out of a fascination with dominant and residual cultural forms and tackle emergent ones. And yet as Williams said, "Our hardest task, theoretically, is to find a non-metaphysical and non-subjectivist explanation of emergent cultural practice."[50]

Part of the answer lies, I think, in a renewal of historicist thought. A skeptical historicism, one which does not imagine it has plumbed the ineffable realities of historical "laws of motion," but one which has developed out of quite specific and local forms of experience a theory or two about the trajectories of the whole. Of course the totality appears differently depending on from where one sees it. One never grasps it in its totality, one grasps only a facet of it, dependent on one's specific cultural grounding, but a facet which one can compare to that glimpsed by others. Moreover, the very globalization of the vector itself provides a common experience of telesthesia for more and more viewpoints, providing the basis for a dialogic approach to understanding the phenomenon itself.

Thus, this book has been organized around a speculative historicism of the vector, developing ever more abstractly, forming a third nature of experience and calculation. This process is not Althusser's "process without a subject or goals."[51] Without a subject, certainly. The automation of the vectors of capital and labor subject human agency to their forms of calculation and movement, but without for all that coming together as an identity. The vector is no more a subject of history than is "man." Particular subjective agencies—businesses, state apparatuses, organizations—pursue the vectoralization of their flows out of particular and different interests. Interests that are incommensurate and antagonistic. There is a process which results from their actions, actions determined in turn by this process, but no subject of history. To look for one is mere nostalgia.

Yet this is a process which paradoxically appears to have goals. (And note that I said *appears* to have goals.) The forces and relations of communication develop historically, through breaks and ruptures no doubt, yet develop they do, and in an irreversible fashion. Ever faster, ever cheaper, ever more flexible—ever more abstract. A goal appears, in spite of itself. As Deleuze and Guattari say in a surprisingly historicist moment:

> It should therefore be said that one can never go far enough in the direction of deterritorialization: you haven't seen anything yet—an irreversible process.

> . . . to the point where the earth becomes so artificial that the movement of deterritorialization creates of necessity a new earth. . . . A little additional effort is enough to overturn everything, and to lead us finally toward other far-off places. The schizoanalytic flick of the finger, which restarts the movement, links up again with the tendency, and pushes the simulacra to a point where they cease being artificial images to become indices of the new world.[52]

I have been thinking about that passage for ten years now, and this book is, I guess, my response to it. A rewriting of the Deleuzo-Guattarian negative historicism of deterritorialization in terms of my own experience, in order to map the difference between my experience and theirs.

So this, then, might be the goal that appears in the trajectory of the vector: a rhizome of pure, abstracted interrelationality. What if the vector becomes so ubiquitous that every point becomes mobile, and every point becomes potentially interconnected with every other point? *What will become of us?* This is the goal that appears in spite of itself and in spite of the contradictory effect of private property on its realization. On the one hand, capital accumulation creates the resources to extend third nature, ever deepening and evening out its mappings. The need to valorize the circuit creates the means. Yet for all that, private property acts as a fetter. Information wants to be free. Material things can become commodities privately appropriated on the basis of their singularity. If you own a silver-gray BMW, then by definition I cannot own the same BMW. Information is not like that. As it becomes ever more immaterial, abstracted from the tangible support of paper or vinyl or magnetic tape, nothing in your possession of a certain information prohibits me from possession of it too. As the media conglomerates buy up every source of information stock and flow to pipe down the next generation of high bandwidth vectors, the fact that this ownership is ultimately an unnecessary fetter appears on the horizon as a possibility.

There is private ownership and restriction, based on private property; there is cultural possession and restriction, based on traditional law and custom. What becomes of culture's ability to set limits, define boundaries, trace ancestries, when all that is solid really does melt into air? The work of Eric Michaels on Aboriginal communities and the way prohibitions on information flow make possible a culture of survival poses this question with the utmost urgency. Michaels worked to foster a culture of indigenous, self-managed video production, compatible with an innovative extrapolation of traditional law, at a time when the shadow of the satellite TV footprint was looming over central Australia.[53] How does a culture maintain its autonomy when, as Michaels makes clear, the self-reproduction of a culture through time requires that it exercise control over the passage of information across its bounds, and that it maintain the dominance of an adaptive form of its own vectors of transmission over and above the information passing along other vectors within the same terrain? I can do little more than pose these problems here, as a prolegomena to a future cultural studies. All I can say is that in the phenomena of the event, one can see an effect for which we can but speculate on a cause. A cause which appears as an emergent tendency. A tendency which requires a return to a certain partly forgotten mode of abstract, speculative thinking to understand.

Logic Bomb

Here is one last story one could tell about weird global media events. We could say that the event is a *logic bomb* hidden away within the dynamic core of the hardware of the vector, programmed by capital. A logic bomb is a species of computer virus. Since one definition of a vector is the trajectory along which a biological virus moves, it seems apt to adopt the terminology for the pathways along which information viruses move—the line of the communication network. A logic bomb, in computer parlance, is a tiny piece of information which passes into a computer system along any vector, be it a network or an "infected" disk. It attaches itself to the operating system of the computer, and there it waits. It may be programmed to "go off" at a preset time. Once the computer's quartz clock oscillates around to that preset time, off it goes. Alternatively, it may be programmed to go off when a certain sequence of commands is activated by the user. Some go off when you use the commands which check your computer system—for logic bombs.

Logic bombs are usually childish pranks performed by adolescent "hackers."[54] Still, the potential is there to, say, hack into major financial organizations and plant logic bombs which might trash their records. "Just as a virus takes over the control mechanism of an infected cell and uses the cell's own biological machinery to do its damage, a logic bomb can fool the infected computer into erasing selected files. . . . In the case of financial information, this kind of erasure could mean the loss of millions or billions of dollars."[55]

This is not the aspect of the logic bomb which interests me here, however. The logic bombs put in circulation along with other kinds of computer virus down the vector of computer networks are a crude toy with the potential to turn information into useless noise with great speed and nuisance. The event, as I have described it in the course of this book, seems to me to be not unlike a logic bomb. Of course, no one plans events in advance. They cannot be blamed on maladjusted teenage boys with low self-esteem and a lack of moral responsibility, except to the extent that the vector field itself, driven by capital, is a perpetual adolescent, innocent of its moral culpability. The event is the youthfully exuberant side of the vector field, when it comes up against its own limitations. The event is a logic bomb without a subject, which takes as its object the whole of third nature rather than a single computer.

Like a logic bomb, the event is programmed in advance to happen. Sometimes historical memory charges a particular date with the role of detonation. The student demonstrations in Tiananmen Square had no choice but to follow the calendar of remembrance. Events are triggered by some particular sequence of instructions passing along the vector. It is difficult to know what these are, even after the event. Why exactly did the Berlin Wall fall on that day and not another? Why did the stock market crash rather than simply slump in a respectable fashion? To a degree, these things cannot be known. The causality is not strict and linear, but systemic and many-factored. Each event is a constellation of noise triggered by the logic bomb which hides within the vector field itself. The vector is programmed in advance to crash, and to reveal something of its structure and workings as it goes down.

In any event, the ever-present threat of noise is the logic bomb within the system. The ethical question is whether noise is always necessarily a bad thing, or whether it has creative uses. The idea of a logic bomb is useful as a suggestive metaphor for how complex information networks function—and dysfunction. There appear to be logic bombs in all kinds of information networks that were not consciously programmed. They happen for an analogous reason to the computer logic bomb. A relative degree of openness means that messages end up lodging in any and every part of the information environment. They are activated when noise traverses the old boundaries and territories that used to characterize social life. Information overshoots the communities which create it. Their more or less shared social codes for interpreting messages, intentions, structures of feeling are not relevant when information passes out of the orbit of one community into another. Something which has very precise meaning in one place might be rendered ambiguous in another. A subtextual mark of no significance in one place might be a detonator of explosive feeling in another, quite unintentionally.

What we require, then, is an approach to the movement of information beyond physically delimited communities, including the accidental and unintended straying of information and the ricochet effect of deflecting from one site to another and on to another made possible by modern, global virtual geography. In other words, when information rapidly and radically overshoots its original context, it makes no sense to insist that the only valid way to interpret information is within its original context. It is important to show how a cultural artifact or text makes sense in its original location, but it is interesting and perhaps increasingly necessary to examine things which stray out of contexts where they make obvious sense into others where they may make perverse sense or none at all.[56] The logic bomb might not be the creation of a nerd individual with a few problems, but of the interface between the remains of vastly different communities and powers, strung together by the vector. The logic bomb might be the product of a communication system which moves information far beyond the thresholds of discrete communities of interpretation who can bind and limit the free play of meaning, preventing its proliferation.

These logic bombs are programmed into the information networks as an accidental byproduct. They are a byproduct of the complexities of power in an information-intensive world. They are an unconscious form of negation. They are the unintended effects of planned rationality and the inevitable byproducts of conflict within the institutions which govern the production and distribution of information. The historian of the "information society" James Benniger talks of a "control revolution" taking place in information systems, necessitated by and parallel to the development of the productive forces during the industrial revolution.[57] Yet every attempt to control the disposition and movement through geographic space and chronometric time of people, goods, weapons, and so on, in short every logistical solution, carries within it the possibility of disorder, disinformation, "discontrol"—the logic bomb.

Audit Trail

I'm particularly attached to the metaphor of the logic bomb because I had one once. It nearly ate this book. A draft of this text was sitting on my hard disk in my computer. There it was, a bunch of quite innocent electrons minding their own business on a magnetic disk. The logic bomb must have sneaked in there on some disk I had inserted into the machine that had a program of some sort on it. Then one day it struck. A little string of digital commands told my disk operating system to erase the hard disk, so it did. No more correspondence files, no more course outlines, no more draft, no more pencils, no more books, no more teacher's dirty looks. All gone.

Fortunately I had some backup disks, but there is a sense in which you never recover from a logic bombing. The idea that chaos can instantly descend into any information order seems to take root, deep in the unconscious.

Events are in a sense fractal. Each event appears as a confluence of noise in the matrix of vectors, but examine that event on a smaller scale and it appears to be made up of little events, all in a certain sense self-similar with the bigger event discovered at a larger scale. No matter where one looks in scale or time, the event appears to have this fractal structure, logic bombs within logic bombs. This is part of the abstraction of the event, that noise and information are abstracted from scale and time. Hence it seems appropriate to name what can be quite vast and global phenomena after something which takes place in the microscopic scale of electrons, nestling next to each other in a program of immaterial information.

On that note it is time to leave this book "finally unfinished," as Duchamp would have put it. I will not try to sum up these essays on such different events with a conclusion, for the form and nature of the work does not lend itself to it. Each of these chapters grew organically out of the constellations thrown up by particular events, and perhaps the concepts and images and analyses which emerged out of the collision of some tools from the humanities and the social sciences with some events of the contemporary global media vector ought to be left as that—collisions. As part of the "audit trail" of detritus left behind by the event itself.

notes

Site #1

1. vector

1. Dilip Hiro, *Desert Shield to Desert Storm: The Second Gulf War* (London: Harper Collins, 1992), p. 154.

2. Quotes taken from "Child Hostages Shown on TV," *Daily Mirror,* Sydney, 24 August 1990, and "The Smile on the Face of the Tiger," *Sydney Morning Herald,* 25 August 1990.

3. Not much has yet appeared on the reality TV phenomenon, pioneered by Steve Dunleavy and other Australian tabloid media stars for Rupert Murdoch's FOX-TV network. According to media researchers Catharine Lumby and John O'Neil, the Gulf war had a significant impact on the thinking of Australian current-affairs producers as to what was acceptable to the public in terms of television violence. See also McKenzie Wark, "You Can Run but You Can't Hide in Real TV Land," *The Australian,* 6 January 1993.

4. Slavoj Žižek, "Eastern Europe's Republics of Gilead," in *New Left Review,* no. 183 (September 1990), pp. 53–54.

5. See Edward Said, *Covering Islam: How the Media and the Experts Determine How We See the World* (London: Routledge Kegan Paul, 1981); William Dorman and Mansour Farhang, *The U.S. Press and Iran: Foreign Policy and the Journalism of Deference* (Berkeley: University of California Press, 1987).

6. Mohamed Heikal, *Illusions of Triumph: An Arab View of the Gulf War* (London: Harper Collins, 1992), pp. 160, 167.

7. Edward Said, *Orientalism* (Harmondsworth: Penguin, 1978), p. 231.

8. Ibid., p. 190.

9. Ibid., p. 312.

10. Heikal, *Illusions of Triumph,* p. 31.

11. Akbar Ahmed, *Postmodernism and Islam: Predicament and Promise* (London: Routledge, 1992), p. 238.

12. Edward Said, *Culture and Imperialism* (London: Chatto and Windus, 1993), p. 359.

13. Apart from the works already cited, see "On the Eve of Iraqi-Soviet Peace Talks," in Brian MacArthur, ed., *Despatches from the Gulf* (London: Bloomsbury, 1991), pp. 318–325.

14. Douglas Kellner, "Television, Crisis of Democracy and the Gulf War," in Marc Raboy and Bernard Dagenais, eds., *Media, Crisis and Democracy: Mass Communication and the Disruption of the Social Order* (London: Sage, 1992). I have read only a section of Doug's *The Persian Gulf TV War* (Boulder: Westview, 1992) in manuscript, but would recommend it nonetheless.

15. Noam Chomsky, "The Media and the War: What War?" in Hamid Mowlana, George Gerbner, and Herbert Schiller, eds., *Triumph of the Image: The Media's War in the Persian Gulf—A Global Perspective* (Boulder: Westview, 1992); "After the Cold War: US Middle East Policy," in Phyllis Bennis and Michel Moushabeck, eds., *Beyond the Storm: A Gulf Crisis Reader* (New York: Olive Branch Press, 1991); "The Gulf in Retrospect," in Nancy J. Peters, *War after War: City Lights Review,* no. 5 (1992), and *Deterring Democracy* (London: Verso, 1991).

16. Avital Ronell, "Support Our Tropes," in Peters, *War after War,* pp. 47–51; *Crack Wars* (Lincoln: University of Nebraska Press, 1992).

17. For a more considered and detailed assessment of the contributions of some of the schools of thought on the globalization of the media, see McKenzie Wark, "To the Vector the Spoils: Towards a Vectoral Analysis of the Global Media Event," in Elizabeth Jacka, ed., *Continental Shift: Globalization and Culture* (Sydney: LCP, 1992), pp. 142–160.

18. George Gerbner, "Persian Gulf War: The Movie," in Mowlana et al., *Triumph of the Image,* pp. 243–265.

19. Previous iterations of the chapters of this book appeared, in radically different form, as "On Technological Time: Virilio's Overexposed City," *Arena,* no. 83 (1987), pp. 82–100; "The News from Beijing," *Arena,* no. 88 (Spring 1989), pp. 50–62; "Europe's Masked Ball," *New Formations,* no. 12 (Winter 1990), pp. 33–42; "Vectors of Memory . . . Seeds of Fire: The Western Media and the Beijing Demonstrations," *New Formations,* no. 10 (Spring 1990), pp. 1–12; and "News Bites: War TV in the Gulf," *Meanjin,* vol. 50, no. 1 (1991), pp. 5–18.

20. Michel de Certeau, *The Practice of Everyday Life* (Berkeley: University of California Press, 1988), p. 87.

21. Michel de Montaigne, *Essays* (Harmondsworth: Penguin, 1985), p. 131.

22. *Roland Barthes by Roland Barthes* (New York: Nooneday Press, 1989), p. 51.

23. Ben Bagdikian, *The Media Monopoly,* 4th ed. (Boston: Beacon Press, 1992).

24. The best-known book on Murdoch is William Shawcross, *Rupert Murdoch: Ringmaster of the Information Circus* (London: Chatto and Windus, 1992), but it's not as good as George Munster's *Rupert Murdoch: A Paper Prince* (Melbourne: Penguin, 1987).

25. Herbert Schiller, *Culture Inc.: The Corporate Takeover of Public Expression* (New York: Oxford University Press, 1989).

26. Quoted in Hamid Mowlana, "Roots of War: The Long Road to Intervention," in Mowlana et al., *Triumph of the Image,* pp. 30–50, at p. 36.

27. Hamid Mowlana and Laurie Wilson, *The Passing of Modernity: Communication and the Transformation of Society* (London: Longman, 1990), p. 210.

28. Mowlana, "Roots of War," p. 43.

29. Heikal, *Illusions of Triumph,* p. 200.

30. John Hartley, *The Politics of Pictures: The Creation of the Public in the Age of Popular Media* (London: Routledge, 1992), p. 207.

31. Ibid., p. 140.

32. There are, of course, exceptions. See, for example, Langdon Winner, *Autonomous Technology* (Cambridge: MIT Press, 1987); David Noble, *America by Design* (New York: Oxford University Press, 1979); David Noble, *Forces of Production* (New York: Oxford University Press, 1986).

33. Andrew Ross has done cultural studies a huge favor by raising the issue of cultural formations and conflicts around technology, in his book *Strange Weather: Culture, Science and Technology in the Age of Limits* (London: Verso, 1991).

34. Marx's *Grundrisse* will be tackled later, but see Winner, *Autonomous Technology.* Raymond Williams, "Means of Communication as Means of Production," in *Problems in Materialism and Culture* (London: Verso, 1989), and *Television, Technology and Cultural Form* (Glasgow: Fontana, 1978); Lewis Mumford, *The Future of Technics and Civilisation* (London: Freedom Press, 1986).

35. Victor Shklovsky, *Mayakovsky and His Circle* (London: Pluto Press, 1978).

36. Paul Virilio, *Speed and Politics,* Semiotext(e) Foreign Agents Series (New York, 1986), pp. 143–144. See also Wark, "On Technological Time."

37. Which may already be happening. See McKenzie Wark, "From Fordism to Sonyism: Perverse Readings of the New World Order," in *New Formations,* no. 15 (1991).

38. Michel Foucault, "Theatrum Philosophicum," in *Language, Counter-Memory, Practice* (Ithaca: Cornell University Press, 1981), p. 172.

39. The coverage of the war in *Far Eastern Economic Review* is a good index of Asian opinion during the event. See "Impact on Asia: Once This Lousy War Is Over . . . ," cover story, vol. 151, no. 10 (7 March 1991). On the press coverage in the Middle East itself, see Caspar Henderson, "The Filtered War," *New Statesman,* 5 April 1991, and Jeremy Seabrook, "View from the South," *New Statesman,* 15 February 1991. For reporting on the refugee situation, see Denis MacShane, "Working in Virtual Slavery," *The Nation,* 18 March 1991, and Al Riskin, "Who Are the Refugees?" *MERIP Middle East Report,* no. 168 (January 1991).

40. On globalization, see Roland Robertson, "Mapping the Global Condition: Globalisation as the Central Concept," *Theory, Culture & Society,* vol. 7, no. 2/3 (June 1990).

41. Ien Ang, *Desperately Seeking the Audience* (London: Routledge, 1991).

42. Gilles Deleuze, *Bergsonism* (New York: Zone Books, 1988). Deleuze's thinking takes the form of a reading of the first chapter of Henri Bergson, *Matter and Memory* (New York: Zone Books, 1991). See also the two volumes on cinema, cited elsewhere.

43. Donna J. Haraway, "A Cyborg Manifesto," in her book *Simians, Cyborgs and Women: The Reinvention of Nature* (New York: Routledge, 1991), p. 150.

44. William Burroughs, "Word," in *Interzone* (London: Picador, 1989), p. 137.

45. This would be my main critical response to the interesting work of Joshua Meyrowitz, *In No Sense of Place: The Impact of Electronic Media on Social Behavior* (New York: Oxford University Press, 1985). He draws some provocative and interesting conclusions from the breaching of the boundaries between public and private space by television. However, he treats television entirely as a naturalistic representation of the "public" world. A consideration of the formal properties of television images leads, I think, to the distinction in modalities between private and public television time I am suggesting here.

46. Patricia Mellencamp, *Indiscretions: Avant Garde Film, Video, and Feminism* (Bloomington: Indiana University Press, 1990), p. 57.

47. See, in particular, the special issue of the journal *Propaganda Review,* no. 8 (1991).

48. On the public sphere, see Alexander Kluge and Oskar Negt, "The Public Sphere and Experience: Selections," and Stuart Liebman, "On New German Cinema, Art, Enlightenment, and the Public Sphere: An Interview with Alexander Kluge," *October,* no. 46 (Fall 1988).

49. Leibman, "Interview with Alexander Kluge," p. 45.

50. See, for example, John Fiske, *Television Culture* (London: Methuen, 1989), and Ien Ang, *Watching Dallas* (London: Methuen, 1985).

51. Kluge and Oskar Negt's writings on the public sphere, such as "The Public Sphere and Experience: Selections," are a critical response to Jürgen Habermas, in this case *The Structural Transformation of the Public Sphere* (Cambridge: Polity Press, 1989).

52. Paul Virilio, *Pure War,* Semiotext(e) Foreign Agents Series (New York, 1983), p. 58.

53. Antonio Gramsci, "The Intellectuals," in *Selections from the Prison Notebooks* (New York: International, 1980).

54. Two recent examples: Schiller, *Culture Inc.,* and Stuart Hall, *The Hard Road to Renewal* (London: Verso, 1988).

55. See, for example, Marion Farouk-Sluggert and Peter Sluggert's "Iraq since 1986: The Strengthening of Saddam," *MERIP Middle East Report,* no. 167 (November/December 1990).

56. Russell Jacoby laments the decline of the public intellectual in *The Last Intellectuals* (New York: Farrar, Straus and Giroux, 1989). He argues that while radical aca-

demics have inserted new content into academic discourses, they have not changed the form. While I agree with this assessment, I am less inclined toward a nostalgia for the public intellectuals of the past.

57. Lawrence Grossberg, in Grossberg et al., *It's a Sin: Essays on Postmodernism, Politics and Culture* (Sydney: Power Foundation, 1988), pp. 57–60.

58. Michel Foucault, "Nietzsche, Genealogy, History," in *Language, Counter-Memory, Practice*, p. 154.

59. Brian Toohey, "Bases Play a Crucial Role," *The Age*, 3 February 1991.

60. Wark, "Vectors of Memory . . . Seeds of Fire."

61. Paul Virilio, *War and Cinema* (London: Verso, 1989); Wark, "On Technological Time."

62. Walter Benjamin, *Charles Baudelaire: A Lyric Poet in the Era of High Capitalism* (London: Verso, 1985), p. 28.

63. Jean Baudrillard, *In the Shadow of the Silent Majorities*, Semiotext(e) (New York, 1983).

64. Ang, *Desperately Seeking the Audience.*

65. Sut Jhally, *The Codes of Advertising* (New York: Routledge, 1987).

66. Pierre Bourdieu, *Distinction: A Social Critique of the Judgement of Taste* (London: Routledge, 1986), chapter 8; Habermas, *The Structural Transformation of the Public Sphere*, chapters 12–15.

67. Sut Jhally, *Propaganda Review*, no. 8 (1991).

68. Jean Baudrillard, *Simulations*, Semiotext(e) Foreign Agents Series (New York, 1983), p. 122.

69. On America's manipulative "realpolitik" in the Gulf, see Noam Chomsky, "The Weak Shall Inherit Nothing," *Guardian Weekly*, vol. 144, no. 14 (7 April 1991); Christopher Hitchens, "Why We Are Stuck in the Sand," *Harper's*, vol. 282, no. 1688 (January 1991), and "Realpolitik in the Gulf," *New Left Review*, no. 186 (March 1991). Less inclined to view the U.S. as a successful regional manipulator is Fred Halliday, "The Crisis of the Arab World: The False Answers of Saddam Hussein," *New Left Review*, no. 184 (November/December 1990).

70. Said, *Orientalism*, p. 28.

71. Burroughs, "Word," p. 138.

72. On this, see John Hartley, *Teleology: Studies in Television* (London: Routledge, 1992), especially Part II: "Truth Wars."

73. This particular detail fits perfectly Slavoj Žižek's interpretation of collective paranoid subjectivity in "Eastern Europe's Republic of Gilead."

74. This perspective owes something to the analysis of media logic advanced by David Altheide, but without the simple distinction between media form and media content this work rests on. Here I have more sympathy with the concept of "discourse." Altheide and Snow criticize John Fiske's use of this term on the grounds that it blurs the distinction between form and content, and privileges the latter over the former. I think Fiske is right to employ the term "discourse" in preference to attempting to distinguish content from form—an impossible task. A concentration on movement rather than form is what is needed, which cuts across the form and content distinction. See David L. Altheide and Robert P. Snow, *Media Worlds in the Postjournalism Era* (New York: Aldine de Gruyter, 1991); John Fiske, *Television Culture* (London: Methuen, 1987).

75. An excellent book on the differentiated subject, both the subject of analysis and the analyzing subject, is Trinh T. Minh-ha, *Woman, Native, Other* (Bloomington: Indiana University Press, 1989).

2. event

1. Dilip Hiro, *Desert Shield to Desert Storm: The Second Gulf War* (London: Harper Collins, 1992), p. 320.

2. Michael Morgan, Justin Lewis, and Sut Jhally, "More Viewing, Less Knowledge," in Hamid Mowlana, George Gerbner, and Herbert Schiller, eds., *Triumph of the Image: The Media's War in the Persian Gulf—A Global Perspective* (Boulder: Westview, 1993), pp. 216–233, at p. 225.

3. Hiro, *Desert Shield to Desert Storm,* p. 308.

4. Samir al-Khalil, *The Monument: Art, Vulgarity and Responsibility in Iraq* (London: Andre Deutsch, 1991).

5. Hiro, *Desert Shield to Desert Storm,* pp. 155, 163.

6. Victor Navasky, *Naming Names* (London: John Calder, 1982).

7. Samir al-Khalil, *The Monument,* p. 51.

8. Mohamed Heikal, *Illusions of Triumph: An Arab View of the Gulf War* (London: Harper Collins, 1992), p. 381.

9. *Mideast Mirror,* quoted in Hamid Mowlana, Danielle Vierling, and Amy Tully, "A Sampling of Editorial Responses from the Middle Eastern Press on the Persian Gulf Crisis," in Mowlana et al., *Triumph of the Image,* pp. 166–172, at p. 172.

10. Douglas Kellner, *Television and the Crisis of Democracy* (Boulder: Westview, 1990).

11. Clayton Koppes and Gregory Block, *Hollywood Goes to War* (Berkeley: University of California Press, 1987).

12. On this privatized domain of what was formerly the public sphere of civil society, see Herbert Schiller, *Culture Inc.* (New York: Oxford University Press, 1989).

13. Walter Benjamin, "Theses on the Philosophy of History," in *Illuminations* (New York: Schocken, 1989), p. 257.

14. Christopher Hitchens, "How Neoconservatives Perish: Good-bye to Totalitarianism and All That," in *Harper's,* vol. 281, no. 1682 (July 1990).

15. Cited in Adel Darwish and Gregory Alexander, *Unholy Babylon: The Secret History of Saddam's War* (London: Victor Gollancz, 1991), p. 63.

16. Edward Said, *Culture and Imperialism* (London: Chatto and Windus, 1993), p. 360.

17. Michael T. Klare, "Policing the Gulf—and the World," *The Nation,* 15 October 1990. See also Michael T. Klare, "The Pentagon's New Paradigm," in Micah Sifry and Christopher Cerf, *The Gulf War: History, Documents, Opinions* (New York: Random House, 1991), pp. 466–476.

18. Cf. McKenzie Wark, "From Fordism to Sonyism: Perverse Readings of the New World Order," in *New Formations,* no. 15 (Winter 1991).

19. Both quotes are from Klare, "Policing the Gulf."

20. Mary Kaldor, "War of the Imagination," *Marxism Today* (March 1990).

21. Bob Woodward, *The Commanders* (New York: Simon and Schuster, 1991).

22. Gilles Deleuze, *Cinema 1: The Movement-Image; Cinema 2: The Time-Image* (Minneapolis: University of Minnesota Press, 1986).

23. Samir al-Khalil, *Republic of Fear: The Politics of Modern Iraq* (London: Hutchinson Radius, 1989), pp. 82–88.

24. Samir al-Khalil, "Iraq and Its Future," *New York Review of Books,* vol. 38, no. 7 (11 April 1991).

25. Max Weber, "The Sociology of Charismatic Authority," in Hans Gerth and C. Wright Mills, *From Max Weber* (London: RKP, 1982).

26. Samir al-Khalil, *Republic of Fear,* pp. 114–115.

27. Hank Wittemore, *CNN: The Inside Story* (Boston: Little, Brown, 1990), p. 124.

28. Stuart Hall, "Encoding and Decoding," in Stuart Hall et al., eds., *Culture, Media, Language* (London: Hutchinson, 1980).

29. See the chapter "Exposition of the Problem of Reported Speech" in V. N. Volosinov, *Marxism and the Philosophy of Language* (Cambridge: Harvard University Press, 1986).

30. Edwin Diamond, *The Media Show* (Cambridge: MIT Press, 1991), p. 57.

31. Dick Hebdige, "Bombing Logic," *Marxism Today* (March 1991).
32. Alexander Cockburn, "Hawks and Doves," *New Statesman,* 7 September 1990.
33. Phillip McCarthy, "Big Shots Look to Small Screen to Get the Message," *Sydney Morning Herald,* 12 January 1991.
34. On Rogich, see Hiro, *Desert Shield to Desert Storm,* p. 251.
35. Martin Walker, "Las Vegas Ad-Man behind the New Improved Image," *Guardian,* 24 November 1990; Andrew Stephen, "Bush of Arabia Flops in the Desert," *Observer,* 25 November 1990.
36. Philip Knightley, *The First Casualty* (London: Pan Books, 1989).
37. Ibid., p. 397.
38. See Noam Chomsky, *Deterring Democracy* (London: Verso, 1991).
39. Mark Hertsgaard, *On Bended Knee: The Press and the Reagan Presidency* (New York: Schocken, 1988).
40. Linda Rocawich, "The General in Charge," *The Progressive,* vol. 55, no. 1 (January 1991); Mark Perry, "Doubts about Desert War: The Pentagon's New Army," *MERIP Middle East Report,* no. 167 (November/December 1990).
41. Quoted in Woodward, *The Commanders,* p. 155.
42. John Pilger, "Myth Makers of the Gulf War," *Guardian Weekly,* 13 January 1991.
43. William E. Burrows, *Deep Black: The Secrets of Space Espionage* (London: Bantam, 1988).
44. Margaret Scott, "News from Nowhere," *Far Eastern Economic Review,* 28 November 1991.
45. From an interview in the "Angry Women" issue of *Re/Search,* no. 13 (1991), p. 131. See also Avital Ronell, *The Telephone Book: Technology, Schizophrenia, Electric Speech* (Lincoln: University of Nebraska Press, 1989).
46. "The Peters Principle," *Penthouse,* October 1991, p. 68.
47. Paul Virilio, "Star Wars," *Art & Text,* no. 22 (1986).
48. Only Edward Said mentioned the historic significance of the city. Cf. "Arabesque," *New Statesman,* 7 September 1990.
49. Darwish and Alexander, *Unholy Babylon,* pp. 85ff.
50. *New Statesman,* 15 February 1991.

Site #2

3. wall

1. *The Guardian Weekly,* vol. 141, no. 20 (19 November 1989).
2. *New York Times,* 13 November 1989.
3. Whereas the fate of Benjamin's angel of history is recorded by Heiner Müller, "The Luckless Angel," in *Germania,* Semiotext(e) Foreign Agents Series (New York, 1990).
4. Zygmunt Bauman, "Living without an Alternative," *Political Quarterly,* vol. 62, no. 1 (January 1991), p. 42.
5. *New York Times,* 10 November and 12 November 1989.
6. Walter Benjamin, "One Way Street," in *One Way Street and Other Essays* (London: Verso, 1895), p. 81.
7. Willy Brandt, "Berlin City Hall Speech," in Harold James and Marla Stone, eds., *When the Wall Came Down: Reactions to German Unification* (New York: Routledge, 1992), pp. 42–45.
8. James Petras, "East Germany: Conquest, Pillage and Disintegration," *Journal of Contemporary Asia,* vol. 22, no. 3 (1992), pp. 341–359.

9. Nicos Poulantzas, *The Crisis of the Dictatorships* (London: New Left Books, 1976).
10. Dorothy Rosenberg, "The Colonization of East Germany," *Monthly Review* (September 1991), pp. 14–33.
11. Anson Rabinbach, "The Return of the Ugly German," *Dissent* (Spring 1992), pp. 150–153.
12. Helmut Kohl, "Overcoming the Division of Germany and Europe," in James and Stone, *When the Wall Came Down*, p. 36.
13. Slavoj Žižek, "Eastern Europe's Republics of Gilead," *New Left Review*, no. 183 (September 1990), p. 50.
14. Theodor Adorno, *Minima Moralia* (London: New Left Books, 1978), pp. 43–45.
15. Stefan Heym, "The Forty Year Itch," *Marxism Today* (November 1989).
16. Helmut Hanke, "Media Culture in the GDR: Characteristics, Processes and Problems," *Media, Culture and Society*, vol. 12 (1990), pp. 175–193.
17. Jürgen Habermas, "What Does Socialism Mean Today?" *New Left Review* (September 1990), p. 7 (emphasis added).
18. Jürgen Habermas, *The Theory of Communicative Action*, vol. 1 (Boston: Beacon Press, 1984). Lawrence Grossberg raises the problem of the dependence on the national framework in cultural-studies approaches in *We Gotta Get Out of This Place* (New York: Routledge, 1992), p. 24. See also McKenzie Wark, "From Fordism to Sonyism: Perverse Readings of the New World Order," *New Formations*, no. 15 (1991).
19. Werner Kratschell, in "The State of Europe: Christmas Eve 1989," *Granta* 30 (1990), p. 144.
20. An extraordinary story in itself. See Desmond Ball, *Policies and Force Levels: The Strategic Missile Program of the Kennedy Administration* (Berkeley: University of California Press, 1980).
21. Peter Schneider, "If the Wall Came Tumbling Down," *New York Times Magazine*, 25 June 1989.
22. Hanke, "Media Culture in the GDR," p. 191.
23. Stephen Spender, in "The State of Europe: Christmas Eve, 1989," *Granta* 30 (1990), p. 169.
24. Timothy Garton Ash, *We the People* (Cambridge: Granta Books, 1990), p. 65.
25. Müller, *Germania*, p. 89.
26. Spender, in "The State of Europe," p. 170.
27. Jean Baudrillard takes over this image of map and territory from Borges in *Simulations*, Semiotext(e) Foreign Agents Series (New York, 1983), but one can already find it in Guy Debord's classic *Society of the Spectacle* (Detroit: Black and Red, 1983). The sense of collective agency implied in this paragraph is of course foreign to Baudrillard, but not to Debord.
28. Timothy Garton Ash, *The Uses of Adversity* (Cambridge: Granta Books, 1989), p. 7.
29. Christa Wolfe, "What Remains," *Granta*, no. 33 (Summer 1990).
30. Wolf Bierman, "Family Arguments," *Granta*, no. 35 (Spring 1991).
31. Debord, *Society of the Spectacle*, epigram 31. Baudrillard develops the theme of the autonomous development of the map of the spectacle in *Simulations*.
32. Debord, *Society of the Spectacle*, epigram 195.
33. Cf. McKenzie Wark, "Spirit Freed from Flesh," *flesh*, intervention publications, no. 21/22, Sydney, 1889.
34. Georg Lukács, "Class Consciousness," in *History and Class Consciousness* (London: Merlin, 1983), pp. 46–82.
35. Harold Innes, *The Bias of Communication* (Toronto: University of Toronto Press, 1991).
36. Michel de Certeau, *The Practice of Everyday Life* (Berkeley: University of California Press, 1988), p. 48.

37. Ibid., p. 117.

38. Comedy is the last form of history, according to Marx. The parody here is of the Manifesto, and less obviously of "The Introduction to the Critique of Hegel's Philosophy of Right," in *Early Writings* (Harmondsworth: Penguin in association with New Left Review, 1975), pp. 247, 250.

39. Habermas, "What Does Socialism Mean Today?" p. 15.

40. Guy Debord's famous parody of Hegel's "that which is real is rational and that which is rational is real" can be found in *The Society of the Spectacle,* epigram 12.

41. McKenzie Wark, "East Meets West at the Wall," *New Formations,* no. 12 (1990).

42. Ash, *We the People,* p. 62.

43. "Floyd's Pink Pomp Plugs a Hole in the Wall," *Sydney Morning Herald,* 16 June 1990.

44. Noberto Bobbio, "The Upturned Utopia," *New Left Review,* no. 177 (1989).

45. Joshua Meyrowitz, *No Sense of Place* (New York: Oxford University Press, 1985), pp. 5–6.

46. Interview with Kluge and Oskar Negt and Kluge, "The Public Sphere and Experience: Selections," *October,* no. 46 (Fall 1988)—the unfortunate term "sphere" is the translator's, not the author's. This work forms a dialogue and a departure from an early work of Jürgen Habermas, *The Structural Transformation of the Public Sphere* (Cambridge: Polity Press, 1989).

47. Jean Baudrillard, *America* (London: Verso, 1988), p. 33; for a critique of Baudrillard's fatal logic of the sign, see Meaghan Morris, "Banality in Cultural Studies," in *intervention,* no. 23/24 (1990), and "Room 101: Or a Few Worst Things in the World," in *The Pirate's Fiancee* (London: Verso, 1988).

48. Peter Sloterdijk, *Critique of Cynical Reason* (London: Verso, 1987).

49. Christopher Hitchens, "How Neoconservatives Perish: Good-bye to Totalitarianism and All That," *Harper's,* vol. 281, no. 1682 (July 1990).

50. Antonio Gramsci, "The Revolution against Das Kapital," in *Selected Political Writings,* vol. 1 (New York: International Publishers, 1973); Victor Serge, *Birth of Our Power* (London: Readers and Writers Co-operative, 1978).

51. Victor Serge, *Men in Prison, Birth of Our Power, and Conquered City,* all published by Readers and Writers Publishing Co-operative.

52. See Foucault's comments on the role which the need to critique the Stalinist conception of power played in his work in *Foucault Live,* Semiotext(e) Foreign Agents Series (New York, 1989).

53. Josef Skvorecky, in "The State of Europe," p. 128.

54. Cf. Stuart Hall and Ernesto Laclau, "Coming Up for Air," *Marxism Today* (March 1990).

55. Andrei Sinyavsky, in "The State of Europe," pp. 151–154; cf. Czeslaw Milosz in the same volume.

56. Stephen Spender, in "The State of Europe," p. 170.

57. Zhores Medvedev, "Soviet Power Today," *New Left Review,* no. 179 (1990).

58. With apologies to Alphonse Alais.

4. site

1. Micha Brumlik, "Light on a Dark Subject," *Guardian Weekly,* 14 February 1993, p. 10.

2. Walter Momper, "Berlin City Hall Speech," in Harold James and Marla Stone, eds., *When the Wall Came Down: Reactions to German Unification* (New York: Routledge, 1992), p. 48.

3. Jean-François Lyotard, *The Postmodern Condition: A Report on Knowledge* (Minneapolis: University of Minnesota Press, 1984).

4. Most of the information on the site of the Achtek comes from Alan Balfour, *Berlin: The Politics of Order 1737–1989* (New York: Rizzoli, 1990).

5. Paul Virilio, *Pure War,* Semiotext(e) Foreign Agents Series (New York, 1983), pp. 44–45.

6. Lewis Mumford, *The City in History* (Harmondsworth: Penguin, 1987).

7. Hegel, quoted in Shlomo Avineri, *Hegel's Theory of the Modern State* (Cambridge: Cambridge University Press, 1980), p. 63.

8. Richard Rorty, "Habermas and Lyotard on Postmodernity," in Richard Bernstein, ed., *Habermas and Modernity* (Cambridge: Polity Press, 1985), pp. 192–216.

9. Carl von Clausewitz, *On War* (Harmondsworth: Penguin, 1985), p. 104.

10. Ibid., p. 105.

11. Göran Therborn, *Science, Class and Society* (London: Verso, 1980), pp. 77–87; Colin Mooers, *The Making of Bourgeois Europe* (London: Verso, 1991), pp. 120–121.

12. Paul Virilio, "The Overexposed City," *Zone,* no. 1/2 (1988).

13. Theodor Adorno and Max Horkheimer, *Dialectic of Enlightenment* (London: Verso, 1979).

14. Karl Marx, "Manifesto of the Communist Party," in Karl Marx, *The Revolutions of 1848: Political Writings Volume 1* (Harmondsworth: Penguin Books in association with New Left Review, 1978), p. 70.

15. Walter Benjamin, "Haussmann or the Barricades," in *Charles Baudelaire: A Lyric Poet in the Era of High Capitalism* (London: Verso, 1985), p. 176. See also Benedict Anderson, *Imagined Communities* (London: Verso, 1989), and Anthony D. Smith, *National Identity* (Harmondsworth: Penguin, 1991).

16. Aldo Rossi, *The Architecture of the City* (Cambridge: Opposition Books/MIT Press, 1986), p. 59.

17. Paul Virilio, *Speed and Politics,* Semiotext(e) Foreign Agents Series (New York, 1986), p. 3.

18. George Grosz, *George Grosz: An Autobiography* (New York: Macmillan, 1983), p. 150.

19. Guy Debord, *Comments on the Society of the Spectacle* (London: Verso, 1990).

20. Guy Debord, *Society of the Spectacle* (Detroit: Black and Red), epigrams 96–98.

21. On the distinction between mediated and immediately constituted power, see Antonio Negri, *The Savage Anomaly* (Minneapolis: University of Minnesota Press, 1991).

22. Debord, *Society of the Spectacle,* epigram 100.

23. Vernon Lidke, *The Alternative Culture: Socialist Labor in Imperial Germany* (New York: Oxford University Press, 1985).

24. Alexander Kluge, "The Public Sphere and Experience: Selections," *October,* no. 46 (Fall 1988), pp. 60–82.

25. Alex Hall, *Scandal, Sensation and Social Democracy* (Cambridge: Cambridge University Press, 1977), pp. 24–40.

26. Ibid., p. 26.

27. Manfredo Tafuri, *The Sphere and the Labyrinth: Avant Gardes and Architecture from Piranesi to the 70s* (Cambridge: MIT Press, 1987), pp. 197–233.

28. Susan Buck-Morss, *The Dialectic of Seeing: Walter Benjamin and the Arcades Project,* Studies in Contemporary German Social Thought (Cambridge: MIT Press, 1989), pp. 34–35.

29. Benjamin, *Charles Baudelaire,* pp. 28–29.

30. Negri, *The Savage Anomaly,* p. 33.

31. Thomas Elsaesser, *New German Cinema: A History* (London: Macmillan in association with the British Film Institute, 1989); Anton Kaes, *From Hitler to Heimat* (Cambridge: Harvard University Press, 1989).

32. Stuart Leibman, "Interview with Alexander Kluge," *October,* no. 46 (Fall 1988), p. 32.

33. Georg Simmel, "The Metropolis and Mental Life," in Kurt D. Wolff, ed., *The Sociology of George Simmel* (New York: Free Press, 1950).
34. "Introduction" to Humphrey Jennings, *Pandaemonium 1660–1886: The Coming of the Machine as Seen by Contemporary Observers,* ed. Mary-Lou Jennings and Charles Madge (London: Picador, 1987).
35. See Bruce Murray, *Film and the German Left in the Weimar Republic: From Caligari to Kuhle Wampe* (Austin: University of Texas Press, 1990); Roswitha Mueller, *Bertolt Brecht and the Theory of the Media* (Lincoln: University of Nebraska Press, 1989); and Buck-Morss, *The Dialectic of Seeing.*
36. Walter Benjamin, "A Berlin Chronicle," in *One Way Street and Other Essays* (London: Verso, 1985).
37. Jean Baudrillard, "The Political Economy of the Sign," in *Selected Writings* (Cambridge: Polity Press, 1988).
38. Patrice Petro, *Joyless Streets: Women and Melodramatic Representation in Weimar Germany* (Princeton: Princeton University Press, 1989).
39. Karl Marx, Economic and Philosophical Manuscripts, *Early Writings* (Harmondsworth: Penguin Books in association with New Left Review, 1975), p. 335.
40. Michel Foucault, *Discipline and Punish* (Harmondsworth: Penguin, 1977), p. 217.
41. Gilles Deleuze, *Foucault* (Minneapolis: University of Minnesota Press, 1988), p. 42.
42. Quotes from *New York Times,* 11 and 12 November 1989.
43. Armand Matellart, *Advertising International* (London: Routledge, 1992).
44. Heiner Müller, *Germania,* Semiotext(e) Foreign Agents Series (New York, 1990), pp. 20, 247.
45. Timothy Garton Ash, *The Uses of Adversity* (Cambridge: Granta Books, 1989), p. 234 (note).

Site #3

5. intersection

1. Geremie Barmé and Linda Jaivin, *New Ghosts, Old Dreams: Chinese Rebel Voices* (New York: Random House, 1992), preface, p. xvii.
2. Nicos Poulantzas, *The Crisis of the Dictatorships* (London: New Left Books, 1975).
3. Raymond Williams, *Keywords* (London: Fontana, 1979), pp. 82–86.
4. Walter Benjamin, "Theses on the Philosophy of History," in *Illuminations* (London: Verso), p. 259.
5. Wei Jingsheng, "The Fifth Modernization: Democracy," translated by Simon Leys in *The Burning Forest* (London: Paladin, 1988).
6. Wei Jingsheng, "Q1—A Twentieth-Century Bastille," in Geremie Barmé and John Minford, *Seeds of Fire: Chinese Voices of Conscience* (New York: Hill and Wang, 1988).
7. Quoted in Barmé and Jaivin, *New Ghosts, Old Dreams,* p. 24.
8. Michael Fathers and Andrew Higgins, *Tiananmen: The Rape of Peking* (London: The Independent in association with Doubleday, 1989), p. 5.
9. Quoted in ibid., p. 7.
10. Lui Xiaobo, "The Tragedy of a Tragic Hero: A Critique of the Hu Yaobang Phenomenon," in Barmé and Jaivin, *New Ghosts, Old Dreams,* p. 43.
11. Quoted in Han Minzhu, ed., *Cries for Democracy: Writings and Speeches from the 1989 Chinese Democracy Movement* (Princeton: Princeton University Press, 1990), p. 7.

12. Liu Xiaobo, "The Tragedy of a Tragic Hero," p. 44.
13. Donald Morrison, *Massacre in Beijing: China's Struggle for Democracy* (New York: Time Books, 1989), p. 197.
14. Michel Foucault, *Discipline and Punish* (Harmondsworth: Penguin, 1979), p. 201.
15. Fathers and Higgins, *Tiananmen,* p. 20.
16. Paul Virilio, *Speed and Politics,* Semiotext(e) Foreign Agents Series (New York, 1986), p. 8.
17. Barmé and Jaivin, *New Ghosts, Old Dreams,* pp. 65–66.
18. George Black and Robin Munro, *Black Hands of Beijing: Lives of Defiance in China's Democracy Movement* (New York: Wiley, 1993), p. 147.
19. Han Minzhu, *Cries for Democracy,* pp. 28–31.
20. Ibid., p. 43.
21. Quoted in Black and Munro, *Black Hands of Beijing,* p. 148.
22. Quoted in Han Minzhu, *Cries for Democracy,* p. 57.
23. Ibid., p. 87.
24. These terms are from George Rudé, *The Crowd in History 1730–1848* (London: Lawrence and Wishart, 1985), p. 4.
25. Han Minzhu, *Cries for Democracy,* p. 339.
26. He Xin, "An Analysis of the Current Student Protests and Forecasts concerning the Situation," in Barmé and Jaivin, *New Ghosts, Old Dreams.*
27. "Some Sayings of Lu Xun," translated by Simon Leys in *The Burning Forest,* p. 206.
28. Virilio, *Speed and Politics,* p. 113.
29. On Chai Ling and the start of the hunger strike, see Li Lu, *Moving the Mountain: My Life in China* (London: Macmillan, 1990), pp. 130–131; Han Minzhu, *Cries for Democracy,* pp. 199–200; Black and Munro, *Black Hands of Beijing,* p. 169; Mok Chiu Yu and Frank Harrison, *Voices from Tiananmen: Beijing Spring and the Democracy Movement* (Montreal: Black Rose Books, 1990).
30. Deng Xiaoping, "Hold High the Banner of Mao Zedong Thought and Adhere to the Principle of Seeking Truth from Facts," in *Selected Works of Deng Xiaoping (1975–1982)* (Beijing: Foreign Language Press, 1984). This speech dates from 1978, before Deng's final victory over the Maoist "whatever" faction.
31. Lawrence Grossberg, *We Gotta Get Out of This Place* (New York: Routledge, 1992), p. 79.
32. Black and Munro, *Black Hands of Beijing,* p. 173.
33. Appropriately enough, both expressions occur in Isaac Deutscher's history of another sclerotic regime of bureaucratic-socialist hue, *Stalin: A Political Biography* (Oxford: Oxford University Press, 1977).
34. Examples of both Dai Qing's journalism and the "River Elegy" script can be found in Barmé and Jaivin, *New Ghosts, Old Dreams.*
35. Quoted in Trevor Watson, *Tremble and Obey* (Sydney: ABC Books, 1990), p. 40.
36. Morrison, *Massacre in Beijing,* p. 173.
37. On the relationship of the Soviet state to the liberal intellectuals, see the work of Boris Kagarlitsky: *The Thinking Reed* (London: Verso, 1988); *The Dialectic of Change* (London: Verso, 1990); and *Farewell Perestroika: A Soviet Chronicle* (London: Verso, 1990).
38. Han Minzhu, *Cries for Democracy,* p. 227.
39. Ibid., pp. 221–222.
40. Black and Munro, *Black Hands of Beijing,* p. 189.
41. Han Minzhu, *Cries for Democracy,* p. 242.
42. Ibid., pp. 294–295.
43. Quoted in Black and Munro, *Black Hands of Beijing,* p. 201.
44. Morrison, *Massacre in Beijing,* p. 169.

45. Ibid., pp. 185–186.
46. "Our Suggestions," in Barmé and Jaivin, *New Ghosts, Old Dreams,* pp. 68–69.
47. Timothy Garton Ash, *The Uses of Adversity* (Cambridge: Granta Books, 1989), pp. 95–108.
48. See David Kelly, "Chinese Intellectuals in the 1989 Democracy Movement," in George Hicks, ed., *The Broken Mirror: China after Tiananmen* (London: Longman, 1990).
49. Han Minzhu, *Cries for Democracy,* p. 327.
50. Ibid., p. 314.
51. Hou Dejian, "Heirs of the Dragon," in Barmé and Jaivin, *New Ghosts, Old Dreams,* p. 153.
52. Jimmy Ngai Siu-Yan, "Tiananmen Days," in ibid., p. 86.
53. Rey Chow, *Writing Diaspora: Tactics of Intervention in Contemporary Cultural Studies* (Bloomington: Indiana University Press, 1993), p. 23.
54. Quoted in Han Minzhu, *Cries for Democracy,* pp. 342–348.
55. Lu Yuan, "Beijing Diary," *New Left Review,* no. 177 (September 1989), p. 7.
56. David Kelly, "Massacre of a Chinese Company: Rise and Fall of the Beijing Stone Group," *Australian Financial Review,* 4 October 1989, p. 13.
57. Or at least that was the judgment of Liu Binyan, who preferred to stay in the United States. Barmé and Jaivin, *New Ghosts, Old Dreams,* p. 48.
58. Geremie Barmé, "Liu Xiaobo and the Protest Movement of 1989," in Hicks, *The Broken Mirror,* p. 69.
59. Gilles Deleuze, *Nietzsche and Philosophy* (London: Athlone Press, 1983).
60. Elias Canetti, *Crowds and Power* (Harmondsworth: Penguin, 1984), pp. 64–65.
61. Morrison, *Massacre in Beijing,* p. 169.
62. Li Lu, *Moving the Mountain,* p. 199.
63. Ibid., p. 200. Hou Dejian's own account is "Blame Me If You Want!" in Yi Mu and Mark Thompson, *Crisis at Tiananmen: Reform and Reality in Modern China* (San Francisco: China Books, 1989), pp. 239–249.
64. For credible independent assessments of the human cost of the crackdown, see Amnesty International, *China: The Massacre of June 1989 and Its Aftermath* (London, 1989); International League for Human Rights, *Massacre in Beijing: The Events of 3–4 June 1989 and Their Aftermath* (New York, 1989).
65. Canetti, *Crowds and Power,* p. 79.
66. Lu Yuan, "Beijing Diary," p. 22.
67. Ibid., p. 18.
68. Yang Lian, "Bloodstains in Heaven," in *The Dead in Exile* (Canberra: Tiananmen Publications, 1990), translated by Mabel Lee, p. 9.
69. For more on the subcultural side of Beijing life, see the story "Rocking Tiananmen" by Liu Yiran and the "Red Noise" section of Barmé and Jaivin, *New Ghosts, Old Dreams.*
70. According to Gang of Four member Andy Gill, "T. J. Clark came around '76 to Leeds. This was somebody who was looking at art production and cultural experiences in a political way. . . ." From an interview in Fareed Armaly, ed., *ROOM* (Milan, 1989).
71. T. J. Clark, *Image of the People: Gustav Courbet and the 1848 Revolution* (London: Thames and Hudson, 1988), p. 13.
72. Gang of Four, "5.45," *Entertainment!* (Warner Bros., 1979).
73. Simon Leys, "After the Massacres," in Hicks, *The Broken Mirror,* p. 156.
74. Black and Munro, *Black Hands of Beijing,* p. 327.
75. Karl Marx, "The Eighteenth Brumaire of Louis Bonaparte," in *Surveys from Exile* (Harmondsworth: Penguin Books in association with New Left Review, 1973), p. 146.
76. Gregor Benton, "Beijing Spring," *New Statesman,* 26 May 1989; see also John Gittings, *China Changes Faces: The Road from Revolution 1949–1989* (Oxford: Oxford University Press, 1990).

77. Greil Marcus, *Lipstick Traces . . .* (Cambridge: Harvard University Press, 1989).

6. *lines*

1. Cf. Gregor Benton, "Beijing Spring," *New Statesman,* 26 May 1989.
2. Elias Canetti, *Crowds and Power* (Harmondsworth: Penguin, 1984), pp. 214–220.
3. Ibid., pp. 54–66.
4. McKenzie Wark, "On Technological Time," *Arena,* no. 83 (1988).
5. "Clear Away All Obstacles and Adhere to the Policies of Reform and of Opening to the Outside World," in Deng Xiaoping, *Fundamental Issues in Present-Day China* (Beijing: Foreign Languages Press, 1987), p. 170.
6. Paul Virilio, *Speed and Politics,* Semiotext(e) Foreign Agents Series (New York, 1986), p. 33.
7. Harrison Salisbury, *Tiananmen Diary: Thirteen Days in June* (London: Unwin, 1989), p. 49.
8. Paul Virilio, "Popular Defense and Popular Assault," in *Italy: Autonomia—Post-Political Politics,* Semiotext(e) no. 9 (New York, 1980).
9. Donald Morrison, ed., *Massacre in Beijing: China's Struggle for Democracy* (New York: Time Books, 1989), pp. 211–212.
10. Karl Marx and Fredrick Engels, *The German Ideology* (Moscow: Progress, 1976), pp. 72–74.
11. From "Some Sayings of Lu Xun," translated by Simon Leys, in *The Burning Forest* (London: Paladin, 1988), pp. 206–207.
12. Chen Erjin, *Crossroads Socialism* (London: Verso, 1984), p. 93.
13. Paul Rabinow, *French Modern* (Cambridge: MIT Press, 1989).
14. Liu Xinwu, "Black Walls," in Geremie Barmé and John Minson, *Seeds of Fire: Chinese Voices of Conscience* (New York: Hill and Wang, 1988), pp. 26–27.
15. Jean Baudrillard, *America* (London: Verso, 1988), pp. 97–99.
16. Morrison, *Massacre in Beijing,* p. 174.
17. In Barmé and Minson, *Seeds of Fire,* pp. 400–401.
18. Henri Lefebvre, *Critique of Everyday Life* (London: Verso, 1991), p. 16.
19. McKenzie Wark, "Speaking Trajectories: Meaghan Morris, Antipodean Theory and Australian Cultural Studies," *Cultural Studies,* vol. 6, no. 3 (October 1992), pp. 433–448.
20. Aldo Rossi, *The Architecture of the City* (Cambridge: Opposition Books, MIT Press, 1986).
21. Simon Leys, *Chinese Shadows* (Harmondsworth: Penguin, 1977), pp. 53–54. Apologies to the author for altering the romanization of chinese names.
22. Cf. "Order and Disorder: Noise, Trace and Event in Evolution and in History," in Anthony Wilden, *System and Structure: Essays in Communication and Exchange,* 2nd ed. (London: Tavistock, 1980).
23. On the problem of the relation between contemporary media and the formation of collective memory, cf. McKenzie Wark, "Just Like a Prayer," *Meanjin,* no. 3 (Melbourne, 1989).
24. Stanley Karnow, *Mao and China: Inside China's Cultural Revolution* (New York: Penguin, 1984), pp. 201ff.
25. Arif Dirlik, *The Origins of Chinese Communism* (New York: Oxford University Press, 1989), p. 60.
26. Ibid., p. 68.
27. Mao Zedong, "Talks at the Yanan Forum on Literature and Art," in *Selected Works* (Beijing: Foreign Languages Press, 1966), vol. 3, pp. 69–98.
28. Anita Chan, "The Reality behind the Cokes," *The Age Monthly Review* (Melbourne, October 1989).
29. Ann Thurston, *Enemies of the People: The Ordeal of the Intellectuals in China's*

Great Cultural Revolution (Cambridge: Harvard University Press, 1988). The events recounted are drawn largely from the first chapter.

30. Michel de Certeau, *The Practice of Everyday Life* (Berkeley: University of California Press, 1988), p. 98.

31. Dong Liming, "Beijing: The Development of a Socialist Capital," in Victor Sit, *Chinese Cities* (Hong Kong: Oxford University Press, 1988).

32. For selections of texts from the period, see David Goodman, *Beijing Street Voices: The Poetry and Politics of China's Democracy Movement* (London: Marion Boyars, 1981); Gregor Benton, *Wild Lillies; Poisonous Weeds: Dissident Voices from People's China* (London: Pluto Press, 1981).

33. Andrew Nathan, *Chinese Democracy* (London: Tauris, 1986), p. 3.

34. Walter Benjamin, "Theses on the Philosophy of History," in *Illuminations* (New York: Schocken, 1987).

35. Merle Goldman, *China's Intellectuals: Advice and Dissent* (Cambridge: Harvard University Press, 1981).

36. Greil Marcus, "Sixty-Eight Eighty-Sixed," *Common Knowledge,* vol. 1, no. 1 (Spring 1992), p. 107.

37. McKenzie Wark, "Vectors of Memory . . . Seeds of Fire," *New Formations,* no. 10 (1990).

38. Nicholas Jose, "China: What Is Going On," *The Independent Monthly,* October 1989, p. 15.

39. James Miller, *The Passion of Michel Foucault* (New York: Simon and Schuster, 1993), p. 169.

40. George Lukács, *The Historical Novel* (London: Merlin, 1989), p. 24.

41. McKenzie Wark, "The Logistics of Perception," *Meanjin,* vol. 49, no. 1 (1990).

42. Greil Marcus, *Lipstick Traces . . .* (Cambridge: Harvard University Press, 1989), and "The Dance That Everybody Forgot," *New Formations,* no. 2 (1987)—one of his finest essays.

43. De Certeau, *The Practice of Everyday Life,* p. 87.

44. Deng Xiaoping, "Clear Away All Obstacles and Adhere to the Policies of Reform and of Opening to the Outside World."

45. Jimmy Ngai Siu-Yan, "Tiananmen Days," in Geremie Barmé and Linda Jaivin, *New Ghosts, Old Dreams: Chinese Rebel Voices* (New York: Random House, 1992), p. 84.

46. Cited in Michael Fathers and Andrew Higgins, *Tiananmen: The Rape of Peking* (London: The Independent in association with Doubleday, 1989), pp. 87–88.

47. I am indebted to the criticisms of Gerry Gill, directed at an earlier, "instant" version of this paper, for this point.

48. Jonathan Alter, "Karl Marx, Meet Marshall McLuhan," *The Bulletin,* 30 May 1989, p. 17.

49. Robert Delfs, "One Stage, Two Plays," and Louise do Rossario, "Safety in Numbers," in *Far Eastern Economic Review,* 25 May 1989.

50. Paul Virilio and Sylvere Lotringer, *Pure War,* Semiotext(e) Foreign Agents Series (New York, 1983), pp. 34–35.

51. Mikhail Gorbachev, *Perestroika: New Thinking for Our Country and the World* (London: Collins, 1987), p. 76.

52. Hans Magnus Enzenberger, in "The State of Europe: Christmas Eve, 1989," *Granta,* no. 30 (Winter 1990), pp. 136–142, passim.

53. Quoted in Robert Donovan and Ray Scherer, *Unsilent Revolution: Television News and American Public Life* (New York: Cambridge University Press, 1992), p. 310.

54. Although I expect it would horrify him, I have to acknowledge that I have borrowed some of the following argument from Rex Butler.

55. James Lull, *China Turned On: Television, Reform and Resistance* (London: Routledge, 1991), pp. 85–86.

56. The typical and the ideal are categories I've borrowed from Bernard Smith, *European Vision and the South Pacific* (Melbourne: Oxford University Press, 1989). The singular is drawn from Paul Carter, *The Road to Botany Bay* (New York: Knopf, 1988). Both these works are concerned with the Western perception of foreign nature and its recording and transformation in second nature. Here I am concerned more with the perception of foreign second nature and its recording and transformation in third nature.

57. See Ien Ang, *Desperately Seeking the Audience* (London: Routledge, 1991).

58. "Mainlanders Tune In for Prizes," *Sydney Morning Herald,* 4 May 1990.

59. Jean-François Lyotard, *The Postmodern Condition: A Report on Knowledge* (Minneapolis: University of Minnesota, 1984); "Rules and Paradoxes and Svelte Appendix," *Cultural Critique,* no. 5 (1986).

60. Deng Xiaoping, "Clear Away All Obstacles and Adhere to the Policies of Reform and Opening to the Outside World."

61. Guy Debord, *Society of the Spectacle* (Detroit: Black and Red, 1983), p. 1.

62. Jean Baudrillard, "For a Critique of the Political Economy of the Sign," in *Selected Writings* (Cambridge: Polity, 1988).

63. Martin Heidegger, "The Question concerning Technology and Other Essays," *Harper's* (New York, 1977), p. 130.

64. Gilles Deleuze, *Cinema #2: The Time-Image* (Minneapolis: University of Minnesota Press, 1986).

65. Heidegger, "The Question concerning Technology and Other Essays," p. 132.

66. Ibid., p. 134.

67. Ibid., p. 136.

Site #4

7. noise

1. *Wall Street Journal,* 20 October 1987; *Financial Times,* 20 October 1987.

2. Mihir Bose, *The Crash* (London: Bloomsbury, 1988), p. 29. Percentage fall figures are from Bose, p. 93.

3. Cf. Robert Sobel, *Panic on Wall Street* (New York: Dutton, 1988). This book was first published in 1968; this is the revised, post-'87 edition.

4. Bose, *The Crash,* p. 49.

5. Jean-François Lyotard, "Les Immatériaux," *Art & Text,* no. 17 (April 1985).

6. Theodor Adorno, *Minima Moralia* (London: New Left Books, 1978), p. 57.

7. J. K. Galbraith, *The Great Crash, 1929* (Harmondsworth: Penguin, 1963), p. 19.

8. *International Business Week,* 18 April 1988.

9. Manuel Castells, *The Informational Economy* (Oxford: Basil Blackwell, 1989).

10. Walter Benjamin, "The Storyteller," in *Illuminations* (New York: Schocken, 1985), p. 90.

11. Monte Gordon, quoted in John Laurence, "How Street Smart Is the Press?" *Columbia Journalism Review,* January 1988.

12. Fredric Jameson, *Postmodernism; or, The Cultural Logic of Late Capitalism* (London: Verso, 1991), p. 269.

13. Karl Marx, "The Power of Money," in *Economic and Philosophic Manuscripts of 1844* (Moscow: Progress Publishers, 1977), p. 132.

14. *Financial Times,* 20 October 1987.

15. Ibid.

16. Craig S. Karpel, "Panic on the Barnhofstrasse," *Harper's,* March 1988.

17. Myra Magnet, "1987 Need Not Become 1929," *Fortune,* 23 November 1987.

18. Guy Debord, *Panegyric* (London: Verso, 1991), p. 11.

19. Karl Marx, "Economic and Philosophic Manuscripts," in *Early Works* (Harmondsworth: Penguin, 1973), p. 366.
20. Fred Block, *Postindustrial Possibilities: A Critique of Economic Discourse* (Berkeley: University of California Press, 1990), pp. 46–74.
21. "Panel Cites Roles of Market Makers and Institutions in Crash," *Wall Street Journal,* 11 January 1988.
22. Hyman Minsky, *Stabilizing an Unstable Economy* (New Haven: Yale University Press, 1986).
23. Adorno, *Minima Moralia,* p. 122.
24. Marx, "Economic and Philosophical Manuscripts," p. 334.
25. This problem is tackled from two different perspectives and at two different levels in Fred Block, "Postindustrial Development and the Obsolescence of Economic Categories," *Politics and Society,* vol. 14, no. 1 (1985); and Grahame Thompson, "The Firm as 'Dispersed' Social Agency," *Economy and Society,* vol. 11, no. 3 (1982).
26. Georg Lukács, *History and Class Consciousness* (London: Merlin Press, 1971), p. 86.
27. Guy Debord, *Society of the Spectacle* (Detroit: Black and Red, 1983), epigram 17.
28. Ibid., epigram 47.
29. Jameson, *Postmodernism,* p. 49.
30. See Susan George, *A Fate Worse Than Debt* (Harmondsworth: Penguin, 1989) and *The Debt Boomerang* (London: Pluto Press, 1992).
31. The phrase is Larry Grossberg's, from his book *We Gotta Get Out of This Place* (New York: Routledge, 1992).
32. John Maynard Keynes, *The General Theory of Employment, Interest and Money* (London: Macmillan, 1967), p. 151.
33. G. L. S. Shackle, *Keynesian Kaleidics* (Edinburgh: Edinburgh University Press, 1974), p. 9.
34. Henri Lefebvre, *Critique of Everyday Life, Vol. 1* (London: Verso, 1991), p. 127.
35. Ibid., p. 154.
36. Susan Strange, *Casino Capitalism* (Oxford: Blackwell, 1986), p. 53.
37. Sobel, *Panic on Wall Street,* p. 428.
38. Ibid., p. 475.
39. D. E. Ayling, *The Internationalisation of Stockmarkets,* Gower Studies in Finance and Investment no. 1 (Aldershot, England, 1986), p. 181.
40. William Greider, *Secrets of the Temple* (New York: Simon and Schuster, 1989).
41. Michel Albert and Jean Boissonnat, *Stop Go Crash Boom* (London: MacDonald, 1989), pp. 19–20.
42. *Fortune,* 23 November 1987; *Financial Times,* 20 October 1987.
43. Tom Wolfe, *The Bonfire of the Vanities* (London: Picador, 1988).
44. *Financial Times,* 20 October 1987.
45. *Wall Street Journal,* 21 October, 1987.
46. William Sheeline, "Who Needs the Stock Exchange?" *Fortune,* 19 November 1990.
47. Lawrence Harris, "The October 1987 S&P 500 Stock-Future Basis," *Journal of Finance,* vol. 44, no. 1 (March 1989); see also Lawrence Harris, "The Dangers of Regulatory Overreaction to the October 1987 Crash," *Cornell Law Review,* vol. 74 (1988/89), pp. 927ff.
48. *Financial Times,* 20 October 1987.
49. Comptroller General of the United States General Accounting Office, in Bernard Reams, ed., *The Stock Market Crash of October 1987: Federal Documents and Materials,* vol. 2 (Buffalo, 1988), p. 73.
50. *The Economist,* 24 October 1987.
51. Alan Cave, "The Electronic Route to Equity," *Financial Times,* 21 October 1987.
52. Alexander Nicoll, "Jury Still Out on Program Trading," *Financial Times,* 21 October 1987.

53. Jean-Jacques Laffort and Eric Maskin, "The Efficient Market Hypothesis and Insider Trading on the Stock Market," *Journal of Political Economy,* vol. 98, no. 1 (1990).

54. Michel Serres, *Hermes: Literature, Science, Philosophy* (Baltimore: Johns Hopkins University Press, 1982), p. 67.

55. Ibid., p. 126.

56. J. Bradford De Long et al., "Noise Trader Risk in Financial Markets," *Journal of Political Economy,* vol. 98, no. 4, p. 704.

57. Ibid., p. 705.

58. Ibid., p. 735.

59. Like the character of Pat Bateman in another great Roaring '80s novel, *American Psycho,* by Brett Easton Ellis (London: Picador, 1991).

60. Max Walsh, "After the Deluge . . . We May Take a Bath," *Sydney Morning Herald,* 8 August 1991.

61. On the concept of feedback see Anthony Wilden, *System and Structure: Essays in Communication and Exchange* (London: Tavistock, 1980).

62. Kathy Acker, *Empire of the Senseless* (London: Picador, 1988), pp. 45–46.

63. I am not interested in this context in orthodox Marxist positions which render price a mere epiphenomenon of value, nor in the arguments of the followers of Ricardo and Sraffa, who want to abolish the category of value in favor of that of the price of production. For a sample of these debates, see Dianne Elson, ed., *Value: The Representation of Labour in Capitalism* (London: CSE Books, 1979); Ian Steedman et al., *The Value Controversy* (London: Verso, 1981).

64. Fredric Jameson, *Late Marxism: Adorno; or, The Persistence of the Dialectic* (London: Verso, 1990), p. 26.

65. Michel Aglietta, *A Theory of Capitalist Regulation* (London: New Left Books, 1979).

66. Alain Lipietz, *The Enchanted World: Inflation, Credit and the World Crisis* (London: Verso, 1985), p. 5.

67. Mike Davis, *Prisoners of the American Dream* (London: Verso, 1986); Barry Bluestone and Bennett Harrison, *The Deindustrialization of America* (New York: Basic Books, 1982).

68. Joan Robinson, *The Accumulation of Capital* (London: Macmillan, 1956), 35.

69. Lipietz, *The Enchanted World,* p. 13.

70. Martin Heidegger, "The Question concerning Technology," in *The Question concerning Technology and Other Essays* (New York: Harper, 1977), pp. 17–18.

71. Nigel Harris, *The End of the Third World* (Harmondsworth: Penguin, 1986).

72. See Connie Bruck, *The Predator's Ball* (New York: Simon and Schuster, 1988).

73. Jeff Madrick, *Marrying For Money* (London: Bloomsbury, 1987), p. 254.

74. Lipietz, *The Enchanted World,* p. 86.

8. crash!

1. Susan Strange, *States and Markets* (London: Pinter, 1988), pp. 131–134.

2. See William Greider, *The Secrets of the Temple* (New York: Simon and Schuster, 1989).

3. Lewis Mumford, *The City in History* (Harmondsworth: Penguin, 1987), pp. 290–297.

4. *Wall Street Journal,* 21 October 1987.

5. Cheol S. Eun and Sangdal Shim, "International Transmission of Stock Market Movements," *Journal of Financial and Quantitative Analysis,* vol. 24, no. 21 (June 1989), p. 243.

6. Mihir Bose, *The Crash* (London: Bloomsbury, 1988), p. 47.

7. *The Australian,* 22 October 1987.

8. Paul Virilio, *Speed and Politics,* Semiotext(e) Foreign Agents Series (New York, 1986), p. 127.

9. On technological determinism, see Landon Winner, *Autonomous Technology* (Cambridge: MIT Press, 1977), pp. 73–100.

10. Cf. Jeanne Hyvrard, "Geonomy," in *Copyright* 1 (Fall 1987).

11. Virilio, *Speed and Politics,* p. 135.

12. William E. Burrows, *Deep Black* (London: Bantam, 1988).

13. D. E. Ayling, *The Internationalisation of Stockmarkets,* Gower Studies in Finance and Investment no. 1 (Aldershot, 1986), p. 193.

14. Barry Riley, "Fewer Controls, Wider Gain," *Financial Times,* 21 October 1987.

15. Ayling, *The Internationalisation of Stockmarkets,* p. 185.

16. On the concept of technofear, see McKenzie Wark, "Technofear: The Terminator Trauma," *21C: The Magazine of the Australian Commission for the Future,* no. 4 (Summer 1991).

17. Paul Stonham, *Global Stock Market Reforms,* Gower Studies in Finance and Investment (Aldershot, 1987), p. 16.

18. James Carey, "Technology and Ideology: The Case of the Telegraph," in *Communication as Culture: Essays on Media and Society,* Media and Popular Culture Series no. 1 (Boston: Unwin Hyman, 1989), p. 217.

19. Ibid., p. 219.

20. Karl Marx and Frederick Engels, "Circular Letter to Bebel et al." (1879), in *The First International and After* (Harmondsworth: Penguin Books in association with New Left Review, 1974), p. 361.

21. Stonham, *Global Stock Market Reforms,* p. 18.

22. Adrian Hamilton, *The Financial Revolution* (Harmondsworth: Penguin, 1986), p. 43; Stonham, *Global Stock Market Reforms,* pp. 45–48.

23. *The Face,* no. 91 (November 1987), p. 37; *Details,* October 1987, pp. 52, 148. On the process of abstraction as it manifests itself in the fashion and culture industries, see McKenzie Wark, "Fashioning the Future: Fashion, Clothing, and the Manufacture of Post-Fordist Culture," *Cultural Studies,* vol. 5, no. 1 (January 1991).

24. Quoted in Hamilton, *The Financial Revolution,* pp. 30–32; Ian Reineke, *The Money Masters* (William Heineman Australia, 1988), p. 16.

25. Stonham, *Global Stock Market Reforms,* p. 19.

26. Ken Auletta, *Greed and Glory on Wall St: The Fall of the House of Lehman* (Harmondsworth: Penguin, 1986), p. 53. Cf. Jeff Madrick, *Marrying for Money* (London: Bloomsbury, 1987).

27. Quoted in Bose, *The Crash,* p. 66.

28. Mike Davis, "The Streets of Los Angeles," *New Left Review,* no. 164 (1987), p. 72. McKenzie Wark, "From Fordism to Sonyism: Perverse Readings of the New World Order," *New Formations,* no. 15 (Winter 1991).

29. Manuel Castells, "High Technology, Economic Restructuring and the Urban Regional Process in the US," in Castells, ed., *High Technology, Space and Society* (London: Sage, 1985), pp. 23, 33. See also his book *The Informational City* (Oxford: Blackwell, 1989).

30. Castells, "High Technology, Economic Restructuring," p. 15.

31. Paul Virilio, "The Overexposed City," *Zone,* no. 1/2 (1988), pp. 19–21.

32. Paul Virilio, "Negative Horizons," *Semiotext(e): USA,* no. 13 (1987), p. 180.

33. On the geography of capital see David Harvey, *The Limits to Capital* (Oxford: Blackwell, 1984).

34. Karl Marx, *Grundrisse* (Harmondsworth: Penguin Books in association with New Left Review, 1973), p. 516.

35. Ibid., p. 517.

36. Ibid., p. 308.

37. Ibid., p. 225.

38. See Gilles Deleuze and Felix Guattari, *Anti-Oedipus* (London: Athlone Press, 1984), pp. 222–240.
39. Marx, *Grundrisse,* p. 524.
40. "Estranged Labour," in Karl Marx, *Early Writings* (Harmondsworth: Penguin Books in association with New Left Review, 1975), p. 325.
41. This is not the time or the place for a discussion of the theory of class which arises out of the views expressed here. They come closest to those expressed by Alvin Gouldner in *The Intellectuals and the Rise of the New Class* (New York: Oxford University Press, 1978). See also Nicholas Abercrombie and John Urry, *Capital, Labour and the New Middle Classes* (London: Allen and Unwin, 1983); Erik Olin Wright, *Classes* (London: Verso, 1987); and Erik Olin Wright et al., *The Debate on Classes* (London: Verso, 1989).
42. Marx, *Grundrisse,* p. 410.
43. Ibid.
44. Mitch Kapor, "Where Is the Digital Highway Really Heading?" *Wired* (July/August 1993).
45. McKenzie Wark, "After Literature: Culture, Policy, Theory and Beyond," *Meanjin,* vol. 51, no. 4 (Summer 1992).
46. Ian Hunter, *Culture and Governement* (London: Macmillan, 1988); Tony Bennett, *Outside Literature* (London: Routledge, 1990); Stuart Cunningham, *Framing Culture: Criticism and Policy in Australia* (London: Allen and Unwin, 1992). See also the debates in *Cultural Studies,* vol. 6, no. 3, and *Meanjin,* vol. 51, no. 3 (Spring 1992).
47. Ian Hunter, "The Humanities without Humanism," *Meanjin,* vol. 51, no. 3 (1992), p. 480.
48. Andrew Ross, *Strange Weather: Culture, Science and Technology in an Age of Limits* (London: Verso, 1991), pp. 169–192.
49. Raymond Williams, *Problems in Materialism and Culture* (London: Verso, 1980), pp. 40–42.
50. Ibid., p. 42.
51. Louis Althusser, *Essays in Self Criticism* (London: New Left Books, 1975), pp. 94–99.
52. Deleuze and Guattari, *Anti-Oedipus,* pp. 321–322.
53. Eric Michaels, *For a Cultural Future,* (Sydney: Artspace Monographs, 1987); *Aboriginal Invention of Television* (Canberra: Australian Institute of Aboriginal Studies, 1986). See also the special issue of the journal *Continuum,* vol. 2, no. 1 (1988). I have elaborated on what I take to be the significance of the late Eric Michael's work in "Autonomy and Antipodality in the Global Village," in A. Cavallaro, R. Harley, L. Wallace, and M. Wark, eds., *Cultural Diversity in the Global Village: The Third International Symposium on Electronic Art* (Adelaide: Australian Network for Art and Technology, 1992).
54. See Ross, *Strange Weather.*
55. Bill Landreth, *Out of the Inner Circle* (Washington: Microsoft Press, 1989), p. 98.
56. See Wark, "From Fordism to Sonyism."
57. James Benniger, *The Control Revolution* (Cambridge: Harvard University Press, 1986).

index

Note: Chinese names are alphabetized without inversion, as given in the text (i.e., Deng Xiaoping), except for those which have been Westernized (such as Jimmy Ngai Siu-Yan, which appears as Ngai Siu-Yan, Jimmy).

McKENZIE WARK lectures in the Masters program in International Communications at Macquarie University. He coedited *flesh* and *Leftwright,* and his essays on communication and culture have appeared in *Cultural Studies, New Formations, New Statesman, Arena, Art & Text,* and *Impulse*. He is a columnist on cultural studies and higher education for *The Australian* newspaper and a regular broadcaster on the Australian Broadcasting Corporation's "Radio National."